C. DAVID MEAD
Professor of English, Michigan State University
ADVISORY EDITOR TO DODD, MEAD & COMPANY

PERSPECTIVES FOR THE SEVENTIES

PERSPECTIVES FOR

Edited by
ROBERT G. NOREEN
San Fernando Valley State College

WALTER GRAFFIN
The University of Wisconsin-Parkside

THE SEVENTIES

DODD, MEAD & COMPANY

NEW YORK   1971   TORONTO

ISBN 0-396-06312-8
LIBRARY OF CONGRESS CATALOG CARD NUMBER: 72-143292

PRINTED IN THE UNITED STATES OF AMERICA

18174

CONTENTS

PERSPECTIVES FOR THE SEVENTIES

INTRODUCTION

ESTABLISHING A PERSPECTIVE

> *"Wonder is the beginning of wisdom. The young are wis-*
> *ing up. All they have not to do is what e.e. cummings*
> *called 'up-grow and down-forget.'"*
>
> MILTON MAYER

Perhaps nothing is more difficult to develop than a good sense of perspective—that is, to develop the ability to view various sides of an issue or an argument with a certain calm detachment. To gain a perspective for the 1970's seems doubly difficult, for in our hurried, uneasy society there is little chance for calmness, let alone detachment. We live in an age of unrest and turmoil. Although many cling to our established institutions and traditions, many more are demanding change, demanding that our institutions become more relevant and more in step with the times. In the distant past, it seems, there was general agreement on what was good for the individual and his society. But today it is clear that agreement no longer exists, if, indeed, it ever did. What once seemed to be meaningful no longer satisfies; what once was important is now irrelevant.

Because so many young people are dissatisfied with the present state of our society, the clamor for change and the demands for relevance are most often heard from them. Refusing to adhere to the old dogmas, many of the young have become impatient with outmoded ideas and institutions, unwilling to accept the traditional patterns and established structures of our society without first determining the importance of these patterns and structures to their own lives. Seeing things differently from their elders, they resist inheriting a world which seems largely irrelevant, one neither meeting their needs nor allowing them to fulfill their lives in meaningful ways. They would rather "do their own thing," like Emerson, than pursue the old American myths of progress and success. They would rather find peace and unity among friends who share their ideas than be superpatriots, supporting their country right or wrong.

While many of those on the other side of the generation gap have not been silent, it is the youth of today who are leading the search for new answers to the complex problems of our society. But whether young or old, any serious individual today shares a common challenge: to find a personal perspective which will best enable him to understand our rapidly changing society and to view it with intelligence and wisdom.

The essays in this text have been chosen to represent a variety of perspectives on five basic issues of our time—the new life styles of our youth culture, the turmoil in our colleges and universities, the conflicts between races, the impact of technology on our lives and environment, and the changing roles of women in our society. Some of the essays can be considered "liberal" and others "conservative"; some essays are from the young generation, others from the old. Some are easy reading, others will challenge the intellect of the best student.

In presenting these essays, the editors make no attempt to dictate what might be the best perspective on any particular issue. Each individual reader must find his own. But he will be most able to do so when he has knowledge of the complexities of the issues, and access to the best that has been thought and said about them; when he has been able to discuss these issues with others and to express his own views in writing. Only as one becomes aware of different perspectives and the arguments supporting them will he be able to make informed judgments for himself; only then will he be able to test his own values, and, indeed, to create them.

Considering a variety of perspectives on the most important issues of our times, and then finding relevant perspectives for oneself, is not an easy task, for it requires an open mind and a capacity for change and growth. To gain the strength of one's convictions requires a responsiveness to one's own changing needs and to the changing needs of our society. But although not easy, the search for viable perspectives is essential. Indeed, it is one of the greatest challenges of the 1970's—one which must be met not only to gain the satisfaction of finding personal meaning in one's life, but even to create the possibility for the survival of the human race on this earth.

The following essay offers one context for this search. Milton Mayer, a distinguished journalist and educator of the older generation, acknowledges the need for new perspectives in our society. These new perspectives, he believes, will come from the youth of our land, who are now conducting a "crusade" to reshape the institutions of our society which are no longer relevant to those they are supposed to serve.

THE CHILDREN'S CRUSADE
Milton Mayer

A distinguished journalist and educator of the older generation acknowledges the desperate need for the current revolution of the young and the blacks; he hopes that it will not be an empty rebellion, but a fruitful one, conducted with intelligence, bearing enlightenment: "If the young do not bring light to the world, if they spurn a little suffering undergone for the sake of intelligence, the wave of the present will roll over them and, like their elders, they will be heard of no more." Milton Mayer is a Consultant to the Center for the Study of Democratic Institutions in Santa Barbara, California, and Professor of the Humanities at Windham College in Vermont.

I am of two minds about this country's present convulsions. My heart is in the highlands with the hellers. But my head tells me . . . It's an old head, mine, without much wool on the top of it in the place where the wool ought to grow. Let me tell you what it is like to be old in the United States of America at the tail end of the nineteen-sixties.

My generation accepted the precepts of its parents, and they were the same precepts our parents had accepted from theirs. We violated the precepts, naturally; but we accepted them. The new generation rejects them. We were wrong and the new generation is right. Our precepts were good precepts, but still the new generation is right. They are right because preceptorial is as preceptorial does. We were—and, of course, are—pious frauds. They are impious Abelards.

That's the one big change. Another one is this: except for the remnantal remains of Gopher Prairie, the America of my youth is vanished without a trace; *Spurlos versunken.* In its perfectly splendid isolation, the rest of the world, being out of sight, was out of mind. My father didn't know whether Korea was in the Caribbean or the Mediterranean, or whether the Congo was a Spanish dance, a Hindu god, or a chocolate bar; he didn't care, and he didn't have to care.

It was an unjust America, of course. Blacks were Negroes, Negroes were niggers, and niggers were ineducable and would therefore always be menial. Jews knew their place and did not take forcible possession of the boardroom of the college or country club that refused to practice participatory democracy. It was an uncouth America, but a generous America and a visionary America. Its golden door was open and the lamp was bright beside it. Its very existence was a terror to tyranny ev-

From *Center Magazine,* Vol. II, No. 5 (September 1969). Reprinted by permission of the Center for the Study of Democratic Institutions in Santa Barbara, California.

erywhere, lest its spirit be infectious. In its pre-scientific and anarchic ardor it cultivated the techniques, if not the arts and institutions, of peace. In the first eight years of my life in Chicago, I never once saw a soldier. America was still, as it was intended to be, a refuge from chauvinistic horrors. If someone had told my father that he had to take a loyalty oath, he would have said, "What do you think this is—Russia?"

Gone, all gone now, to be replaced by the garrison state and the last best hope of preserving the status quo ante all over the world. If, then, you can understand what it is to be old in this country at the tail end of the nineteen-sixties, you will be able to understand why I am of two minds about the present convulsions: on balance, the changes I have seen in my time have been for the worse. I am afraid. But about certain aspects of the situation I am of one mind.

First: The revolution of the young blacks, formerly Negroes, is nothing but the Jim Crow branch of the American Children's Crusade. What the American Negroes are saying to the American whites is what the American young are saying to the American old: "I don't dig you. I don't love you. I don't honor you. I don't obey you." Whether it's Vietnam and "Hell, no, we won't go," or the ghetto and "Hell, no, we won't stay," the message is the same. The parochial concern of the Negro should not obscure the common cause against an America whose promises were made with its fingers crossed.

Second: The revolution of the young Americans—white, black, red, or pink—is nothing but the American branch of the world revolution of the rising generation—and the American branch is behind the times. The French branch has pulled down de Gaulle. The Spanish and Japanese branches have driven Franco and Sato up the wall. The Italian branch has made it impossible to govern Italy. The German branch has paralyzed Prussianism, and the Czech branch has immobilized communism. In our characteristic American provincialism we suppose that we have something special going here. The only thing that is special, indeed unique, is the elders' effort to persuade the young to call themselves kids in the hope that they won't take themselves seriously.

Third: The revolution is overdue—the revolution which Jeremiah and Jefferson invoked when they said that God's justice would not sleep forever. The evils that were containable under kings are no longer containable under politicians. A world that spends more on war than it does on health and education combined is not susceptible of reform. It calls for revolution. But revolution is not the same thing as rebellion. The aftermath of the Russian Revolution instructs us that revolution is not a matter of systems but of men; as the men are, so will the revolution be.

John Locke never heard of law and order, but he had heard of divine right. "When men are miserable enough," said Locke, "they will rebel, cry up divine right how you will." I think he should have said "desperate enough" instead of "miserable enough." The difference between submissive misery and desperate rebellion is hope. And the difference between rebellion and revolution is intelligence. The young everywhere, black, white, poor, rich, have the desperate certitude of hope along with the adolescent possibility of intelligence. The young don't need God *or* the big battalions on their side. All they need is the actuarial table, and they've got it. My object here is to persuade them to win a revolution instead of a rebellion—to make their victory stick. No revolution—not the French, not the American, and not the Russian—has ever stuck.

What is wanted is intelligence. That the status quo is unintelligent is superbly self-evident. But the revolution against it is not *ipso facto* intelligent. If it strikes with the wrong weapons at the wrong people for the wrong reasons, it will prove to have been unintelligent. If it assumes that there is nothing wrong with power and that a transfer or redistribution of power will improve the human condition, it will prove to have been unintelligent. He who says, "This ruler is a fool, but when I am a ruler I will not be a fool" is already a fool. It is not power that corrupts, but the unintelligent belief that power is not necessarily corrosive.

The revolution has to be intelligent, and the Negro's revolution has to be especially intelligent because he is its natural leader and is fighting in an exposed position. If he acts unintelligently he will go down faster than the white revolutionary whose pallor restrains (though it does not disable) the counter-revolution. To ask the Negro to be more intelligent than the white is only to ask him to use the intelligence he already has. But if all he has learned through his suffering is how to burn, baby, burn, he hasn't learned anything more than the white man, whose technological triumph consists of burning babies.

If the Negro does not use his superior intelligence, he is lost, because an ignorant little man cannot beat an ignorant big one. Whitey has overkill; blackie has underkill. The inference is inescapable. Along toward the end of 1941—but prior to December 7th of that year—Professor Morris Cohen listened while a Jewish colleague said, "I just want to bash in a few Nazi heads before I die." Somebody turned to Cohen and said, "And what do you think?" "I think," said Cohen, "that bashing heads is for the ninety-six per cent—not for the four per cent."

Even the ninety-six per cent cannot win that way now. It took the winners of the First World War fifteen years to realize that they had lost it. It took the winners of the Second World War only five. What keeps the winners of the third world war from launching it is the suspicion that they have lost it in advance of its launching. They can't bash in a few Russian or American heads without being bashed back. Their unintelligent alternative, as every schoolboy knows, is a balance of terror which is ruinous in any terms and in its own terms unreliable. Their only hope is to save their faces: It is an open secret that the Americans will agree to surrender to the Vietcong if the Vietcong will agree to proclaim an American victory. Old whitey seems to be at the end of the road. The inventor of the lynching bee at Calvary, the auction block at Charleston, and the shoot-out at Verdun seems to have no more inventions.

The young—above all, those who are non-Caucasian and therefore preconditioned to use their intelligence—are called upon to go out and turn the world upside down. Like the Apostles of Jesus, they do not need any baggage. They do not need black studies, because intelligence is not absorbed through the epidermis. They do not need black dormitories, because intelligence is not contracted by sleeping with people. They do not need black awareness, because intelligence is aware of itself and everything else. They need the intelligence they acquired in the course of their suffering, nothing more.

It is not enough for them to do their thing; the thing has to be the sensible thing to do. The sensible thing to do is not to demand a debased education on the ground that a debased education is what the young, and especially the Negro young, are fit for. The sensible thing to do is to demand a good education plus the compensatory qualifications of which they have been deprived.

A good education is not vocational training. The purpose of education is human freedom. We don't want Dow Chemical or R.O.T.C. off the campus; we want everything off the campus that has nothing to do with education for human freedom. That takes care not only of Dow Chemical and R.O.T.C. but also the placement office, home economics, physical education, business administration, journalism, speech, fraternities, and all the other goodies with which the old have tricked out higher learning in the hope of keeping the young quiet in a rest home for rich adolescents. We don't want war research off the campus; we want everything off the campus that has nothing to do with education for human freedom—including war research and industrial and commercial and labor research. We don't want theology, law, medicine, and engineering off the campus, but across the street where we can take advantage of pure research without diverting it from its purity.

Their motto has to be the motto of my alma mater, and it has to be properly parsed. The motto of my alma mater is, "Let knowledge grow more and more, that human life may be enriched." My alma mater abandoned the enrichment for the knowledge, the end for the means, and achieved the first self-sustaining nuclear chain reaction; the enrichment of human life in Hiroshima astonished the world.

There is nothing the young can do to disrupt the American college campus that hasn't been done by their elders. They should not connive with their elders in its disruption. They should revolutionize it—revolutionize it intelligently on the intelligent ground that it has forfeited its legitimacy and prostituted its independence. A university fifty per cent of whose budget is provided by the producers of overkill is monopolized by them and every one of its procedures tainted. (The Supreme Court once held that control of six per cent of the market for automobile magnetos was enough to constitute a monopoly in the industry.)

Education has always presupposed authority—the rightful authority, in respect of teaching, of those who know over those who don't know. It has lost its authority because its practitioners have lent themselves to the production and perpetuation of deadly error. Authority stripped of its rightfulness is authoritarianism. The young are right in repudiating authoritarianism. But they are mortally wrong if they think that they will improve their situation by replacing their elders' authoritarianism with their own.

Their intelligence, as it rejects authoritarianism, rejects the struggle for Negro rights as such and for student rights as such. Such a struggle is self-interested and is therefore no different in principle from the self-interest that disgraces their elders. There is no such category as Negro rights or student rights because there is no such category as Negro or student. Either there are human rights or there are none. Either we are first of all men, and only then black men or white men, or we are nothing. Because blacks are men, they are not to be badgered. Because they are men, they are not to be manipulated. Because they are men, they are not to be conscripted or enslaved. When the Negro was a slave, and the white man called him a black, he said, "I am a man."

The Negro does not have to be superhuman or saintly. He has only to be intelligent. What was good about Martin Luther King was his intelligence. He would not lift a finger to save one man or one country. His race was the one race, man, without regard to the amount of melanin in his skin. He knew the perdurable agony of man in his own person. Persecution was his teacher, and he learned from his teacher how to speak for man.

Who else will speak for man? Not whitey. Whitey has battened on partiality—on racism, on nationalism, on the exploitation of his brother, black and white. Whoever fights for partiality is playing whitey's game and playing into whitey's hands, perpetuating the intolerable separation of man into species. Separatism is for the birds; there is only one surviving species of the class *Homo,* and that is *Homo sapiens.* Whoever speaks for man must refuse to let any man be segregated by anybody—even by himself.

Just as there must be one world or none, so there must be one culture or none. That culture is man's. Asian and African and European studies in America are justified only by the American's ignorance of Asia, Africa, and Europe; that is, they are not justified at all. The black culture of the African-descended American, like the Irish culture of the Irish-descended American, is an atavism that denies the common manhood and asserts a tribalism which is always and everywhere barbarian. If I cannot understand the writings of Eldridge Cleaver because of my skin color, then Eldridge Cleaver cannot understand the writings of Shakespeare because of his. Everybody, and not just the Nazis, will burn the books.

What is wanted here is unanswerable argument. Attack education for its present debasement, and you are unanswerable. Assert your right to live without killing, and you are unanswerable. Demand justice and not advantage, and you are unanswerable. Call upon the church, not for five hundred million dollars in special reparations for the Negro but for five hundred billion dollars in general justice for the poor, and you are unanswerable. But call policemen "pigs" and you are answerable by those who remember the Nazis calling the Jews *Schweinehunde*. Call public officials "fascists" and you are answerable by those who remember fascism. Call for power and you are answerable by those who remember the Caesars and the Hapsburgs and the Romanovs. Call for black faculties and black curricula and you are answerable by those who call for humanistic faculties and humane curricula. Call for separatism and you will have on your side—though they kill you—the supremacists who have the necessary overkill to maintain the separatism you call for. Do you want separate but equal opportunity? You will get the separate opportunity and suffer the inequality that follows ineluctably from the separation of the minority from the majority.

The Negro racist, like the white racist, bases his racism on dignity. But men cannot shoot or burn or brawl their way to dignity; if they could, the American white man would be the most dignified man on earth. Does it make the young feel good to occupy an administration building and horrify the straights and terrify the timid and license the governor to turn on the tear gas? Do they want to feel good or to be intelligent? Do they want a rebellion or a revolution? Dignity is not a matter of feeling good—of the mumbo-jumbo of "black is beautiful" or "America the beautiful." America is no more beautiful than Africa and black is no more beautiful than blue.

I wish that the young could make their demands negotiable, but I don't see how they can if they make them intelligent. I don't see how overkill can be negotiated. I don't see how a ghetto or nerve gas research or the C.I.A. can be negotiated. But properly non-negotiable objectives cannot be achieved by throwing a rock through a window on the ground that the owner of the window understands nothing but force. He understands force, all right, and he has it. His level of intelligence has to be raised to the point where he can comprehend that the travesty of the campus and the ghettos and the battlefield is finished. A generation which elects a Lyndon Johnson or a Richard Nixon has no visible intention to negotiate. It will pay lip service to negotiation, provided that the shape of the table is right and as long as it doesn't have to stop doing the only thing it knows how to do. Harvard University had three hundred years to clean house on the basis of negotiable demands. The people who rightfully deplore the claim of the riotous young to amnesty have amnestied themselves since the world began. There may be those who recall Cain's general demurer to the complaint that he had failed to discharge his responsibility to his brother.

Old whitey may be unintelligent and out of steam, but he still has his pristine cunning. If he is persistently pushed he will propose gradualism, by which he means gradually wearing blackie down. Whitey isn't wicked. He is unconcerned. His unconcern is not immoral. It is unintelligent. By power possessed, he cannot understand what Paul meant by saying that we are all members one of another. He cannot understand what Jesus meant by saying that he who takes the sword will perish by it. He cannot understand what the prophet meant by proclaiming the greater damnation of those who devour widows' houses and make long prayers for a pretense. He didn't mean to be like this. Power benighted him, and he walks in the noonday as in the night. If I may paraphrase an eminent Harvard alumnus—a hundred generations of people like us is enough. If the new generation turns out to be the hundred and first, it is lost.

The old have torn down Vietnam and kept the ghettos in their place, and now they say that the young want to tear things down without having anything to put in their place. The old are not competent to complain, and the complaint is an empty one anyway. The young don't have to have anything to put in the place of the present shambles. The Lord God Jehovah did not tell their ancestors and mine what to put in the place of Sidon and Tyre; he told them, "You shall walk in My path and I will show you My way." It is easy to think up the right thing. What is hard is to stop doing the wrong one. The Lord did not tell their ancestors and mine to do good. He told them, "Cease to do evil—learn to do good." They need only to be intelligent.

If they are intelligent, the totalitarian spirit—which unintelligently obeys all laws—will call them anarchists. But they should not be dismayed. True, anarchy is the second worst condition of human society. The worst is tyranny. He who, like the intelligent founders of this republic, will not have tyranny, must take his chances on anarchy. The Nuremberg decision of the International Military Tribunal in 1946 *requires* anarchy of the soldier who is ordered to perform inhuman acts. Disorder is no worse than injustice, which is the institutionalization of disorder. When the laws are rooted in violence and maintained by violence, they must not be obeyed. Socrates was right, not wrong, when he said, "Men of Athens, I love you, but I shall obey God rather than you." John Brown was right. Mohandas Gandhi was right. Martin Luther King was right. And Thomas Aquinas was right seven centuries ago when he said that an unjust law is no law and does not bind a man in conscience.

There is a higher law. The higher law does not have to be very high to be higher than the Selective Service Act or the Internal Revenue Act, only more intelligent. The young should study the German experience of the nineteen-thirties, when the most literate nation on earth, mistaking literacy for intelligence, elevated ignorance to power and cut its own head off. They should study the German experience and learn that neither the government nor the majority is by definition a good judge of justice. Civil disobedience may be treasonable. It is not necessarily unpatriotic. A patriot will set his country right if he can, but in no case will he contribute to its continued delinquency.

I am one of the elders of whom I speak. The young terrify me. They terrify me because I have mine, which I got by the exercise of the good precepts I learned from my parents plus being white and landing on my feet every time I fell on my face. The young do not terrify me with their popguns; I have ten machine guns for every one of their popguns. They terrify me because they show some small sign of social maturity, of civic responsibility and human concern. Their elders, like me, are nice people, but they did not mature. The young have seen them playing cops and robbers at home and overkill in their worldwide playpen. Television reveals the infantilism of the adults' attention span. They cannot talk; they can sit mesmerized, or they can shout or mumble. They made the young mumble, "One nation, indivisible," and after they had mumbled it a few thousand times, some subversive told them that five per cent of the American people have twenty per cent of the nation's income and twenty per cent have five per cent of it, and they began to become what their elders call cynical; that is, intelligent. The day the young complete the process their elders will fall off the stage of history; they won't even have to be pushed.

The President of Notre Dame says that "we need a rebirth of academic, civic, and political leadership——a sharing of those youthful ideals and dreams, whether they are impossible or not." The President of Notre Dame is right. But whose fault is it that we need such a rebirth? How did we come to be so needy, with so rich a heritage and so profligate a land? How are we to be reborn? What does "a sharing of those youthful ideals and dreams" mean? What have the elders got to offer as their share? Not youth or ideals or dreams.

The ideals of the elders are money, fame, and power, and they dream of bigger and better sugarplums. They are starved for soul food, and chicken every Sunday has not filled them. They are obese, but unfilled. Now they have run out of time. They have run out of time to choose to free the Negroes or to fight a civil war to enslave them. All they can do now is cry up the divine right of law and order and shudder for themselves as they see it in action and observe the lawlessness and disorder it brings in its train.

Our black brethren are freeing themselves impatiently. For three centuries they waited patiently—so patiently that whitey, who takes impatience for manliness, took them for sheep who look up to be fed and look down when they aren't. They waited at the end of the line, and no matter how short the line got they were still waiting. They waited at the back of the bus, and no matter how empty the bus was they were still at the back. Their patience is beginning to be exhausted.

Whitey had no intention of living up to his profession that all men are created equal. As this country's sovereign he could not and can not pass the buck for its derelictions. What the country was was his doing; was, and is. His tragic flaw was his possession by power and the consequent corruption of his intelligence. He did not understand that no man can free another because no man can enslave another. Whitey wanted blackie to act like a freedman. But blackie isn't a freedman; no man is. He is a free man, and a free man because he is a man. Therein lies his dignity—not in the grace of his master—and he loses it not by being in chains but by chaining himself to the humiliating values of his master. Whoever would want to be and do and have what the American white man is and does and has is not a man but a slave and, like the American white man, an unhappy slave at that.

The only hope of the old is the intelligence of the young. Their intelligence may be undeveloped, but it is not yet corrupted. They are still young. They have been forced by the American educational process to undertake their own education. They are not to be put down or put off, because they have been set to wondering. What set them to wondering was, I suppose, the two victorious world wars their elders waged and lost in the process of winning them. Coming in the wake of these wingless victories, they would have had to be catatonic epileptics not to have wondered. Wonder is the beginning of wisdom. The young are wising up. All they have not to do is what e. e. cummings called up-grow and down-forget.

Their intelligence tells them that the only solution to racialism is miscegenation. There was a time when an Irishman could not be elected President. There was a time when a Catholic could not be elected President. There was even a time when a fighting Quaker couldn't be elected President. The change in our national attitude was the result of what we Dixiecrats call mixing. Hybrid corn and hybrid pigs are of higher quality than the original stocks, and there is no evidence whatever that hybrid man is not. Since seventy per cent of all the American "blacks" are part "white" and millions of American "blacks" have passed unknowingly into the so-called white race, the racist who says he wouldn't want his daughter to marry a Negro—or a white man—has no way of knowing whether she does or doesn't and neither has she or her fiancé. As long as pigmentation provides our society with the one discernible other, and as long as whitey is ineducable by anthropology, psychology, and theology, the only solution is to make indiscernible others of us all.

Five hundred years would do it. But then five hundred years of education for freedom would make intelligent human beings of us and it wouldn't matter anymore what color we were. But we have run out of time. It isn't the future that's dark—it's the present. If the young do not bring light to the world, if they spurn a little suffering undergone for the sake of intelligence, the wave of the present will roll over them and, like their elders, they will be heard of no more.

PART ONE

LIFE STYLE: YOUTH CULTURE

"Youth culture." The phrase appears so frequently today that it has acquired the recognition and the ambiguity marking such words as "cool,"
"heavy," and "relevance." Youth extol their culture; the media exploit it;
and politicians, depending on their constituency, condemn or praise it. All
use exaggerated terms: this generation will save or ruin . . . the individual,
the nation, the world. But what is this supposedly revolutionary culture?
How widespread it is?

It is easier to ask these question than to answer them. Indeed, the category "youth" defies description when it is used in the context of "youth culture." A recent study by *Fortune* defined "young adults" as "those people
between the ages of eighteen and twenty-four." But when critics of drug use
discuss its dangers to the "young," they stress the problems confronting high
school students. *Esquire,* on the other hand, has discussed the life style of
the "micro boppers," the pre-teen segment of the youth culture. Furthermore, not all young people between the ages of ten and thirty identify with
a counter culture. Conversely, many "youth" leaders—including such lumi-
naries as Timothy Leary, Allen Ginsberg, Abbie Hoffman, Jerry Rubin, and
Tom Hayden—have passed the supposedly crucial age of thirty; and some,
including Herbert Marcuse and Chairman Mao, will never see seventy
again. It seems, then, that people are a part of the youth culture if they simply agree with its aims. So we use the phrase loosely, its imprecision serving
to remind us of the youth culture's ambiguous and contradictory nature.

Just as the exact boundaries of "youth"—and therefore the size and influ-

ence of the youth culture—are elusive, so is it difficult to explain defini-
tively what that culture consists of. Theodore Roszak, who contributes the
first article in this part, calls it a "counter culture," meaning that its values
and life styles are in opposition to our competitive, materialistic, impersonal
culture. In "The Making of the Yippie Culture," Garry Wills sees the youth
culture as one in which aesthetics has replaced ethics. Abbie Hoffman
sounds a key note of the individualism of this movement when he says, "Do
your thing," with equal emphasis on the first and second words.

As useful as these views are for an understanding of the youth culture,
closer scrutiny of it reveals certain contradictions. In the most visible aspects of youth culture—pop music and clothing fashions, for example—
youthful innovations are not much of a counterforce or threat to the establishment. Instead, the music industry has simply incorporated the new music
and now relies on it for financial success. The record sales of Dylan, the
Beatles, and the Rolling Stones alone demonstrate the size and importance
of the youth market. Furthermore, titles such as "Mozart's Greatest Hits"
and "Bach's Greatest Hits" indicate the youth culture's ability to alter established practices. But the new music has not markedly changed the materialistic, competitive nature of the recording industry. Rock musicians are
businessmen, and the most successful ones become corporations. The same
trend appears in the clothing industry, in which boutique fashions have become a staple even of discount department stores and youth styles influence
every aspect of fashion. Instead of being in opposition to big business, much
of the youth culture *is* big business. The problem the new culture faces is, in
one sense, not how to overthrow the establishment, but how to prevent itself
from being absorbed by the establishment. Today, even rebels and convicted
criminals become celebrities and famous authors.

The notion that the youth culture promotes aesthetics instead of ethics
also seems debatable, especially when reading the idealistic statements made
by Tom Hayden, Mark Rudd, and Abbie Hoffman. The most radical protesters want revolution, not theatrical gestures; and they want it in order to
correct society's flaws—prejudice, poverty, and injustice. While detractors
of the youth culture lament its lack of a constructive program, many commentators see the same culture's revolutionary zeal as society's only hope
for moral and social regeneration.

Another contradiction or ambiguity present in the counter culture results
from the simultaneous emphases on individualism and collectivism. In an effort to announce its individuality and to differentiate itself from another
generation, a segment of youth has turned to field jackets and Indian garb
—with the result that the youth movement has a uniform just as surely as
the business culture of the 1950's had its gray flannel suit. The young want
to do their own thing, but they seem to enjoy doing it most when in the
company of 500,000 other young people at a rock festival or in a particular
section of a city, such as the East Village in New York or Old Town in
Chicago.

These contradictions are not cited as weaknesses; in fact, they may represent the strength of the youth movement, showing that it is flexible enough
to accommodate opposing ideas and tendencies. The contradictions are men-

tioned, rather, because that is what the essays in Part One emphasize. Positive views on the youth culture vie with negative ones. Liberal, conservative, and radical viewpoints are all present; and the reader himself must decide which views are most accurate.

In "How Wide is the Generation Gap?" the three essays place the youthful discontent in a broad historical perspective. Readers of the modern novel know that the generation gap did not suddenly appear on the contemporary scene in the 1960's and 1970's. Stephen Dedalus rejected father, church, and country. Thomas Sutpen drove his sons away from him. Holden Caulfield saw adults as "phonies." Theodore Roszak and Jacob Bronowski both trace generational conflict into the more distant past, and agree that such conflict and the protest it produces are important parts of human progress. In opposition to these optimistic interpretations, Louis J. Halle thinks that today's protest movements differ from previous revolutionary movements because the current ones are, in his view, based on a negative image of man. The essays in this section implicitly agree that a generation gap exists, but they disagree on this important question: Is it a detrimental or a beneficial phenomenon?

"The Young Radicals" offers the statements of four articulate men—three young radicals and a critic of radical reform. Each essay calls for revolution. But Daniel Sisson's insistence on a revolutionary movement based on American models establishes an interesting test to apply to the views of Tom Hayden and Mark Rudd. Do their ideas seem to be outside of the American heritage; and, if so, do their calls for action seem to be falling on deaf ears, as Sisson contends ideologies not founded on the American experience must? The piece by Abbie Hoffman shows revolution to be a psychological phenomenon and gives a feeling for the kind of freedom that the radical movement aims for.

If movements and cultures were like poems (which, in Archibald MacLeish's words, "should not mean/But be"), the third section in this part, "What Do the New Life Styles Mean?" would not be necessary. But we crave to know what something signifies. The seven essays in this section try to satisfy that desire. Garry Wills gives a negative reading of many aspects of the youth culture and contends that it has its most similar counterpart not in the ancient centaurs or Christians, as Theodore Roszak says, but in the Nazi youth movement. When Russell Kirk looks at the new life styles at a liberal college, he sees only signs of decadence and chaos. But Jack Richardson is more optimistic about the new morality, as his article about Joe Namath's "heroic virtue" shows. Two articles about drugs and the drug culture, and two about rock festivals, focus on highly-publicized aspects of youth culture. French journalist Suzanne Labin's emotional article stressing the "tragedy" of children taking drugs, is balanced by the mild, undramatic statements of two actual drug users. The closing essays in this section concern the rock festival—one of the most representative events in the youth culture. Both essays agree that Woodstock, like the culture it embodied, was paradoxical: as Andrew Kopkind says, it was "paradise and concentration camp, sharing and profiteering, sky and mud, love and death."

HOW WIDE IS THE GENERATION GAP?

"Don't trust anyone over thirty."

AN INVASION OF CENTAURS
Theodore Roszak

Born in 1933, Theodore Roszak is one of many people who look to the under-thirty generation for social and moral reforms. Besides teaching history at the college level, he has also written *The Making of a Counter Culture* and numerous magazine articles, and edited *The Dissenting Academy*. In this essay he provocatively compares today's youthful revolutionaries to the early Christians, who unexpectedly toppled the established Roman culture.

In the "today," in every "today," various generations coexist and the relations which are established between them, according to the different condition of their ages, represent the dynamic system of attractions and repulsions, of agreement and controversy which at any given moment makes up the reality of historic life.[1]

If we agree with Ortega that the fitful transition of the generations is a significant element in historical change, we must also recognize that the young may do little more than remodel the inherited culture in minor or marginal ways. They may settle for alterations that amount to a change of superficial fashion, undertaken out of mere pique or caprice. What is special about the generational transition we are in is the scale on which it is taking place and the depth of antagonism it reveals. Indeed, it would hardly seem an exaggeration to call what we see arising among the young a "counter culture." Meaning: a culture so radically disaffiliated from the mainstream assumptions of our society that it scarcely looks to many as a culture at all, but takes on the alarming appearance of a barbaric intrusion.

An image comes at once to mind: the invasion of centaurs that is recorded on the pediment of the Temple of Zeus at Olympia. Drunken

From *The Making of a Counter Culture* by Theodore Roszak. Copyright © 1968, 1969 by Theodore Roszak. Reprinted by permission of Doubleday & Company, Inc.

[1] José Ortega y Gasset, *Man and Crisis,* trans. Mildred Adams (London: Allen & Unwin, 1959), p. 45.

and incensed, the centaurs burst in upon the civilized festivities that are in progress. But a stern Apollo, the guardian of the orthodox culture, steps forward to admonish the gate-crashers and drive them back. The image is a potent one, for it recalls what must always be a fearful experience in the life of any civilization: the experience of radical cultural disjuncture, the clash of irreconcilable conceptions of life. And the encounter is not always won by Apollo.

Toynbee has identified such cultural disjunctures as the work of a disinherited "proletariat," using as his paradigm the role of the early Christians within the Roman Empire—a classic case of Apollo being subverted by the unruly centaurs. The Christian example is one that many of the hip young are quick to invoke, perhaps with more appropriateness than many of their critics may recognize. Hopelessly estranged by ethos and social class from the official culture, the primitive Christian community awkwardly fashioned of Judaism and the mystery cults a minority culture that could not but seem an absurdity to Greco-Roman orthodoxy. But the absurdity, far from being felt as a disgrace, became a banner of the community.

For it is written [St. Paul boasted] I will destroy the wisdom of the wise, and will bring to nothing the understanding of the prudent. . . . For the Jews require a sign, and the Greeks seek after wisdom. . . . But God hath chosen the foolish things of the world to confound the wise; and God hath chosen the weak things of the world to confound the things which are mighty. (I Cor. 1:19, 22, 27)

It is a familiar passage from what is now an oppressively respectable source. So familiar and so respectable that we easily lose sight of how aggressively perverse a declaration it is . . . how loaded with unabashed contempt for a long-established culture rich with achievement. And whose contempt was this? That of absolute nobodies, the very scum of the earth, whose own counter culture was, at this early stage, little more than a scattering of suggestive ideas, a few crude symbols, and a desperate longing. It was the longing that counted most, for not all the grandeur of Greco-Roman civilization could fill the desolation of spirit Christianity bred upon. Since we know now with an abundance of hindsight what the Christian *scandalum* eventually led to, the comparison with the still fledgling counter culture of our youth is bound to seem outlandish. But then, all revolutionary changes are unthinkable until they happen . . . and then they are understood to be inevitable. Who, in Paul's time, could have anticipated what would come of the brazen hostility of a handful of scruffy malcontents? And what would the nascent Christian movement have looked like under the merciless floodlights of any then-existing mass media? Would it even have survived the saturation coverage?

Perhaps the young of this generation haven't the stamina to launch the epochal transformation they seek; but there should be no mistaking the fact that they want nothing less. "Total rejection" is a phrase that comes readily to their lips, often before the mind provides even a blurred picture of the new culture that is to displace the old. If there is anything about the ethos of Black Power that proves particularly attractive even to young white disaffiliates who cannot gain access to the movement, it is the sense that Black Power somehow implies an entirely new way of life: a black culture, a black consciousness . . . a black soul which is totally incompatible with white society and aggressively proud of the fact. Black Power may build any number of barriers between white and Negro youth, but across the barriers a common language can still be heard. Here, for example, is Bobby Seale of the Oakland Black Panthers speaking to a meeting of the Center for Participative Education held at the University of California at Berkeley in September 1968. The crisis at hand stemmed from a decision of the UC regents to deny a Black Panther spokesman access to the campus. But for Seale, as for the students, the issue had deeper cultural implications. Everything— the meaning of authority, of personal identity, of Judeo-Christian ethics, of sexual freedom—was somehow involved in this single act of administrative censorship.

Archie and Jughead never kissed Veronica and Betty. Superman never kissed Lois Lane. We are tired of relating to comic book conceptions. Adam should have defended the Garden of Eden against the omnipotent administrator. Life, liberty, and the pursuit of happiness don't mean nothing to me if I can't go home and feel safe with my wife in bed replenishing the earth.[2]

At first glance, it may not be apparent what sentiments of this kind (and they were the substance of the address) have to do with an issue of academic freedom. But Seale's audience had no trouble understanding. They readily recognized that authoritarianism in our society operates overtly or subtly at every level of life, from comic strip imagery to Christian theology, from the college classroom to the privacy of the bedroom—and they were prepared to discard the culture that relied on such sleazy coercion, root and branch.

Or to take another example of these apocalyptic yearnings that beset our young. When the Antiuniversity of London, the first English version of our free universities, was opened in early 1968, its prospectus was filled with courses devoted to "anti-cultures," "anti-environments," "anti-poetry," "anti-theatre," "anti-families," and "counter institutions." Seemingly nothing the adult society had to offer any longer proved acceptable. The superheated radicalism of the school was eventually to

[2] From a recording of the address presented over KPFA (Berkeley) on September 24, 1968.

reach such a pitch that even the age-old student-teacher relationship came under fire as an intolerable form of authoritarianism. So it too was scrapped, on the assumption that nobody any longer had anything to teach the young; they would make up their own education from scratch. Unfortunately—but was the misfortune more comic or more tragic?—the school failed to survive this act of radical restructuring.

Such white-hot discontent always runs the risk of evaporating into a wild, amorphous steam—so that it becomes difficult to tell the chiliastic illuminations from mere inanities. The typical fare offered at the Anti-university can be sampled in one of the "courses," called "From Comic Books to the Dance of Shiva: Spiritual Amnesia and the Physiology of Self-Estrangement." (Again one notes the bizarre but cunning association of the comic strip and high religion.)

Description of course: A free-wheeling succession of open-ended situations. Ongoing vibrations highly relevant. Exploration of Inner Space, de-conditioning of human robot, significance of psycho-chemicals, and the transformation of Western European Man. Source material: Artaud, Zimmer, Gurdjieff, W. Reich, K. Marx, Gnostic, Sufi, and Tantric texts, autobiographical accounts of madness and ecstatic states of consciousness—Pop art and twentieth century prose.

Heavy weather indeed. But altogether representative of the free-university style. Often enough, such madcap brainstorming under the auspices of instructors hardly out of their teens degenerates into a semiarticulate, indiscriminate celebration of everything in sight that is new, strange, and noisy; a fondling of ideas that resembles nothing so much as an infant's play with bright, unfamiliar objects. The appetite is healthily and daringly omnivorous, but it urgently requires mature minds to feed it. It will in large part be my purpose in the chapters that follow to examine a few of the more important figures that are now doing just that. But to make my own point of view quite clear from the outset, I believe that, despite their follies, these young centaurs deserve to win their encounter with the defending Apollos of our society. For the orthodox culture they confront is fatally and contagiously diseased. The prime symptom of that disease is the shadow of thermonuclear annihilation beneath which we cower. The counter culture takes its stand against the background of this absolute evil, an evil which is not defined by the sheer *fact* of the bomb, but by the total *ethos* of the bomb, in which our politics, our public morality, our economic life, our intellectual endeavor are now embedded with a wealth of ingenious rationalization. We are a civilization sunk in an unshakeable commitment to genocide, gambling madly with the universal extermination of our species. And how viciously we ravish our sense of humanity to pretend, even for a day, that such horror can be accepted as "normal," as "necessary"!

Whenever we feel inclined to qualify, to modify, to offer a cautious *"yes . . . but"* to the protests of the young, let us return to this fact as the decisive measure of the technocracy's essential criminality: the extent to which it insists, in the name of progress, in the name of reason, that the unthinkable become thinkable and the intolerable become tolerable.

If the counter culture is, as I will contend here, that healthy instinct which refuses both at the personal and political level to practice such a cold-blooded rape of our human sensibilities, then it should be clear why the conflict between young and adult in our time reaches so peculiarly and painfully deep. In an historical emergency of absolutely unprecedented proportions, we are that strange, culture-bound animal whose biological drive for survival expresses itself *generationally*. It is the young, arriving with eyes that can see the obvious, who must remake the lethal culture of their elders, and who must remake it in desperate haste.

PROTEST—PAST AND PRESENT
Jacob Bronowski

Jacob Bronowski, born in 1908, is a senior fellow and trustee of the Salk Institute for Biological Studies in San Diego. He is also an eminent humanist who has written on such topics as William Blake, science and human values, the Western intellectual tradition, and the identity of man. In the following essay, Bronowski defends protest movements but warns that they must be based on a widely accepted ethic if they are to bring positive and permanent changes.

The title of this essay is meant as a reminder that protest is not a new invention . . .—and this whether we think it a divine invention or a satanic one. On the contrary, protest has always been the normal apparatus to initiate change in human societies. Whenever we say of some historic pioneer that he was *original,* we imply that he was at odds with the traditional view of his time, and that he ultimately persuaded others to his view by voicing his dissent.

This is most obvious in the sciences which, from Galileo to Albert Einstein, have always had to question the established explanations and replace them by new ones. So one reason for the growth of heterodoxy has no doubt been the spread of scientific education. Yet the same

From *The American Scholar,* Vol. XXXVIII, No. 4 (Autumn 1969). Copyright © 1969 by the United Chapters of Phi Beta Kappa. Reprinted by permission of the author and the publisher.

march of innovation, the same process of dissent and challenge, is evident in other intellectual fields: for example, in the arts and in philosophy. It has been equally important in politics and social reform; there could have been no American Revolution and no French Revolution without such unorthodox men as Benjamin Franklin and Thomas Jefferson and Voltaire.

Lest that remark be passed over lightly, I pause to recall that I speak as an Englishman to what George III would have called a parcel of rebels—that is, an audience of Americans. You are a republic today because your forefathers were impatient of social wrongs, what they called "a long train of abuses and usurpations," and revolted against them in 1776. This country was made by political dissenters and, even before that, by religious dissenters. Unlike most of you, I am not a Christian either: so it is fair that I remind you also that you would not be what you are if Christ had submitted to the religious authority of his elders—or if Luther had done so later. It is a sobering lesson in history that millions of people who dislike the contemporary forms of protest still call themselves Protestants.

Progress by dissent then is characteristic of human societies. It has been responsible for the growth and success of democracy in the last four hundred years, and the decline and failure of absolute forms of government. For the crucial feature of democracy is not simply that the majority rules, but that *the minority is free to persuade people* to come over to its side and make a new majority. Of course, the minority is abused at first—Socrates was, and so was Charles Darwin. But the strength of democracy is that the dissident minority is not silenced; on the contrary, it is the business of the minority to convert the majority; and this is how a democratic society invigorates and renews itself in change as no totalitarian society can.

Finally, it is natural that all through history the protesters have belonged to the younger generation, and the defenders of tradition have been the older men. This is one reason why dissent has usually come from the centers of learning, and has often begun as an intellectual movement before it became a popular one. It was so, for example, in the time of Erasmus, and again in the decades of ferment that preceded the Russian Revolution. There are several new factors that underline this tendency today to which I shall point later.

We see in general that protest is the age-old instrument for human progress. Yet when this has been said to link past to present, it remains evident that there are also differences, and that protest today has some features that are special and contemporary.

One feature that is peculiar to America is that the movement of dissent here is greatly occupied with getting justice and equality for racial minorities. I shall refer to this important aim again, but I shall not speak about it much, because I cannot do so at first hand. I am a new-comer to this country; my experience is almost wholly in European uni-versities; and I shall therefore concentrate on those aspects of student dissent that American universities share with European universities.

The striking and universal feature in the protest of the young all over the world is that *it is not doctrinal*. We have been used in the past to associate new movements with some specific dogma: with women's suf-frage, or socialism, or land reform, or even National Socialism. There are no such ideological cure-alls in the minds of students today. Cer-tainly they dislike the existing organizations of government pressure and social conformity, and they want them replaced by something more egalitarian, more personal, less rigid and manipulating. But the very fact that the students' protest runs across the existing political bounda-ries, from Berkeley to Warsaw, and from Prague to Paris and London, shows that there is no ideology that they think will solve the problems of the world overnight. The young now do not expect to reform society by a ready-made program with the points numbered from 1 to 14.

In particular, it is wide of the mark to think that dissent in this coun-try is inspired by communism. Most students now find that idea laugh-able: they consider communism in East Europe to be a mechanical and dictatorial system of state that is as repugnant to them as any other au-tocracy. Otherwise, why would the universities in Poland have made their remarkable protests in 1968? The Polish establishment called those demonstrations a capitalist plot, of course, and that makes a neat match to the fears of our establishment. But the students in Poland and Czechoslovakia are not rooting for capitalism, and the students in the West are not rooting for communism; they are united in *rejecting both establishments*.

It is easy to be scornful of all this, and to say that the students' lack of dogma is an impractical and romantic approach to changing the world. Indeed it is: the heroic pictures of Mao and of Che Guevara on the walls of dormitories show that. It may even be called negative and, worse, a purely destructive approach. But these easy criticisms miss what is crucial in the outlook of the young now, and new. They are not merely criticizing the systems of state in which their elders live, either east or west of the Berlin wall. They are criticizing the *systems of val-ues* by which their elders live everywhere.

So the students' protest is not doctrinal because it goes much deeper: it is concerned with ethics. In the past there was a simple difference be-tween the generations, all the way from politics to sports: the old were usually in favor of the status quo and the young were usually in favor of change. But simple differences like these, simple labels like conservative and liberal, will no longer do now. Now the difference between the generations is a total difference in posture—a rejection by each of the norms by which the other lives.

The generation gap is now a moral chasm, across which the young stare at their elders with distrust, convinced that the values that make for success are fakes. Evidently the first field in which young people are struck by this suspicion is public life, and there the undeclared war in Vietnam has had a disastrous impact. Who indeed could have believed that, twenty-five years after Pearl Harbor, national policy would be carried on like this?

Young people would like to be proud of their own nation (that, after all, is what the students from the minorities exemplify) and they were shocked to find that they could not be proud of the policy of America and her allies in Asia. This was coupled with a second shock, when they found that they could not be proud of the weapons and methods with which the war was waged.

But the greatest shock of all to the idealism of the young is the way in which official spokesmen manipulate and even hoodwink the public opinion that they are supposed to lead. A whole apparatus of evasion has been developed in which nothing is an outright lie, and yet nothing quite means what it seems to say. The very words are unreal: de-escalation, ultimate deterrent, agonizing reappraisal—a tasteless vocabulary of plastic which George Orwell prophetically called Newspeak.

Plainly this language is not designed to *state* a policy but to *sell* it, and accordingly it is tailored to each audience in turn: the patriots here, the realists there, and the credulous everywhere. No wonder that students on both sides of the Iron Curtain think that politics is a career for actors rather than principals. This state of affairs has become so notorious in some countries that it has been christened with a euphemism all its own: it is called the credibility gap. That politely evasive phrase describes what is the fundamental outrage to democracy, namely, the concealment of knowledge: and more than anything else (I believe) this has been responsible for sapping the trust of the young in public standards.

It would be comforting if we could stop there and say, yes, some men in high places have disappointed the young, but after all they have their parents and teachers to look up to still. Unhappily, it is just here that the generation gap is different now from what it was thirty years ago. I can speak for this from my own experience, and I will do so.

I was brought up in Europe in an orthodox Jewish household. My father was a devout believer, who was meticulous to the point of obsession in the practice of every detail of his religious faith. By the time that I went to college I no longer shared his beliefs, which seemed to me an anachronism. But I did not doubt for a moment that my father was sincere in what he believed and practiced. No one, not even the mutinous son that I was, could have thought my father a hypocrite. And as I respected him, so he respected me—in spite of my skepticism. My father thought me a hothead, but he did not doubt that I was sincere, too.

Today the generation gap cleaves through families and colleges, and there is little respect left in it. I need not trouble to spell out for you what the fathers think—and worse still, the grandfathers: they are the ones who write to the papers with such venom every day. Yet I must not quite neglect the phenomenon of those letters to the newspapers. Here we are in the country that prizes education more than any other country in the world; and in that country, here we are in the state of California, which prizes education more than any other state. And yet exactly here the correspondence columns are filled with such hatred against the young, such hysterical fear of change, that one cannot imagine how the writers picture a university. Do they expect education to run backward? Do they think that there can be progress without originality, and originality without dissent? Or would they really like to burn heretics?

Perhaps senior citizens always felt like this, and their grandsons paid no attention. But now the same gap has opened between fathers and sons. Whatever the generation, the sons no longer believe that the standards by which their elders judge them are genuine; on the contrary, they strike them for the most part as bald hypocrisy. I knew that my father lived by the precepts that he tried to impose on me. But most students today are convinced that their parents and teachers deceive themselves, and profess a traditional set of principles without even being aware that they do not live by them. In the eyes of the children, the generation gap now is a hypocrisy gap.

If those whom the young stigmatize were all reactionaries and anti-intellectuals, it would be easy to concur. Unfortunately, things are not so simple. A whole generation of liberals and humanists, to which I belong, is bewildered at the discovery that the young include us in their charge of hypocrisy. We made liberalism respectable by our labors, and turned it into an intellectual faith; and now we are distressed to find that our heroic memories of the hungry thirties and the Spanish Civil War are dismissed as an out-of-date mythology.

The fact is that we, the generation of intellectuals, have been a success, and our liberal and even radical ideas have not stood in our way on the road to affluence. And the young are suspicious of affluence: they do not believe that success comes so cheap to those who hold their principles dear. Success is a commodity sold on television in shatterproof bottles at bargain prices, and the children are no longer impressed by those trappings of authenticity. They know in their hearts that the successful man is a prisoner of the status quo, whatever high principles he may avow in the family circle or on the rostrum.

When the French historian La Popelinière died in obscurity in 1608, his biographer wrote that he had died "of a disease common to men of learning and virtue, that is, of misery and of want." But that was in the past. Now men of learning fare much better, and their sons and students are correspondingly less certain of their virtue.

So it is not to be wondered that the young are restive when they hear us pay lip-service to intellectual truth. For in the thirty years in which we have preached that, the world has changed, and we have somehow forgotten to find new foundations for the old truths. The economic exploitation and social inequality of thirty years ago have been transformed since then, and will no longer do as grounds for the human and liberal morality in which we still believe—and believe rightly. As intellectuals, we have done little to formulate afresh *an ethic of liberalism on foundations that are modern* and valid now. In my view, this is the central criticism that can be directed against intellectuals today, in and out of the universities.

Here I must pause in my argument to say something about the practical discontents in the universities. For, of course, there are direct and practical causes that turn the moral scruples of students into the bitter hand-to-hand clashes with campus authority. Three causes are specifically modern, and illustrate how education now differs from the past—even the past of thirty years ago.

First, there are vastly more students now than there have ever been before. There are about seven million students in America at this moment, which is more than went to college in the whole world in all the hundred years of the last century. What students in these numbers want from university education must be different in kind from the academic programs of the past. So we are now engaged by necessity in the experiment of finding a core curriculum and a culture to embody the aspirations of mass democracy. This is the cardinal problem to which I shall come back at the end of this essay. The demands of the minority groups for higher education are one part of the problem we have to solve. But the problem is the same for the majority, and is worldwide: what is the central content of contemporary knowledge that every young man and woman (and not just a few) ought to have in order to feel and act as educated citizens?

Second, young people now become physically and emotionally mature almost two years earlier than they did in the past. Yet while the age of biological maturity has fallen steadily, the age of university education has remained almost unchanged. As a result, the campuses are now peopled by grown men and women, yet are governed by traditions of organization and discipline that were made for adolescents. No wonder that the parents who remember themselves as striplings at college are outraged by the beards and the bosoms that they see there now—and by the intransigence that is natural in the bearded and the bosomed, especially when they have to be treated as children. The university system as it is, historically, is two years out of step with the attitudes and emotions of contemporary students, and is only suited to the young who are now in high school.

And third, the trouble on campus is a microcosm that reflects the troubles of administration and organization that dog any mass democracy. I have already said that democracy is a very special philosophy. It expresses the mind of the majority, yet it gives the minority the right to try to change the mind of the majority. That is, democracy is an instrument for change and progress.

But to make that philosophy work, democracy has to have an administration that is receptive to change. It has to be sensitive to what people want *before* they break the rules. And this is where organizations of state and government are failing us, and where most seriously the campus administrations are failing the students. I have been an administrator myself and I know the temptations. There is always some piece of business in the office that seems more urgent than the complaints of people. So the awkward issues are postponed; the grievances accumulate; and we stumble from crisis to crisis, never acting until the strike notices have been posted and people's blood is up. We never tackle a frontier dispute until there is shooting; a labor demand until the garbage is piled high in the streets; and the restlessness of the young until they invade the president's office.

The trouble on campus has a tremendous message: that we must discover how to run mass democracy so that things are changed *before* people get mad. In an age of technology, of constant practical change, this is a practical message to shake the world. Because if we do not get this right, then the process of peaceful change will break down, and people will turn to violence and minority rule everywhere. The trouble on campus is a storm signal to warn us that the philosophy of democracy will only survive if we reform the *practice* of democracy.

Yet when these practical things have been said, the intellectual problem comes back to meet us. We need to find a philosophical foundation for the ethics of democracy that the young can believe in. What divides democracy from its enemies is not a dogmatic distinction as between good and bad, your faith and mine, but is the basic distinction between tolerance and fanaticism—between persuasion and violence. When the students turn to disruption and hooliganism they show that our generation has failed to make the liberal values real to them. Instead we have demonstrated to them in a dozen political precedents, all the way from Ireland to Israel, that only men with guns get their demands. And calling out the National Guard will only reinforce that ugly lesson.

The young are looking for a universal ethic now as much as in the past, and here as much as in Czechoslovakia. If they strike you as amoral, look again: they are in search of a morality that shall be idealistic and realistic at the same time. And if we think we have it in humanism, we shall have to find modern foundations for that.

It is pointless to exhort students to law and order, and to lecture them about rights and duties, in the absence of any foundation for human respect—and worse, in an atmosphere of cynicism that claims that human nature is a caged beast. Law and order are not ends in themselves; they are the means that society has invented to preserve justice, which is the harmony between individual freedom and communal need. Since only man among the animals is both individual and social, he has constantly to re-create the balance between these two sides of his nature. What we have to ask then of people, young and old alike, is not blankly that they respect the law, but that they respect every man as a man (whatever his opinions or his social function). And to bring that about, we have to make a modern analysis of the nature of man, derived from the natural and social sciences and equally from its expression in the arts. Only so shall we establish for everyone that the identity of man demands respect as an essential and, as it were, an existential condition of his being.

This is in a sense an academic program, and none the worse for that; and the universities are to be blamed for failing to attempt it. In a time of bold technical progress and of brilliant scientific discovery, one might have expected that humanists in the universities would also be eager to move into new fields, and that the study of the ethical nature of man would be most attractive to them. After all, many of the protesting students are suspicious of science and disillusioned by it, and are ready to look to the humanities for a lead. But in fact the departments of humanities have done little to move away from their traditional studies and toward the ethical content of their own subject matter. And yet that is surely what the arts can teach: the sense of identity with the inner lives of all men.

It is particularly sad that philosophy has remained remote from any genuine inquiry into the human mind and the dilemmas of personality. At a time when young men hunger for principles to guide their lives, philosophy has been preoccupied with forms of analysis in which, it rightly assures them, there surely are none to be found. So for thirty years now no philosopher has commanded, or has aspired to, that combination of intellectual and moral respect which made Bertrand Russell a giant in his generation.

I believe that there are principles to be found today to guide human conduct, as there were in the past. Today they must come out of modern knowledge of what makes us the creatures that we are, specifically human. We do not know the whole answer to that, of course, and no doubt we never will; but we know more than we ever did in the past. And what we know is not exclusively in science, and not exclusively in the humanities, but is a combination of both in which each illuminates the other. Only in this way, by understanding as exactly and as sympathetically as we can what men are, can we make the generations (past and present) agree to try to be what men should be.

In my view, this is a very practical task: for an agreed ethic must be based on a common culture, and a common culture must be expressed in what is taught in schools and universities. The great need, the great experiment in education now is therefore to put together a core curriculum for all students, whose parts truly represent the constituents of modern culture. I think there should be three parts: science, anthropology (as representative of social study) and literature.

In science, students need in the first place to learn enough physics, chemistry and mathematics (including some statistics) to make a foundation for biology in its contemporary form. As soon as they have the foundation, they should go on to biology as the central science in the core curriculum. The accent in biology should be on evolution: the evolution of life, of molecular structures and processes, of organs, of species and their behavior, and in the end, of man. The purpose should be to build up a picture of man as he is by nature, within the order of nature: what I have called elsewhere "an understanding of the evolution and the place of man" as a single conception. I will go on to quote what I said there:

He is, like the other primates, noisy, inquisitive, cooperative, intelligent, skillful, thoughtful, and as busy with himself as with his environment. These features are not common in the rest of the animal world, singly or in combination. They have been a great deal more important in the evolution of the primates than the territorial imperative and the aggressive drives which we share with other animals. And in the remarkable order of primates, the evolution of man is most remarkable and spectacular. His gifts of discrimination and judgment, the ability to speak, to remember, to foresee, to imagine and to think symbolically, his carriage and the freedom that it gives to hands and face, his face-to-face relations and his way of making love, his family life and the intimacy of his social values, are an incomparable biological equipment. They have evolved him, and in turn have been evolved by his own progress, within at most a few million years. From them he has his creative skill and his imaginative breadth of outlook, in which are intertwined his need for the society of others and his urge to think for himself.

As the second leg in what I will call my tripos curriculum, I have chosen anthropology. I prefer it to other branches of social study in a core curriculum, because I think students should not be preoccupied only with the forms of social institutions (including government) but should unravel the underlying beliefs and values that those express. Anthropology is the best discipline for the study of values, not as arbitrary social norms, but as expressions of human aims. In this sense, it carries on the scientific purpose of my first leg, and I can go on with my quotation:

It goes without saying that the picture of man that science presents to a bewildered and downcast public must be truthful. But that does not mean that it turns him either into a beast or into a computer. On the contrary, what makes the biological machinery of man so powerful is that it modifies his actions through his imagination: it makes him able to symbolize, to project himself into the consequences of his acts, to conceptualize his plans, and to weigh them one against another as a system of values. We are the creatures who have to create values in order to elucidate our own conduct and to learn from it so that we can direct it into the future.

For the third leg of my tripos I propose literature as the most accessible representative of the arts. The arts are important in the curriculum because they *express* the human condition directly, and as powerfully as the sciences *expound* it. Literature in particular should give the student a sense of the immediacy of human problems, an open door into the minds and passions of men, within which he finds himself to be both singular and universal. The gift of imagination makes man able to live his own life and a thousand others, and to draw from that network of experience a central concept of himself that can be a better guide to conduct than any book of moral precepts. Since I have presented these views in *The Identity of Man* I need not argue them here; I think they leave no doubt that literature can be as important a constituent in founding a modern ethic as can the sciences of biology and anthropology.

The need for a modern ethic of this kind, securely founded, is patent: because precisely the lack of it has turned the movements of protest toward self-righteousness and violence. Otherwise we are simply on the way to confronting dogma with dogma, force with ferocity, my right with your wrong. But these do not constitute the real division in human conduct. The fundamental distinction is between liberal and bigot, and at bottom it is the distinction between human and inhuman. At the base of any educational reform, this is the distinction for which we have to find a secure, contemporary, and universal foundation.

THE STUDENT DRIVE TO DESTRUCTION
Louis J. Halle

Unlike the authors of the two previous selections, Louis J. Halle, who was born in 1910, casts a cold and critical eye on the youthful generation and its leaders. To Halle, who is a specialist in world affairs and the author of *The Cold War as History* and *Civilization and Foreign Policy,* many spokesmen for the young exemplify the twentieth century's negative image of man.

" 'We shall destroy because we are a force,' observed Arkady. . . . 'Yes, a force is not to be called to account.' . . .

" 'Allow me, though,' began Nikolai Petrovitch. 'You deny everything; or, speaking more precisely, you destroy everything. But one must construct too, you know.'

" 'That's not our business now. The ground wants clearing first'."

Turgenev, Fathers and Sons

To understand the implications of the students' revolt for the future of our civilization one should place it in its historical setting. As a movement of rejection it represents the nihilism that has been developing for over a century now, to the point where it is at last becoming the dominant intellectual drive of our time.

The word "nihilism" was introduced into the common language in 1862, when Turgenev published his *Fathers and Sons,* a compassionate novel dealing with the gap between the generations. Bazarov, the young nihilist who is its hero, represents the revolt of the new generation against the old, against its whole traditional culture.

By the second half of the nineteenth century that traditional culture was losing such innate authority as it had once had. It was the possession of a ruling élite, expressed in the affectation of high ideals that took no account either of the findings of science or of the impoverished lives of the great majority of people, on whose labor the élite lived. Nihilism, in these circumstances, was not entirely without point. According to Bazarov's disciple, the student Arkady, "a nihilist is a man who does not bow down before any authority, who does not take any principle on faith, whatever the reverence in which it may be enshrined." Such nihilism stood for a frank recognition of reality, for a society based on science rather than on an obsolete idealism.

Those who affected the culture that the original nihilists opposed took an optimistic view of human nature—that is, they made a polar distinction between their own noble nature, which was soulful, and the nature of the brute beasts. Man, in their view, was essentially divine, created in the image of his maker, and if he had fallen into evil he was still capable of the redemption that they, themselves, pretended to represent. The nihilists, responding to the initial impact of Darwinism, denied this distinction between men and beasts. (Turgenev began writing his great novel just as *The Origin of Species* was published.) For the piously optimistic view of human nature they substituted a new view in the name of scientific realism. Their denial that man was the divine creature he pretended to be took a particularly persuasive form, at last, in the works of Freud and the Freudians, who concluded that men are governed by the destructive forces that represent their basic animal nature, however either sublimation or hypocrisy may cover them up.

Throughout the Victorian Age ladies and gentlemen had pretended to be exempt from the bestial impulses that are, in fact, common to us all. The way new generations were produced was an unmentionable secret, not to be acknowledged—above all, to be kept from the members of the new generation until, inevitably, they at last learned about it in the shame of the wedding night.

With the revolt against Victorianism that followed World War I, Freudianism became a religion among the advanced intellectuals. The zeal with which it was adopted and preached in the 1920's can be understood only if one appreciates the release from former shame and inhibitions that it provided. Those of the new generation who had secretly entertained "wicked thoughts," believing that decent people did not have them, suddenly learned that everyone had them, including their hypocritical elders. The Freudian psychoanalyst, to whom so many of these people now turned, relieved them of the moral burden they had borne. They confessed to him and he took away the shame. The experience was that of an ineffable liberation.

There were other forms of liberation as well, stemming from the thesis that everyone should rid himself of his inhibitions, inhibitions associated with the hypocritical tradition of the Victorian generation. The extreme exponents of this thesis organized free-love camps and nudist communities. For the most part, however, what it produced was greater verbal frankness, together with a more relaxed and informal relationship between the sexes. Women got off the pedestal that had held them at such a distance from men, and by dressing and behaving so as to reduce the differences between the sexes they made possible a camaraderie with men that, a generation earlier, would have been regarded as improper. (They gave themselves a flat-chested appearance by means of the newly invented brassieres, which were simply tight bands; they cut their hair short, and they smoked cigarettes.) All this was the beginning of what we call permissiveness.

These two trends—the disposition to regard man as essentially beastly, and permissiveness—have both continued through the half century since the First World War, until they have at last reached the predominance they are manifesting today. Today, books advancing the thesis that man is a predatory aggressor by nature are welcomed and acclaimed by the intellectual community. At the same time, all censorship and most of the traditional restrictions on sexual indulgence are denounced.

There is a paradox of disastrous implications here. At the same time that man is represented as being an aggressive beast, incapable of moral responsibility, the inhibitions that society has hitherto imposed on his freedom to indulge his nature are to be removed.

Throughout the history of political philosophy, an optimistic view of human nature has been associated with the advocacy of freedom, a pessimistic view with authoritarianism. The pessimistic view that Plato took, in consequence of the disasters that popular rule had just brought upon Athens, was the basis of the authoritarianism advocated in *The Republic*. In ancient China, the optimistic view of human nature led the Mohists to advocate a society based on love rather than force, while the pessimistic view led the Legalists to advocate a police state. Russian authoritarianism, alike under the czars and their successors, is associated with the accepted view that men are destructive creatures who, if only for their own sakes, have got to be held down.

Our own Western tradition of liberalism, which goes back through Thomas Jefferson to John Locke, was justified by the optimistic view of man's nature that prevailed in the eighteenth century. This is also true of the Jacobin tradition, which goes back through Karl Marx to Rousseau. Marx was explicit in his conception of human nature as basically creative rather than destructive. Consequently, he looked forward to the day when, capitalism having been liquidated, the coercive state would wither away, after which men would enjoy in perpetuity perfect freedom for the indulgence of their natural creativity.

In the face of the logic these cases exemplify, how can one explain the present advocacy of permissiveness by those who regard man as an irremediably greedy, aggressive, and predatory beast? This stands opposed to the logic I have cited, which also takes the form of the principle that men can be free only to the extent that they make a disciplined use of their freedom. It is only where men are prepared to deal tolerantly with the diversity among them, and to abide voluntarily by "the rules of the game," that freedom is possible. Where men will not tolerate the expression of opinions different from their own, and where they refuse to accept decisions reached in accordance with "the rules of the game," the impositions of the police state become unavoidable. Anyone who has raised children knows, from direct experience, that freedom is a function of the capacity for socially responsible and considerate behavior.

It is the tradition of civility in the United States and Britain, expressed in self-restraint, that has hitherto made possible the relative freedom enjoyed by their peoples, and it is the extreme moderation of the Swiss in resolving their internal differences, which are great, that makes possible the freedom they enjoy today. Here we have demonstrations of the fact that human nature, at an advanced stage of civilization, is capable of such self-discipline as a free society requires.

If one looks at the mixed historical record of mankind, or if one consults one's own experience of the people one has known, it is quite impossible to believe that man is either all bad or all good. He may be properly described, it seems to me, as a beast with a soul. Even if I were willing to concede that the evil was predominant in him—in the sense that he was governed by his animal appetites, by a desire to destroy, by a lust for power—even so, if there is only one spark in the darkness of his nature, there is, in that spark, a basis for unlimited hope. In spite of the fashionable anthropology of our day, which identifies him as a predatory beast, it seems to me clear that man, in his evolution, has already made noticeable progress in rising above the level of his pre-human ancestors.

This is a view for which abundant evidence could be adduced, but it is not a view that can gain a hearing today because it is, for the depressing reasons I have already cited, so unwelcome to those who represent the intellectual fashions of our day. If I should write a book showing that man, like the great carnivores, is predatory by his unchangeable nature, I could be sure that it would be widely read and acclaimed; but if I wrote a book that took an optimistic and teleological view of man's evolution, regarding it as an ascent from the level of the beasts to something ethically and spiritually higher, it would hardly be well received and few would read it. The burden of living up to a high standard is something men can do without. I do not think that this situation will change in what remains of this century, for we seem to be in one of those long periods when civilization, in decline, produces the kind of thinking appropriate to such decline. But if the Phoenix ever rises again, its rise will be accompanied by the general optimism that periods of progress always produce.

Men tend to be what they think they are. If they accept a view of themselves as self-indulgent they will tend to be self-indulgent; if they accept a view of themselves as morally responsible beings they will tend to be morally responsible. I do not think that the widespread denial of social inhibitions on human behavior, which we call permissiveness, is altogether unrelated to the prevalent view of what our human nature really is. Here is a logic that does, in fact, associate the two trends of our time: the hopeless view of our human nature and the assault on social inhibitions. If we are really pigs, rather than fine ladies and gentlemen, then we should not be asked to behave like fine ladies and gentlemen. We should be free to use language regarded as obscene, and there should be no restrictions on theatrical exhibitions of sexual and sadistic practices, no matter how sickening some of them may be. (Whatever may be said in favor of freedom for obscenity, I submit that it is not on the same level of importance as the freedoms guaranteed by the first ten amendments of our Constitution.)

I do not offer this, however, as the primary explanation of how it is that those who regard man as fundamentally bestial are, nevertheless, the advocates of permissiveness. A further explanation is that they are not really interested in the maintenance or enlargement of a régime of freedom that, on the one hand, they tend to take for granted (having never experienced anything else), and that, on the other, does not in itself cure the intractable problems of our societies. The causes they nominally espouse are not necessarily causes they believe in, but mere pretexts for action that has other ends than their success. Any number of activist students admit in private that when they shout for Marx or Mao or Castro that does not mean they care anything about what these figures stand for. They do not carry intellectual responsibility that far.

Some of the student leaders have, on occasion, made it clear that what they really want is power for themselves (thereby exemplifying the fashionable anthropological view of human nature). At other times they have not bothered to deny that destruction is, for them, an end in itself —relieving them, as such, of any need to think beyond it. If they invoke causes that are genuinely idealistic and progressive, such as human equality or freedom, they do so for tactical purposes only. They invoke them as pretexts on the basis of which they can confuse men of good will and rally the forces of destruction. When German student leaders led their followers, last September, in a violent physical assault on the Leipzig Book Fair, the reason they gave was that the directors of the Fair had chosen President Senghor of Senegal as the recipient of the Fair's peace prize when they might have chosen, instead, Mr. Stokely Carmichael, the apostle of violence. Here the cynicism is patent.

No one, I gather, doubts the intelligence of these student leaders, however gullible their followers may be. In preferring violence to free speech they know, as the Nazi leaders knew, that its success would spell the end of such free speech as I am exercising in this article. When they deliberately and skillfully provoke a bewildered police force into acts of brutality, and then denounce its "fascism," they know the equivocation in which they are indulging. When they denounce the authorities of New York City as being the rulers of a "police state," and oppose them on that basis, they know that a police state is what their movement, if carried to the lengths they intend, would bring about.

It is no answer to say that there are real and important matters for grievance. Of course there are! The point is that the proponents of violence are not really acting, as they pretend, to eliminate these matters. Their leaders, at least, know that, if there are stupid professors (a grievance one student offered me as justification for violent demonstrations), destroying the universities is not the way to get intelligent ones. They know that white discrimination against blacks will not be overcome by a course of action that makes votes for Wallace and pushes the American society in the direction already taken by South Africa. The leaders who know these things are acting cynically, however idealistic what they are doing may seem to older intellectuals who think themselves back in 1848.

Violence and destruction for its own sake prepares the way for the police state, as violence and destruction in Germany prepared the way for Hitler's dictatorship. Specifically, they prepare the way for brutal and ignorant leaders to assume the power of a state that, in our case, possesses a nuclear armament with which it could destroy the world. For those who pursue destruction as an end in itself, the possibilities are now unlimited.

One thing that separates my generation from the generation of my children is the experience it has had of the great depression and of the decade during which the tyranny of the fascist police state seemed likely to engulf the world. My generation has vivid knowledge of how easily the structure of civilization can collapse, and of how terrible the consequences can be in terms of human suffering. Our children, on the other hand, have at best read about these experiences in history books. All that most of them have experienced at first hand is full employment, unlimited opportunity to make a living, and the remarkable freedom of speech and behavior that they have enjoyed in an increasingly permissive society. (On the Berkeley campus, a couple of years ago, I saw earnest-looking boys and girls, righteous indignation written on their faces, sitting behind a table marked "Committee for Sexual Libertinism," and I wondered who was preventing them from simply going ahead and engaging in it.)

I cannot imagine that many of those who say they are willing to face the eventuality of a police state, as the consequence of their actions, would not change their minds if ever they found themselves living under one. I have emphasized the element of cynicism in their conduct—but it is accompanied by an innocence of either experience or knowledge that contributes to their moral irresponsibility. (It was Irwin Cobb who said: the trouble with the younger generation is that it hasn't read the minutes of the last meeting.)

I have no doubt that, if mankind is on a long upward path over the millenia, that path will continue to be marked, in the future as in the past, by great crashes of civilization. I cannot quite believe that one of these crashes will spell a final end to the hopes of mankind; but we are now entering a period of human history when new dangers, produced by scientific progress, require us to exercise a greater self-control than ever before. It is not impossible, as a consequence of the breakdown in the discipline of civilization, that Mr. George Wallace or someone like him will become President of the United States in 1973, with responsibility for its international relations and with control over its nuclear armament.

I have talked to students who believe that the basic procedure of democracy is represented by violence in the streets, and that freedom means doing whatever one pleases. To the extent that each generation is responsible for educating the next, my generation must regard itself as a notable failure.

THE YOUNG RADICALS

"We intend to make a revolution."

MARK RUDD

"TWO, THREE, MANY COLUMBIAS"
Tom Hayden

While the 1968 strike at Columbia has already well receded into the past, similar disturbances looming in the future at many universities promise to make this essay still relevant for the 1970's. The author—a founder of S.D.S., someone who manned the barricades at Columbia, a member of the Chicago Seven—has credentials that would make an aspiring leader of radical youth envious. As this article and the next one by Mark Rudd show, some of the most publicized revolutionary spokesmen are not hedonistic barbarians who advocate orgies and nihilism. If these men are "guerrillas," they are very idealistic ones. Tom Hayden talks of "transforming," not destroying the university, and he wants to do so in order to establish "decent values."

The goal written on the university walls was "Create two, three, many Columbias"; it meant expand the strike so that the U.S. must either change or send its troops to occupy American campuses.

At this point the goal seems realistic; an explosive mix is present on dozens of campuses where demands for attention to student views are being disregarded by university administrators.

The American student movement has continued to swell for nearly a decade: during the semi-peace of the early '60s as well as during Vietnam; during the token liberalism of John Kennedy as well as during the bankrupt racism of Lyndon Johnson. Students have responded most directly to the black movement of the '60s: from Mississippi Summer to the Free Speech Movement; from "Black Power" to "Student Power"; from the seizure of Howard University to the seizure of Hamilton Hall. As the racial crisis deepens so will the campus crisis. But the student protest is not just an offshoot of the black protest—it is based on authentic opposition to the middle-class world of manipulation, channeling and careerism. The students are in opposition to the fundamental institutions of society.

The students' protest constantly escalates by building on its achievements and legends. The issues being considered by seventeen-year-old freshmen at Columbia University would not have been within the imagination of most "veteran" student activists five years ago.

Columbia opened a new tactical stage in the resistance movement which began last fall: from the overnight occupation of buildings to permanent occupation; from mill-ins to the creation of revolutionary committees; from symbolic civil disobedience to barricaded resistance. Not only are these tactics already being duplicated on other campuses, but they are sure to be surpassed by even more militant tactics. In the future it is conceivable that students will threaten destruction of buildings as a last deterrent to police attacks. Many of the tactics learned can also be applied in smaller hit-and-run operations between strikes: raids on the offices of professors doing weapons research could win substantial support among students while making the university more blatantly repressive.

In the buildings occupied at Columbia, the students created what they called a "new society" or "liberated area" or "commune," a society in which decent values would be lived out even though university officials might cut short the communes through use of police. The students had fun, they sang and danced and wisecracked, but there was continual tension. There was no question of their constant awareness of the seriousness of their acts. Though there were a few violent arguments about tactics, the discourse was more in the form of endless meetings convened to explore the outside political situation, defense tactics, maintenance and morale problems within the group. Debating and then determining what leaders should do were alternatives to the remote and authoritarian decision-making of Columbia's trustees.

The Columbia strike represented more than a new tactical movement, however. There was a political message as well. The striking students were not holding onto a narrow conception of students as a privileged class asking for inclusion in the university as it now exists. This kind of demand could easily be met by administrators by opening minor opportunities for "student rights" while cracking down on campus radicals. The Columbia students were instead taking an internationalist and revolutionary view of themselves in opposition to the imperialism of the very institutions in which they have been groomed and educated. They did not even want to be included in the decision-making circles of the military-industrial complex that runs Columbia: *they want to be included only if their inclusion is a step toward transforming the university*. They want a new and independent university standing against the mainstream of American society, or they want no university at all. They are, in Fidel Castro's words, "guerrillas in the field of culture."

How many other schools can be considered ripe for such confrontations? The question is hard to answer, but it is clear that the demands of black students for cultural recognition rather than paternalistic tolerance, ·and radical white students' awareness of the sinister paramilitary activities carried on in secret by the faculty on many campuses, are hardly confined to Columbia. Columbia's problem is the American problem in miniature—the inability to provide answers to widespread social needs and the use of the military to protect the authorities against the people. This process can only lead to greater unity in the movement.

Support from outside the university communities can be counted on in many large cities. A crisis is foreseeable that would be too massive for police to handle. It can happen; whether or not it will be necessary is a question which only time will answer. What is certain is that we are moving toward power—the power to stop the machine if it cannot be made to serve humane ends.

American educators are fond of telling their students that barricades are part of the romantic past, that social change today can only come about through the processes of negotiation. But the students at Columbia discovered that barricades are only the beginning of what they call "bringing the war home."

COLUMBIA'S STRIKE LEADER: "WE WANT REVOLUTION"
Mark Rudd

Like Tom Hayden, Mark Rudd was a leader of the original S.D.S. Since 1969, however, he has been associated with the more militant Revolutionary Youth Movement ("The Weatherman"). While this article is as idealistic as the previous one, it relies more openly on an economic interpretation of history than Hayden's. Not everyone will accept the terminology and ideology Rudd uses to explain why "student power" must confront capitalism. But everyone should note the moral imperative he uses to justify direct and sometimes extreme action: "either you support oppression of human behavior or you fight against it."

Despite the inordinate number of reporters and commentators who have "analyzed" the New Left and the events at Columbia, despite mountains of words and endless theories about conspiracies, no one outside S.D.S. (Students for a Democratic Society) and the New Left has yet to make a reasonably knowledgeable statement about the meaning of the Columbia rebellion and the rise of the New Left student movement.

There has been a qualitative shift in the purpose and identity of the student movement since the Berkeley rebellion of 1964. Young people no longer see social problems in the same light. The war in Vietnam, for example, is viewed by the New Left as an inherent part of the political-economic system that dominates our country, not as the product of one man's policies, nor the result of general "aggressive drives" in men's personalities.

The direction of S.D.S. was set in 1965 at the first March on Washington in opposition to the war. Paul Potter, at the conclusion of his speech, advised that we must take our abstract notion of "the system," ". . . analyze it, understand it," and, on the basis of what we ourselves find, change that system. Our ideas come out of our experiences with this society, not out of the dogma of any political sect. Our anger and our hopes, just as much as anyone else's, have been created by this society. Anyone who wants to understand the New Left must look at America, not Fidel Castro or Chairman Mao, to discover what we are about.

What are the realities of America's political-economic system? Why do we consider it to be our enemy and the enemy of most of the people of the world?

Everyone knows that the United States has a "capitalist" system. Theoretically, it functions through free competition for profits. Ac-

From the *Saturday Evening Post,* Vol. 241, No. 19 (September 21, 1968). Reprinted by permission of the Curtis Publishing Company.

tually, the system runs by concentrations of capital, by monopolies open to very few. John Doe, next door, cannot start an automobile plant, or a railroad or even a supermarket, for want of capital, connections and political pull. But those who control the monopolies exercise tremendous power on society both economically, through the production and capital of their corporations, and politically, through their ties with the Government—they are the main contributors to Democratic and Republican Party funds, they are sponsors of intermediate institutions such as the Council on Foreign Relations, and they have personal influence as individuals.

In order for American capitalism to sustain its profits and power, it has developed two main forms of domination—racism and imperialism. The latter, working on an international scale, is the economic domination of underdeveloped countries by U.S. corporations for markets, raw materials and new areas of investment. Sometimes it is necessary for the United States Government to engage in direct political interference in order to maintain economic interests, as in Guatemala, in 1954, when the Central Intelligence Agency overthrew the Arbenz regime to protect the United Fruit Co.; and the Dominican Republic, in 1965, when Johnson sent Marines to help overthrow the legal reform regime that threatened American sugar interests. In all forms of imperialism, United States domination works against the well-being of the underdeveloped countries, limiting their freedom, sapping their wealth and restricting their development. Imperialism works against our own well-being, too. We have seen the domestic effects of the war in Vietnam—the tremendous waste of our manpower and economic resources to fight a war to maintain United States political hegemony.

Racism, far from being the product of the "American character," is, like imperialism, the result of the necessities of the capitalist system. Ghettos exist because they are profitable—they provide a source of cheap labor. For several generations white Americans have been trained to adopt racist, discriminatory attitudes, sometimes out of immediate economic self-interest. These attitudes themselves are perpetuated by policy decisions of those who control government and big business. Columbia University's expansion into Morningside Heights, to cite one such policy, is designed to create a white "respectable" neighborhood around Columbia, driving poor blacks and Puerto Ricans from one of the few integrated neighborhoods in Manhattan.

Given this analysis of our society and the workings of capitalism, New Leftists have chosen to fight imperialism and racism in order to fight capitalism—to free ourselves and others. We work where we are —in high schools, universities, unions, factories.

Many have called us a "student power" movement, implying that our goal is student control over the "educational process," taking decision-making power away from the administrators and putting it in the hands of "democratic" student groups. Presumably, the guiding principle in a university where student power is a reality would be to make possible the greatest fulfillment of human potential. Student power used to be the goal of S.D.S., but as our understanding of the society has developed, our understanding of the university's role in it has also changed.

We see the university as a factory whose goal is to produce: 1) trained personnel for corporations, government and more universities, and 2) knowledge of the uses of business and government to perpetuate the present system. Government studies at Columbia, for example, attempt to explain our society through concepts of pluralism and conflicting group interest, while the reality of the situation is quite different.

Clark Kerr, president of the University of California at Berkeley in 1964, in his book, *The Uses of the University*, explains that the purpose of universities like Berkeley and Columbia is to train the technicians who will administer our society. The University of California "educates" aeronautics engineers in the latest techniques for private aircraft companies. Columbia has received a $1.5 million "gift" from I.B.M. for an expansion program. It is no accident that graduate professional schools of universities are growing most rapidly. Columbia, for example, is constructing a vast new International Affairs building to train future C.I.A. agents, State Department officers and corporate specialists, at a time when the undergraduate liberal-arts college is overcrowded and fires good teachers for lack of money. Within this university factory, students are manipulated and channeled, stripped of creativity and energy, ready at the end of the assembly line to take their places in deathlike offices or still more educational factories.

Student power is not the way to achieve a university structured to benefit humanity, since the problems of the university originate elsewhere. Because power and money are concentrated in corporations and government, it is impossible to create a "free" university within a society as unfree as ours; the university is the tool of society, or, in the American case, those who dominate our society. At Columbia, the all-powerful board of trustees, composed of men from banks, corporations and government, act as the representatives of this ruling class. To be sure, certain reforms are possible within the university, but these are mostly either to give the illusion of democracy, as in student or faculty senates and judicial boards, or to grant more privileges to students, such as longer dormitory visiting hours or later curfew. University administrators can well afford to make such concessions, because of their lack of social significance.

Far from being internally oriented, the rebellion at Columbia was "political" in the most important sense of the word. Our strike gave people a chance to act directly against imperialism and racism—to engage in political activity that went far out into society and linked students with other groups in the country and the world. We demanded that Columbia sever its ties with the Institute for Defense Analyses, which does weapons research for the war in Vietnam and American military ventures around the world. We demanded a stop to the construction of the university gymnasium in Morningside Heights, a demand first raised by people of the Harlem community. This was a case of white and black students at Columbia supporting the right of the people of Harlem to control their own community. We demanded an amnesty to all who participated in the demonstration. This would have forced the administration of Columbia to say we were right. If we had settled for a bipartite student-faculty committee to make decisions on discipline for the students engaged in the demonstrations, we would have been co-opted, neatly and efficiently, because Columbia president Grayson Kirk and the board of trustees could well afford to accommodate all our other demands. What they could not afford was to be among the first members of the ruling sector to be defeated on the field of political battle by a motley mob of rebelling students.

Again, this was not a question of student power; we had gone much farther. We had questioned the very foundations of our society—the capitalist system itself. And we did this in the institution where we are located—the university.

Why did so many thousands of students risk so much for issues primarily outside the university, issues that did not affect their immediate self-interest? The answer lies in the dissatisfaction we students feel with this society and our identification with the most oppressed groups—the people in the ghetto, the people of Vietnam. The young understand more clearly the oppression of others because we too are oppressed, though rarely as directly as by napalm or the National Guard. At Columbia we hit out at the people responsible for the manipulation of our lives at the university, as well as the oppression of blacks and Vietnamese, by seizing the buildings. This action told the university that we would no longer allow the exploitation of our brothers or of ourselves. Ours was no group of liberals fighting for the rights of others; we felt, the entire time, that we were fighting for our own lives, for our present and future, which up to now had appeared meaningless.

Most of those who participated in the demonstrations, a number reaching into the thousands, felt that the lines were very clearly drawn —either you support oppression of human beings or you fight against it. Liberalism is bankrupt because of its inability to deal with the realities of racism and imperialism and their fundamental causes. The options are limited: to stand in the middle, to be "neutral," constitutes support for the *status quo.*

Many of the hundreds who seized the Columbia buildings said that they had never experienced such a feeling of personal liberation as during the strike; this came not only from the knowledge that they were fighting an oppressive enemy but also because we were in the process of building real communities within the buildings, which far surpassed the stiff, repressive life of Columbia.

Young people feel more strongly, too, the gap between the possibilities and the realizations of this society. The richest economy the world has ever known depends on waste production—production to satisfy created needs, not real needs—for a great part of its national income, while it leaves unbearable and degrading slums in every city. Our factories produce at a fraction of their potential capacities, yet thousands of people starve to death in the world every day. The potential for liberation from toil and want, leaving people free to create, is enormous, yet men must still work in meaningless, wasteful jobs to keep themselves and this economic system going. How meaningful, in terms of real human needs, is the work of a market research analyst developing an advertising program for a new brand of toothpaste? Or that of a worker making a part for a car he knows is designed to become obsolete in two years, working in a factory over which he has absolutely no control? We students see the huge gap between potential and realization in our lives. We see that the university prepares us for meaningless work and we see that so much remains to be done.

It is true that a relatively small number—perhaps as few as 500—started the demonstrations at Columbia. Yet thousands supported the strike because the issues we were raising made sense to their own lives.

In our strike, we united with many of the people who have been affected by the university's policies—the tenants in Columbia-owned buildings, the Harlem community, the university employees. Many other people throughout the world saw us confront a symbol of those who control the decisions that are made in this country.

In France, the workers and students united to fight a common enemy. The same potential exists here in the United States. We are attempting to connect our fight with the fight of the black people for their freedom, with the fight of the Mexican-Americans for their land in New Mexico, with the fight of the Vietnamese people, and with the exploited and oppressed throughout the world. We intend to unite with all people who believe that men and women should be free to live as they choose, in a society where the government is responsive to the needs of all the people, and not the needs of the few whose enormous wealth gives them the political power. We intend to make a revolution.

THERE IS NO WAY TO RUN A REVOLUTION
Abbie Hoffman

Like fellow young radical Jerry Rubin, Abbie Hoffman often assumes a comic or bizarre stance to gain attention and to signify rejection of standard behavior. A member of the Chicago Seven, Hoffman's confrontations with authority have resulted in more than twenty-five arrests. While his style and language are obviously more humorous—and at the same time, may *seem* to be less serious—than the style and language of the other articles in this section, they serve the same serious purpose. Abbie Hoffman is telling us that "You are the Revolution," that we must encourage a humane individualism, and that action ("Do your thing") speaks louder than words ("Listen to silence").

Revolution is in your head. You are the Revolution.
Do your thing
Do your thing
Do your thing
Do your thing
Do your thing
Be your thing
Practice. Rehearsals come after the act. Act. Act. One practices by acting. Billy the Kid strides with 6 guns blazing, receding into his inner space. What does he find? Another Billy the Kid striding with 6 guns blazing, receding into his inner space. There are no rules, only images. Only a System has boundaries. Eichmann lives by the rules. Eichmann, machinelike, twitching nervously, pushes at his steel-rimmed glasses, takes his neatly folded handkerchief from the breast pocket of his gray-flannel suit and mops his sweating bald forehead (AN ELECTRICAL ENGINEER: *"My goal in life is to make myself replaceable"*—DOT—DOT—BEEP—BEEP).

"My God was a pink memo. Uh . . ." he stutters, "excuse me, my God was a pink memo on Tuesdays, on Wednesdays it was a blue memo. . . . It's hard to remember exactly. Yes, yes, that was it. Pink memo on Tuesdays, blue memo on Wednesdays."

Eichmann lets out a huge sigh of relief, smiles a little pince-nez smile, carefully refolds his handkerchief and replaces it in his pocket.

"I was a careerist. (s l o w) I   was   only   doing   my   death."

Behind Billy the Kid stands Abraham. Grand old man of 9,000

years, striding across the desert lands, sweat crushed against his brow by a huge sun-baked forearm of golden fleece, the same golden fleece that hung from his head and face in cascading waves of hard times.

God says, "Abraham, take your beloved son Isaac to the land of Moriah and place him upon an altar and make of him a sacrifice."

And Abraham tightens his fists and gnarls his teeth and cries out, "How do I know that is the God that has guided me and my people all these years?"

Inside he knows because He is God, which is to say, a Man and not a machine. He bids goodbye to Sarah, whom he truly loves, and he walks, holding his young son's tender hand, the three miles to Moriah. Placing his son upon the carefully constructed altar, he binds and gags him to let his son know that he loves him, and yet he does not need to do that because the boy too loves his father and needs no bindings. There would be no pain. Then Abraham dabs the boy with holy water that he had carried from his holy well and recites a few ritual prayers, mumbling them rotely because three days ago when he talked to God, he had already decided he would do what he must do. He holds his left hand over his son's eyes and raises the long well-used knife in the air, poising it for that final plunge. One plunge, quickly, for the steel in his mighty arm—sword will need but one thrust upon the young lad's frail body.

"Abraham, I am your God."

He slumps, exhausted with joy. It was an orgasm of consciousness, pulsating down rows upon rows of mankind.

Trust   your   impulses.   Trust   your   impulses.   TRUST   — TRUST — TRUST — TRUST — TRUST — TRUST — TRUST TRUST — TRUST — TRUST — TRUST

    Test

      Test

        Test

          Relax

The trouble with liberalism and bull-shit American middle class DOT–DOT–BEEP–BEEPs is that they run the myth backwards.

"God is dead," they cry, "and we did it for the kids."

Conversation with the Reader

What goes through your head when you read this pudding? Images? Images of who? Me? You? I am a myth. Besides I can't write and words are all bullshit anyway. I don't know how to write. Here is an example of what I mean. It is called a poem. I didn't call it that, someone else did. I called it a brown manila envelope. It is a manila envelope about meetings. It was fun to write.

DIGGER CREED FOR HEAD MEETINGS

MEETINGS ARE

INFORMATION
MEDITATION
EXPERIENCE
FUN
TRUST
REHEARSALS
DRAMA
HORSESHIT

MEETINGS ARE NOT

PUTTING PEOPLE DOWN

Shhhh!   LISTEN AT MEETINGS   Shhhhhh!

LISTEN TO eye movements
LISTEN TO scratching
LISTEN TO your head
LISTEN TO smells
LISTEN TO singing
LISTEN TO touches
LISTEN TO silence
LISTEN TO gestalt vibrations
LISTEN TO a baby born in the sea
LISTEN TO the writing on the wall

DON'T LISTEN TO WORDS
DON'T LISTEN TO WORDS
DON'T LISTEN TO WORDS

meetings are life
surrender to the meeting . . . the meeting is the message

MEETINGS ARE CONFRONTATION —
MEETINGS ARE RELAXATION —
DIG OTHER HEADS —
DIG YOUR HEAD

dig disrupters, dig poets, dig peacemakers, dig heads who mumble, dig heads who don't go to meetings, dig heads who fall asleep, dig andy kent, dig clowns, dig street fighters, dig heads who scribble on paper, dig hustlers, dig heads that admit they are wrong, dig heads that know they are right, dig doing, dig changes, dig holy men, DIG HEADS who do everything AT MEETINGS DIG HEADS WHO DIG MEETINGS
all meetings are the same same same same same same same same same same same same same — DIFFERENT meetings are rivers   —   don't build dams

BEWARE OF STRUCTURE FREAKS
BEWARE OF RULES
BEWARE OF "AT THE LAST MEETING WE
DECIDED . . ."
DON'T GO BACK — THERE WAS NO LAST MEETING
DON'T GO FORWARD — THERE IS NOTHING
meetings are Now   you are the meeting   we are Now
WITHOUT MEETINGS THERE IS NO COMMUNITY
COMMUNITY IS UNITY
AVOID GANGBANGS . . .   RAPE IDEAS NOT PEOPLE
MAKE LOVE AT ALL MEETINGS
MEETINGS TAKE A MOMENT — Time is Fantasy —
MEETINGS TAKE FOREVER
there is no WAY to run a meeting
use meetings to help you DO YOUR THING
Go naked to meetings   —   Go high to meetings
BE PREPARED
PREPARE BY meditation
PREPARE BY doing
COME PREPARED TO DROP OUT   —   COME PREPARED TO STAY
FOREVER
IF YOU ARE NOT PREPARED MEETINGS ARE NOT YOUR THING
ONLY DO YOUR THING
mene, mene, tekel, upharsin

(meetings are a pain in the ass)

TOWARD A NEW PATRIOTISM
Daniel Sisson

"Violence is the last refuge of the incompetent." With this quotation from
the Stoics, Mr. Sisson, a graduate student in political science when he wrote
this essay, dismisses the most radical elements of the current revolutionary
movement. Extolling the American Revolution as the only suitable model for
contemporary revolutionaries, he disdains "anarchistic radicals who capture
today's headlines" and looks, unsuccessfully, for men like Adams and Jefferson, who displayed a complete and intellectual "commitment to revolution."

Perhaps every successful revolutionary group in history has inaugurated
a "new order," meanwhile claiming some historical tradition to legiti-

From *Center Magazine*, Vol. II, No. 3 (May 1969). Reprinted by permission of
the Center for the Study of Democratic Institutions in Santa Barbara, California.

mate its power. Indeed, the claim to tradition has often served to rally the people to the cause, and more often than not it has determined the success or failure of the revolution.

Curiously, this claim to represent an historical tradition has been singularly lacking among revolutionary movements in this country. With the exception of the first American revolutionary generation, there has been little or no attempt by those who wished to overthrow the power structure to identify themselves specifically with the nation's revolutionary tradition. This may explain why we have failed to produce a genuine revolutionary movement for almost two hundred years. We have, instead, suffered one great, and many minor, rebellions.

The current revolutionary generation in America is no exception. It has, so far, refused to associate itself—even remotely—with the American past. Yet, within the radical movement today increasing numbers of American youths assert that they are actively promoting a violent revolution. This assertion assumes, first of all, that in their minds a revolutionary situation exists and, secondly, that there is sufficient strength and support among the young for such a rebellion to take place. There is, however, a major difference in the historical condition of our time and those that may have been present in the past.

If a revolutionary situation does exist today, then there is one overwhelming danger that many have cause to fear. It is that in a technological society enjoying the support of the police and the armed forces, it may be impossible to bring about revolution without its also culminating in an American version of fascism. In fact, the signs of such a development are already apparent. President Nixon's endorsement last January of "preventive detention" has been widely construed by students as the first step toward legalized fascism. If their analysis is correct, to make a judgment based upon the violent opposition they have encountered at every level of confrontation with the System, the American version of fascism cannot be far off. There is no mistaking the fact that many self-styled revolutionaries have now committed themselves to pursuing a course of violence in the hope that it will lead to revolution. They are determined to destroy the System—whenever and wherever possible—whatever the consequences.

The consequences of unleashing massive violence in an abortive attempt at revolution can only be tragic for all—for the revolutionaries as well as the society at large. For if fascism would be the most likely result of such a rebellion, we will all become immersed in a cauldron of violence from which we may never escape. Moreover, if the history of revolution means anything at all, the revolutionary group that controls its violence entertains the greatest possible chance for success. But there is little evidence, if any, that today's revolutionaries wish to control the level of violence. On the contrary, their rhetoric insists that they wish to escalate it as much as possible.

"Violence is the last refuge of the incompetent." This was an axiom among the ancient Stoic philosophers. The phrase may become the epitaph of the current radical movement. For, in refusing to consider our indigenous historical tradition, the modern revolutionaries have demonstrated more than just a degree of incompetence; they have unwittingly and unnecessarily alienated a goodly percentage of the population. In doing so they have indicated that their revolutionary theory, as formulated, is concerned with promoting their own interests, not that of the entire society, its history, or its traditions. If the American past has any relevance, their revolution is doomed to certain failure.

The charge of incompetence goes far beyond these two basic requirements for any successful revolution. For what characterizes the present movement is its mirroring of the failures of the past. The movement has become mired in a confusion of strategy and tactics; it has no grand strategy. It has become anti-intellectual, ignoring its own Western revolutionary tradition. Incredibly, it has concentrated its energies on varying foreign ideologies. As a result, it is frustrated in its haphazard opposition to the Establishment for lack of a tradition which would appeal to most Americans. It is thwarted in reaching and converting these people, despite its frenetic activity, by the lack of a nationwide organization. It is hampered in offsetting its organizational vacuum by a lack of total commitment among its leaders, who change faces every four to five years. It is obsessed with the idea of violent confrontation at any cost, and the pursuit of an impossible dream—the imminent destruction of the central government. Finally, the movement has become so fractured in its vast array of groups, aims, and objectives that it remains vulnerable to that classical strategy employed by every government against a revolutionary group in the history of man—*divide et impera!*

I suggest, then, that unless the radicals make a significant change in their approach to revolution they are destined to become the objects of bewildered curiosity within a few years. They must somehow break the cycle of alienation that characterizes their relationship with most of their peers and with practically all their elders. They must begin to identify with their own people. The radicals of today, to be successful, should begin to search American history to formulate a revolutionary theory that will encompass the country's revolutionary tradition. Finally, in order to validate their claim as the vanguard of the new order, they should turn to the nation's past. One might say that, with few exceptions, the past becomes a controlling factor in the inauguration of a new order. The sentiments, loyalties, and tendencies of a population to become attached to a wave of the future depend in large part on how that future looks in the light of the past. The majority of Americans will not commit themselves to a revolutionary ideal if they cannot imagine themselves believing in and participating in the realization of that ideal. There must be something familiar, something positive to latch on to. People must be able to identify with the revolution. Otherwise there will be no revolution, there will only be rebellion.

The task of providing a rationale familiar to the American people will be impossible if it does not take account of the tradition associated with America's history. Any attempt to impose on Americans an ideology whose roots lie hidden in Russian, Chinese, or Cuban nationalism will be futile and self-defeating.

If foreign ideologies have failed to produce a revolution in America, what kind of ideology will? If we disregard the New Left, the Old Left, the Socialists, the Communists, the Wobblies, and Syndicalists as being offshoots of European ideologies, there is little left to choose from. The Populist movement incorporated a fine tradition, but though a few individual Populists were radical their platform was more liberal than revolutionary. The Abolitionists were radicals, but in the end they, too, became reformers. Neither pledged themselves to overthrowing the system. And the remaining protest groups have been political parties, none of which has been truly revolutionary.

All this serves to remind us that the American political tradition has been flexible enough to absorb every radical movement in the nation's history. Therefore, to find the only genuine revolutionary in our history one has to go back to the second half of the eighteenth century. Oddly enough, that tradition has been lost to most Americans. It has been usurped and perverted by ultra-patriotic groups whose reactionary views are totally inconsistent with the logic of the tradition they exalt. For within the writings of Thomas Jefferson and of Sam and John Adams is the call to a continuing democratic revolution—the same democratic revolution that has swept the world ever since 1776 and is continuing now in the Third World. I suggest that we revive that tradition and reinterpret it. It is one that every American—young or old—can identify with, understand, and appreciate. If it is presented skillfully enough, it is a tradition capable of fomenting a political revolution in conservative America.

Contained within the seeds of our Revolutionary period is the key to the American mind. It is the one era in our history with which everyone, regardless of his beliefs, can readily identify. Furthermore, it contains an inspiring tradition that is radical and revolutionary, to be sure, but yet communicable to the majority of the people. It is also a period that contradicts the main body of our history which, since the death of the last member of the Revolutionary generation, has been mainly conservative. It is, moreover, the one period that corresponds more closely with the present than with any other time in the nation's past. For that reason alone it should bear closer scrutiny by today's radical students.

Contemporary Americans, like their Colonial predecessors, are concerned with defining a revolutionary situation. In fact, although many of the young sense that a political revolution may be coming in their lifetime, they are unable to say what conditions might bring it about. Despite this, they still see themselves caught up in a hostile situation that is likely to explode at any moment. A brief look at history might tell them why.

They are confronted with an empire in the guise of a nation whose administration has gone sour and with a monopolistic economic system in which a few pile up wealth at the expense of the many. They observe with anger a political system that through "royal favor" denies opportunity and stifles talent. They turn away in disgust from a Constitutional framework that has become irrelevant because the authorities who interpret that document no longer believe, understand, or respect its true values. These young people find, too, that the tradition of respecting protest and dissent is withering away. Like the Colonists of the eighteenth century, they sense that they are slowly losing their liberties.

Other parallels might be drawn, but what is most important is the tradition within that period which every revolutionary group in our history has sought for in vain—the tradition capable of producing a revolution in this country that will insure a decent way of life for all people, regardless of race, color, or creed. For this was what the American Revolution was all about. It should be what the current radical movement is all about.

The Colonists were attempting to conserve the values and ideals of a system that gave them the freedom to pursue their own life, liberty, and happiness. They felt that the British body of laws, the famous "unwritten constitution," had enabled them to do this. But after 1688, when the Parliament gained supreme power and upset the balance of the British constitution, those who interpreted the laws no longer respected their underlying values. Instead, the Parliament began gradually to destroy those values. No longer were citizens of the Empire guaranteed their natural rights as Englishmen. And as each new administration, comprising advisers to King and Parliament, seemed to formulate an even harsher policy than its predecessor, the Colonists began to fear for even their basic rights as free men. A few predicted that they might even become slaves to the British imperial system.

Rather than argue for the overthrow of the entire system, the Colonists realized (strategically) that the basic values of British law were still valid. The freedoms of Magna Charta and the Petition of Right would guarantee the conditions necessary for the preservation of life and liberty—at least if they were interpreted justly. Thus the revolutionaries focused upon the King's "evil ministers," and placed the responsibility of perverting British law upon them.

The same argument can be justifiably made today from the viewpoint of the "loyal opposition," in which body I include myself. In the main, it is not the basic values of the Declaration of Independence or even the American Constitution that we oppose. It is, rather, what they have become—instruments of corrupt power in the hands of incompetent men. For the most part, we are for limiting the power of government and for the government's using that power we do grant to help the masses of dispossessed citizens. We are for maximizing individual freedom in the face of an increasingly despotic economic system that disregards the public interest and disdains governmental regulation. We crave more justice and deplore the sick appeal to "law and order" without its related virtue of justice. We want to create a peace-loving nation in which American nuclear power does not threaten the world with a holocaust. In short, we demand, or should demand, a model government and hope that the world might follow our example.

These were exactly the demands made by the first American Revolutionaries. They did not have to worry about nuclear war, of course, but they were quite aware of the consequences of an aggressive foreign policy. The founding fathers knew from their study of history that the acquisition of territory abroad and the "uniting of the sword and the purse" at home were a deadly combination for any form of government. They also knew that increasing the power of government would transform the republic into an empire.

Moreover, they considered that end a betrayal of their ideals; for empires (such as Rome) put an emphasis upon military power that reverses the civilian supremacy over the military. They knew that if military influence continued to grow in a free society it would create bellicose men who would tend to subvert the liberties of the people.

In order to become an effective revolutionary one must devote his entire life to the cause of revolution. The commitment must be total. It makes imperious demands upon one's time, energies, loyalties, and abilities. Above all else, it claims absolutely the resources of the potential revolutionary. Significantly, Sam and John Adams and Thomas Jefferson made an intellectual commitment of that kind. They were the youngest members of the power structure in their Colonial society. They had received the best educations then available. They were being groomed for leadership in their respective Colonial assemblies and spent most of their time organizing political action groups. They were the inheritors of their system. They should not be compared to the anarchistic radicals who capture today's headlines.

Sam Adams' intellectual commitment to revolution began at an early age when he entered Harvard and made revolution the core of his study program. His thesis topic for an M.A. was a prelude to revolution, entitled "Whether It Be Lawful To Resist the Supreme Magistrate If The Commonwealth Cannot Be Otherwise Preserved." Adams concluded that rebellion was justified, and for the next thirty-three years he put his theories into practice by organizing and directing political activity in the area of Boston. Sam Adams' organizing genius was responsible for such inventions as the caucus and the idea of the Sons of Liberty. He was also behind the effectiveness of the New England Committees of Correspondence and the Association—the latter an economic group that effectively boycotted Loyalists. He labored in this fashion for almost half a century before his work bore fruit; he was fifty-three when that first confrontation, the battle of Lexington, occurred.

Sam's cousin John, like Sam, had attended Harvard. Instead of committing himself to revolution he chose to teach and to study the law. Adams' subsequent legal career influenced his politics for years. He was a conservative until about 1760. Meanwhile, he came under the influence of such radical-liberal stalwarts as James Otis and Oxenbridge Thatcher—the finest legal minds in Massachusetts. Even then, after being converted to their point of view, Adams had such a difficult time becoming radicalized that he suffered a nervous breakdown. But once he had committed himself to the cause his zeal was unequalled.

For over fifteen years John Adams wrote and pondered the problems of revolution. His diary is evidence that throughout his life he studied history, politics, and philosophy, becoming the most learned political philosopher of his time. And it ought to be noted, too, that John Adams was almost forty when the first blood was shed at Lexington.

Forty years after that confrontation, John Adams wrote to Thomas Jefferson asking him to define the nature of the American Revolution. He wrote: "What do we mean by the Revolution? The war? That was no part of the Revolution; it was only an effect and consequence of it. The Revolution was in the minds of the people, and this was effected, from 1760 to 1775, in the course of fifteen years before a drop of blood was shed at Lexington. The records of thirteen legislatures, the pamphlets, the newspapers in all the Colonies, ought to be consulted during the period to ascertain the steps by which the public opinion was enlightened and informed concerning the authority of Parliament over the Colonies."

When John Adams sent this query to Jefferson he referred to an historical period when conditions in America distinctly paralleled those of the present. His advice, therefore, may be even more relevant today than it was in 1815. For the course of study he offers is nothing less than a grand strategy for revolution in America. His suggestions include: the commitment of radical leadership to the idea of revolution, the basic organization of revolutionary activity, the role of theory in revolutionary activity, the strategy of violence versus non-violence, psychological warfare, a revolutionary educational process, and the insights that his generation provided into the true character of the American mind.

However, it was Jefferson more than the Adamses who saw into the future and articulated the doctrine of a continuing democratic revolution. Jefferson's philosophic commitment to the cause of revolution and his scholarly pursuits are storied. What is not as well known is that Jefferson continued to refine the idea of revolution in America long after his contemporaries had become conservative. He helped produce the first Revolution, in the end a violent one. But after the overthrow of British rule, unlike many of his contemporaries, he refused to conservatize the Revolution. After the Constitutional Convention he wrote to Madison and others, attempting to perpetuate the idea of revolution by putting in a clause that would give each generation the right to determine its future. Jefferson wanted the Constitution rewritten every twenty years. If he had had his way the educational process that each generation would have experienced in writing their own constitution might have preserved the revolutionary tradition. His efforts ended in failure, but Jefferson never ceased his revolutionary activity. As Minister to France he held endless conversations with the future leaders of the French Revolution. Then upon his return to the United States he served in Washington's Cabinet. When it became evident that the reactionary Federalists might subvert the republic and install a monarchy, Jefferson organized and brought about what has been called the peaceful revolution of 1800.

His second revolution was based on the assumption that the people had the right not only to choose their leaders but to throw corrupt and reactionary governments out of power. There is evidence, in fact, showing that the revolution of 1800 was saved from being violent by the last-minute actions of the Federalists. That Jefferson and his party meant to preserve liberty by peaceful means if possible is clear. Jefferson's supporters, however, were quite willing to risk plunging the country into civil war if the popular will was rejected.

That second revolution was this nation's first example of participatory politics. Jefferson and Madison successfully put into practice a decentralized political organization that mobilized the energy of the people. In addition, their activity might also be construed as the first attempt at the politics of confrontation. For by using the framework of the Committees of Correspondence they had systematically organized small factions, coördinated them into a network, and directed each one to confront the Federalists at various points throughout the nation.

It was the desire to curb a party in power that impelled Jefferson to write another potential revolutionary document—the Kentucky Resolutions. The Resolutions argued for the right to rebel against the central government if certain basic liberties reserved to the states were denied. What Jefferson sought to do was to constitutionalize the right to revolution through the idea of states' rights. While he knew, as did Madison, that invoking those Resolutions might lead to bloody revolution, the preservation of liberty became even more important to both. Through Constitutional language, both attempted to perpetuate the course of a revolutionary tradition. In essence they said that the popular will, and its ability to "submit despotic power to democratic controls," must be the real meaning of any revolution in America.

It would appear, then—especially in the late twentieth century—that if any revolution is to be successful in this country it must follow a pattern similar to that which shaped the American Revolution. Both Adamses and Jefferson offered us a revolutionary heritage. It was philosophical, reflecting the Age of Reason; at the same time, it relied upon the Western constitutional tradition. They provided us with a model for revolution in America. It is still useful, still relevant.

WHAT DO THE NEW LIFE STYLES MEAN?

". . . the youth rebellion is not a monstrous incursion from nowhere; it is just the next step, a little more thorough, a little more honest, on the way our culture is moving."

GARRY WILLS

THE MAKING OF THE YIPPIE CULTURE
Garry Wills

Garry Wills's inclusive survey of the "now" culture ranges from participatory democracy to nudity to street theater. His thesis states that we live in an "experimental" culture in which no *a priori* standards exist, in which aesthetics—hence the theatrical gestures in politics and life styles—have replaced ethics. In criticizing this state of affairs, Wills, a free-lance writer, turns to the recent past for a parallel. What, he asks, explains the popularity

From *Esquire*, November 1969. Copyright © 1969 by Esquire, Inc., and reprinted by permission of Esquire Magazine.

of Hitler and Mussolini? "They were both, unquestionably, masters of street theater."

In Chicago, with the nomination of "Pigasus" for President, Americans were exposed to the playful fringe around the edges of our radical youth movement. It has always been there, though it rarely gets as much attention as it did in Chicago. The freaks and crazies have a para-political role to play. The difference between them and staid radicals like Rennie Davis and Tom Hayden was symbolized when the University of Chicago's administration building was occupied early in 1969. Inside were the real guerrillas; outside was a group that called itself Chicken-shits, who were afraid to go in. They wore yellow armbands, and carried a yellow flag, and played kazoos (popular instrument with the freaks). When they crashed administration hearings, it was to read parts of *Catch-22*. Instead of seizing the Dean's files, they went and *asked* him for them. When he turned them down, they dropped to the floor and crawled out mumbling, "Grovel, grovel, grovel, who are we to ask for power?"

Most such guerrilla theatre is not merely propaganda for the revolution, enacting little moral lessons (though there are some dead-serious propaganda teams like the San Francisco Mime Troupe). The spirit of play, of put-on, is important for its own sake, and related to the nonpolitical "Merry Pranksterism" in groups like Ken Kesey's and the Hog Farm, groups that did not even bother to go to Chicago. The Yippies' heroes are Antonin Artaud (for his "poetry of festivals") and Marshall McLuhan ("Myth means putting on the audience"). Even the pig as candidate was not meant solely as a symbol of the cops, of Daley, of Humphrey, of Nixon ("There would be a pig in the White House in '69, no matter what"). It was also a symbol of the Yippie movement ("We love the pig, our candidate and hero"). The original plan was to roast and eat him as a kind of communion rite. Death of the Pig meant the death of Yippie—and to kill Yippie was the stated purpose of the Yippies' trip to Chicago. A funeral was actually held on Thursday, Paul Krassner presiding.

There had been earlier funerals for Hippie and the Flower Children. The first thing the freak movement must do, once it establishes itself, is kill itself off. Abbie Hoffman wrote, after Chicago: "There never were any Yippies and there never will be. It was a slogan YIPPIE! and that exclamation point was what it was all about. It was the biggest put-on of all time." Krassner writes: "The Crazies have a rule that in order to become a member one must first destroy his official membership card." There should be nothing surprising in all this, if we remember Dada and the Surrealists. The Yippies—wearing American Revolution uniforms to H.U.A.C. hearings, exorcising the Pentagon, burning money at

Wall Street, nominating Pigasus, trying to turn Chicago on with LSD in the water supply (it was counteracted by chlorine), holding an "In Hoguration" in Washington, calling for Indecency Rallies, taking the arms off the clock in Grand Central Station (perhaps their best symbolic blow at the System)—are modern Dadaists. And Dada was always devoted to the destruction of Dada. Its principles were often enunciated: The real Dadaists are against Dada. Everyone is a leader of Dada. No one is a leader of Dada. The Dadaists and Surrealists wanted to kill Art, which degenerates inevitably into Culture. But Dada's own gestures were continually being framed off as artifacts and hailed as "the new art," so the movement had to keep killing itself ("Dada is not new, not modern, not art"). This was the time when Duchamp made a practice of "incompleting" works; and at a Dada "manifestation," André Breton went along behind Francis Picabia, erasing the drawings he had just made. The Dada manifestation was like modern street theatre, even in details—death's heads, toy guns, mocking use of uniforms, elaborate put-ons, gestures obscene or obscure, incantations, nudity. At the International Dada Fair in 1920, the principal attraction was a dummy in German officer's uniform, topped with a stuffed pig's head—the first incarnation of Pigasus.

Like Dadaists, Yippies represent the aesthetic side of a revolutionary movement. It was the custom to distinguish between "radicals" at the Chicago convention, and Yippies, and liberal McCarthy kids. The distinction is real, but partial—more a question of mood, of style, than of doctrinal divisions. In fact, the code of the Yippies is simply Castroism applied to art. Fidel's view of revolution is that one acts and, through action, discovers the aims of the revolution. Only by forswearing ideology—even the revolutionary ideology of Marx—does one discover radically new roles for society. Dada took the same approach to art; only by forswearing art does one open up new creative worlds: "Thought is made in the mouth" (Tristan Tzara). The Yippies' form of anti-politics is not simple negation (curse the pig). It is also support for all anti-political symbols (we *love* the pig). Anti-politics becomes a positive thing. In just this way, Dadaists lionized the piggish Père Ubu, creation of their favorite ancestor, Alfred Jarry.

The Yippie events take place within an aesthetic context established over the last decade or so, beginning with the motion from Action Painting to Pop Art and Happenings. A trickle-down effect spread Happening philosophy out from the Reuben Gallery onto the street. The critical rationale of the movement was popularized by Susan Sontag in her essay *Against Interpretation,* which criticizes "the hypertophy of the intellect at the expense of energy." She is merely picking up the standards of Dada and Surrealism, which tried to free energy from the trammels of Art. But more to the point today, she is giving us a Castro aesthetic, the artistic equivalent of Debray's maxims: he wrote, "The intellectual will try to grasp the present through preconceived ideological constructs and live it through books. He will be less able than others to invent, improvise. . . ." Since interpretation sets up categories of the possible before all the possibilities have been broached, Miss Sontag claims that "a great deal of today's art may be understood as motivated by a flight from interpretation." Just as a great deal of radical action is motivated by a flight from ideology. "Abstract painting is the attempt to have, in the ordinary sense, no content; since there is no content, there can be no interpretation. Pop Art works by the opposite means to the same result; using a content so blatant, so 'what it is,' it, too, ends by being uninterpretable." Rubin and Hoffman and Krassner, when they are not making fun of ideology, portray themselves by put-on as "Commie freaks." In Chicago Hoffman passed out dime-store bits of paper with Chinese figures on them, to show his "tails" that he was one of Mao's men. This is making a message so blatant that it is uninterpretable.

The Surrealists, too, wanted to go "beyond art" by a destruction of Culture, which is an elaborate set of expectations—expectations that limit, structure, contain experience much as ideology hedges revolutionary action. But where Dadaists depended, like the street kids, on direct unstructured action, Surrealists relied on the newly discovered subconscious. If the aim is to "cut back content" by living entirely in one's first virgin grasp of things, the subconscious becomes a kind of pre-primary grasp of reality, existing before actual sensation. Thus the Surrealists concentrated on dream-reporting, on automatism, on cultivated delirium and hysteria (Dali's "paranoia-criticism"). They even threw a birthday party for hysteria, on the fiftieth anniversary of its discovery. Action Painting was, on one side of it, a return to such automatism.

The Surrealists even *sound* like today's kids. Breton pointed to "the conviction that here we all share—i.e., that modern society survives by a compromise so serious as to justify any excess on our part." The second-generation Surrealist magazine, *Le Grand Jeu,* declared: "Our discoveries are those of the explosion and dissolution of all that is organized." The artists had a joint interest in astrology, in Eastern mysticism. They demanded an end to military service and release of all "political prisoners." They indulged in what came later to be known as Camp; Maurice Nadeau recounts how they sought out vapid popular performances: "The most ridiculous shows were the most prized, for they put on stage the popular sentiments and emotions that had not yet been spoiled by culture." And they were resolutely Against Interpretation: *La Révolution surréaliste* proclaimed that "Surrealism does not present itself as the exposition of a new doctrine. Certain ideas which serve it today as a point of departure must not be allowed to prejudice its later development."

If the Yippies are the advance guard of the youth culture, the youth culture is the advance guard of our popular culture. And the whole thing is anticipated and embodied in an official culture of the museums. We are living through an aesthetic revolution that is entirely Castroite. That was borne in on me during a 1969 stroll through the museums clustered in one block on West Fifty-third Street. The Museum of American Folk Art had a show of Pennsylvania artifacts from the eighteenth and nineteenth centuries—intricate toys, large wedding chests, rich mazy samplers like postage-stamp Renaissance tapestries. The most interesting thing was the mechanical bent of the artists— sprocketed, wheeled, drilled, dowel-in-hole smooth rub of wood on wood; axle turn, mesh, catch; windmills, whirligigs, model grinding mills; seesaw worked up and down (and dwarfed) by a huge wheel-and-pulley apparatus; a wrought-iron squirrel cage, big ribbed drum swinging easily. The artists obviously liked to invent little worlds of programmed action for real or imagined small denizens, worlds outside their maker, controlled by him.

A few doors east on Fifty-third, the Museum of Contemporary Crafts had a show called "Feel It," where one moved in a suspended April rainstorm, sunlit, of translucent clinging plastic strips (two hundred fifty miles of the stuff cut up into lengths that just brushed the floor, descending everywhere in dazzling sheets). There were murky revelations made by mirrors, blipping electric lights and sounds, lucite cones and coils. Here was a new squirrel cage which the artist builds to *enter,* along with his audience (who all become artists). It is the perfect way to escape interpretation. What is the artifact to be interpreted—the strips of plastic? the lights or mirrors? But these do not function until people stir and intercept them, are tangled or reflected in them. If there is an artifact, it is put together, disassembled, redone constantly in each person as he gropes, snow-blind in the lucite, toward or away from others. Not only is the audience the artist. The artist is also audience: Allan Kaprow says of his Happenings, "I need to be part of it to find out what it is like myself." And both audience and artist are, as well, the artifact—hundreds of discrete "products" of the process, successfully defying interpretation. Miss Sontag wrote: "Interpretation takes the sensory experience of the work for granted, and proceeds from there. This cannot be taken for granted, now." The Feel-In neatly solves that problem: it offers *nothing but* the sensory experience. "Our task is to cut back content." A task accomplished, here. Art is now an experiment one performs upon oneself—not standing outside or above it, like the makers of toy wooden worlds in Pennsylvania. The promise of the new art, like that of the new politics, is that you need not make a revolution; the revolution, if you simply act, will make you. The artist need not make an artifact. Art, if you simply act, will shape the true, the authentic artifact within you. This was the new element Action Painting added to Surrealist concepts of automatism. The painting is not so much a product as an act—paint*ing*. This means the audience must be present at the act, either actually or in imagination, or with the help of TV or movie cameras. The Japanese Gutai painters became a kind of repertory theatre of painting, and developed many of the props used in Happenings (transparent walls to be painted on, balloons, smoke). When the French action-painter Mathieu painted the Battle of Bouvines, he did it in period costume on the battle's anniversary, with an audience and with the cameras grinding.

The big gallery on Fifty-third was still waiting for me—the Museum of Modern Art, then holding its popular exhibit on The Machine. That term was stretched to include many things. There, for instance, was Duchamp's piston-slide blurred nude of mechanical outline, clicking her way downstairs, perfectly audible across the room despite trip-hammer sounds of metamatics and other chugging devices. There were walls of Futurist paintings trying to be movies. Photographs (not themselves machines, but the result of mechanical play with sunlight). Léger's mechanics made extensions of the machines they work on. Dada machines for doing nothing. Their ideal was finally achieved in Claude Shannon's Little Black Box, which involves the audience (one must throw the box's switch to an On position) and erases the artist-audience's effort (all the On switch does is activate a hand that pops out of the box and turns the switch back Off). Drawings and photographs of Jean Tinguely's Homage to New York, a vast happening-contraption, a "self-destroying machine," part of which was meant to drag itself over to the museum pool and drown itself; appropriately, it did not make it all the way to the water (Tinguely said he was constantly thinking of New York as he put together his guilty and suicidal Frankenstein of a "city").

But there were real machines, too: one of the six surviving "Golden Bugs," the finest car ever made—chassis by Bugatti, coach by Weinberger, tires by Royal. TV sets (tubes by RCA). Lights by G.E. There was even a perfect working model of an elevator button cleverly placed beside the elevator. The famous car by Kienholz still has its rickety lovers in the backseat, their papier-mâché passion wired in taut frustration. But they were not nearly as good as the crumpled papery figures in the museum restaurant, masterpieces of a jaundiced realism (sneakers by Keds). There were Coke bottles on the restaurant tables, too, much better in that setting than the one on the second floor of the museum, where a section is devoted to design: Trimline phones, stainless-steel knives, racing helmet. The racing helmet goes with Andy Granatelli's STP car, downstairs in the Machine exhibit. And the omnipresent Coke bottle reappeared down there in Claes Oldenburg's green plastic profile of a Chrysler Airflow, which looks like a Coke bottle sawed in half.

But Oldenburg's most spectacular contribution to the show was his Giant Soft Fan, the old propeller sort inside its cage, with flabby blades drooping in the droopy cage, ready to stir in any breeze, reversing the order of things ("I am a technological liar," says Oldenburg). It was perfect in detail, but bloated and gone soft like a dream fan, dwarfing passersby. It is not so much an artifact, enclosed, as a dream prop creating an aura, around it, of life thrown off-scale, grown weirdly malleable, marshmallowy. Walk into the magic zone, and you are back in Feel It, doing experiments on yourself.

And the true masterpiece of the show was not the puffy Oldenburg fan; it was a Soft Girl made, it seemed, of mattresses—thermal underwear, shepherd boots, sheeps'-wool cape. She too seemed to inhabit, hypnotically, a dream: I followed her; it was a working model that dragged itself *all the way* to the pool—I mean the door. And on out where, in the New York streets, she looked perfectly at home, endangered—another self-destroying machine.

Our whole culture is a kind of street theatre. That was the real point of the machine exhibit, mixing everyday artifacts with the new art's anti-artifacts. If one cannot say *what* art is (cannot "interpret"), then one cannot even say *that* it is; cannot define it, find its boundaries, seal it off as something separate, to be judged. The Dadaists were right: the only way to get free of art is to destroy it. Back to Breton-Picabia: now an "Erased de Kooning by Robert Rauschenberg" is exhibited. Yet one cannot destroy Art—all the attempt does is turn *everything* into art, into a giant squirrel cage man runs in, having experiences, a huge laboratory for doing experiments on himself. The world of the Feel It show is also that of a nightclub like Cerebrum, where one is to float, seen and seeing, in diaphanous stuff; of the Joffrey Ballet and its dance-rub through plastic bubbles and tunnels; of Barbarella's adventures in the same stuff; of an increasing number of shows where one froths through a suds of various synthetics—for that matter, the world of a rock concert, where one is immersed in dense undulant sound; or the world of disorienting light thrown off by strobes, mixed media, Expo '67 camera work all around one. Yoko Ono, a veteran of Happenings before she moved on to bed-ins with John Lennon, puts it simply: "I think they should turn everywhere into a museum. It is a museum. They just need to put a label on it all, don't you think?"

Our aesthetics is Castroite because our culture, like radical politics, drifts toward total empiricism, where all norms are provisional, to be tested; where no authority exists except majority will at the moment (and our majority seems, for the moment, to have no will). There is no *a priori* set of standards; one must pick up or produce a set for oneself, *ambulando*. Seen in this light, the youth rebellion is not a monstrous incursion from nowhere; it is just the next step, a little more thorough, a little more honest, on the way our society is moving. Life is being absorbed into street theatre, devoted to what Tzara called "the poetry of the street." As Richard Goldstein says, the Living Theatre turns every building where it performs into a street (even when it does not, as in New Haven, actually take to the street). Yayoi Kusama has given up museum work (phalloi pinned to couches) for the painting of polka-dot nudes—real nudes—in the street. When the brothers Berrigan, priest war-protesters, lugged draft records into the street to pour napalm and blood on them, it was treated as a kind of Action Painting—Pollock doing his famous drip act—and given "reviews": Paul Velde wrote, "The details, it is clear, are those of a guerrilla action, the smallness of the numbers, suggestive of professional cadre, an underground; the very apparent concern of the participants with the media possibilities of their action, with the outrageous; surprise, shock, blatant symbol manipulation." Even church services are now happenings with a touch of Yippie gesture: at St. Clement's Episcopal Church, according to The New York *Times,* "Communicants were blindfolded, ordered to take off their shoes and led through a forty-minute maze that included a period of crawling on their hands and knees over bread crumbs as a sign of 'humble access' to the Holy Communion." (*Grovel, grovel, grovel, who are we to ask. . . .*) At one of the more famous Happenings of modern recent years, the march on the Pentagon, Norman Mailer one-upped the Yippies' exorcism rite by turning the whole thing into a movie of him-as-hero writing about him-as-hero getting arrested. It was action-art carried to its logical goal—as if Mathieu had a camera watching him paint the Battle of Bouvines *at the actual Battle of Bouvines.*

As the rest of society is drawn into the ongoing street drama, the impresarios react in various ways. Some see such participation as a threat —as when Abbie Hoffman complained that Bobby Kennedy's ghetto appearances were turning into better shows than his own troupe could supply. Others welcome the "conversion" of society to their norms— Jerry Rubin, for example, wrote: "The cops are a necessary part of any demonstration theatre. When you are planning a demonstration, always include a role for the cops. Cops legitimize demonstrations." The cops, of course, played the main role (though not the hero's) in the well-managed morality play on Chicago's streets. When Robert Brustein protested to Judith Malina, "That's not theatre, it's politics," she answered, "You can't separate the two, can you?" Rubin criticizes the university by reviewing the classroom as theatrical set: "You can always tell what the rulers have up their sleeves when you check out the physical environment they create. The buildings tell you how to behave. . . . They designed classrooms so that students sit in rows, one after the other, hierarchically, facing the professor who stands up front talking to all of them. . . . Classrooms should be organized in circles, with the professor one part of the circle."

The experimental character of our culture has a number of facets, the most obvious of which can be listed:

1. Perhaps the first sign of a constant need for fresh experience in our people is the power of youth fashion to set all fashions. In the past, teen-agers left behind a world of nursery rhymes and children's books in order, progressively, to listen in on adult talk and entertainment. The big bands, the pop singers of the Thirties, belonged to adults and were merely shared by teen-agers. In Elvis and The Beatles, the kids possessed, briefly, a culture of their own. But only briefly; for the situation is now reversed, and adults listen in on the kids' world. Clothes, decoration, music, literature—all take standards and new directions from the young. And the leaders of the youth culture are under terrific pressure to keep changing, starting over, reconstructing themselves in radical ways—following the example of Bob Dylan and The Beatles. There is more to this than America's tendency to look on itself as a young nation; more to it than liberal openness to one's children or modern permissiveness. A society that has lost its own certitudes and sense of self is coming to rely on the defiance, the bluff and arrogance, of a newly found or asserted self; on adolescents. Even things that were part of a criminal subculture, like drugs and violent protest, are moved up to respectability through the filter of the youth subculture. Extremes become part of a spectrum that grades imperceptibly toward the official center of fashion. The activism of radicals and the theatrical "act" of Yippies are two different readings of the same experimental approach to life. This is underlined by the way Jerry Rubin "updated" Tom Hayden's famous opening to the Port Huron Statement. The original went this way: "We are people of this generation, bred in at least modest comfort, housed now in universities, looking uncomfortably to the world we inherit." Rubin's version: "We are a new generation, species, race. We are bred on affluence, turned on by drugs, at home in our bodies, and excited by the future and its possibilities." One could construct a series of such creeds moving out from the Yippies to the whole Beatlemaniac youth culture and from there to the universities, movie houses, museums, theatres, and suburbs of America—each giving the doctrine a different inflection, but working from the same text.

2. Another sign of our empiricism is the need for participation. If experience is the only authentic test of reality, then one cannot simply be told something. One must undergo it. The classroom must become a

circle, eliminating the gap between teacher (who only tells things) and students (who get told). The gap must be eliminated everywhere— between artist and onlooker in the museum, actors and audience in the theatre, leaders and followers in the street, "newsmakers" and crowd in the televised event. When Robert Brustein told members of the Living Theatre they were destroying drama as the arena of supremely gifted individuals, he got a shouted reply, "We are all supremely gifted individuals." This, too, was the code of Dada and Surrealism; both movements adopted Lautréamont's slogan, "Poetry must be made by all, not one."

The techniques of participation are being developed and expanded on all sides. Group therapy, "sensitivity training," social dynamics are extended from clinical to everyday use. Scenarios are written for domestic fights; the "games people play" are thought of as street theatre or bedroom theatre—at any rate, as role-playing, enactment, drama. Even that key word "scenario," used by the war-gamers, suggests the way society is conceived as a laboratory in which we all do experiments on ourselves. The Rand Corporation, advertising its simulated wars "to guard the nation and the free world"—wars that are waged constantly "in our labyrinthine basement, somewhere under the Snack Bar"—invites members of the general public to sign up as hypothetical missile commanders: "To understand the game one should participate, for understanding is 'in the experience.' "

The ruling metaphor behind social thought like McLuhan's is of society as a mechanical arrangement of meshing parts that must give way to an electronic field of forces. Men must become attuned to each other (rather than mesh), become remote-control extensions of their own TV sets, adjust the circuitry of their nerves to history's shift from mechanics to electronics. To "tune in," to join the global village, to become part of our whole culture's message (which *is* its electronic structure), we must, above all else, participate.

3. A third sign of this empiricism is the spread, out of a subculture and into the main culture, of shocking life-styles (exotic clothes, drugs, unkempt and hirsute experiments with the human shape and its sexual differentiations). And one extreme of this—as such, a good test of it— is the shocking use of nudity in street theatre, then in legitimate theatre, and then in the fashion world at large. Nudity has always been a weapon in the arsenal of shock. Both Dadaists and Surrealists used it —the former, for instance, in the Picabia-Satie event, Relâche, the latter when they opened a Paris show with a banquet eaten off a naked girl. There is a combination of risk and challenge, of vulnerability and effrontery, in the act of public nudity that makes it a natural experiment for a culture that is, precisely, devoted to performing experiments on itself, testing its own reactions, trying everything out. Nudes often ap-

peared in Happenings. Then nudity (as opposed to *Playboy's* pastry bare breasts) spread through the underground press, where it was often used as a political weapon. Finally, it went onto the street in "guerrilla theatre" performances and demonstrations—first on the West Coast, then at the Chicago convention and in New York, as well as at the Washington Inauguration. Significantly, nudity first made a timid appearance on Broadway as part of a simulated "Be-In" by the young cast of *Hair*. Then, as happens with most youth fads, it spread to the rest of our culture. One of the style-setting plays of 1968 was especially good at presenting nudity as a human *experiment*. In Terrence McNally's *Sweet Eros,* a deranged fellow captures a girl, ties her in a chair, undresses her, and for a long time studies her as a laboratory specimen, going over her with a magnifying glass, watching her reactions, referring to her as an insect. For the audience, too, she was an object, an alien "prop" on the stage, so unusual was complete nudity at the time. Author and director did not allow her to move or react for a long period. Only after the novelty wore off, both for her dramatic captor and for the audience, was she by stages "humanized," becoming a character in the play rather than a shocking part of the decor. It was an experiment performed on the audience, making it overcome a whole series of distractions and obstacles to accept her as simply another person in the story.

Then several groups invited audience participation to the point of shared nudity—accepting a new dare, performing a new experiment. And, always, there is the note of menace or insult: the boy whipping his penis out at the Guardsman in Chicago, kids coming forward nude and with a pig's head to insult Professor Galbraith—mocking others who will not be so exposed, so free, so "committed." Richard Goldstein heard one breathless woman, who had stripped during a Living Theater performance, murmur as she put her bra back on: "I feel like I've done something. You know, I can't stand the war. They're killing babies over there." *She'll* get even with the napalmers. *She'll* show them. *She'll*— take off her panties!

The logic seems elusive, but is not. Though the stripping takes place under a rationale of openness and love, it gets its real edge of excitement as an antisocial defiance of "Establishment" norms. It is a political act, and it keeps its vitality only in groups (like the Becks' Living Theater) that are openly revolutionary. This is not, despite the vapid apologia offered for it, a nudity of the health clubs, offered as something natural and normal. It is a defiance of norms—a push off into normlessness which the true empiricist hopes will open up new worlds. That is why the stripping grows out of a litany of frustration and resentment in the Becks' show (*"I am not allowed* to travel without a passport. *I am not allowed* to smoke marijuana. I don't know how to stop the war. *I am not allowed* to take my clothes off"). The nudity comes in a froth of blood and slaughter in *Dionysus in '69.*

4. A fourth sign of the empirical society is a reversion to superstition, magic, astrology, fortune-telling, tarot cards, I Ching, omens, spells ("Om"), Vedanta, witchcraft, mysticism. Not only do these supply a street theatre of liturgy, symbol and vestments; thay are also, like all magic, basically experimental. Magic is a way of getting certain things done. Say the right spell, and an automatic response is assured. Be born under the right star, and things will demonstrably happen. When authority has been drained from conventional religion, when the social symbols no longer signify anything, no longer promote communication, men are forced to invent private myths; they are thrown back on their own resources, no longer saying a social creed based on pure faith, on undemonstrable mysteries. Belief in astrology is mere acceptance of a working hypothesis, which allows endless experiment, verification, personal adaptation, analogical extension. Magic is also "against interpretation." Who knows what machinery makes the doors swing wide at "Open sesame"? And who cares? The real question is not how astrology works, but whether it works; and that is a question each person must answer in his own case, by experiment, by the daily lab work of checking one's life against one's horoscope.

5. Another sign of the spontaneous culture—acute interest in community as such—might seem to be at odds with the egocentric ethic of "authenticity." But the conflict is only apparent. Since the total empiricist is not bound to others by social-contract doctrines, the ties with others must be existential, based on experiences shared; a oneness that stands (in theory) apart from ideological agreement, principles negotiated, demands met or compromised. Thus arranging for the experience of community becomes a great concern of the empirical culture. Mechanisms must be set up for acquiring shared experience: group gropes, be-ins, feel-ins, festivals of life, Esalen Institute, Om circles, group therapy, living theatre, hippie communes, all leading up to the overarching experience of participatory democracy. New rituals must be invented, hieratic dress, symbols of shared experience. As James Kunen says, defending his long hair and hippie dress, "I like to have peace people wave me victory signs and I like to return them, and for that we've got to be able to recognize each other."

6. The most ominous sign of the empiricist society is a taste for violence. The need always to test oneself by new experience leads almost inevitably to shocks greater than nudity, nonconformity, or verbal violence. It leads to actual violence. Breton, the "Pope" of Surrealism, said, "The simplest surrealist act would be to go out into the street, revolver in hand, and fire at random into the crowd." Lafcadio's murder

as a gratuitous act, Raskolnikov's murder as an experiment performed on himself, haunt the Surrealists, and must always fascinate any explorer of the nerves' boundaries, of one's own system's tolerance (not to mention the tolerance of *the* System). For Lafcadio and Raskolnikov, violence is a form of asceticism, of self-testing. Stavrogin cruelly marries the crippled girl, as Auden's Tom Rakewell marries Baba the Turk, to *defy* desire, to exist "beyond desire." The gratuitous act is the only way to achieve this superman status. An act not "corrupted" by considerations of desire or morality, selfishness or altruism—the random pistol shot in the crowd—is the only act that is demonstrably "disinterested"; and to avoid covert moralism or cowardice one must seek out the revolting, the dangerous, the violent.

A culture bent on authenticity and self-experiment is bound to move toward violence. Seen in this light, the young assassins of our time—not only Oswald and Sirhan, but Charles Whitman and Richard Speck—are explained less by TV violence than by the whole stimulus-culture of which TV is only a part. Both Oswald and Sirhan were egocentric, compulsive diarists, students of themselves, performers before the mirror. They resemble the generation of European terrorists in the Eighties and Nineties of the last century—a group of introspective young people Camus analyzed as "fastidious assassins." These assassins were students, disoriented, idealistic, "trying to escape from contradiction and to create the values they lacked." Obsessed with themselves, they hardly recognized the existence of their victims as people: the *delendi* were merely symbols—which is why they turned out to be heads of state or other "charismatic" figures. The assassins did not act from hatred—as Perry Smith did not hate Nancy Clutter, Charles Whitman could not have hated individually all those he shot—but to test a wavering reality by testing themselves. They had to pursue the Feel It experience to the point where they not only witnessed the violence of our times but participated in it. Perhaps wielding that power would give them some power over it, make them less the audience and more the author-artists of this unstructured world of cruel experience. "Necessary and inexcusable—that is how murder appeared to them (the fastidious assassins)."

The Surrealists took as one of their heroines—and applied to her Baudelaire's saying, "Woman is the being who projects the greatest shadow or the greatest light in our dreams"—Germaine Berton, who murdered the royalist Marius Plateau. The original terrorists made a Joan of Arc out of Vera Zassulich, who shot General Trepov in 1878. American students have not, of course, made a hero of Oswald—perhaps because of his target. But what if he had succeeded in his first assassination attempt, on General Walker? It was more than a joke, with some people, to ask during Johnson's last months in power,

"Where are you, Oswald, now that we need you?" The underground press was full of targets superimposed on Johnson's face, and Humphrey's; of "Wanted" signs describing various members of the military-industrial bogey. A sense of vicarious assassination was being created in the Movement; and it was probably a normal enough college student who cried with ecstatic hope, when he saw a fire down the street in Chicago, "Is it a *pig* car?"

Violence is now openly defended on the Left, and rather lovingly analyzed. Jack Newfield found that more than half the S.D.S. members he canvassed on their reading habits had read some Frantz Fanon, the apologist for terrorism in Algeria. Fanon, a psychiatrist, constructed a simple hydraulics of violence, which he imagines as seeking its own level. All the violence of colonialism's history must be quantitatively balanced off by anti-colonial violence. This is the equivalent, in psychological terms, of "purging" and the balance of humors in a primitive medicine; for Fanon thinks violence is a psychic necessity for those who have been colonized. Only a therapeutic rage and catharsis of destruction can give back to "the wretched of the earth" their pride and manhood, make them throw off the alien culture imposed on them, that white mask on their black faces which does violence to their natures. Che said that revolution educates a man; first act, and out of action will come enlightenment. Fanon makes the same promise for violence; first be violent, and wisdom will blossom from that explosion: "Violence alone, violence committed by the people, violence organized and educated by its leaders, makes it possible for the masses to understand social truths and gives the key to them."

It is not surprising that anger and frustration should bring forward such a spokesman in the time of the Algerian tortures and official acts of terror. It would be useless to criticize Fanon "outside the situation"—his purge-theory of the mind's health, his belief that history's violence can be cut into quantitatively exact segments and balanced off, his hope that violence is healing rather than addictive. All these matters were explored centuries ago, when Aeschylus wrote his trilogy of "justified counter-violence" leading to an endless "chain of crimes." But the truly fascinating thing about Fanon is the willingness of our young people to transfer his analysis from Algeria to America. The obvious analogue, partially justified, is the position of the black man still suffering the historical violence of slavery and discrimination, the institutional racism still evident in American life. But the students take the matter much farther: middle-class rebels at the best universities, resorting to tactics of force, claim *they* are the oppressed, the wretched of the earth, who are merely returning a violence first inflicted on them. This violence, of course, has to be described as covert and diffuse—the institutionalized militarism and imperialism of our system; the manipulative, exploitative, brainwashing influence of the political parties and mass media; the inbuilt essential violence of capitalism; even the "violence" of liberal compromise and negotiation. In the students' view, American imperialism is not only exercised against the Vietnamese, who like Fanon's Algerians, are justified in a counter-terrorism of guerrilla war and torture. It is exercised also, even especially, against the American students, who are not merely spokesmen of the exploited Vietcong, but are themselves exploited. The System, not those who resist it, is responsible for all violence. In Marcuse's words: "The students have said that they are opposing the violence of society, legal violence, institutional violence. Their violence is that of defense. They have said this, and I believe it is true."

The terrorists Camus described were—like our current apologists of violence—Leftists; not so much because of political doctrine, but because the terrorists must strike out at the Establishment. That means, in America as it did in nineteenth-century Russia, revolution from the Left: it was the Bay of Pigs that made Oswald lump Kennedy with General Walker. Russia and Cuba were the logical outlets for his flight from America. Sirhan wrote in his diary: "I advocate the otherthrow of the current president of the f—ing United States of America . . . I firmly support the Communist cause and its people—wether [sic] Russian, Chinese, Albanian, Hungarian or whoever."

But murder as self-experiment is not inherently political. It can come from the Right, too—as it did when Germany's Dada and Surrealist period came to an end with the collapse of the Weimar Republic. Students then were taking the lead in society, forming the backbone of new parties, making demands on the university, asking for changes in the curriculum (especially the introduction of courses on race). Many people, in 1968 and 1969, read with a shudder of recognition Peter Gay's description of these young people in his book, *Weimar Culture:* "But all *Wandervogel* except the most casual attached an enormous importance to their movement, an importance dimly felt but fervently articulated; as solemn, rebellious bourgeois—and they were nearly all bourgeois— they saw their rambling, their singing, their huddling around the campfire, their visits to venerable ruins, as a haven from a Germany they could not respect or even understand, as an experiment in restoring primitive bonds that overwhelming events and insidious forces had loosened or destroyed—in a word, as a critique of the adult world. . . . Hans Breuer, who compiled the songbook of the youth movement . . . insisted . . . that he had gathered his folk songs for 'disinherited' youth, a youth 'sensing in its incompleteness—*Halbheit*—the good, and longing for a whole, harmonious humanity.' What, he asks, 'What is the old, classical folk song? It is the song of the whole man, complete unto himself.' . . . The *Wandervogel* sought warmth and comradeliness, an escape from the lies spawned by petty bourgeois culture, a clean way of life unmarked by the use of alcohol or tobacco. . . . The result was a peculiarly undoctrinaire, unanalytical, in fact unpolitical socialism—it was a 'self-evident proposition,' one observer noted, for all people in the youth movement to be Socialists. Young men and women, seeking purity and renewal, were Socialists by instinct; the *völkisch,* right-wing groups demanded the 'reawakening of a genuine Germanness— *deutsches Volkstum*—in German lands,' while the left-wing groups called for 'the restoration of a *societas,* a communally constructed society.' Everywhere, amid endless splintering of groups and futile efforts at reunion, there was a certain fixation on the experience of youth itself; novels about schools and youth groups exemplified and strengthened this fixation. . . . Flight into the future through flight into the past, reformation through nostalgia—in the end, such thinking amounted to nothing more than the decision to make adolescence itself into an ideology. . . . The hunger for wholeness was awash with hate; the political, and sometimes the private, world of its chief spokesmen was a paranoid world, filled with enemies; the dehumanizing machine, capitalist materialism, godless rationalism, rootless society, cosmopolitan Jews, and that all-devouring monster, the city."

All the needs of that society were soon met. The cult of youth became a celebration of the "new man" who would rule a thousand years. The need to participate was satisfied in therapeutic group rallies. The thirst for shock and primitiveness came about through state terrorism. Superstition was fed with the myth of a magic race. Community became the invincible *Volk.* And violence was *Blitzkrieg.* It was, as the kids say, "Beautiful."

The last thing left, to a society that rejects imposed standards as unauthentic, is the aesthetic sense. Even those far gone in nihilism have a feel for the striking, the dramatic, the gesture made with flair. Fascism was, in this way, a substitution of aesthetics for ethics: Aryanism was a code of the beautiful, enacted with uniforms, gestures, music, lights and rallies. Mussolini's neo-Renaissance of *Italianità* went along with Hitler's chiaroscuroed world of Leni Riefenstahl visions, Wagnerian "moments." In retrospect, it is difficult to understand what made men like Mussolini and Hitler respected and loved. They were not great political thinkers or admirable beings; not even very talented schemers. What were they then? They were both, unquestionably, masters of street theatre.

NO FEET ON THE FLOOR
Russell Kirk

Nudity is not new. People have been disrobing ever since they invented clothing. But Russell Kirk sees it as a detrimental comment on our permissive culture when nudity appears in coed dormitory lounges and even classrooms. A prominent spokesman for conservatism, Kirk is syndicated columnist ("To the Point") in over one hundred U.S. newspapers, a professor, and the author of many books, including *The Conservative Mind* and *Political Principles of Robert A. Taft.* He is a regular contributor to the *National Review.*

At Oakland University, in Michigan, last term, a male student obtained considerable attention, in the press, and in the state legislature, by stripping off all his clothes before a mixed class. He had been reading some verses of Yeats aloud to his fellow students, and he said he would feel more free if he were naked. (William Butler Yeats would have kicked him downstairs.) Since then, this young exhibitionist has departed to "study" in India, I am told.

In immediate consequence of this performance, a member of the Michigan Senate demands an investigation of Oakland University. This senator, living in Oakland County, hears many rumors of the carryings-on at Oakland U. Well, I know a number of Oakland students—and nearly anything you hear about Oakland is true.

This curious institution, situated amidst the affluent northern suburbs of Detroit, was founded as a branch of Michigan State University, but is now virtually autonomous. In the beginning, Oakland was supposed to emphasize quality of instruction; the first dean declared that he wanted "not well-rounded men, but men with hard, abrasive edges." Quality went out of the window in the game, however, because the typical Oakland student—permissively reared and schooled, and suffering from all the ills of suburban affluence—wasn't eager for the works of the mind.

Quantity, however, Oakland has—growing by leaps and bounds, on the model of its parent Michigan State. With its nine-story dormitories, Oakland is educational collectivism; also it is Brave New World, in mind and morals. There survive some good students—most notably, successful people of mature years who live in Oakland County and take courses in their leisure hours. (These middle-aged students often are resented by the typical Oakland undergraduates, on the ground that the suburban junior executives and housewives, being able to study at

From *National Review,* Vol. XXI, No. 13 (April 8, 1969). Reprinted by permission of *National Review,* 150 East 35th Street, New York, New York 10016.

home, earn better grades and therefore force up the grading "curve.")

This complaint is not altogether unreasonable, in that the undergraduate dwelling in Oakland's monstrous dormitories—supposing he wishes to read books or write papers—can find silence and solitude nowhere. The students are packed four or five to a bedroom; the nominal rule that quiet should prevail in the dormitories from seven in the evening to seven in the morning never is enforced; the dormitory lounges are equipped with big television sets, seldom turned off; and the couches in those lounges are pre-empted by ardent couples "making out," almost round the clock. There remains the library; but that, too, is noisy and disorderly. Such, on more campuses than Oakland's, has become our higher learning.

A number of girl students, vexed at finding no place to sit in the dormitory lounges and being somewhat embarrassed when compelled to receive visiting parents in lounges which looked like bordellos, recently proposed that some restrictions be imposed upon the makers-out in one of the residence halls. Should it not be required that courting couples in the lounges keep one foot on the floor—that is, one foot out of two feminine and two masculine feet? Heartened by this ethical discussion, other girls suggested that perhaps regulation should be carried even farther: *two* feet, per couple, on the lounge floor at all times. This would make more space on the couches, for one thing.

All nine floors of the dorm were consulted, and sentiment seemed to favor such an infringement upon absolute liberty. But the requirement has not been adopted—because the senior housemother flatly refused to enforce any such bothersome provisions.

Along one corridor, even liberal-minded girls were somewhat vexed by the fact that the female inmates of one room were entertaining, every night, all night, for weeks on end, a gentleman-caller. They objected to curious odors—presumably of narcotics—emanating from that room; to hysterical or ecstatic screams in the wee hours; to obscene conversations which penetrated through the partition-walls; to the gentleman-caller's custom of peering into other girls' rooms as he passed along the corridor.

At length a housemother was prevailed upon to remonstrate with the offending coeds. She declared mildly that if such visitations continued, she might feel it necessary to report to higher authority. Then the gentleman-caller ceased to call; but soon there appeared another lodger in the same room—a baby, said to belong to friends, who took up regular residence and who rends the night with its wails. So much for hard, abrasive edges at Oakland.

Last term's orientation at that institution of higher learning consisted principally of exhortations against Demon Racism. All entering freshmen were given copies of the Kerner Report to study, and there occurred much related indoctrination by lecture. Thankful for small favors, nevertheless, some of the better freshmen report to me that there was one orientation period devoted to a talk about books the new students should read.

It is so pleasant, in the Academy, to talk grandiosely about a better social order for the busy world; and so painful, of course, to recover order within the Academy itself—let alone to impart those principles of right reason that make possible the ordering of the soul. At Concupiscence U., where freshmen enroll in a dreary survey-course in "social psychology," there is all manner of freedom except freedom of the psyche. Doubtless such institutions work to produce a society as free as that of *Brave New World*.

JOE NAMATH AND THE PROBLEM OF HEROIC VIRTUE
Jack Richardson

Jack Richardson, who has written many articles for national magazines, is only partially facetious when he discusses Joe Namath in terms of "heroic virtue." Underlying the superficial details of the celebrated quarrel between the famous quarterback and the football commissioner, there is a contrast of life styles. Joe Namath's preference, momentary as it was, for the more honest style qualifies him, in Richardson's eyes, for at least a footnote in a history of cultural heroes.

Joe Namath cried! The phrase didn't topple parliaments around the world, but in the quixotic land of American sports, where morals and manners still affect in public the uncomplicated sentimentality of Victorian melodrama, *Joe Namath cried!* became a sort of touchstone, an objective correlative to the ethical puzzle that had sportswriters and commentators, fans and players scattering about such words as "loyalty" "integrity," "obligation," and engaging in musings on morality as intricate and hazy as any medieval debate on a matter of theological punctilio. Asked by professional football's commissioner Pete Rozelle to divest himself of his interest in a New York restaurant because known gamblers were often found leaning against its bar, Namath's first choice was to divest himself of football instead. An unholy decision, it would seem, had not the man who gave the American Football League a dignity equal to its National League rival claimed that what he was doing was a matter of principle and then gone on to display deep, lachrymose evidence that principled action is a painful, demanding experience.

Now there are many ways of regarding this banishment from football of one of its most expensive possessions. The large, historical perspective might well be that there was a certain spiritual inevitability in the clash, that Namath and professional football were destined to quarrel because the latter is too involved with American myth to tolerate a Namath and must finally expel him in the manner of an organism instinctively rejecting an alien body, no matter how indispensable to the organism's life the intruder might prove to be. Boxing, after all, with a burst of righteous frenzy, reduced itself to moribundity by expelling Cassius Clay because of moral and social idiosyncrasies, so there is good reason to suspect that football, too, could have a collection of zealous antibodies which rush suicidally and compulsively to defend their system against any anomalous invader. Namath, although certainly an exciting adornment to the game, was still a nettlesome figure in the professional sports world, a world which, for all its venality, still wants to appear driven by altruistic yearnings to a public eager to believe it is not watching the corporate hustling, trading and hiring of a few hundred well-conditioned mercenaries. Along with this desire to keep the pursuit of money in the background, the makers of the game have a precious notion of image, a notion which tries to keep its heroes crew-cut, clear-eyed, happily married, politically antiseptic and, in all outward respects, examples of the American Way as it might be dreamed of by Senator Dirksen after a heavy, fried-chicken lunch. Thus, no matter how excellent and exciting Namath might have been as a player, it was still true that his unaccommodating ways gave rise to a great many suspicions that each pass he completed caused, somewhere in our land, another sideburn to sprout or another love-in to take place. For there was no doubt that if Namath stood for anything besides good football, it was hair and hedonism, qualities which cause pathological reactions among those who want their sports heroes to be symbols of denial and models of indifference to any personal vanity that cannot be disguised under the respectable term "competitiveness."

Yes, it could be that Namath and the American sports world were not meant to fuse and that the incident of sinister gamesters in his restaurant was simply something epiphenomenal to a deeper, more metaphysical rupture in our society. And yet, Namath wept! He did not turn his back on the pomposities of his profession and, with resignation, head off for the fleshpots and franchises of the world. No, he agonized, invoked principle and in every way presented a case as morally baroque as that of any Racine hero.

Do not walk among gamblers and those who would cleave unto you so that they might advantage themselves on the point spread, said the Commissioner. And the Quarterback answered: You do not want me to live in this world, for there is in it no place where there are not those who seek an edge over their fellow men. Banish gamblers, and you banish all of life.

Thus the moral battle lines. One man who weeps and sees the world as it is; another who makes laws based on a world as it might have been had the roses in Eden never faded. The philosopher against divine authority: it is no wonder that Namath left the public hearing and retired with his friends to sip, if not hemlock, at least a goodly portion of Johnny Walker Red and to talk of the Blessed Isles around Las Vegas where the truth of human nature is catered to and honored.

Suppose then that this was the principle over which Namath wept. It is, after all, finally a question of reality, a question which someone of Namath's exuberance could easily turn into a moral battle, for he had never been tolerant of opinion, no matter how prevalent, which contradicted the facts as he knew them. Thus when the Baltimore Colts—a team of grim, collective excellence, whose symbol was the old, wounded hero, Johnny Unitas, a man who calls everybody "Sir"—became seventeen point favorites in the Super Bowl, Namath forcefully let it be known that reality was being abused.

In that instance it was fairly simple to prove that the establishment has miscalculated the truth of the matter, and Namath did just this by turning the Colts into a stunned, sulking, conquered people before millions of spectators. The confusion in the commissioner's office, however, would not be so easy to undo. How to convince him that in the great world beyond filled stadiums and pre-sold television rights there are pleasures almost as supreme as a goal-to-goal kickoff return? How to make clear that no matter what the generally accepted pieties may be, people *do* bet on football (I would guess that at least half the spectators at any game during the seaon have some sort of wager going) and to avoid all of them would mean a straight flight from the locker room to an underground cell guarded by Jesuits fanatical in their hatred of those who deal in the laws of probability.

Also, since I have been known to gamble a bit myself, I would like to think that Namath was striking a blow for a more enlightened public attitude toward this way of life. For the most part, gamblers do not advocate the overthrow of the government, are indeed conservative and anti-Maoist in their politics, and at least when winning, make good companions and tolerant friends. They deserve a better fate than that of being marked as carriers of a moral typhus which forces restaurants to close and careers to end as soon as they make an appearance.*

So then, what the Namath affair actually produced was two realities, two notions of the world that were fundamentally irreconcilable. In-

---

* I am here, of course, talking about honest gamblers, not bad, bad men who would try to fix a game. If the latter possibility with Namath is admitted, then, naturally, the whole affair escalates into moral absurdity.

deed, such an impasse does make for tears, for at such moments one discovers that there is no honorable way of maintaining a public and private self in this country without becoming either an outlaw or a politician. And so Namath honored a part of him that football's officialdom could not tolerate, and in so doing he made his point that athletes may be contractually indentured, but they are not bound to bow before the myths of public actuality. In the real world, people eat, drink, screw, gamble, wheel-and-deal, and that is the world Namath chose, without apology, to defend.

What would Joe have done without the Jets? Probably nothing more spectacular than make a few bad movies and flit in and out of honest business investments. However, there were rumors about his opening a casino in Las Vegas, and that is where I should like to see him. Perhaps with those teammates who promised to defect with him working as pit bosses, dealers and bouncers. Namath could finally preside, like some heavy-lidded, brooding angel, over his notion of what the world is really about.

TURNING ON: TWO VIEWS
Time Magazine

These personal accounts of drug use make no pretense of being "expert" testimony or of settling the controversy over the desirability of legalizing marijuana and LSD. Their interest originates from their lack of scientific, legal, and moral terminology. While facts and expert opinion are needed, so too are the feelings and subjective truths present in these personal statements.

A Teen-Ager's Trip

Eerie visions, horror, and a real or imagined new awareness of self crowd a teen-ager's mind when he gets on the drug kick. With chilling casualness, a 17-year-old starting college this fall, describes for *Time* his three years of drug taking. Brought up in the East in a middle-class suburban family, he was sent to a private school in Colorado because his parents hoped the experience would buck up his sagging attitudes and grades. He obviously knows some of the perils inherent in drugs, but is alarmingly heedless of others, notably LSD, which can be extremely dangerous. He graduated last June in good academic standing with a B average. When he turned on for the first time:

This guy down the hall happened to give me 500 ground-up morning glory seeds and he told me to eat them. He said I'd get stoned. I really

From *Time,* The Weekly News Magazine, September 26, 1969. Copyright 1969 Time, Inc. and reprinted by permission.

didn't know what drugs were all about then, but I took them and waited about two hours and I couldn't feel very much. Then I walked over to one of the school buildings and the same cat was up in a loft blowing grass. I didn't know what that was then either. I thought it was like heroin. I thought it was really bad. This chick who was a friend of his said, "Why don't you come up and smoke some?" So I went up there and started smoking it out of this Chinese opium pipe. We smoked it for a long time. Finally I climbed down.

The doors have glass windows with chicken-wire in them. I looked out the windows and I saw two suns in the sky. They were opposite each other and one was purple and one was some other color which I can't really describe. And they both were shooting down these long, thin poles made of light. When the poles hit the snow they broke like ice or glass and then the pieces melted like mercury and disappeared. I started to smile and I thought how strange everything was. This was something that never had happened to me before.

That was the first time. Only about five people at the whole school smoked any grass. It felt good to be one of them. That was one of the main reasons that I smoked, I think, and because I really wanted to try it. It was a nice thing. I probably smoked about 20 or 30 times that school year. Pretty soon about 85% of the kids smoked. It got to be a really statusy thing. A lot of the kids who smoked would come and tell you when they were stoned just to impress you. The school kind of overlooked all the grass smoking.

I stopped taking ground-up seeds, though, because once I took them before a vacation and had a bad trip [frightening experience]. I had to take a six-hour bus ride and then a plane. I took about 550 seeds just before the bus left. A lot of kids from school on the bus were stoned too. Some had grass and one guy drank two bottles of cough syrup. And it was really good for about an hour but then I started to freak. I felt like jumping off the bus. I just had to move. There were pine trees along the road and they all started to move really fast. They were moving too fast for me so I closed my eyes. But I had to open them all the time because if I didn't, I couldn't tell where I was.

I thought I was going insane and would have to be committed. When I finally got on the jet, I really started to freak because there was no one to talk to. I really wanted to talk to someone I knew. So I just sat there gripping the seat when the hallucinations got bad. The next day I was feeling really strange. I was psychotically paranoid. I thought people were trying to kill me and that they were behind huge plots against me. When I got back to school about two weeks later, I was pretty normal except that I never wanted to take seeds again.

Just before I left school that spring, two cats got a kilo of grass in the mail. They sold lids [packages containing roughly one ounce] and I bought two. I put them in my suitcase and the first night home, I smoked and left the bag under the bed instead of hiding it. One of my brothers found it and brought it to my parents. They were really horrified and they thought I was a real drug addict. They threw all of it down the toilet. They are really paranoid about drugs. They suspect me of being stoned when I am not.

The next summer I smoked only about three times a month because I didn't want to spend much money on it, and also because I fell in love and then I hardly smoked at all. For me, I think, grass is a substitute for love.

At the end of my senior year, everything was relaxed and nobody suspected me, and one weekend this cat came from Alaska and he offered me some acid [LSD]. I was pretty uptight. I didn't think it would wreck my mind, but I was still scared. Then when it started to come on, I thought, "How could such beautiful stuff hurt me?" I really dig acid raps. That's when you talk to the cat you took acid with about anything that comes into your mind. Once a big Day-Glo ribbon materialized and hovered three or four inches above the ground. It was about 7 ft. long and 2 ft. thick. Everything that I was going to say was written on that ribbon in pink letters before I was going to say it, so I just read the ribbon to talk. Acid has taught me a new way. You have to dig anything that happens to you, even if it's not what you wanted. And it taught me to appreciate more things. Things are really beautiful if you look at them or think about them enough.

After I took acid, I told my parents I had dropped [taken it]. They got really really uptight and said acid could make you go insane. But at least they didn't care about grass any more. They're just worried about grass because it's against the law. They never threatened to call the heat [police] or anything. They never even told me never to use drugs again. They just said: "Not in the house."

I haven't been stoned on anything for about a month, and I don't plan to take anything in the near future. Just to groove on reality for a change. I was born straight, so I think I should be straight for most of my life. But I will take acid again. When I'm on acid, I am as stoned as I could ever hope to be. The heavy drugs, like acid or mescaline, totally destroy reality. If I want to get the hell out, I'll just drop some of that good old LSD.

But some people can have a bad time with dope. Acid can make you flip out. One classmate of mine was disowned by his wealthy parents after he got busted from school for using grass. He started to do acid every day by shooting [with a hypodermic needle] and snorting [inhaling the powder], and he started to deal [push it, sell it] too. His parents thought he was going insane, and they talked of committing him. So he ran away from home. Nobody knows where he is now. Also, another cat I know got busted in Carmel [Calif.] for using weed. He couldn't leave the town for a year and had to spend every Saturday in jail.

A Straight Adult

How does marijuana affect a normal, successful adult? The following account was written for *Time* by a married 29-year-old Ivy League college graduate. He is levelheaded and ambitious, and works a taxing 50-hour week at a responsible job. He began turning on eight months ago, now uses marijuana twice a week on the average. He is not trying to persuade anyone else to follow his example.

Rashly, perhaps, I decided to risk the multiple legal and professional dangers of smoking pot. But how to find the stuff? My first discovery was that one turns out to have a lot of Jekyll-Hyde friends, who jekyll in the straight world and hyde when they are smoking grass.

Next came the props. These are purchasable at hundreds of "head" shops—those freaky emporia with psychedelic posters in the windows and incense pouring out of the door. I stopped at the grass counter and asked for some regular white Zig-Zag cigarette-rolling papers. Friends had also suggested a Rizla rolling machine if I felt too clumsy to roll my own. Another important purchase was a roach clip, used to hold the "roach" or butt of the joint after it has burned down and concentrated all those good resins at the end.

Then I went home and waited for the right mood. Almost any will do, although it's best not to smoke if you're extra anxious or depressed, since grass can amplify these feelings. I was also warned to be careful if I mixed pot in food—Alice B. Toklas brownies or "apple turn-on." These concoctions can take as long as two hours to have any effect, and if you get impatient and eat more, you can start feeling paranoid and even vomit. I learned to smoke with friends. Pot is best when shared with other people, and they can reassure you if you panic, as some people do when they first find their normal thought patterns beginning to change.

I inhaled deeply, holding the smoke down as long as possible, and passed the joint. The chances are excellent that nothing will happen to any first-timer, mostly because he has such fear about marijuana that he fights off its effects.

Eventually I did get stoned. Your feet and arms may seem a little cold, and you begin to feel and see things very intensely. Suddenly you wish that everyone would cluster in a small corner of the room because you almost feel that everyone near you is in some magic bubble, whereas the people over in the other part of the room seem very far away. Time slows down in the most felicitous way: an hour can seem like three, but yet I have suddenly seen the sun coming up when I thought it was only one in the morning.

Conversation tends to become diffused. When people throw out feelings and images, you don't just nod and say politely that you understand —you are right there with the fellow who is talking, looking at the same thing. Once, in a group of people listening to the Moody Blues, the music suddenly seemed to swell, as if it were the sound track of *Cleopatra* just at the point where the slaves are rowing her barge down the river. Someone suggested that the music made him think of the monumental effort a snail makes in pulling itself across a lawn, and instantly everyone was grooving on this image of those huge blownup snails painstakingly but nobly pulling themselves across the wet grass. There is probably no better way to understand Andy Warhol's pop art Campbell's Soup cans than to get stoned and look at everyday objects.

If there are partners around with whom people would like to sleep, chances are some of them will. If there is a pool near by, one of the first things people want to do is to go swimming in the raw. Then suddenly you realize you are both thirsty and hungry. The wise pot hostess, Author Jack Margolis advises in his new book, *A Child's Garden of Grass,* should have "plenty of munchies and suckies around the house when the gang drops in."

One has to be prepared to laugh at himself. I find I tend to deliver lines like Moses standing with the Ten Commandments under his arm. One night a bunch of us were somewhat stoned at a restaurant. A man at the next table leaned over and said to his wife, "If there is no view, why don't you frost the windows?" I dutifully informed my table of the remark, and we spent most of the evening on it: it seemed to sum up religion, Communism, even drugs. Unfortunately, the next morning it was simply another phrase—a good one, but not something that would knock straight people out for the count.

I learned not to walk into a store stoned. A pot-high woman friend had to go shopping for a few hot dogs, rolls and a six-pack of Coke. She came back an hour later $60 poorer, with six bags of groceries: things like brandied peaches, cans of baby shrimp, caviar and lots of pickles. It's not so much that your powers of discrimination are diminished—it's just that your powers of appreciation are enhanced.

A pot high is quite different from a liquor high. Alcohol dulls the senses whereas pot sets them on edge. If a child were screaming in the next room, I'd take a drink, not a joint. If I were sitting with an arm around Jane Fonda and she had just told me I had beautiful eyes, I'd light up. Drink is for tuning out. Pot is for tuning in.

Well, that's my view, anyway.

KID KILLERS:
A NIGHT WITH THE DRUGGED CHILDREN OF AMERICA

Suzanne Labin

Born in 1913, Suzanne Labin is a French journalist with a degree in advanced social and international studies; she has written many books on Soviet-American relations. Her essay shows little sympathy for those who debate the legality of drug use. Instead, she focuses on the "human tragedy" of children taking marijuana and LSD.

It wasn't until I had spent a night at a police station in West Hollywood that the figures I had read on drug addiction among the young in America were translated into human tragedy.

I would have thought that things would be slow at night at a police station. What I found was the tension of a fort under military attack. Three years earlier, I was told, this same precinct had three cars patrolling the streets on weekend nights. Today there are twenty, with forty policemen and detectives on night duty—all the result of the hippie phenomenon and the rise in drug use. And the police are overworked despite a fivefold increase in personnel in three years.

In the room to the left of the entrance hallway I noticed two men behind bars and was appalled as I always am when I see human beings in such surroundings. But my pity for them—the thieves and the drunks that make up much of the night-time occupancy of a city precinct station—was soon submerged by a far more distressing sight: coming through the door, escorted by policemen, was a group of children, picked up on the streets at night, all of them having on them drugs of some sort. Neither the children nor the women were put in cells—they present no physical danger to the police officers. They are questioned either in the entrance hall or in the offices of the detectives.

It's one o'clock and I watch a continuous stream of children being brought in. First two boys, then three young girls. The oldest girl is fifteen, cute with a tight short dress that outlines her adolescent breasts and leaves her skinny shoulders bare—it's hot in Los Angeles even at this hour. The two other girls, slovenly dressed and with messy hair,

From *National Review*, Vol. XXI, No. 17 (May 6, 1969). Reprinted by permission of *National Review*, 150 East 35th Street, New York, New York 10016.

look more like schoolgirls than delinquent children of the night. They refuse to give the police their parents' addresses, pretending that they don't know where they live. They lie brazenly, arrogantly. One bursts into laughter: "My mother? If you know where she is, please tell me."

A detective tells me that more often than not when the parents of a sixteen-year-old runaway, who has been picked up smoking marijuana, arrive at the station their reaction is: Well, she's sixteen. She's old enough to know what she's doing. The child is then often sent to a psychiatrist—who solves nothing. She runs away again, is picked up again, the parents are called in again, they take the child home and send her back to the psychiatrist—and the cycle is repeated. That is the story of the daughter of a minister friend of mine in Chicago.

In the United States the number of runaways is reaching tragic proportions. These runaways are comfortably and warmly dressed, well fed, and more often than not well supplied with pocket money. They have usually left home over a small matter, often to protest a parental injunction of one sort or another. For the most part they have nothing against their parents. They have run away for adventure, to see the world, and because in many circles in the past couple of years it has become the thing to do.

In contrast to the girls, the boys who are brought in tonight seemed scared. Police are apt to be tougher on boys than girls. One boy is on the verge of tears. He gives the police his mother's address. He comes from Quebec and is fourteen years old. I speak to him in French. I tell him he can confide in me because no one else in the station house speaks French. He's a nice boy, shy and polite. He finds it hard to contain his tears at the prospect of a night behind bars. I ask him what led to this night that he will never forget.

His story is not even dramatic. He lives with his older sister and his mother, very happily, he tells me. One day he went to a birthday party. Instead of going home from it he stayed out that night, wandering around the streets, observing the night life. Nothing so serious about that. But in the course of the evening he got hold of some marijuana. He was given the cigarettes free—a number of the children questioned tonight say they got theirs free, too. And he didn't go home. He drifted into the hippie life, and ended, tonight, in the West Hollywood police station.

I leave the police station for a while to make a tour of Sunset Strip with a couple of detectives. We go into a hippie discothèque. The music is so loud it makes my head ache. Brasses blare out over a background of discordant sounds, but all is subordinated to the hysterical shrieks of a singer who twists and turns, pulling her long dark hair out in front of her to the full length of her arms. She tosses the mop of hair across her face so that there are no eyes, no mouth, nothing but the voice: the mad voice that comes through the mass of hair. My eardrums are about to burst and my eyes are assailed, wounded, tortured by an orgy of light, of screaming images that flash on and off so rapidly that you can't tell what they are. You just about recognize the face of a young girl with an open mouth when a gangster fires a pistol into your face; a horse gallops over you; and you're about to scream when you find yourself in the Garden of Eden where a beautiful naked girl appears, only to be engulfed immediately in a raging sea. And always, all the time, superimposed on everything else the face of the young girl with the open mouth whose features, whose expression you never get because of the speed with which it flashes on and off. Our optic nerves are the target of ten projectors which simultaneously beam images on different surfaces of the dark walls, images that flash with the speed of lightning and with all its brightness. Colored designs, sometimes violet, sometimes brown, but with red always dominating the colors, cross, clash, torture us.

Then I notice human forms on the darkened dance floor moving to the beat of the orchestra. I am told that these are what were known in earlier days as dancers. They are squeezed like sardines in a can and yet these are the most solitary dancers in the world. Each one sways alone. None of them watches the *grand guignolesque* spectacle on the walls. They watch their feet. No girl smiles at a boy, no boy at a girl. But then there is nothing to see, nothing to touch: these swaying, undulating, bending, stretching phantoms wear shapeless pants on their nether parts, outsized Indian vests with fringes around the middle, are covered on top by long hair to which the incessant movement of the head seems to give a life of its own. They are shadows without substance, asexual, shadows in constant movement, engulfed in incessant sound. I can't take this machinegun fire of sound and light for more than fifteen minutes. How, I ask my detective friends, can the habitués stand this hell all night long? It's because they've smoked marijuana or are on other drugs, they tell me, and their senses are dulled.

I return to the police station. New faces behind the bars; more children waiting to be questioned. A small boy, slim, with fine features and the rosy skin of a very young girl, with large chestnut eyes, the pupils dilated. I approach him and he asks: "Are you the fuzz?" I ask him to repeat the question, my knowledge of English not being up to hippie slang. I finally understand that he wants to know whether I am connected with the narcotics squad. I laugh and tell him that I am a French journalist doing a story on the hippies. My French accent convinces him and he tells me his story.

In front of him is a table on which lie the things they found on him: a dozen marijuana cigarettes rolled in yellow paper; some loose shreds of marijuana, some ashes from the cigarette he had been smoking when arrested. There are also some rose-colored beads that contain drops of

LSD, "acid" as it is called. He tells me that he takes LSD trips regularly and that they last from twelve to fourteen hours.

"Aren't you afraid of ruining your health?" I ask.

"Everyone does it," he replies.

"Not everyone. Just people in the groups you run around with. It's a very small group."

"What's the difference, whether it's acid or drink? Why is society so anxious to keep me from ruining my health with drugs while doing nothing to keep me from getting cancer from tobacco?" (This argument is going the rounds of the underground press.)

He tells me that he's just one of three billion people in the world so why is the Establishment so concerned about him. He tells me that all the Establishment wants is to keep him healthy until he is twenty so he can be shot in Vietnam. I ask him if he doesn't think there is anything worth fighting for. Yes, he admits, but adds why not have a good time before he's called up. I ask him if he can't find the amusement he craves in travel, or movies, or sports or girls—in things that won't ruin his health.

I could, he tells me, but they are all expensive. His mother works behind a soda fountain and he doesn't want to end that way.

While we are talking, a policeman brings in something else they have found in his pockets. It is evidence that will convict him. A schoolboy notebook covered with childish writing. On the first page he has listed, in alphabetical order, the names, addresses and telephone numbers of his "clients." On another page is written, in different colored ink, the prices he charges, according to the quality, for grass (marijuana), acid (LSD), speed (methedrine).

On still another page he has totted up his earnings for the month and then subtracted his expenses. There is a large debit notation in the LSD column, and this sentence, followed by two exclamation marks: "I could have cleared $75 more if I had had the strength not to use so much!!"

I am aghast. Seventy-five dollars! One dose of LSD costs five dollars. That means that in the course of a single month he has taken fifteen trips. On another page he has listed the names and addresses of certain wholesalers. On still another the names of new clients to be contacted, and new areas to be explored. Finally across the whole of a blank sheet of paper, and in much larger block letters, this commentary from the future Napoleon of drugs: "I MUST EXTEND MY EMPIRE. . . ."

They come to take him to his cell. Tears start to come to his eyes. Our conversation had made him forget his situation—for the moment. The other boys are going home to their parents, he is going to jail.

He turns toward me politely: "It helped me to talk to you," he says and goes out leaden-footed.

He is fifteen years old.

This parade of drugged children took place in the middle of a Friday night, a Friday night of Friday nights, in a single precinct of a single American city. If you put together all the nights in all the precincts in all the big cities of America you realize that tens of thousands of American teen-agers have and are tasting the forbidden fruit.

And the argument continues to rage between those who insist that marijuana is not addictive and that it should be legalized and those who believe that a good number of young marijuana-users escalate up the ladder to the more dangerous drugs: hashish, LSD, STP, mescaline and the amphetamines, finally heroin.

A night at the West Hollywood police station might help some of the disputants bring the argument down to its least common denominator, the runaway child.

UPON A TIME IN WOODSTOCK
Philip P. Ardery, Jr.

Although the youth culture prizes individualism, it also promotes collective activities. Beginning with Woodstock in 1969, the rock festival has taken its place alongside of the "be-in" and the demonstration as meccas of experience for young people. Philip P. Ardery, Jr., a young writer whose work frequently appears in the *National Review,* sees Woodstock as a glorious anomaly in a commercialized culture and sadly implies that similar festivals will not be so disorganized, so free, so utopian.

No stars that night over our outdoor city, and we, a half million of us, sat fitfully up in our amphitheater turned bog, hearing singers and guitars below but not really listening. Behind the stage, across a country road, a field stretched out, the fence around it laced with a string of red Christmas tree bulbs—our own, private constellation. The lights, blurred by rain, glowed eerily and took our attention, because sound was there too, a whipping whine, much louder than the music. A spotlight shot its bright cone earthward, a visible sign of something hovering, blowing up wet grass, and then, finally, touching ground. Many in our city—who knows why?—suddenly broke into applause.

One young man, half-high on marijuana, offered a stoned reading of the scene: "You see, the Martians announced they would pay earth a visit, and all these people came out to greet them, and some bands got together to play a few songs of welcome." Far. Out. But then the scene,

From *National Review,* Vol. XXI (September 9, 1969). Reprinted by permission of *National Review,* 150 East 35th Street, New York, New York 10016.

like other scenes during those three days, invited wild interpretations. The Woodstock Music and Art Fair fit no one's expectations, and we groped to give it form and purpose—and continued groping until the end.

True, the focus, the central interest of the weekend was not this landing on the helipad. But then—and this created our confusion—neither was it the music, the single attraction that had lured one of every seventy Americans from fifteen to 25 to an isolated New York farm. So many came to listen that we overwhelmed the performers, however well some of them played. Our cars, our tents and ourselves improvised a city, twenty-second largest in the United States, and the fact of this city, its weather, its privations, its confusion and its civility, dominated our senses. We shared a formless experience, one we had not prepared for, and it gratified immensely.

There are, really, only three groups of people who disapproved our pleasure. First, and justifiably, the farmers and townspeople of upstate New York, who did not engineer their own inconvenience. Our improvised city, without enough land, shelter, food, warmth or sanitation to sustain itself, took over their roads, parked its cars on their lawns, pitched its tents in their fields, rustled their crops, stole their fenceposts for firewood, used their creeks as garbage dumps and latrines. We wronged them. Eight thousand of us hung around on Monday to clean up, make amends.

The Left, too, hated the Fair, what it was supposed to be and what it actually was. The idea of holding it was an affront, a fantastic wager that the revolution of youth is far less political than cultural. Eight, maybe ten thousand people swept into Chicago last summer to see Hubert Humphrey and Richard Daley. Nowhere, New York, offered Jimi Hendrix and Janis Joplin, and the promoters needed 200,000 customers to break even on their investment. When the bet paid off to handsomely (our overlarge crowd broke down the gates, the ushers never sold or collected tickets, the promoters lost more than $1 million), and, swelled to city size, we transformed ourselves from an audience for music into participants in a muddy void, we filled that void not with rebellion and angry talk but with drugs and quiet friendship. Our uninvolvement, our frivolity maddened the Left. We did not even collect pennies for SANE.

Some locals, the Left—and then many ordinary Americans disliked us too. Our city's drugs were illegal. Its citizens unkempt. And, worst of all, the city was a mob, the nemesis of all purposeful men, all believers in American individualism. But it was not planned that way. Most of us by far had come for music, to enjoy a one-to-one relationship with the stage, not to be lost in a muddy commune. Else why would we have chosen Woodstock? There have been other festivals this summer, and hundreds of "be-ins," but none drew close to our half million. None offered so many fine musicians.

We became a mob, but only because our extreme disorientation, our fear of being trapped there, the pleas to share, be cool, *it's the only way to make it,* forced a collective consciousness upon us. What made us a mob made us good, too, because our fears and needs pushed the limits of togetherness beyond our city of peers, to the gracious and generous police and townspeople. The worst of us learned that cops and rednecks are more angel than pig.

Our city depended on them, and they on us. We behaved well so that the squares could help us survive. Doctors healed wounds, treated illnesses, smoothed out rough "trips." Police helicopters flew in our food, flew out our sick. Farmers shared their produce. And the promoters, after having made the one gigantic mistake of conceiving the idea of Woodstock, spared no expense to make us less uncomfortable, even when they knew we had robbed them of their profit.

The few very hip ones among us came away from it all positively glowing. Had not the rest of us failed to find purpose in being there, had not we simply existed communally, and yet enjoyed it? It seemed to some that the ideal hippie, killed in San Francisco by methadrine and angry politics, had been reborn, and in such numbers that he might survive, multiply, maybe even prevail.

But that—the root of the individualists' fear—is making too much of Woodstock. It was only a moment of glorious innocence, and such moments happen only by accident, and then not often. Had everyone known we would be a city, there would have been more toilets, more food, more tents, more water, more comfort generally. And therefore less confusion and fear, less need to band together and be good. Had the East Coast known there would be a complete electrical failure on November 9, 1965, workers would have stayed at home, housewives would have stockpiled canned foods and candles, and no puzzled, gay and loving people would have flooded downtown streets.

And these accidental bursts of aimless solidarity do not last forever. America take heart. By Sunday afternoon, most of us had abandoned Woodstock, eager for a return to form, purpose and individuality. The same thousands who waved gaily from their cars, hardly creeping away from the mudpile, were driving furiously and honking horns by the time they got back to New York City.

COMING OF AGE IN AQUARIUS
Andrew Kopkind

Since the other essays in Part One of this book present contrasting—and sometimes contradictory—views of the youth culture, it is appropriate to end with Andrew Kopkind's report on the Woodstock festival. Here was an event which embodied the paradoxical aspects of the new culture. It was "paradise and concentration camp, sharing and profiteering, sky and mud, love and death." But the author refuses to be pessimistic, despite the festival's mistakes, and concludes that the paradoxical and disturbing qualities of the new culture will decline as the youth culture develops its own institutions. Kopkind, who was born in 1935, is the founder and editor of *Hard Times* and the author of *America: The Mixed Curse.*

> I looked at my watch, I looked at my wrist,
> I punched myself in the face with my fist;
> I took my potatoes down to be mashed—
> And made it on over to that million dollar bash.
> > Dylan

The Woodstock Music and Art Fair wasn't held in Woodstock; the music was secondarily important and the art was for the most part unproduced; and it was as much of a fair as the French Revolution or the San Francisco earthquake. What went down on Max Yasgur's farm in the low Catskills last weekend defied casual categories and conventional perceptions. Some monstrous and marvelous metaphor had come alive, revealing itself only in terms of its contradictions: paradise and concentration camp, sharing and profiteering, sky and mud, love and death. The urges of the ten years' generation roamed the woods and pastures, and who could tell whether it was some rough beast or a speckled bird slouching towards its Day-Glo manger to be born?

The road from the Hudson River west to White Lake runs through hills like green knishes, soft inside with good earth, and crusty with rock and wood on top. What works of man remain are rural expressions of an Other East Village, where the Mothers were little old ladies with sheitls, not hip radicals with guns. There's Esther Manor and Siegel's Motor Court and Elfenbaum's Grocery: no crash communes or head shops. Along that route, a long march of freaks in microbuses, shit-cars and bikes—or on thumb and foot—passed like movie extras in front of a process screen. On the roadside, holiday-makers from the Bronx looked up from their pinochle games and afghan-knitting and knew that the season of the witch had come.

From *Hard Times*, August 25–September 1, 1969. Reprinted by permission of the publisher.

"Beatniks out to make it rich": Woodstock was, first of all, an environment created by a couple of hip entrepreneurs to consolidate the culture revolution and (in order to?) extract the money of its troops. Michael Lang, a 25-year old former heavy dealer from Bensonhurt dreamed it up; he then organized the large inheritance of John Roberts, 26, for a financial base, and brought in several more operatives and financiers. Lang does not distinguish between hip culture and hip capital; he vowed to make a million before he was 25, beat his deadline by two years, and didn't stop. With his Village/Durango clothes, a white Porsche and a gleaming BSA, he looks, acts and *is* hip; his interest in capital accumulation is an extension of every hippie's desire to rip off a bunch of stuff from the A&P. It's a gas.

The place-name "Woodstock" was meant only to evoke cultural-revolutionary images of Dylan, whose home base is in that Hudson River village. Woodstock is where The Band hangs out and the culture heroes congregate; it's where Mick Jagger (they say) once ate an acid-infused Baby Ruth right inside the crotch of a famous groupie. A legend like that is good for ticket sales, but the festival was always meant to be held in Wallkill, 40 miles away.

By early summer, Woodstock looked to be the super rock festival of all time, and promoters of a dozen other summertime festivals were feverishly hyping up their own projects to catch the overflow of publicity and enthusiasm: Rock music (al fresco or recorded) is still one of the easiest ways to make money off of the new culture, along with boutique clothes and jewelry, posters, drugs and trip-equipment, Esquire magazine, Zig-Zag papers and Sara Lee cakes. But the Woodstock hype worried the burghers of Wallkill, and the law implemented their fears by kicking the bash out of town. Other communities, however, were either less uptight or more greedy; six hard offers for sites came to the promoters the day Wallkill gave them the boot. With less than a month to get ready, Woodstock Ventures, Inc., chose the 600-acre Yasgur farm (with some other parcels thrown in) at White Lake, N.Y.

Locals there were divided on the idea, and Yasgur was attacked by some neighbors for renting (for a reported $50,000) to Woodstock. But in the end, the profit motive drove the deal home. One townsman wrote to the Monticello newspaper: "It's none of their business how Max uses his land. If they are so worried about Max making a few dollars from his land they should try to take advantage of this chance to make a few dollars themselves. They can rent camping space or even sell water or lemonade." Against fears of hippie horrors, businessmen set promises of rich rewards: "Some of these people are shortsighted and don't understand what these children are doing," one said. "The results will bring an economic boost to the County, without it costing the taxpayer a cent."

The vanguard of freaks started coming a week or more before opening day, and by Wednesday they were moving steadily down Route 17-B, like a busy day on the Ho Chi Minh Trail. The early-comers were mostly hard-core, permanent dropouts: Their hair or their manner or their rap indicated that they had long ago dug into their communes or radical politics or simply into oppositional life-styles. In the cool and clear night they played music and danced, and sat around fires toasting joints and smoking hashish on a pinpoint. No busts, pigs or hassle; everything cool, together, outasight.

By the end of the next day, Thursday, the ambience had changed from splendor in the grass to explosive urban sprawl. Light and low fences erected to channel the crowds without actually seeming to oppress them were toppled or ignored; cars and trucks bounced over the meadows; tents sprung up between stone outcroppings and cow plop. Construction went on through the night, and already the Johnny-on-the-Spot latrines were smelly and out of toilet paper, the food supply was spotty, and long lines were forming at the water tank. And on Friday morning, when the population explosion was upon us all, a sense of siege took hold: Difficult as it was to get in, it would be almost impossible to leave for days.

From the beginning, the managers of the festival were faced with the practical problem of control. Berkeley and Chicago and Zap, N.D., were the functional models for youth mobs rampaging at the slightest provocation—or no provocation at all. The promoters interviewed 800 off-duty New York City policemen for a security guard (Sample question: "What would you do if a kid walked up and blew marijuana smoke in your face?" Incorrect answer: "Bust him." Correct answer: "Inhale deeply and smile."), chose 300 or so, and fitted them with mod uniforms. But at the last minute they were withdrawn under pressure from the Police Department, and the managers had to hire camp counselors, phys ed teachers and stray straights from the surrounding area.

The guards had no license to use force or arrest people; they merely were to be "present," in their red Day-Glo shirts emblazoned with the peace symbol, and could direct traffic and help out in emergencies if need be. The real work of keeping order, if not law, was to be done by members of the Hog Farm commune, who had been brought from New Mexico, along with people from other hippie retreats, in a chartered airplane (at $16,000) and psychedelic buses from Kennedy Airport.

Beneath the practical problem of maintaining order was the principal contradiction of the festival: how to stimulate the energies of the new culture and profit thereby, and at the same time control them. In a way, the Woodstock venture was a test of the ability of avant-garde capitalism at once to profit from and control the insurgencies which its system spawns. "Black capitalism," the media industry, educational technology, and Third World economic development are other models, but more diffuse. Here it was in one field during one weekend: The microcosmic system would "fail" if Woodstock Ventures lost its shirt, or if the control mechanisms broke down.

The promoters must have sensed the responsibility they carried. They tried every aspect of cooptation theory. SDS, Newsreel and underground newspapers were handed thousands of dollars to participate in the festival, and they were given a choice spot for a "Movement City"; the idea was that they would give hip legitimacy to the weekend and channel their activities "within the system." (They bought the idea.) Real cops were specifically barred from the camp grounds, and the word went out that there would be no busts for ordinary tripping, although big dealers were discouraged. There would be free food, water, camping facilities—and, in the end, free music, when attempts at crowd-channeling failed. But the Hog Farmers were the critical element. Hip beyond any doubt, they spread the love/groove ethic throughout the farm, breaking up incipient actions against "the system" with cool, low-key hippie talk about making love not war, the mystical integrity of earth, and the importance of doing your *own* thing, preferably alone. On the other hand—actually, on the same hand—they were the only good organizers in camp. They ran the free food operation (oats, rice and bulgar), helped acid-freaks through bad trips without Thorazine, and (with Abbie Hoffman) ran the medical system when that became necessary.

The several dozen Movement organizers at the festival had nothing to do. After Friday night's rain there was a theory that revolt was brewing on a mass scale, but the SDS people found themselves unable to organize around the issue of inclement weather. People were objectively trapped; and in that partial aspect, the Yasgur farm *was* a concentration camp—or a hippie reservation—but almost everyone was stoned and happy. Then the rain stopped, the music blared, food and water arrived, and everyone shared what he had. Dope became plentiful and entirely legitimate; in a soft cool forest, where craftsmen had set up their portable headshops, dealers sat on tree stumps selling their wares: "acid, mesc, psilocybin, hash. . . ." No one among the half-million could not have turned on if he wanted to; joints were passed from blanket to blanket, lumps of hashish materialized like manna, and there was Blue Cheer, Sunshine acid and pink mescaline to spare.

Seen from any edge or angle, the army strung out against the hillside sloping up from the stage created scenes almost unimaginable in commonplace terms. No day's demonstration or political action had brought these troops together; no congress or cultural event before produced such urgent need for in-gathering and self-inspection. The ambiguities and contradictions of the imposed environment were worrisome; but to miss the exhilaration of a generation's arrival at its own campsite was to define the world in only one dimension.

Although the outside press saw only masses, inside the differentiation was more impressive. Maybe half the crowd was weekend-hip, out from Long Island for a quick dip in the compelling sea of freaks. The other half had longer been immersed. It was composed of tribes dedicated to whatever gods now seem effective and whatever myths produce the energy needed to survive: Meher Baba, Mother Earth, street-fighting man, Janis Joplin, Atlantis, Jimi Hendrix, Che.

The hillside was their home. Early Saturday morning, after the long night of rain—from Ravi Shankar through Joan Baez—they still had not abandoned the turf. Twenty or forty thousand people (exactitude lost its meaning: it was that sight, not the knowledge of the numbers that was so staggering) sat stonily silent on the muddy ground, staring at a stage where no one played: petrified playgoers in the marble stands at Epidaurus, thousands of years after the chorus had left for the last time.

No one in this country in this century had ever seen a "society" so free of repression. Everyone swam nude in the lake, balling was easier than getting breakfast, and the "pigs" just smiled and passed out the oats. For people who had never glimpsed the intense communitarian closeness of a militant struggle—People's Park or Paris in the month of May or Cuba—Woodstock must always be their model of how good we will all feel after the revolution.

So it was an illusion and it wasn't. For all but the hard core, the ball and the balling is over; the hassles begin again at Monticello. The repression-free weekend was provided by promoters as a way to increase their take, and it will not be repeated unless future profits are guaranteed (it's almost certain now that Woodstock Ventures lost its wad). The media nonsense about death and O.D.s has already enraged the guardians of the old culture. The system didn't change; it just accommodated the freaks for the weekend.

What is not illusionary is the reality of a new culture of opposition. It grows out of the disintegration of the old forms, the vinyl and aerosol institutions that carry all the inane and destructive values of privatism, competition, commercialism, profitability and elitism. The new culture has yet to produce its own institutions on a mass scale; it controls none of the resources to do so. For the moment, it must be content—or discontent—to feed the swinging sectors of the old system with new ideas, with rock and dope and love and openness. Then it all comes back, from Columbia Records or Hollywood or Bloomingdale's in perverted and degraded forms. But something will survive, because there's no drug on earth to dispel the nausea. It's not a "youth thing" now but a generational event; chronological age is only the current phase. Mass politics, it's clear, can't yet be organized around the nausea; political radicals have to see the cultural revolution as a sea in which they can swim, like black militants in "black culture." But the urges are roaming, and when the dope freaks and nude swimmers and loveniks and ecological cultists and music groovers find out that they have to fight for love, all fucking hell will break loose.

PART TWO

EDUCATION IN THE SEVENTIES

We are living in the age of the "multiversity," an age in which our colleges and universities have extended their influence into nearly every area of our national life. That our universities have become powerful and important forces in our society cannot be denied; but in recent years, more and more voices have been raised in protest against this development, challenging and criticizing the many roles which our universities are now playing. Many believe that as our universities have grown larger and more powerful, they have gotten out of step with those they are supposed to serve, becoming less relevant to the concerns of the individual students and less responsive to the real needs of society.

Most of the complaints have come from the students themselves, reflecting a greater degree of student unrest than at any other time in our history. The complaints have been made for a variety of reasons. Some students are simply impatient; they see little sense in spending four valuable years pursuing a degree which means little more to them than a union card providing the proper credentials for entry into the world. Some students are frustrated by required courses which seem to bear little relation to their own values or to the future professions they want to enter. Some complain that they have too many general education requirements, and that their courses in the sciences or the humanities are vague, irrelevant, and a waste of time; others value these requirements, finding instead too great a stress on specialized courses and too much emphasis on narrow research during their undergraduate years. Many students complain about the loss of identity they feel upon entering college: at their first registration they are assigned a number which seems to become far more important to the school than their name. Many students complain about mediocre teaching; those who attend large universities may have more poorly prepared, poorly paid teaching assistants during their first two years than they have professors. And the professors, many of whom are caught up in a publish-or-perish syndrome, may seem to care little for their students. Those professors who are well-liked are frequently so busy that they have no time to talk informally with their students. Many students have complained about their school's close ties with the government; with up to seventy percent of some university budgets being supported by the government for research and defense projects, it seems apparent to them that their universities are much more concerned with government contracts than with education.

Whether or not these complaints are legitimate, there has been a general cry for reform, for change, for a more relevant education. There is no doubt that many students have flourished under the present educational system and have found it quite adequate to meet their own needs. But a growing number of students, like the first essayist in this part, Roger Rapoport, have agonized over the education they are receiving; and they have been willing to take risks in order to change the structure and the style of their schools.

The most visible sign of growing student dissent can be seen in the many student protest movements which have arisen in recent years. By organizing, students have found a new sense of power, a new strength which they had never exerted collectively before. They have fought for many causes—to force changes in curriculum, to have some say in how their schools are run, to establish programs for students from minority groups, to gain better control over the administration of student funds, and to ensure free speech. Not only campus issues have galvanized students into active protest. Increasingly, students have used their power to agitate for political causes not directly related to their education—in speaking out against the draft, in protesting American involvement in Vietnam, in registering their concern over continuing racial injustice, in expressing their alarm over the pollution of our environment.

The student power movement has posed a real threat to many members of our society, which is perhaps an indication of its effectiveness. As students have exerted their muscle, administrations have toppled, legislatures have trembled, fearful governors have called out the National Guard, and the general populace has reacted with suspicion, distrust, and recriminations; and, as Joseph Lyford describes, all of this has been minutely recorded by the press and television, as if the whole student protest movement were one giant, continuing TV spectacular.

Some serious thinkers have begun, however, to question the use students are making of their newly found power. George Kennan asserts, for instance, that students who are engaged in the power movement are wasting their time and their educations, for they do not yet have clearly formulated goals for the use of their power. Nathan Glazer, on the other hand, believes that students are aware of their objectives, but he advises students to use their power wisely, avoiding the complete politicization of their campuses.

While student power continues to pose a threat and its use continues to be seriously questioned, it is very likely that in the 1970's power will still be exerted by students to force reform; it seems now to be only a question of what shape the reforms will take. In the essays that follow, a number of specific proposals for reform are made in response to the many questions students are asking. How can we make our studies relevant to our own personal lives? To the kind of society we would like to create? Should our schools do away with grades, thus lessening some of the pressures which afflict students? Should we abandon the traditional lecture system and replace it with discussion groups and tutorials? Some students, believing that what their teachers force them to learn is irrelevant, would establish "free universities" in which the students themselves would plan and develop their own courses. Certain educators, like Harold Taylor, would support at least one aspect of this idea, urging students, as he does, to become more involved in teaching each other and to share in the excitement of communicating their newfound knowledge to their peers. But other educators, like Henry Steele Commager, caution that the narrow insistence of students that the university be relevant to their own concerns (in the same way that, say, a newspaper is) will be damaging to education.

While the essayists in Part Two propose many different specific reforms, most of them would agree that the university should be preserved as a place where ideas can be freely interchanged, without suppression and without recriminations. It should be a place for criticism and a place for creativity. It should be a place which will not only preserve values, but will also foster the continuing search for new truths; provide the knowledge appropriate to prepare one for a career; and provide the wisdom necessary for man to survive on this earth. The university should above all be the place where, in the spirit of freedom and inquiry, one establishes his values and develops his potential.

IS A COLLEGE EDUCATION RELEVANT?

"Unless I was going to become an academic, a lawyer, a C.P.A., or some other carefully defined careerist, school was a liability. So I began to treat it as a part-time job. By no means was I a dropout, I still took my courses and passed. But like my friends I shifted my commitment outside the classroom."

ROGER RAPOPORT

LISTEN TO THE WHITE GRADUATE,
YOU MIGHT LEARN SOMETHING

Roger Rapoport

More and more students today are questioning the value of spending four or
more years in college. In this essay Roger Rapoport, a 1968 graduate of the
University of Michigan, provides an articulate account of the disillusionment and frustrations he experienced while at Michigan. He sought intellectual stimulation, but found classes boring, course requirements senseless, and
professors pedantic or remote. Those professors who did seem exciting were
far too busy to spend time talking with him. With his assertion, "college
never led me on to anything," he expresses the feeling of many students that
college training has become a liability rather than an asset.

Historians will doubtless rank April 27, 1968, as a landmark in the annals of American education, second only to passage of the Morrill Act.
On that day I completed seventeen years of study, graduated from the
University of Michigan and resigned my commission in the nation's
school system. I knew education would never be the same without me,
nor I the same without it. Still, I would have preferred sleeping through
my own commencement like one more eight-o'clock class. But my parents were flying in for the occasion. So I woke early and hurried over to
the administration building to get their graduation tickets.

Inside, a secretary explained she didn't have the advertised tickets
and directed a long line of seniors to the site of the ceremony, the
domed University Events Building. While janitors obscured the basketball court with maize and blue bunting, ushers ran us around the perim-
eter of the building to the ticket window. A uniformed guard said:
"There are no tickets left and besides you're not supposed to be inside
this early."

In frustration I drove directly to the home of University President
Robben Fleming. His wife opened the door just as the President descended the staircase with houseguest and commencement speaker Robert Weaver. After being introduced to the Secretary of Housing, I sat
down on the living-room couch and explained the dilemma. Fleming
made some unsuccessful phone calls and sent me back to the administration building. There a university administrator directed me to a
ticket clerk at the Events Building who was dubious about the authenticity of my yellow plastic I.D. card (362-44-9616-5). I helplessly
flipped him my entire wallet—Social Security card, driver's license,
draft card and all—in a final effort to get the tickets for my parents, by

now stranded at the airport. Tickets in hand, I rushed to pick them up, coming back too late for the pomp and circumstance but soon enough to hear Mr. Weaver talk of promising career opportunities for today's graduates: "So I say to you that the urban frontier, with all of its complexities and problems, is an avenue to exciting and meaningful careers."

Afterward we rushed off to a friend's party and pondered our glorious futures. Here, amidst piles of potato salad, cold cuts, and brownies, was the educational elite of civilization's most advanced state —the breast-fed generation off to conquer the world. In one corner a comely history major was taking her degree to the advertising department of a Boston false-teeth manufacturer. Another friend, a flaming blonde Marxist, had landed a taskless secretarial post with a New York ad agency. And I was heading for San Francisco and a free-lance writing career. But I wasn't optimistic, for I was following the path of an old friend, a sociology major who had graduated the year before and was now floundering. My new room-mate had been forced to supplement his writing income as a guinea pig for N.A.S.A. in Berkeley. He was paid $25 a day for eating a special diet and depositing the resultant gaseous human waste into a rubber bag stuffed into the back of his pants. The results were used to simulate the effects of astronaut exhaust fumes in the Apollo space capsule. At one point rumor had it that an evaluation of his fumes nearly prompted the scientists to delay the entire Apollo project.

Before embarking upon these remarkable careers, it was natural for our conversation to drift into anecdotes about the good old days. Graduating from college is not just completing a four-year cycle, it's like ending an era. Suddenly you are rid of that inner demon which has been controlling your actions since seventh grade when an adviser waved a manila folder and said in halitosis-filled remarks: "This is C-49—your academic file where we keep records on everything you do in school. To get into college you must build a good one." I studied hard and my teachers wrote soaring evaluations for C-49. Admission to Michigan in my senior year was automatic: B average, student council member, honor society member, editor school paper. So one steamy August afternoon I piled my belongings and a friend in the family Falcon, backed out the driveway and honked good-bye, drove slowly through North Muskegon, Michigan, the town I knew so well, sniffed the sulphurous paper mill, saw the foundry smoke darkening the sky, and said farewell to Muskegon Lake. Soon we were on the superhighway slicing across the Michigan farmland. Three hours later we descended into the Huron River Valley, a forested depression in which nestled Ann Arbor, the technological center of the Midwest and home of the university.

I drove directly to my new residence, South Quadrangle. Built in

1951, it was a classic piece of neo-penal architecture—nine stories of cinder block sheathed in red brick. The name South Quad lent proof to Marcuse's theory that words have lost all meaning. It was actually north of East Quadrangle and adjacent to West Quadrangle (the planners gave up and named the northern quadrangle Mary Markley Hall). The quad itself was only a stubby patch of grass virtually consumed by adjacent parking lots reserved for staff. I parked on a side street and lugged my suitcases up to my fourth-floor quarters, which offered a splendid view of the football stadium.

The Quad was drab but never boring. A week after I moved in someone bombed the cafeteria. Upstairs, wrestlers rattled windows and shook walls during nocturnal practices. When lighted cigarette butts incinerated our mailbox, the postmaster put up a warning notice which was promptly burned down. The dim brown corridors were livened by jars of urine splashed under doors, heads jokingly stuffed in flushing toilets, boxes of manure placed on elevators and butyric acid poured into ventilators. Maids opened doors to find naked rear ends mooning them.

Amidst all this horseplay the silver-haired president was kind enough to remind us at our opening convocation that we were "the most talented freshman class in the history of the university." Stressing the quality control which had gone into the selection of our class, he gestured as if he were Moses parting the Red Sea, and summoned wave upon wave of my fellow students to their feet: first the high-school valedictorians, then the salutatorians, finally the student-body presidents.

Orientation week followed. First we learned how to find the health service and get football tickets. Then came a battery of placement tests. I was particularly nervous about the French test (in high school my teacher had passed me on the promise that I would never reveal she was my instructor). I almost flunked the oral part of the placement exam read by a professor from Japan with an unusual French accent. Next came psychological testing with true-false questions like: "I prefer eating raw carrots to cooked carrots." (The test presumed a correlation between personal preference and career motivation.) These results were slipped into a folder with my high-school record, which I took to Angell Hall auditorium. My counselor was one of twenty conferring in the auditorium. He had the third aisle and I sat down beside him. We turned sideways and shook hands. It took him a mere five minutes to sign me up for history and political science (which I didn't want but needed for a social-science requirement), journalism (which I didn't want but needed for a sequence), and French (which I simply didn't want). I tried to protest but he smiled and said: "Don't worry, you've got to take 120 credit hours in four years and that's a lot of hours."

Next was registration, which was like going to camp, a concentration camp. We were herded into the basement of Victorian Waterman gymnasium in small groups. Our pictures were shot in the basement weight room. In the wrestling room student clerks handed out our I.B.M. cards and steered us to the locker room, temporarily fenced into a maze. At a checkpoint, student guards stamped and sorted our papers. The shower room, our next stop, turned out to be a tuition check for in-state students who pay lower fees. Passing under the harmless nozzles we were guided up a stairway to sign up for "psychological experiments." Upstairs, we paid tuition, made last-minute adjustments on courses, and then dribbled off the basketball court with a smudged carbon "class schedule" for the dorm bulletin board.

Although I didn't know who my new teachers were, I figured they would certainly beat my high-school instructors such as the one in world history who ran dry halfway through the period and turned on a radio for the Paul Harvey midday news. But I soon discovered my college professors didn't have much to say either. In Political Science 101, sixteen dull lectures led to a midterm examination asking: "Briefly compare the origins, theory and practice of Communism and Democracy." Small discussion classes weren't better, just harder to sleep in. Under orders from the departmental hierarchy, teaching fellows taught as if we were retarded. In French we got a bowdlerized version of *Candide* and a time card to punch in at the language laboratory three hours a week (where a technician just in from Argentina feebly tried to give aid in Spanish). In English composition we had to write 1500 words on "How to Make a Succulent Hamburger." There was little reassurance when I discovered a copy of the departmental manual which advised the teaching fellows: "Socially, the teacher has to recognize that the students in his section, however inept their prose and surly their manner, are basically reasonable human beings."

In order to fulfill the natural science sequences, I elected astronomy. Class turned out to be a varsity-club meeting. All the athletes sat like the *Playboy* All-America Squad draped across the front row. "The Doc," as we knew her, was a short, elderly woman passionately devoted to the Wolverines. She dressed like a cheerleader in saddle shoes, bobby sox, bulky sweater and pleated skirt. Her grading system was rumored to be "A" for athlete, "B" for boy, and "C" for coed, an exaggeration, of course, but athletes seldom failed.

The Doc's tests were said to be based on old exams. When midterms came along, every Xerox machine in town hummed. The jock fraternity houses kept up their files of old exams as faithfully as they polished their trophies. During my freshman year, Michigan went to the Rose Bowl. The Doc was so excited that she didn't bother to turn in semester grades by the Christmas deadline. The registrar tracked her down in California but she stood her ground: "Fire me if you don't like it," she told them.

Sometime during my first year, I realized the biggest headache was not "depersonalization" but "overpersonalization." If you leave them alone, 30,000 students can probably coexist happily with each other. But like any bureaucracy, a large university has too many of the wrong kind of people in the wrong place. A "resident adviser" with a powerful antenna for marijuana was one example. A dorm "housemother" was another pest. It was rumored she had once dated a young Army officer named Dwight Eisenhower. Now she was a nasty lady muttering like a psychology instructor about "anxiety" and "deviance" and "Spock babies" whenever an ashtray was missing.

Privacy didn't exist. Girls were sequestered on the other side of the dorm and allowed in our rooms for three hours a month during "open-opens" (provided three legs were kept on the floor). The girls often circumvented this nonsense by dating older boys with apartments, since there were no boys around with three legs. (Under dorm rules at the time, a girl coming in five minutes after curfew was penalized; a girl who stayed out all night would not be punished.) We had no place to go. Those freshmen with steady girls resorted to cars, music rooms, church basements or lounges. One couple, a disheveled pair whom we called "Cyclone and Flopsy," used to have a nightly encounter on a high-backed sofa in a main-floor lounge. I'd be reading and suddenly notice a crescent shape rising above the sofa and then disappearing behind the back.

Despite the setbacks in the dorm and the classroom, I never would have comprehended the total frustration of college without the four-story undergraduate library, a sterile, glass-enclosed cage fronted by a gravel-pit lawn. The UGLI, as it was called, was more lonely-hearts club than library. Girls flocked there to distract boys from their studies. The sorority girls who gathered in the art-print gallery were a typical diversion. They were checking out Rubens, Giotto and Brueghel—all I could see was Odalisque lying there waiting for me. Downstairs wasn't much better. My concentration was broken by the creaking chairs and clacking typewriter rooms, the whirring library computer and vulturous cleaning ladies slamming down ashtrays. I usually ended up at a table looking out at the revolving Ann Arbor bank sign down the block. The electric lights enumerated my failure: 7:30 and 20 degrees (page 1), 8:02 and 15 degrees (page 8), 10:35 and 12 degrees (page 22).

Because it was impossible to study efficiently, I would end up in the UGLI seven days a week. By Sunday night, after eight straight hours, the world would be closing in on me. Exhausted and depressed I would try to clear my head by standing out in the chill wind peering through the glass. Amidst the bubbly lights inside I would see thousands of students bent over their books.

One Sunday, something snapped off inside of me. I had been studying an astronomy problem. But hung up on a logarithm, I couldn't begin to do the assignment. So finally I just crossed out my name in the front, shut the book, and left it on the table where the cleaning woman would nosily swoop it up.

After freshman year I moved out of the dorm into a series of old, cluttered houses and dilapidated apartments. While the Quad experience gives shape to my memory of freshman year, the remaining three years are a blur. College never led me on to anything. I felt the same as a senior as I did when I was a sophomore. The days were indistinguishable. I spent nights on couches while room-mates and girl friends took the bedroom. In the morning I rose, stretched to the ceiling and a piece of acoustical tile popped out. I ate Life Savers for breakfast, went back to bed for a noonsie at lunchtime, and then feasted on a hamburger for dinner, or I would open a can of lard, flip a glob into the skillet, and then throw in a half pound of frozen ground beef from the freezer. As the hamburger thawed in the bubbling lard, I gradually sliced off melting chunks and formed them into a patty that finally crumbled into a greasy sloppy joe. Afterward I threw the dishes into the three-day-old puddle in the sink and headed for the language lab, which was closed. So I came back, conjugated French, watched Johnny Carson and fell asleep again on the couch.

The days passed emptily and then suddenly slammed smack into the examination period. I can remember the feeling at two a.m. when the snow was falling outside—and only six hours remained before a final exam. I'd put aside lists of key facts, thinking back on those early semester resolutions. Like all courses, it had begun well. The professor had an international reputation and an exciting reading list. But somewhere it all fell apart. The books proved to be scholarly treatises only an author's mother could finish. The first-day jokes gave way to disorganized soliloquies. I wanted to assimilate material, fitting facts into concepts. The professors wanted overall knowledge accumulation as told to a computer via multiple-choice tests. So at the end of the semester I was not pulling together what I had learned—I was taking it apart. I broke down all the concepts into isolated facts, dates, treaties, and names, the stuff grades are made of. In the morning my class met for the exam. The professor handed out mimeographed questions. When I had filled in all the computer blocks, I turned in the answer sheet (silently, so as not to disturb those still working). Then I went home for vacation to recuperate. Two weeks later a postcard arrived from the professor. No inscription, not even a signature, just a scrawl: "Political Science 110, Grade: C."

As I talked with older, graduating friends it became clear that I had to unpin my hopes from the university classroom. To think of going on to graduate school meant being professionalized into an academic automaton. A friend in dentistry was forced to shave his modest sideburns lest they "pick up infectious bacteria from the spray of the high-speed drill." Unless I was going to become an academic, a lawyer, a C.P.A. or some other carefully defined careerist, school was a liability. So I began to treat it as a part-time job. By no means was I a dropout, I still took my courses and passed. But like my friends I shifted my commitment outside the classroom. There were a variety of alternatives like S.D.S. and student government. As an aspiring writer I chose the student publications building and the campus paper, *The Michigan Daily*.

No prerequisites were required for admission to *The Daily*. There were no examinations or term papers. The hours were ideal—noon to two a.m. A clattering A.P. machine kept *The Daily* contemporary as radical students and staffers engaged in endless discussions where I found both the intimacy and intellectualism lacking in the classroom. Nor was the paper bogged down in the academic seniority system. As a freshman I was sent to Selma to cover the civil-rights demonstrations and wrote numerous signed editorials on how to better mankind.

Outraged administrators accused *Daily* writers and radicals of naïveté. I always felt the *Daily*'s most powerful weapon was its ability to unite the journalist's nose and the child's eye: applied to the stench and confusion of corporate university management, the combination was devastating. My own awakening came in following a tip about one of the most powerful Regents, Eugene Power, who ran a microfilm company with a parasitic relationship to the university's library. Power's firm, University Microfilms Inc., was converting 5000 "borrowed" books a week into salable microfilm copies. In addition, two special microfilm cameras had been installed in the UGLI to copy rare books, some of which would disappear off the shelves for months. When I asked the library director why Power's firm wasn't at least paying a fine for overdue materials, he didn't appreciate it. Regent Power himself stalled on an appointment for three weeks. Finally, flanked by obsequious aides, he sat down with me. He shed little light on his business affairs, ushered me out like a rebellious servant, and admonished, "Behave yourself, son." The story ran (despite a plea by the library director's physician that his coronary patient would suffer a fatal heart attack) and a subsequent attorney general's investigation found Power in conflict of interest. He resigned his post.

The other Regents were no improvement. They were absentee landlords who visited the plantation two days a month. Their ephemeral presence was the clue that the university was not run by its constituents, but by corporate ambassadors. Chauffeured limousines swept them off campus to deliberations in a baroque mansion blessed by tranquil oaks, rolling lawns, reflecting pools, and a panoramic view of the Huron River Valley. The deliberations normally began on Thursday. All decisions had to be completed by noon Friday in order to give the news service time to prepare releases in advance of the formal two p.m. "public meeting."

The public meetings were required by constitutional statute. The vice-presidents offered faithful little soliloquies while the sleepier Regents dozed behind sunglasses. "A new French house is going into the Oxford Housing Unit," declared the Vice-President for Student Affairs. "Will there be French plumbing," inquired a Regent, convulsing his colleagues.

At first many students thought they could crack this anachronistic structure with liberal administrative allies. It seemed logical that a bright young administrator could work from within to subvert the system to the benefit of the students. Accordingly student radicals worked hard to put a popular liberal psychology professor in office as Vice-President for Student Affairs. On taking office he promised to be a "vice-president presenting the student interest to the Regents and the President." But we soon learned otherwise.

When the House Un-American Activities Committee subpoenaed the names of sixty-five students and faculty members of radical groups he gave in (and withheld announcement of the decision until after *The Daily* had suspended publication for the summer). He refused to honor a campus referendum that had gone two to one against the university's practice of ranking students for the draft. Then he tried to ban sit-ins and finally wound up making secret attempts to discipline S.D.S. leaders for anti-war protests.

Naturally, he was showered with abuse for having "sold out." But rather than try to explain himself to students (he was, after all, still vice-president), he withdrew into his Danish-modern office and brooded. *Daily* reporters were denied interviews. Radicals noticed that he had even drawn the shades and locked his door to thwart imaginary sit-ins. Eventually he became tired of his role and quit, only to be rewarded by an appointment as special adviser on urban problems.

Like adults everywhere he wanted students to reinforce his own expectations, confirm what his generation had done and stabilize his lifetime. At heart the campus administrators were only subtler versions of the forty-two-year-old Ann Arbor police lieutenant who arrested campus cinema leaders for showing a suggestive underground movie. His critical review seemed to be based less on artistic judgment than fear. "The students are going down the same path that caused the Roman Empire to fall," he explained. "When laws break down, that promotes anarchy which leads to dictatorship. Now think what that could do to a man like me. Say I'm in my twenty-fourth year on the police force here and looking forward to my retirement pension after twenty-five years service. Some dictator could come and cancel that plan and I'd be out of luck. That's why when you have a good system you have to support it."

But I hadn't signed up for any pension plan yet. Unlike the lieutenant I was not committed to perpetuation of the Ann Arbor police. Unlike the administration I was not committed to perpetuation of the university in its present form. I saw that obedience to the school system required people to forget about each other. One had to get out of school to be human. For taking school seriously meant wrapping oneself up in a meaningless schedule that did not allow time to know or talk to others. It meant teachers knew their students better by their handwriting than their faces. It meant students had to compete with each other needlessly on the grade-point battlefield. It meant locked offices and silent libraries to preclude conversation. College cut people instead of bringing them together.

I recall running into a favorite poetry teacher on pulling out of the Thompson Street parking ramp at the end of a hectic day. For the past few weeks I had unsuccessfully been trying to fit into his tight schedule. But now we had our chance. We talked hurriedly through my car window until impatient drivers honked me out of the six-story structure.

Still I tried to reassure myself from time to time—only to have the truth thrown back at me. I remember the night I spent cramming for my last set of finals with a friend. Lying bewildered on a couch amidst study guides, Xeroxed notes, and dog-eared old exams I mused: "It's tough now. But I'll bet twenty-five years from now we'll look back on these as the best years of our life." My friend, wrestling with incompletes, a late paper, and the final, could only grimace. "Go ahead and think that if it makes you feel good. But my memory is better than that."

Disquieting thoughts for a graduation celebration—but they were honest ones. When the party ended I took my parents back to the airport, and devoted my last evening in Ann Arbor to packing. In the basement I found forgotten piles of notebooks, paperbacks, love letters and exams. The ash cans filled quickly, so at midnight I quietly piled the overflow into a neighbor's backyard. The next morning I called a cab for the airport. On the way out of town, there was a last sentimental stop. The driver pulled up in front of UGLI and I raced inside to pay a $3.25 library fine which was blocking my diploma. Now I was free.

THE CRISIS OF THE UNIVERSITY

Henry Steele Commager

Students who demand that what their university teach be relevant may be asking their school to assume an inappropriate and impossible role. In this essay, eminent historian and editor Henry Steele Commager, Professor of American History at Amherst College, attempts to clarify what the role of the university has been in the past and what, in his opinion, it should be today. Professor Commager is the author of many books, including *The Growth of the American Republic* (with Samuel E. Morison); *Freedom, Loyalty, and Dissent;* and *The Search for a Usable Past.*

The crisis of the university today is a tribute to its importance. Within a quarter century the university has moved to the very center of American life—the center of ideas, the center of research, the center of criticism and of protest. Students who once went to the university to prepare for a career or, as we amiably say, to prepare for life, now find that the university is life. Parents who looked upon the university as a golden interlude before their children faced the hard realities of life are confronted by the fact that college years are not an interlude but the real thing and that they are not golden but iron. The public, which thought students should be protected from disturbing ideas and should provide vicarious happiness and public entertainment for those outside the university, is discovering that students are far more interested in making people unhappy than in making them happy. Student population has grown to 6 million—rather larger than the total number of farmers —and university teachers probably number half a million: a formidable phalanx. If professors ever thought of the university as an ivory tower (which may be doubted), they no longer do: they are involved in everything from advising Presidents, who rarely listen to them, to conducting seminars for businessmen, attending conferences in Asia and Africa, or mediating between capital and labor and between whites and blacks. The scientists, said Lord Snow, have the future in their bones, but it is no longer the scientists alone; it is the whole army of scholars, in all areas. The future promises no relief from this situation but rather more of the same: the university population is bound to grow, and as society and economy become increasingly complex, scholars, who stand at the levers of control of a technological society, will play an increasingly vital role.

No one bothers to attack institutions without significance or power.

From *Newsday,* Garden City, New York, June 7, 1969. Reprinted by permission of the author.

As long as the college was small and pastoral it could be ignored or tolerated but not taken very seriously. Now that it occupies the vital center of society it is inevitable that the winds of controversy should swirl about it, that the din of national politics and international controversies should shatter its peace, that all of its members—students, faculty, and administration—should be shaken out of their complacency and required to justify themselves.

The student protest against the university is, in a sense, a flattering gesture, though there is no doubt that most universities would gladly forgo the flattery. What students are saying, in their somewhat incoherent way, is that they no longer have any confidence in government, politics, business, industry, labor, the church, for all of these are hopelessly corrupt. Only the university is left. Clearly it is corrupt, too, but not hopelessly; it can still be saved, and if it is saved it can be made into an instrument to reform the whole of society.

Student dissent and revolt in the United States have two clear dimensions, though the students themselves are aware of only one of them. Vertically it is rooted in some two centuries of American experience with colleges and universities, experiences quite different from those of Old World nations. Horizontally it reflects the pervasive frustration, outrage and despair of the young at the Vietnam war, the draft, the armament race, the destruction of the environment, racial injustice—at all that is implied in that epithet "the establishment."

It is the heritage that largely explains why the revolt of youth against the establishment is directed against the university rather than against government, parties, the military, or Dow Chemical or Chase Manhattan or the Automobile Workers of America; it explains, too, why students who revolt against the university claim special exemption because they are part of the university and demand that it protect them and care for their every need.

The university as it emerged out of medieval Italy, France, and England and developed over the centuries, had three clear functions.

The first was to train young men for essential professions: the church, the law and medicine, and perhaps teaching.

The second was to preserve the heritage of the past and pass it on to the future generations intact.

The third—first clarified by Gottingen and her sister universities in Germany in the 18th and 19th Centuries—was to expand the boundaries of knowledge through research.

The two ancient universities of England added a fourth which was never quite clear: to train a social elite to the tasks of governance.

Because the American colonials were unable to establish genuine universities, they created instead something quite new: the college—and the college remains, to this day, a unique American institution, occupying a twilight zone between the high school and the university. As American students were very young—boys went to Harvard or Pennsylvania or Yale at the age of 12 or 13, though a really bright lad like John Trumbull could pass the entrance examinations to Yale at the age of 7—they had to be treated as children: hence the early practice *in loco parentis* and its persistence through the years and even the centuries. As they came from simple middle-class households, without (for the most part) learning or sophistication, they had to be taught elementary subjects, and the plan of study had to be laid out for them with utmost circumspection. Hence the long tradition, still very much with us, that the college is a kind of extension of the high school, that students must be taught everything in formal courses, and that students were intellectually, as well as socially and morally, *in statu pupillari*.

These characteristics of the American college persisted into the 19th Century and when, in the 1860s, Americans created their first universities, they established them not as substitutes for the college but as continuations of the college, and adapted them, very largely, to collegiate rather than to university standards.

Just as the antecedents of the colleges had been Cambridge and Edinburgh, so the antecedents of the university were Gottingen and Berlin and Leipzig. But this could not last, or, where it did, it produced a kind of academic schizophrenia. Actually the university was bound to develop otherwise in a democratic and equalitarian society than in an aristocratic society. Because the United States did not have the scores of other institutions to carry on much of the work of science and research or even of ordinary cultural activities (as did most Old World countries), almost everything that society wanted done in these areas was handed over to the university. Thus the schools of agriculture, of engineering, of library science, of nursing, of hotel management, of business administration, of almost anything society or government wanted. Thus, too, came the multiversity, the university that did not confine itself merely to four faculties or to the traditional functions of professional training and research, but took on the most miscellaneous activities, academic and otherwise.

Thus by the 20th Century the special character of higher education in the United States was pretty well fixed. It was an education that was to be open to all, that was dominated by the collegiate idea, that inevitably took on the habits of *in loco parentis*. It was required to teach everything society wanted taught or special interest groups in society were strong enough to get taught; and it was expected to acquiesce in the democratic notion that all subjects were equal; it was expected to respond to all the demands of government or society, to serve these masters in every way that it could serve—as a sanctuary for the young, as a moral training ground, as a social and matrimonial agency, as a social welfare center, as an agency for entertaining the community, as a center for research in all fields, and as a handmaiden of government. Some of the private institutions escaped the most onerous of these demands, but even they fell easily into the habit of accepting them.

The pattern of the college-university worked well enough as long as almost all elements in the community agreed on the basic assumptions that were implicit in it: that the university was to reflect American life (the current formula is that its student body is supposed to be a reflection of the whole of American society), that it was to train character as well as the mind, that it was to inculcate all the going values of American life, that it was, in short, an integral part of the establishment and that the establishment itself was sound, just, and enlightened.

Now the situation is different, and the mood is different. Students no longer accept the establishment but repudiate it. They are too old and physically too mature for *in loco parentis*. They are not interested in the historic functions of the university, and are revolted by the dependence of the university on government or its ready response to economic interests or social demands.

They no longer believe in these traditional functions, nor do they accept these traditional objectives, but they cannot free themselves from them or from the expectations which they have encouraged. They reject the right of the university to interfere with their private lives, insisting that they be treated as adults, but they reject with equal fervor the notion that when they violate the laws or public mores they are to be treated precisely as other adults. They say, in effect, that as long as they are students, trespass isn't trespass, arson is not arson. They reject the tyranny of courses, but assume that they cannot possibly learn anything unless some professor (preferably of their own choosing) gives a course in it, and they clamor for more and more courses. They reject the connection of the university with government and with the establishment, but demand that government support the university—and its students too.

What they are really concerned about is not, in fact, the university, but society, government, the economy, even the moral order. They know perfectly well that the university did not make the Vietnam war, and cannot end it. They know that the university did not institute the draft, and cannot end it. They know that the university is not responsible for the Cold War or the armaments race, not responsible for the destruction of the environment, not responsible for racial injustice, and cannot cure these ills. Even more, they know—most of them, anyway—that in the past two decades it is from the university that has come the most penetrating and effective criticism of all of these things, and that long before they themselves were old enough to protest against the shocking evils and immoralities of our society, university professors were voicing such protests. But they still direct their hostility and their attacks on the university. For the university is *there,* and it is *theirs.*

Nothing is more depressing than the gap between the evils that the young object to and the changes which they propose to the university —nothing except, perhaps, the pervasive triviality of the demands. If every academic demand student rebels have made were to be granted tomorrow, nothing would be any different—nothing, that is, that they really care about. The war would still rage, the draft would still work its injustices, the environment would still submit to ruin, the cities would still decay, racial discrimination and racial injustice would still flaunt themselves everywhere. For the students do not, on the whole, have a program, certainly not one that they have been able to make clear to the university or to society. They are passionate in protest but paralyzed when it comes to constructive achievements.

This is not to say that the demands on the university itself are inconsequential. Here the students are, for the most part, either misguided or pernicious. Consider, for example, the *cri de coeur* of the young, that the university be involved and that what it teach be relevant.

Consider this matter of involvement. Students assume that it means being involved in all the things that they suppose important—involved, that is, in opposition to the war, in opposition to the antiballistic missile proposals, involved in the plight of the cities and in racial discrimination and in the lawlessness of government. And so it does. But if this were all that it meant, why bother with the university? It cannot, in the nature of things, make decisions in these areas; these are the areas of government, for government.

But university involvement is something quite different. It is the duty of the university to be involved with the past and to preserve it and its contributions to civilization. It is the business of the university to be involved with the welfare of future generations, as far as imagination can reach. It is the business of the university to be involved in the welfare of the whole of mankind, not just of this local segment of it.

Suppose all the great geneticists and biologists turned away from their laboratories and went into the hospitals: they would doubtless alleviate much suffering, but we should never find the cause of cancer. Suppose all the great jurists left their legal studies and enlisted in the work of the legal aid societies: they would doubtless help many a poor wretch now the victim of racial discrimination. But we would never come to an understanding of the law, to a reassessment of the penal code, to the construction of effective system of international law. Suppose the painters and musicians turned from their easels and their pianos and devoted themselves to work with deprived children or, for that matter, to playing folk songs designed to inspire youth revolt. All very well, but would we have any Serkins or Rubensteins, any Krieslers or Elmans, any Lili

Kraus or Clara Haskel in the next generation? And without these, and their equivalents in every area of art, would we have any civilization?

No, the obligation of the university is not that of the doctor or lawyer or engineer or social welfare worker. It is to train doctors and lawyers and engineers and welfare workers, and this it does. It is to create an intellectual and moral atmosphere which will persuade the young to study medicine and law and to serve mankind, and this it does. But more, it is an obligation to the great commonwealth of learning, an obligation to the past, and to the future.

There is this to be said, too: it is perilous for the university to be *involved* as a university. Involvement is a personal affair. Professors have always been, and doubtless always will be, involved: indeed, just a few years ago it was a familiar charge that professors were neglecting their scholarly duties and involving themselves far too much in public concerns. But just as the university cannot be permitted to speak for its members, certainly not for its professors, so professors cannot be permitted to speak for and thus commit the university, nor can presidents nor trustees. It is the essence of the university that each of its members speaks for himself.

So, too, the demand for relevance misconceives the nature and the function of the university. What do students mean by relevance? What they mean is that the university has failed to make clear the relation of what it teaches to their own deep interests and anxieties, that it has failed to excite their minds or to lift their spirits; that it has not brought them that warm and sympathetic relationship with their society and their fellowmen that they had hoped for.

Insofar as this is true, and insofar as the failure is not in the student himself, this is a just criticism of the university, or of its teachers and its administrators. Students at large universities who are fobbed off with graduate students rather than learned scholars, who are treated impersonally, who are not taught to use the resources of the library, or of the museum, or of the record collections, or of the scores of other enterprises through which the university attempts to widen the horizons and deepen the sensibilities of the young, have a right to be outraged at what they consider a betrayal.

But usually students mean something a good deal more specific than this. They mean that the university is not relevant to their own concerns, that it is not relevant as, say, The New York Times or a television documentary is relevant.

But it is not the business of the university to be relevant in the way that a newspaper or a television station is relevant. It is not the business of the university to allow itself to be captured by the immediate, the momentary, the sensational. The university has other relevancies. It is —or should be—relevant to the whole of the past and the whole of the future. It finds a place for scholars who think classical archeology or the civilization of the Incas is relevant. It finds a place for those who are sure that there can be nothing more relevant than art, music, philosophy. It has, too, another very special function. It must create an atmosphere in which students can discover what is relevant to them, and provide the facilities for them to enlarge that relevance. For relevance is essentially subjective. It is something that happens to an individual, as a result of experience. That experience may be hearing a Mozart trio, or solving a difficult problem in mathematics, or getting to know Voltaire or Goethe; it may be falling in love; or having a child, or writing a poem. Do the young really suppose that only Prof. Herbert Marcuse or Stokely Carmichael are relevant, only sociology and black studies? All experience is against them, including their own.

Now, how does a university go about creating an atmosphere in which students can discover what is relevant to them? This is a very complicated business, one that cannot be summed up in a formula. It may do it, as Oxford and Cambridge do, by antiquity and beauty. It may do it, as Harvard and California do, by attracting great scholars and building up great libraries. It may do it as so many of our smaller colleges do, by teaching that helps students to find themselves: teaching by a Robert Frost at Amherst that made poetry relevant, teaching by a Lionel Trilling at Columbia that made criticism relevant, teaching by a David Riesman at Harvard that makes sociology part of philosophy. The university is not an institution which is, itself, relevant to any particular time or place of interest; it is an institution where students and scholars can discover what is relevant to them and find encouragement and guidance in exploring and possessing it.

There is, to be sure, one area where students want not more involvement, but an end to involvement: that is the area which the university and government occupy jointly. Disillusioned by what they see of university tie-ins with the Defense Department, the State Department, the Central Intelligence Agency; outraged by university cooperation in research on chemical or bacteriological weapons, they turn to violence to dramatize their indignation. They demand that the university break with the government, that it break with all branches of the government that are themselves tainted by participation in an unjust and immoral war.

But all European universities and most American are in fact supported by government; all have in the past cooperated with government on research in a thousand fields. Nor has this research always been designed only for the purposes of peace. Universities enlisted, as it were, in the struggle against Nazi Germany; their scholars and scientists threw themselves into governmental service, and their administrators hastened to make available their library and laboratory facilities. None demurred at the time, and few now would have had it otherwise. The explanation of the alliance between the university and government in World War II was not innocence. It was rather the all-but-universal assumption that the war was a just war, and one that had to be won if civilization were to survive.

What this experience suggests is the danger of absolutism in judging the relation of government and universities, even in time of war. For there are wars, and wars. Some, like World War II, had to be won. Others, like the war in Vietnam, have to be lost if we are to survive. It was right for scholars to enlist in World War II; it is wrong for scientists and universities to suppose that no moral issues are involved, or that they are to be neutral in moral issues, or that the government can decide these issues for them, and thus to defend participation in the Vietnam war.

Here protesting students—and professors (who were after all, first in the field)—have performed an invaluable function. They have resisted the automatic conscription of the university to the purposes of government in time of war. They have rejected the immoral principle of secrecy in scientific research. They have insisted that the university itself must be in charge of its scientific investigation, and have repudiated the efforts of government to bribe, seduce, tempt or intimidate scholars and administrations to serve on terms the government lays down. They have steadily reminded the government, and the public, that the community which the university serves is not just the immediate local or national community, but the larger community of man and the longer community of succeeding generations.

As for the minor, though vexatious, problem of recruiters on campus —recruiters from the military or the CIA, recruiters from Dow Chemical or others of that ilk—here, too, there is a fairly simple formula that will resolve most of the difficulties. The university is not an employment agency. It is not under any obligation to supply facilities to any organization that comes along and asks for them. It is an educational institution. It should open its gates to all who are engaged in the business of education; it should close them to those who are engaged in making money or in fighting wars or in other irrelevant activities. That there are borderline cases here is, of course, clear; there are always borderline cases in life and law. But sensible administrators and faculty committees can be trusted to deal with these.

What students want of the university is that it be independent, and that is just what professors and administrators have been fighting for for many years. Students reject what they call the establishment, and ask the university to divorce itself from this. No great segment of society can wholly divorce itself from that society, but allowing this, must it not be said that for centuries the university has stood aloof from society? Students, and critics, charge that the university is itself part of the establishment and that it is therefore corrupt. But the university has been for generations the chief critic of the establishment, and still is. It is the university that has been the generator of new ideas, the powerhouse of new programs: that is the reason it is always in trouble with the establishment, always being attacked by the stout defenders of the status quo.

Independence means independence of all improper pressures— improper pressures from students as well as from government or industry or patriotic organizations. And in the past few years, the pressures from students have been more grossly improper than those from any other element in society.

One thing that should be beyond dispute is that the university is a citadel of reason; if it is not that, it is not a university. The use of force —closing buildings, assaulting or intimidating members of the faculty, setting fire to chapels or libraries—these are the very antithesis of reason and the deepest repudiation of the university.

There is a sobering analogy between the use of force by students against the university and the use of force in Vietnam by President Johnson and his associates. Johnson, Dean Rusk, Walt Rostow, and others were sincerely convinced that the cause they espoused—the cause of containing Communism—was good. So too students are no doubt sincerely convinced that their own cause—the attack on the establishment—is good. The Johnson administration did not, however, whether out of prudence or out of cowardice, attack Communism at its center, China. Instead it attacked Communism on its periphery, Vietnam, which was innocent and vulnerable. So rebellious students do not attack Dow Chemical or Chase Manhattan Bank, nor do they boycott labor unions that practice discrimination; they attack the university, which is both innocent and vulnerable. Johnson and his associates were convinced that because their cause was just they were justified in disregarding international law, flouting existing agencies for the adjudication of international disputes, and using terror against the enemy. So students, sure that their cause is just and their heart pure, think it entirely proper for them to ignore the potentialities of discussion and debate— which have never been refused—to repudiate due process and to resort to force.

They hate Johnson and perhaps President Nixon too; they hate the war in which they find themselves involved. But, as so often in history, they have succumbed to what they hate, and have adopted the methods of those they reject and despise.

What we are witnessing now is the most reckless attack upon academic freedom in our history. In the past, academic freedom has been threatened by the church, the state, private filiopietistic and interest groups. Now for the first time it is threatened not from without but from within, and that is perhaps more a betrayal than a threat.

Students assert now that they are to dictate courses and even appointments and tenure. This is precisely what the Nazis said to the universities back in the 1930s, and the state dismissed Jewish scholars while bands of Nazi youths roamed the universities attacking professors who were supposed to be unsympathetic with Nazi racial creeds. Students tell us now what is to be taught, and their demands are not based primarily on intellectual considerations but on nonacademic considerations. Students demand now that others be admitted not on the basis of intellectual or artistic capability or potential but on the basis of color: that is, in reverse, the equivalent of excluding students on the basis of color. Students ask now that the university dispense with grades and even with standards. Grades themselves are of little importance, but standards are: imagine dispensing with standards in medicine or law. If the academy is to put the stamp of approval on students not on the basis of competence but of race, or of needs, or of compassion, then it can no longer maintain any standards at all.

Once you accept the assumption that powerful minorities, using intimidation and force, can dictate university policies and faculty appointments, prescribe courses of study, select students—that they may even take over the universities physically to enforce their demands—you have established precedents that it will be very difficult to resist at a later day. You have, in effect, endorsed the principles of totalitarianism, the principles which made a mockery of higher education in Nazi Germany, in Fascist Italy, in Communist Russia.

The university is the most honorable and the least corrupt institution in American life. It is, with the church, the one institution that associates us with the past and the future, the one institution that has, through all of our history, served, or tried to serve, the interests of the whole of mankind and the interests of truth. No other institution can perform the functions which the university performs, no other can fill the place which it has for so long filled, and with such intellectual and moral affluence. If we destroy the university we shall destroy a unique institution. As the integrity of civilization depends in part on the university, we will be dealing an irreparable blow to a civilization now in moral peril.

THE STUDENT REVOLT AND THE STRUGGLE FOR POWER

"One cannot, therefore, on looking at these young people in all the glory of their defiant rags and hairdos, always just say, with tears in one's eyes: 'There goes a tragically wayward youth, striving romantically to document his rebellion against the hypocrisies of the age.' One has sometimes to say, and not without indignation: 'There goes a perverted and willful and stony-hearted youth by whose destructiveness we are all, in the end, to be damaged and diminished.' "

GEORGE KENNAN

STUDENT POLITICS IN A DEMOCRATIC SOCIETY
Nathan Glazer

To what extent should a student become involved in politics? In this essay Nathan Glazer describes and analyzes three positions on the role of the student in a democratic society. He believes that a student should be prepared for a political role, but that he should not try to transform his university into a bastion and base of political activity. When he wrote this essay, Glazer was Professor of Sociology at the University of California, Berkeley; he is now at Harvard. He is the author of *The Social Basis of American Communism* and coauthor (with David Riesman and Reuel Denney) of *The Lonely Crowd*.

Ten years ago our topic would have been a very bland one indeed. At that time the wave of serious G. I. student veterans had already passed through the schools; students were seen as passive, uninvolved, uninterested in society, and concerned only for their own careers and their own security. The most influential descriptions of the students of the mid-fifties were, I believe, those of David Riesman, who described their premature caution in questioning the recruiting agents of corporations about pension and retirement plans. If anyone had raised then the question of the role of students in a democratic society, it could only have been to answer that their role should be larger; that students should

From *The American Scholar*, Vol. XXXVI, No. 2 (Spring 1967). Reprinted by permission of the author.

concern themselves more with public affairs, with the large problems of society, should involve themselves in social and political action.

But after the revolutionary role played by Southern Negro students and Northern white students in the South, after the explosion at Berkeley in which students overthrew the administration of one of the country's great universities, who could simply repeat these platitudes, and not feel forced to examine the question closely, considering not only the impact of student political involvement on society, but on one of the major institutions of society itself, the college and university?

Let me try to describe in order three positions on the role of the student in a democratic society, and to analyze their content and their consequences.

The first position is the simplest and the most cautious. It is that the student should learn about all the problems of the society and in effect prepare himself to act in the society. This on the face of it would seem to be an inevitable and necessary part of the education of the student, and it would seem reasonable that all those who accept the underlying premises of higher education, and who assume it has more than purely vocational and training functions, would accept this point of view. Unfortunately, as we know, this has not always been the case. In America, our universities have a very distinctive form: they are run by trustees, public and private, not by faculty, and not by students. And we have a long history of interference by trustees in the running of the university —private trustees and public trustees. Certain ideas—arguments in favor of socialism or communism, arguments in favor of full racial equality, criticisms of the American economic system and its capacity to create the best society, criticisms of America's foreign policy and participation in war—are capable of arousing violent and emotional reactions. These reactions are one of the permanent dangers of a democratic system. They lead the powerful to interfere in the teaching function of the university; and they lead the people to interfere, too, through their legislators. If the people were in a position to act directly on their feelings all of the time, democracy, we know from various studies, would be in very bad shape.

Substantial majorities of the American people are against having atheists or even Socialists teach in American universities. Concerning Communists, there is an even more overwhelming rejection. Sidney Hook and others have made a powerful case on intellectual grounds against allowing Communists to teach, because they are under discipline and cannot teach the truth as they see it. I believe this argument is somewhat exaggerated, certainly when it comes to Communist teachers of mathematics and science, and even when it comes to Communist teachers of humanities and the social sciences, where Communist doctrines have a more immediate impact. Someone who is formally under discipline is not under discipline at all times and for all purposes. If this were the case, Catholics might also be considered unqualified to be university teachers. And additionally, one might argue against this position that Communists change; even in the Communist world there is today an argument going on over the limits of freedom.

So even the position that the university is a place in which students are freely prepared to play an active role as citizens in the world is itself always, in most places, and in some measure, controversial. This controversy breaks out when the university administration—either in its own right or under the pressure of trustees and of public opinion—limits students' access to certain ideas. Must everything be taught in the university? Of course not, and there is no easy way to ensure that it should. But when a group of teachers feels that they should add someone to their number who is qualified to teach, and who expounds either in the course of his teaching or outside the classroom unpopular ideas, I think no one should interfere to prevent such an appointment. If a group of students or professors feels they want to listen to someone speak on the campus, no one should prevent them from having that opportunity. This is the position that the university teachers of America have developed, and despite the fact that this is the mildest form in which students participate in a democratic society, we know that it is continually threatened.

There still remain serious problems when we consider this relatively simple form of participation. Does the university have the right to require that faculty members guide student groups and approve their action in inviting off-campus speakers? Does the university have the right to require that one view presented on campus be balanced by another? Does the university have the right to require that questions be allowed at meetings? Does the university have the right to require that faculty members chair meetings? Does the university have the right to decide where in the university a meeting shall be held, thus limiting effectively the size of the audience? Does it have the right to require student groups to pay for police protection, if the off-campus speaker is so controversial that disorder or violence may be feared? Must the university provide loudspeakers for the speaker? May the university deny the most prominent locations on the campus to the speaker?

These are all real questions at Berkeley, questions that have been debated endlessly, and that have mostly been answered, "no." Even when we raise an apparently unobjectionable principle—the right to be informed and educated about the chief issues and positions in conflict in society, the right to be prepared to be a citizen—we cannot answer all questions on the basis of the application of a simple principle and simple rule alone. Any principle, when it becomes absolute, brings other principles into question.

On most campuses the answer to the questions I have raised has been "yes." That is, it is agreed that the university does have the right to restrict in various ways, and by the setting of various rules, the freedom to hear a variety of opinions expressed on campus. If these rules exist in order to restrict the freedom to be informed, to learn, then there is no question that they violate the chief function of a university. But there is another ground on which such rules are imposed and defended —the ground that the university has a duty to ensure the broad education of the students. This duty requires that faculty supervise in some manner the activities of student organizations, that the university ensure that there is free discussion and the presentation of alternative views, and even that the university, through the assignment of facilities for speakers, consider the overall educational impact of the pattern of speakers and the degree of their prominence. Thus, one could argue, on educational grounds, that the university should be concerned if the only points of view on our military involvement in Vietnam presented on campus are critical of American policy. But if there is such a concern, what is the proper form of procedure? Does the university encourage student groups who support American policy to form and present programs? Does it sponsor its own programs? Does it restrict the activities of the critics? These are all real questions, and real possibilities—once again, they become more evident on politically active campuses than on others.

On these questions, just as on the questions of free speech generally, there are many disputed marginal areas, and in our society we have developed forms for the settlement of these marginal cases—principally courts of law. Once one raises these issues seriously and passionately on the campus, however, the question that properly arises is: what forms exist to settle such matters? The decisions of the state legislature? The board of trustees? The president? The faculty? Or the students themselves? It is because on a politically active campus such as Berkeley the question of the limit of free speech and political activity is continually raised, and we have frequent conflicts between the vital principle of free speech and such other principles as public order and the primacy of educational objectives, that the question of the rules, how they are set and who sets them, has become so important.

Thus, even such a mild and apparently cautious formulation of the student's role in a democratic society as the one I have first posed—that the student should be prepared to act better as a citizen—raises serious questions for a university. How much more serious then are the questions raised by the next position, which is rather stronger. The second position is that the student should actively participate in the political and social conflicts of the society. The argument here is that first, society needs him—the student is better educated, less bound by responsibility of occupation and family, more generous and more flexible in his political and social attitudes, than other citizens. And the argument continues, the student needs action in society to make his education really complete. Certainly it is easy for us to find examples that support both arguments. The part of my own college education that was most vital, most important to me, was participation in a radical student political organization. I learned not only how to speak, how to write, how to edit a newspaper, how to organize a conference—and these are all valuable skills; I also learned an ideology. Certainly the way I learned it was not the way I would want to teach anyone—for I learned in a political organization, not a university, and I was indoctrinated rather than taught. And yet on the basis of further experience in the world, the indoctrination wore off. It became possible for me to learn then how indoctrination itself works, why at one stage in one's life one is ready to believe what, in the course of further experience, one rejects as nonsense.

This is a fairly extreme form of participation. But the participation of students in the work of political parties, in the work of social and political organizations, can add a dimension to their education that is quite beyond the power of the classroom and the teacher. A university should not limit such participation. Indeed, I believe many universities should find ways to encourage such participation, despite all the difficulties such encouragement might bring. Thus, I think universities might well grant time off and perhaps even credit for participation in political campaigns, although I imagine this would be easier for small private colleges than for large state-supported institutions. It would not do to have it turn out that more students were supporting the campaigns of one party than of another!

I have said too that society needs this participation. And it is scarcely necessary to spell this out in the South, where to my mind the greatest and healthiest change that has occurred since the Civil War has been brought about by the activism, the heroism, of students, South and North. The South was and is still in large measure afflicted by the terrible contradictions between the principles of democracy and equality and the reality of the treatment of the Negro, both officially and unofficially. The rest of the country remained in large measure ignorant or unmoved by these injustices. It was students, unencumbered by adult responsibilities and rationalizations, committed to a greater justice and equality, who played a significant role in bringing long-maintained injustices to the attention of the nation, and in overturning them.

To my mind two problems are raised by the position that the student should participate, for his good and for the good of society, in the social and political conflicts of his time. The first problem is presented by the fact that the participation of the students may be so energetic and effective that powerful forces in the society will move against the university.

I do not in the slightest suggest that the antagonism of powerful forces who are the targets of student actions should be a sufficient reason for the university to restrict this action. Yet in the concrete situations in which colleges and universities are placed, this is a serious problem indeed. At certain times in recent years the presidents and boards of trustees of Negro colleges in the South have moved against students who have engaged in political action off the campus. The dilemma of these administrators must be understood. They feared that if they allowed the students to continue to participate in demonstrations they would draw upon their institutions the enmity of governors and state legislatures, see their budgets cut, and perhaps worse. Thus they faced the tragic choice between maintaining the growth of their institutions and curbing their students, or allowing their students to participate in off-campus political activity and facing loss of necessary support.

This, in a far less serious form, was also one of the problems faced by the administration of the University of California. Many hundreds of California students had been active in sit-ins, clearly illegal, undertaken in San Francisco during the 1963–64 academic year. The targets of these demonstrations were the hiring practices of San Francisco businessmen. From the point of view of the businessmen, as taxpayers and citizens of California, the business of the students was to study in the university that the state's taxpayers had so lavishly equipped. Many citizens and government and law enforcement officials were angered by the sit-ins. Many people demanded that the university restrict the off-campus political activities of its students. President Kerr answered that what the students did off campus was their business, and the university could not be responsible for them. It would not discipline them; neither would it protect them or intercede for them if they got into trouble for breaking the law.

This seemed at the time a clear and strong position. But even this position, I believe, cannot be maintained unequivocally. In the course of the following year, the year of the student uprising on the Berkeley campus to protest restrictions on their freedom to engage in political activities on campus, a second problem became evident in the position that urges students to participate in community politics.

All through that tense year, the student political leaders insisted that they could not be held responsible for any off-campus political action, legal or illegal, because that would affect their constitutional rights. But after campus sit-ins and arrests, after the faculty had voted overwhelmingly in support of the student position, after endless meetings and consultations, the rules at the university still assert that a student *may* be held responsible for off-campus actions. Was it only because of the stubbornness of the regents of the university that this principle is still maintained in the rules—although no action has been taken under it against students? I do not believe so, although certainly their stubbornness is important. It is rather that as the range of political action has widened to include not only illegal actions to test the constitutionality of laws, but illegal actions to force public officials and private citizens to accept the views of certain groups, and illegal actions to extend the realm of permissible moral behavior—as this expansion of the traditional notion of permissible political behavior has widened, it has become increasingly clear that there is a limit at which the university may and should discipline students for off-campus behavior. This has long been clear in the case of standard college fun and games, brutal hazings, destructive pranks, and so on. These are now less common than they were. But politics may take over where the fraternities and football rallies left off. The question then arises, should the term "political" cover and exempt every action that students undertake under that name?

I am convinced that the university—in any case, the American university—cannot accept the principle that it is indifferent to the actions of its students off the campus, that it is indifferent to the character of its students, and that any action they perform will be left to the civil arm to handle. For the university is also based on certain principles—respect for ideas, freedom of speech and inquiry, the elimination of prejudice and intolerance; and it is possible for student actions in the community to undermine and attack these principles. At that point, the university cannot be indifferent to the actions of its students.

The problem here is that the university will often be urged by the pressure of its contributors and supporters, by the citizens of the state, by legislators and governors, to act against students who engage in political and social actions in the community. Its own interests may often lead it to restrict student rights, claiming it is doing so to maintain the authority of the administration, the order of the campus and the very principles that are necessary for higher education. There are serious dangers involved in the principle that, at the margin, student actions in the community may be a basis for university action against them. For students should be free to experiment, to make mistakes, to expand the area of political action. But the danger that students will be restricted to quiet public opinion should not lead us to deny the reality that students at some times and places have in the past and may again in the future engage in actions that they will defend in the light of some political position or perspective, but that will require university action against them. If one group of students were to attack or break up the meetings of another group because of their race, religion or opinions; or if one group of students were to outrage the religious sensibilities of another group—these might well be matters for the courts, but they would also be matters for the conscience of the university. I remain convinced of this principle because it is inconceivable to me that our major private institutions, which are freer than state institutions of either student or public pressures, would ever accept the principle that the off-campus actions of their students were not subject to their concern.

The third position on the student's role in a democratic society raises the most serious considerations. Let me recall that the first position is that the student should be *prepared* to participate as a citizen in the political and social conflicts of society; the second, that he should be *encouraged* to participate even as a student in the political and social conflicts of society; the third position is that the university campus is a *key source of activists* for the various political and social positions in conflict in society. Thus, according to this position, the campus should be open to active recruitment and preparation of students for enlistment and leadership in the significant political and social camps of society.

Characteristically, the American student has not been considered fully adult, or fully mature. This has been a consequence of such factors as the role in American higher education of the need to train ministers, and, of course, seminarians have always been subjected to a severe discipline; of the influence on American higher education of the English rather than the continental model, so that students live in colleges under teachers who also act in lieu of parents; of the influence in American higher education of the characteristic location of university campuses in small towns or in the country, which has meant that the college or university has had to supply housing and has therefore had some concern with the life of the student. In view of this background, which brings American higher education closer to the cloister or the preparatory school than to the European university, it would indeed be strange to view the university as one of the chief sources of political activists for immediate participation in the struggles that face society.

Yet as we know, in underdeveloped countries today, the universities do play this role. When the students of Vietnam or South Korea or Indonesia decide to move against their governments, those governments tremble and are indeed in jeopardy. In the more advanced states with very large urban universities—such as Japan and France—the students are also an important political force, although not so important as in the underdeveloped world. The reason is that in the advanced states, even though there are many more students, there are politically active classes that have much greater importance in the political life of society than do the students. There are organized industrialists and businessmen, an organized trade union movement, professional societies of all sorts that may take a role in politics. Under these circumstances, while the students of Japan and France may shake a government, they alone cannot overthrow one. In the underdeveloped states, on the other hand, there is a mass peasantry, a small middle class devoted to its own security, leaving the students and the army to form the chief participants in the active political life of society.

Under these circumstances, every important party must pay attention to its student base. If the Communists had succeeded in capturing the leadership of Indonesian students, there would have been no way of preventing that country from going Communist: but apparently non-Communist nationalist and Moslem elements were also strong among the students. Thus in certain nations the political outlook of students— the relative strength of certain political groups among them—is critical for the political fate of the nation.

In this country, until recently, students have been much less important politically than even in Europe. They did not develop the political activism of the students of underdeveloped countries, certainly, or of Continental Europe. And since they were not the sharply defined future elite of the country as in England—for here our elite has been more open and mass higher education has been a reality for generations— there was no great interest in how their political views were developing. The only political groups that have ever shown great interest in the students have been radical groups—Communists, Socialists and more recently the groups of the radical right, ideological conservatives. All these groups play a relatively minor role in American politics; they are incapable of developing any substantial support among the major social strata of the country, whether businessmen, professionals, workers, farmers, white collar workers, or what you will. Consequently they have been attracted to the campus, where in addition they may find among students the rational and ideological outlook that may make their consistent if extreme positions attractive. Thus student politics—unlike national politics—has often consisted of the conflict between radical groups.

What has all this to do with the present situation? It is my feeling that in recent years we have seen the beginnings, in a number of very different events, of the potential politicalization of the American campus. Let me point to three events.

The first is the major role that the Negro students of the South played in the last seven years in breaking the pattern of official and unofficial discrimination against the Negro. Here we had a situation similar to that which we find in the underdeveloped world. The Negro student was in a position to play a key role. The larger part of the Negro people in the South were uneducated and apathetic or beaten, and accepted their inferior role. The Negro middle class also accepted for the most part an inferior status. Just as in the underdeveloped world, the Negro students formed a class available for the political work of society, their society. Perhaps only one element in the political constellation of underdeveloped societies was missing among Negroes in the South—there was no army. So the Negro students held the field unopposed and were able to become the political leaders of their people.

There were other important political parallels between the position of the Negro in the South and the position of the people in an underdeveloped country: the formal political structure offered few effective means for improving it, because so many were excluded from the vote. I would say that when these three circumstances prevail: when the students are the only or the chief class available for political activity; when the problems of the nation are desperate; and when there is no effective democratic procedure for reform—under these circumstances, I believe, the students become one of the dominant political classes in society, and become the target for recruitment by the chief political forces in society.

Was the involvement of Negro students in the fight for equality only an exceptional case? For our society as a whole certainly does not show the features of an underdeveloped society; the students are not the only available class to do the political work of society; our problems are not desperate; our democracy functions, and change, even extensive and radical change, has been and can be brought about through the democratic process.

We should realize, however, that there is a growing political viewpoint in this country, the viewpoint of the New Left, which actually does see America in these terms: the New Left believes the people are corrupted by the mass media dominated by business interests, and that therefore their participation in our democracy is meaningless and ineffective; they believe the American people are corrupted by the opportunities for a high standard of living, and therefore are indifferent to the poverty and misery of most of the world and their fellow citizens as well; they believe democracy is ineffective because even those social groups that in the past have fought for the extension of equality—intellectuals and the labor movement—have been corrupted and bought by what they call the power structure, and consequently only among the students does one have the political forces potentially available for solving the problems of society, which they also see as desperate.

It is this viewpoint that has been, in a number of variants, dominant among politically active students at Berkeley and that has been to my mind at the base of the turmoil on that campus. For if the campus is a chief source of recruits, and indeed may be the salvation of the society, then every means of access to students must be exploited, and the question of the rules that govern that access becomes crucial. For the rules may limit the number of meetings a group may hold in a week, or deprive them of loudspeakers, or of the best locations on the campus, or may deprive them of using nonstudents to aid in the political work of propaganda and recruitment.

Is Berkeley the sport, the exception, of the sixties, just as City College was the sport of the thirties? Or does it reflect some deeper underlying trends on the American campus, which are transforming the campus into one of the chief sources of political activists, one of the chief centers of political debate and decision? Certainly many observers have seen in Berkeley a portent, and they have been proved right in the spread of student demands to other campuses that have been influenced by Berkeley. But let us distinguish two rather different things that happened at Berkeley: one was a free speech movement, which involved the active participation of thousands of students, and which struck at the whole system of university rules that treated students in some ways as children and as less than citizens. These rules are to be found in universities across the country. The students also struck at the conception that students should be excluded from formulating the rules under which they live. Thus we have seen a growing demand for greater student freedom on campus—freedom not only to participate in politics but to govern their own social activities; we have also seen a growing demand for a greater student role in university government. I believe both these demands are justified. The American university still bears in too many cases the marks of its origins in the seminary, in the high school, and in the cornfields; and as adult students, who in many ways become adult earlier than their teachers and the administrators did, come into the universities, the rules must become less restrictive, and the student role in university government must become greater.

This was one aspect of the free speech movement at Berkeley, but it was closely linked to something else. A relatively small group of students, supported by large numbers of former students and prospective students, had flocked to the university primarily to make it a chief center of political creativity and activism in society. They fought against the rules not only for the same reasons that other students opposed them, but because the rules limited their access to students whom they wished to recruit for political activity. In addition, this struggle gave the radical leaders an opportunity to teach their view of American society to other students by attacking the rules as reflecting the restrictions, the bureaucratization and hypocrisy of that society.

This part of the Berkeley story has not been understood or told too clearly, and this part of the struggle is still going on. Thus, student and nonstudent political leaders sometimes see students as the chief force that might change the course of American policy in Vietnam. This is an ambitious perspective indeed; it is also in large measure an arrogant perspective, for it ignores the reality of a politically sophisticated society, in which many strata, many people, many groups, will have their say on Vietnam and will play a role in determining American policy there. This is also a perspective that inevitably has brought the student leaders in conflict with the university and its faculty, as they press for the widest possible opportunities to spread and indeed impose their views on the campus. Most of the faculty, despite its interest in and concern for political problems, does not favor or see as possible any such ambitious role for the university in American political life. Indeed, they fear such a role, for then the university might well lose what limited degree of distance it now has from the problems of the society.

There is unquestionably a tension—there should be a tension—between the university and society. This tension exists in the fact that the university should not take as seriously and immediately as those actively engaged in society the problems of society. It can look at these problems in historical perspective; it can try to strip these problems of the emotions that invest them; it can try new and strange and even playful alternatives, in thought and in experiment. Thus, I would argue, there is still some virtue in the independence of the university in some measure from the immediate problems of society, although these virtues are not often exploited.

This independence is threatened from a number of quarters. One threat is from the insistent demand that the university be helpful—the demand from business and government that it offer practical aid, which continually diverts the research time and teaching of universities into areas of immediate payoff. Another threat is from the vocational conception of the university. The university must prepare students for jobs —and the student demand for an immediate vocational payoff from higher eduction, even though there are more forms of support outside of work than there used to be, has become more and more insistent.

But the independence of the university will also be threatened by turning it into a chief center of political activity. The universities have recently played an important role in this country in making the war in Vietnam a subject of national debate—I can think of no other major issue in this country's history in which the universities have played such an important role. They have developed a means of bringing this subject to national attention that is ideally suited to the nature of the university—the teach-in, in which the problems are analyzed and a broad array of fact and analysis is brought to bear upon them. But on many campuses, on the politically most active campuses, the teach-in becomes a political weapon; when it does, speakers who support our policy in Vietnam are booed and shouted down; those who oppose our policy bring into play the most powerful emotional appeals, not in order to make the issues clearer, but to arouse the strongest possible response—in other words, they become propagandists and recruiters. At this point, the university brings nothing of its own to the discussion and understanding of our problems. Indeed, the political leaders of the New Left criticize the faculty for being insufficiently emotional in their discussion of key issues. They criticize the faculty too for its effort to maintain objectivity and its refusal to join them in a warm bath of emotion and anti-intellectual communal togetherness. This is also a danger to the university.

Thus, this third position on the student's role in a democracy raises troubling questions. I do not think the university in a democratic society ideally should be a chief target of political forces, seeking to find recruits and activists, to seize the political leadership of students, and to use student organizations and the university name as a weapon in political combat. I can envisage situations when such an all-out use of all available resources in society for a political struggle to prevent some great evil is necessary, and I appreciate the views of those who believe the American involvement in Vietnam presents such a threat, and thus does require us to ignore the special character of institutions in bringing all of them into the battle. I do believe the situation of the Negro in the South in the early sixties did justify the use of every resource the Negro posessed—the church, the college, the tactics of civil disobedience—to overcome the grave injustices in his position.

The same orientation, it is now argued, must affect all the universities of the country in overcoming a grave threat to American democracy. Just as enlistment in a war means that much must stop in a man's life, just as involvement in a war for a nation means it must stop building schools and hospitals, so, at least on my campus, I am told by some of our students and faculty colleagues, we must invest all the resources of the university—its students, its faculty, its classrooms, its capacity to command public attention—in the struggle against American policy in Vietnam. As I listen to these voices, I think of the problems of the past and of the problems of the future, and I see that there will always be a problem that to some will justify this mobilization of the resources of the university for some political end. There are situations when the university must indeed be mobilized in the defense of human ends, must become a seat of struggle, with all that means for the independence of the university, for which so many hard struggles have been fought, and which even today is achieved only in measure in some universities. I do not believe we face such a situation in this country today. I think our democracy does function, even if with many difficulties; many of our people are alert to our problems; and there are many hands willing to take up the necessary political work of society. Under these circumstances, I believe that the first two positions I have described form a sound basis for answering the question, what is the student's political role in a democracy? He should be prepared for a political role, he should learn from involvement in political activity—but he should not try to transform his university into a bastion and base of political activity.

STUDENT POWER: ON THE OTHER HAND . . .
John R. Coyne, Jr.

In this essay John R. Coyne, Jr., author of *The Kumquat Statement* and a
frequent contributor to the *National Review,* considers the student power
movement and the current unrest on campus; he feels that one of the main
reasons for unrest on campus is that students feel they are being gypped out
of a good education: "somewhere along the collegiate assembly line . . .
they find they are not being educated."

The script is, by now, drearily familiar. SDSers and their allies scratch
around for an issue, stage a demonstration and force a confrontation
with police. Mobs of students throw bricks, destroy property, and another college president flees to Addis Ababa. A tired script, yet it always seems to work, and many people must wonder why small groups
of campus radicals can at the crucial moment muster sufficient nonideological student support to carry off these confrontations.

There are numerous answers, of course, ranging from faculty-inspired
disgust with what the professors like to call "middle-class values" to
loneliness and tension brought on by a pack of punched cards or a rude
form letter from the library threatening terrible reprisals if an overdue
book is not returned. But perhaps the most convincing explanation for
student alienation is the one that only a few men such as Russell Kirk
choose to discuss: the American college student, especially the undergraduate, gets gypped. Most undergraduates, at least at the outset, are
not potential rioters who want to overturn the whole academic structure
just for the hell of it. But, somewhere along the collegiate assembly line,
something happens to too many of them. They find they are not being
educated.

Several years ago, former President Barnaby Keeney of Brown
summed up the common academic view of the student's role in the educational process. "Students," said Keeney, "tend to forget that they
have, in a way, 'hired themselves educated,' and that, having hired an
institution, they are well advised to abide by the decisions of the institution." Now this is certainly true to a point. But granted that students do
hire an institution to perform a specific service, surely one must concede that they have the right to complain if the institution fails to do the
job it was hired to do.

Some colleges and universities still do sell the undergraduate what he
pays for, of course, but many others, among them a large number of the

From *National Review,* Vol. XXI, No. 17 (May 6, 1969). Reprinted by permission of *National Review,* 150 East 35th Street, New York, New York 10016.

state universities, offer little return for the fees they charge. Students flock to these universities, usually because they are residents of the state and cannot afford to pay out-of-state tuition at other institutions. For despite the assumption implicit in Keeney's statement, the assumption that there is a free market of choices for the student, relatively few parents are able to finance out-of-state educations for their children. And while it is true that there are more scholarships today than ever before, it is also true that the competition for them is fiercer. And, in any case, these scholarships are increasingly being reserved for either exceptionally intelligent or exceptionally underprivileged students. And with the advent of federal work-study programs, it has become nearly impossible for students whose families are not destitute to find part-time jobs on campus. The result, then, is that the average high school graduate from an average family must usually either choose to attend his state university or else forget about a college education. And what this university sells him is more often than not a deficient product, not worth even the relatively modest price charged for it.

The typical undergraduate is cheated in a number of ways. His fees, usually funneled into graduate programs, buy him lectures not by high-salaried professors, whose services are reserved for graduate seminars, but instead by teaching assistants, underpaid graduate students who usually work one jump ahead of their classes and who provide the slave-labor base upon which most state universities build their idealistic programs. (One former graduate student likes to tell of the day he asked his department head at a large Midwestern university to raise his $1,-650 assistantship because both of his children had pneumonia and the medical bills were piling up. The department head responded with a lecture on the value of thrift.)

These teaching assistants, overloaded with children and debts, usually must moonlight to make ends meet. The case of one such t.a. at the University of Iowa, who taught three sections in the morning, washed dishes in a cafeteria in the afternoons, and cooked most of the night in a restaurant, is not untypical. And in addition, of course, these graduate student-teachers must at the same time drudge along through an obstacle course of unnecessarily petty and harassing Ph.D. requirements. Such people can seldom do a good thorough job of teaching the undergraduates delivered into their care. Their knowledge of the subjects they teach is limited, they have little practical classroom experience, and they usually find themselves adopting the same obfuscating techniques used by their own poorer professors in order to hide their ignorance and lack of preparation. And let it become necessary to choose between finishing up a term paper for a major professor or preparing a lecture for an undergraduate, any graduate student who wants to keep margarine on the family bread will finish up the paper. Of such stuff are comic novels made. And poorly educated undergraduates. And one should not suppose that this is a minor problem. Recently, one typical large Midwestern state university revealed that over half of its undergraduate courses were being taught by graduate assistants.

The undergraduate is cheated in numerous other ways: Examples are legion, familiar to anyone who has attended large public universities: the huge upper-division courses, open both to graduates and undergraduates, in which one of those rare birds, a senior professor, drones old lectures from note cards yellow with age; the young firebrand instructor whose sole mission seems to be to destroy whatever values students have brought with them from home ("Got to shock them out of their middle-class values," thinks the lecturer, the only son of a Crete, Nebraska druggist, as he reads the spicier parts of *Pamela* aloud); and, most pitiful of all, the older professor who wants to make his lectures "relevant." "Sarah Orne Jewett would not be entirely unsympathetic to today's student protests.")

Anyone who has lived in academe knows that the list of abuses of higher education is endless. The problem is, however, what to do about them. One expects little help from administrators, most of whom these days spend all their time conducting monologues with small groups of radicals. And the faculty, who adopt liberal political ideas in the same way they buy button-down shirts and pipes, is perhaps the single most reactionary group in the land when considering any sort of educational reform which might modify traditional faculty prerogatives. (A great wave of faculty protest recently swept over the Berkeley campus when Governor Reagan, attempting to balance his budget, discovered tenured professors at Berkeley taught only five hours per week. Thinking he could shave the university's request for funds to hire new faculty, the Governor suggested that each professor teach an additional class. The reaction was one of shocked outrage.)

This would seem, then, to leave it up to the student. And his options are sharply limited. University offices are too often staffed by men to whom it is useless to complain, epitomizations of Kafka's bureaucrats. For these men, literally, students are only numbers. Department heads are inaccessible, and college presidents, when they are not fleeing to Ethiopia, are busy serving on various commissions which study how to improve society. Keeney would tell students not to rock the boat; faculty would say that the student lacks the academic expertise necessary to improve things; and the tyrants of the administrative offices would tell him to go home and memorize his ID number. The student, then, usually has three options. He can be quiet, he can drop out, or he can protest.

Until recently, the drill was to keep quiet. Those of us who came back from Korea to find that we were not only older than our instructors but knew a good deal more about life than they, were usually content to treat them as we had treated commanding officers. Keep our mouths shut, let them think they were fine fellows, and do what we wanted to do. We earned our degrees, but many of us carried away a bad taste which was to linger and, at the very least, make us a bit cynical about those high-flown statements of purpose composed by pr men from college catalogues. Recently, however, students have begun to follow the advice of those educators who used to chide us for our "apathy." How such men as Grayson Kirk must regret those speeches of the Fifties.

It is difficult to condemn today's nonideological undergraduate for his noise precisely because he has so few alternatives. He is automatically assigned to a section in each of his classes. If the instructor is a lemon, it proves as difficult for the student to switch sections as it would have been for Thackeray to divorce his lunatic wife. Such a student knows that he must invent some sort of excuse such as a schedule conflict, for if he tells the truth, if he says the instructor is a nitwit, he will probably not only fail to get his section changed but will be singled out by that instructor for the rest of the term. And the free choice of programs is similarly mythical. At most universities everyone takes the same courses for the first two years and often beyond. There is, therefore, little chance to choose among programs. And the other alternative, that of leaving and going elsewhere, is equally impractical. It is, for instance, very difficult to transfer in the middle of the first year, although that is the ideal time to bail out of a bad university. Deans and admission officers view such transfer applications with great suspicion and, at any rate, the financial problems involved would probably be too great. University bursars, the undergraduate learns, are as diligent as collection agencies.

If the average undergraduate at the average state university is not content to follow Keeney's advice, then, and if he decides that he deserves the product which the university purports to sell and for which he has paid, chances are that he will look around for a way to make his grievances heard. It is particularly unfortunate that at present the only people who seem to get a hearing are the SDS types, for the student, frustrated at being cheated out of his education, finds that in order to force someone to listen to him he must throw in his lot with the radicals, for whom, in most cases he probably feels little more than contempt.

The tragedy is, of course, that when the confrontations end and when the SDSers and their ilk are appeased, the same old abuses will continue and the average student will be as frustrated as ever. Many of these abuses—administrative rigidity, indifference to individual human needs—should be capable of relatively easy solution. Other abuses, however—over-reliance on graduate students to prop up over-extended programs, professors unable to talk about esoteric interests and content to read from notes taken in graduate school decades before, other professors more interested in changing society according to some textbook recipe than in teaching their subjects—those abuses, in short, which fall solely within the academic sphere, are probably more difficult to cure.

Nevertheless, if officials and faculty do not want to see scores of thousands more of disenchanted students marching beneath the SDS banner, they should be cured, and the attempt must be made by those men who run the academy. At present the only source of any sort of educational reform seems to be the student body. This is a shame, for most of them are, after all, children, but children with legitimate grievances which they are, in the end, unable to remedy by themselves. One suspects that if faculty and administrators made a genuine attempt to provide the leadership expected of them, the SDS would find its supply of cannon fodder drastically curtailed.

WHO'S BRAINWASHING WHOM?
Joseph P. Lyford

What we hear about the student protest movement is often distorted. Joseph Lyford, Professor of Journalism at the University of California, Berkeley, contends that the outbreaks of violence on America's campuses are being tailored for television as carefully as network and sponsor mount a TV special. "If the day comes when television is freed from its dependence on what this or that angry crowd is doing, we will get a very different perspective on what is going on inside this country and inside our heads."

I suspect that my four-year-old son sees the world as a series of television commercials, which are about the only things he watches on TV these days. In Jody's opinion a banker who carries a briefcase around is automatically a flunky for the Master-Charge credit card people, and when his mother lights up a Kent, he is there at her elbow humming "That's What Happiness Is." One day, watching a C.B.S. documentary film showing the workings of the human stomach, he began talking about aspirin tablets. Lately, in an effort to bridge the generation gap, I have been studying television all over again from my son's point of view, and I can report that he has something. For one thing, the commercials are about the only programs left that aren't running over with violence. And in a symbolic, subliminal way, the commercials seem to

From *Center Magazine*, Vol. II, No. 2 (March 1969. Reprinted by permission of the Center for the Study of Democratic Institutions in Santa Barbara, California.

be telling us more about American life than all the news and movies and laugh-ins that come in between. There is the big success message from the automobile companies, with their chromium bumpers and headlights-with-eyelids, that it's what's up front that really counts. Then there are the messages within messages. One can't help noticing, for instance, that those suburban homeowners who collect insurance when their houses burn down are always white people.

My new look at TV has also unsettled my ancient assumption that the public is being brainwashed by the mass media. It may be the other way around. Far from being the helpless victims, the citizens are just as often busy manufacturing much of the bad entertainment and fake news we complain we are getting from the local station or our favorite newspaper. The TV cameramen are merely in there video-taping our carryings-on, and if we don't like what we see on Huntley-Brinkley, well, we can remember that David Brinkley says he doesn't, either. The citizens have been assaulting the TV people with all sorts of propaganda devices, which the media can't ignore even if they want to. One of the most successful of these gimmicks is a type of group theater whereby go-getters with a message simply organize a repertory company and play the mass communications business for all it's worth. Group theater, of course, is nothing new. The first Senator McCarthy and his coterie ran successfully on Capitol Hill for years as long as they played to the print media, but the Senator was not ready for television and it destroyed him. However, the current group theater, especially as it is put on by super-militant people on our warm-weather campuses, is more sophisticated, and it has the TV and press people on the run—literally. Perhaps this is some sort of rough justice, for the media brass has been telling us for years that nothing is news unless it entertains and has plenty of suspense and violence. These days they are getting much more than they are able to handle.

Ironically, the man who did the most to bring out the possibilities of group theater was someone who did not believe in four-letter words or violence, and who did not consciously write for television. In a sense, Martin Luther King's scripts were open-ended, and the conclusions were supplied by people who hated him, such as the white citizens of Montgomery, Alabama, and Cicero, Illinois, and Bull Connor, the sheriff of Birmingham, with his police dogs and fire hoses. Dr. King merely added a comment now and then to make sure nobody missed the point. Dr. King's way was founded on the principle of judo—that with just the right amount of enticement the unfriendlies can always be relied on to throw themselves to the mat. In retrospect this helps explain why nonviolence turned out to be practical.

There are vast differences between the improvised and often wordless theater of Dr. King's people and the dramas of planned violence being played out now at such places as San Francisco State, the College of San Mateo, and elsewhere by super-militants—black and white—who are scarcely able to hide their contempt for the assassinated Dr. King. The King demonstrations laid heavy demands on the discipline and conscience of each individual involved. Emphasis on personal self-control, the maintenance of one's special identity even in collective action, was absolutely necessary to the successful practice of non-violence. Non-violence sometimes also placed a premium on silence much in the manner of the Quakers. Some of us still remember Dr. King's people kneeling in prayer in their moments of extreme crisis. It was required that the act be a vehicle for the moral statement of the movement—the means had to be at one with the goal. Thus it was that the demonstrations sought to inform us about ourselves by posing questions rather than presenting us with dogma. Finally, of great political significance, the King demonstrations were *legal* assertions of human rights specified by the Constitution and fortified by the Supreme Court of the United States. The interposition of the demonstrators' bodies was a plea for, not against, the dialogue; a defense of, not an attack upon, the democratic process.

Whatever we may think about television, it must be recognized that while Dr. King held the stage, television relayed the quality of his demonstrations in a manner that shocked the conscience of millions of Americans. Today television is relaying versions of a group theater which has completely reversed the King principles. The purpose of the new play is, largely, the play itself. The script has concerned itself with proclamations and ultimata rather than questions. The language is loud and verbose and increasingly aimed at the destruction rather than the restoration of the dialogue. Where Dr. King sought eventual union with the uncommitted—even with his adversaries—the super-militants are interested only in union among themselves as a strategic necessity. Dr. King constantly prospected for some common ground of understanding as a place to begin; the super-militants have committed themselves to polarizing the conflict, to emphasizing that they cannot be reconciled with those who withhold full acceptance of their prescriptions. The in-group language of the handbill and the chant, the stress on mass behavior and mass articulation, are the means by which the super-militants achieve internal conformity in their movement. What Eric Severeid has called the tactics of "stylized violence" means that the participants must have first abandoned their individuality and personal conscience. In short, the super-militant demonstration is devoting itself to consistent violation of the very rights to which the King activists laid claim. Whatever uncertainty there may have been about the reality of this strategy of violence, it has been pretty well dispelled by the events at San Francisco State and the College of San Mateo, and by the success of the super-militants in forcing cancellation of a University of California con-vocation on racial justice last December in San Francisco. The off-campus coördinator of the Black Students Union at San Francisco State is frank about the matter. "We have no illusions about using force," he says. "If armed strength is what we need to seize power to determine our own educational destiny, then that will be done."

The new theater of violence has been tailored for television as care-fully as network and sponsor concoct an entertainment program; this helps explain why the line between TV entertainment and "news" has become almost indistinguishable at times. The demonstrations even meet the requirement for proper timing to make the seven o'clock news-casts. Like major-league baseball, revolutions are postponed in case of rain as much out of deference to the camera crews as to the health of the demonstrators. It goes without saying that the symbolic rituals of group theater are not a monopoly of the Third World or the Black Panthers, for with every strophe ("Pig!") an Eldridge Cleaver has led at Stanford or Berkeley, there have been antistrophes from such people off-stage as the Governor, the Superintendent of Public Instruction, and various posts of the American Legion.

Like other types of air pollution, the rise in the noise level resulting from such exchanges, here and elsewhere, has obscured the whole American landscape. Time given by television and the press to the staged event is time taken away from reporting the happenings that are not contrived—the invisible illnesses afflicting all levels of our society, the erosion of personal well-being in the suburbs as well as the inner cities, and the few but significant experiments that provide some hope for dealing with these problems. A rare glimpse at some subterranean reality, such as C.B.S.'s "Hunger in America" or N.B.C.'s look at a Negro family in Dooley County, Georgia, is seen once and then van-ishes into limbo.

One subject left untreated by television that especially interests this writer, who persists in his admiration for the undaunted libertarianism of Justice Black, is the state of mind of the political liberals who used to carry the burden of dissent in this country and provided much of the intellectual drive for reform of the democratic process. There are rather depressing indications that a good percentage of them have lately ac-commodated themselves to the violent and separatist doctrines of the super-militant Left, apparently in the belief that the Bill of Rights is a fraud perpetrated by the white racist establishment.

One can speculate endlessly about the reasons for the liberal toler-ance of the violent confrontation and the black super-militant's ludi-crous proposal to oppose integration and Africanize black America. Perhaps some liberals have been so conditioned to seeing the extreme Right as the source of all evil that they have, almost without realizing it, committed themselves so completely to the Left that they will not criticize its wildest excesses. Perhaps, in their knowledge of the crime white America has visited on the Negro, they feel it necessary to indulge in the sort of guilt-wallowing that leads them to support without remonstrance the most manifest absurdity if it is uttered by a black man. Or perhaps the liberals' historic overdependence on the young has made it impossible for them to criticize their moments of irrationality. Whatever the reason for their change in values, many liberals are suffering from a psychic infection that has undermined their courage to take issue with those super-militant claques increasingly addicted to violence.

The collapse of liberal dissent has had its most tragic repercussions in the field of education—in the public-school system of New York City as well as on our college campuses. When, in 1966, New York's liberal mayor turned over the power to hire and fire teachers to community pressure groups that had promoted racist violence against white teachers in an experimental Harlem school, almost all the city's liberal leadership remained silent. The "community control" concept—part of the mayor's so-called "decentralization plan" which tormented I.S. 201—has had its inevitable aftermath in the 1968 Ocean Hill-Brownsville school district explosion, where teachers were fired in violation of due process, inflamed crowds harassed teachers at the instigation of the local governing board of the district, and racial tensions were escalated beyond control. Again, with the exception of a few people like Michael Harrington and Daniel Bell, the liberal establishment—white and black —has remained silent on a vital issue of academic freedom or, like the New York Civil Liberties Union, has taken sides against the teachers and misrepresented their case. It has remained for Robert Hutchins, in one of his columns, to describe that case fairly. "No program of decentralization should be permitted to destroy the meager independence that teachers are granted in American schools. . . . The Ocean Hill-Brownsville community succeeded in giving the impression that teachers should immediately reflect and carry out whatever views on education the community might entertain. . . . Decentralization should not permit children to be sacrificed to the whims of their parents."

In California, liberals and civil-rights groups, who have been extremely sensitive to police misbehavior, have exhibited little or no public concern over calculated student violence at San Francisco State, the College of San Mateo, or San Fernando Valley State. San Francisco State faculty members who have organized a group called FORCE demand due process for a dismissed black faculty member (who is serving a six months suspended sentence for participating in an assault on some student editors) at the same time they support a "non-negotiable demand" for the firing of a college administrator without a hearing. Some

faculty members who oppose, as an invasion of their academic prerogatives, Governor Reagan's ill-advised attempt to bar Eldridge Cleaver as
a lecturer at Berkeley are willing to shut down their classes and lock
out students who want their instruction to continue. Last year at Berkeley there was not the slightest outward sign of faculty or student outrage
when a group of black super-militants used the threat of violence to
force cancellation of a Sproul Hall rally by Volition, a conservative student group. Perhaps the most dismal illustration of their tolerance of
force has been the silence of the white and black liberal leadership in
the aftermath of an organized rampage of a hundred and fifty super-militants, who last December invaded the College of San Mateo and beat
faculty and students with pipes and clubs. (The "violent trouncing,"
boasted one of the super-militant leaders at a press conference, was
"long overdue.") The view of some faculty liberals that one should not
get up-tight about the methods of the super-militants because they have
real grievances brings back memories of the people who defended Joseph McCarthy on the ground that he had the right objectives.

The reflexive opposition of many liberals to the use of police on campus in any situation also brings back memories of the days when we ap-
plauded the dispatch of National Guardsmen to the University of
Mississippi to protect James Meredith, and supported the occupation of
Little Rock by soldiers sent there to make *Brown vs. Board of Education* a reality for a handful of Negro children. For those liberals who
still feel that the police are the main threat to academic freedom or the
dialogue personal immersion in one of the campus conflicts generated
by the Students for a Democratic Society, the Third World, and its allies, is recommended. At still another rally at Berkeley last fall, when
the crowd was being exhorted to "take over" the university, my request
for a vote on the matter was shouted down by the leadership, the micro-
phone was denied to opponents of the takeover, and students with plac-
ards telling the rally to "cool it" were pushed around and their signs
ripped down. Attempting to argue the issue in the flesh in the center of
the crowd only increased the feeling of the absurdity of the affair: one
felt almost apologetic for raising questions. There were no shades of
opinion in the conversations; there weren't even any conversations.
Language disappeared until nothing was left but a roar composed of the
four-letter words that constitute the basic English of the *Berkeley Barb*.

Faculty members have little interest in these encounters, which is too
bad. Sometimes the phalanx does break down, as it did on the day of
Berkeley's Moses Hall sit-in. In the confusion, a few hundred students
found themselves in another building listening to a professor arguing
against the use of force with Peter Camejo, one of the sit-in organizers.
When somebody suggested that everyone sit on the floor and let the two
men talk it out, the crowd became an assembly of individuals who lis-

tened, asked questions, and made intensely personal statements in controlled, beautiful language. Camejo seemed to miss the point of what was happening, and shouted his calls to revolution as if he were still on Sproul steps with his audio equipment. After Camejo had a half hour to predict such things as the imminent installation of gas chambers on campus, the students told him he talked too much. Television was not there, of course: the reporters were at Moses Hall where the "action" was.

Except for an occasional ten-second interview on the run, the reporters gave little time to the type of students in that gathering who by no means accepted the claims of the hyperactivists. In fact, the student who has kept his critical wits about him is not adequately represented in any public way by his teachers or the general liberal community. Instead he is lumped with the "silent majority" so often referred to contemptuously by the liberal, the implication being that the non-militant student is apathetic, smug, and—worst of all—middle-class. It is rarely suggested that the inability of the "silent majority" to mobilize in the mass may have something to do with its diversity, a quality quite absent in the super-militant phalanx. The fact that the vast percentage of Berkeley students choose not to demonstrate their awareness of social crisis by breaking a window doesn't tell us very much about them, nor does their decision to be silent in certain situations. Some of them are, of course, the comfort-seekers and fraternity types, but large numbers of them tutor children in the West Oakland schools or later join the Peace Corps or VISTA—which is called finking for the Establishment by the super-militants.

If the "revolutionaries" are the most intelligent and highly motivated students, as a current academic cliché would have us believe, the assumption remains unproved in my experience, as I have found that the students with the most enduring commitment to realizing their creative capacities are not usually the ones who want to tear down the university. In fact, the confrontationist confronted in the classroom frequently turns out to be dogmatic and humorless, addicted to the trite and the oversimplified, and absorbed in self-dramatization.

The mass media pass over the unaffiliated student for the same reason they tend to overlook the other unaffiliated people in our society. Such people are, practically speaking, invisible and inaudible. They lack the stage provided by a group allegiance and do not have the demonstrably large numerical constituency that impresses the people who put news shows together. Because they speak with an individual rather than an organizational voice, it is hard to classify them or reduce their attitudes to the sort of "representative" views for which reporters and poll-takers are always looking. Television (the press, too) concerns itself with demonstrations in the mass rather than the human condition in the particular, and it has far less courage in tackling the abstract than the concrete and the easily perceived. This is why we rarely get a look via television at the momentous things happening to us that can't be filmed the way we can photograph a riot or the surface of the moon. It is why television is not telling us very much about the nature of power, about the ideas that are quietly generating enormous changes in life, about the "shy thought, shyly expressed by shy men" to which Peter Ustinov has referred, or about the essential fraudulence of violence. If the day comes when television is freed from its dependence on what this or that angry crowd is doing, we will get a very different perspective on what is going on inside this country and inside our heads. Until then, one can do worse than study the television commercials for clues to the mystery.

REBELS WITHOUT A PROGRAM
George F. Kennan

The student movement has been criticized by many who are alarmed by the violence and apparent irrationality of protest demonstrations. In this essay, George F. Kennan, a professor at Princeton and the Institute for Advanced Studies, criticizes the student rebels for their lack of a responsible, constructive program of reform. A former diplomat (ambassador to the Soviet Union and to Yugoslavia), Professor Kennan is the author of many distinguished books on foreign policy and Soviet-American relations.

There is an ideal that has long been basic to the learning process as we have known it, one that stands at the very center of our modern institutions of higher education and that had its origin, I suppose, in the clerical and monastic character of the medieval university. It is the ideal of the association of the process of learning with a certain remoteness from the contemporary scene—a certain detachment and seclusion, a certain voluntary withdrawal and renunciation of participation in contemporary life in the interests of the achievement of a better perspective on that life when the period of withdrawal is over. It is an ideal that does not predicate any total conflict between thought and action, but recognizes that there is a time for each.

From *Democracy and the Student Left* by George F. Kennan. Copyright © 1968 by George F. Kennan. Reprinted by permission of Atlantic-Little, Brown and Co.
This essay was originally prepared for the dedication of a new library at Swarthmore College. It was printed in *The New York Times Magazine* for January 21, 1968, and drew an unprecedented response from students and teachers all over the United States. The essay and the reactions, both favorable and unfavorable, have been compiled in *Democracy and the Student Left* (Boston: Little, Brown and Company, 1968).

No more striking, or moving, description of this ideal has ever come to my attention than that which was given by Woodrow Wilson in 1896 at the time of the Princeton Sesquicentennial.

"I have had sight," Wilson said, "of the perfect place of learning in my thought: a free place, and a various, where no man could be and not know with how great a destiny knowledge had come into the world—itself a little world; but not perplexed, living with a singleness of aim not known without; the home of sagacious men, hardheaded and with a will to know, debaters of the world's questions every day and used to the rough ways of democracy; and yet a place removed—calm Science seated there, recluse, ascetic, like a nun; not knowing that the world passes, not caring, if the truth but come in answer to her prayer. . . . A place where ideals are kept in heart in an air they can breathe; but no fool's paradise. A place where to hear the truth about the past and hold debate about the affairs of the present, with knowledge and without passion; like the world in having all men's life at heart, a place for men and all that concerns them; but unlike the world in its self-possession, its thorough way of talk, its care to know more than the moment brings to light; slow to take excitement, its air pure and wholesome with a breath of faith; every eye within it bright in the clear day and quick to look toward heaven for the confirmation of its hope. Who shall show us the way to this place?"

There is a dreadful incongruity between this vision and the state of mind—and behavior—of the radical left on the American campus today. In place of a calm science, "recluse, ascetic, like a nun," not knowing or caring that the world passes "if the truth but come in answer to her prayer," we have people utterly absorbed in the affairs of this passing world. And instead of these affairs being discussed with knowledge and without passion, we find them treated with transports of passion and with a minimum, I fear, of knowledge. In place of slowness to take excitement, we have a readiness to react emotionally, and at once, to a great variety of issues. In place of self-possession, we have screaming tantrums and brawling in the streets. In place of the "thorough way of talk" that Wilson envisaged, we have banners and epithets and obscenities and virtually meaningless slogans. And in place of bright eyes "looking to heaven for the confirmation of their hope," we have eyes glazed with anger and passion, too often dimmed as well by artificial abuse of the psychic structure that lies behind them, and looking almost everywhere else but to heaven for the satisfaction of their aspirations.

I quite understand that those who espouse this flagrant repudiation of the Wilsonian ideal constitute only a minority on any campus. But tendencies that represent the obsession of only a few may not be without partial appeal, at certain times, and within certain limits, to many others. If my own analysis is correct, there are a great many students who may resist any complete surrender to these tendencies, but who nevertheless find them intensely interesting, are to some extent attracted or morally bewildered by them, find themselves driven, in confrontation with them, either into various forms of pleasing temptation, on the one hand, or into crises of conscience, on the other.

If I see them correctly (and I have no pretensions to authority on this subject), there are two dominant tendencies among the people I have here in mind, and superficially they would seem to be in conflict one with the other. On the one side there is angry militancy, full of hatred and intolerance and often quite prepared to embrace violence as a source of change. On the other side there is gentleness, passivity, quietism—ostensibly a yearning for detachment from the affairs of the world, not the detachment Woodrow Wilson had in mind, for that was one intimately and sternly related to the real world, the objective, external world, whereas this one takes the form of an attempt to escape into a world which is altogether illusory and subjective.

What strikes one first about the angry militancy is the extraordinary degree of certainty by which it is inspired: certainty of one's own rectitude, certainty of the accuracy and profundity of one's own analysis of the problems of contemporary society, certainty as to the iniquity of those who disagree. Of course, vehemence of feeling and a conviction that right is on one's side have seldom been absent from the feelings of politically excited youth. But somehow or other they seem particularly out of place at just this time. Never has there been an era when the problems of public policy even approached in their complexity those by which our society is confronted today, in this age of technical innovation and the explosion of knowledge. The understanding of these problems is something to which one could well give years of disciplined and restrained study, years of the scholar's detachment, years of readiness to reserve judgment while evidence is being accumulated. And this being so, one is struck to see such massive certainties already present in the minds of people who not only *have not* studied very much but presumably *are not* studying a great deal, because it is hard to imagine that the activities to which this aroused portion of our student population gives itself are ones readily compatible with quiet and successful study.

The world seems to be full, today, of embattled students. The public prints are seldom devoid of the record of their activities. Photographs of them may be seen daily: screaming, throwing stones, breaking windows, overturning cars, being beaten or dragged about by police and, in the case of those on other continents, burning libraries. That these people are embattled is unquestionable. That they are really students, I must be permitted to doubt. I have heard it freely confessed by members of the revolutionary student generation of Tsarist Russia that, proud as they were of the revolutionary exploits of their youth, they never really learned anything in their university years; they were too busy with politics. The fact of the matter is that the state of being *enragé* is simply incompatible with fruitful study. It implies a degree of existing emotional and intellectual commitment which leaves little room for open-minded curiosity.

I am not saying that students should not be concerned, should not have views, should not question what goes on in the field of national policy and should not voice their questions about it. Some of us, who are older, share many of their misgivings, many of their impulses. Some of us have no less lively a sense of the dangers of the time, and are no happier than they are about a great many things that are now going on. But it lies within the power as well as the duty of all of us to recognize not only the possibility that we might be wrong but the virtual certainty that on some occasions we are bound to be. The fact that this is so does not absolve us from the duty of having views and putting them forward. But it does make it incumbent upon us to recognize the element of doubt that still surrounds the correctness of these views. And if we do that, we will not be able to lose ourselves in transports of moral indignation against those who are of opposite opinion and follow a different line; we will put our views forward only with a prayer for forgiveness for the event that we prove to be mistaken.

I am aware that inhibitions and restraints of this sort on the part of us older people would be attributed by many members of the student left to a sweeping corruption of our moral integrity. Life, they would hold, has impelled us to the making of compromises; and these compromises have destroyed the usefulness of our contribution. Crippled by our own cowardice, prisoners of the seamy adjustments we have made in order to be successfully a part of the American establishment, we are regarded as no longer capable of looking steadily into the strong clear light of truth.

In this, as in most of the reproaches with which our children shower us, there is of course an element of justification. There is a point somewhere along the way in most of our adult lives, admittedly, when enthusiasms flag, when idealism becomes tempered, when responsibility to others, and even affection for others, compels greater attention to the mundane demands of private life. There is a point when we are even impelled to place the needs of children ahead of the dictates of a defiant idealism, and to devote ourselves, pusillanimously, if you will, to the support and rearing of these same children—precisely in order that at some future date they may have the privilege of turning upon us and despising us for the materialistic faintheartedness that made their maturity possible. This, no doubt, is the nature of the compromise that millions of us make with the imperfections of government and society in our time. Many of us could wish that it might have been otherwise—that the idealistic pursuit of public causes might have remained our exclusive dedication down into later life.

But for the fact that this is not so I cannot shower myself or others with reproaches. I have seen more harm done in this world by those who tried to storm the bastions of society in the name of utopian beliefs, who were determined to achieve the elimination of all evil and the realization of the millennium within their own time, than by all the humble efforts of those who have tried to create a little order and civility and affection within their own intimate entourage, even at the cost of tolerating a great deal of evil in the public domain. Behind this modesty, after all, there has been the recognition of a vitally important truth—a truth that the Marxists, among others, have never brought themselves to recognize—namely, that the decisive seat of evil in this world is not in social and political institutions, and not even, as a rule, in the will or iniquities of statesmen, but simply in the weakness and imperfection of the human soul itself, and by that I mean literally every soul, including my own and that of the student militant at the gates. For this reason, as Tocqueville so clearly perceived when he visited this country a hundred and thirty years ago, the success of a society may be said, like charity, to begin at home.

So much, then, for the angry ones. Now, a word about the others: the quiescent ones, the hippies and the flower people.

In one sense, my feeling for these people is one of pity, not unmixed, in some instances, with horror. I am sure that they want none of this pity. They would feel that it comes to them for the wrong reasons. If they feel sorry for themselves, it is because they see themselves as the victims of a harsh, hypocritical and unworthy adult society. If I feel sorry for them, it is because I see them as the victims of certain great and destructive philosophic errors.

One of these errors—and it is one that affects particularly those who take drugs, but not those alone—is the belief that the human being has marvelous resources within himself that can be released and made available to him merely by the passive submission to certain sorts of stimuli: by letting esthetic impressions of one sort or another roll over him or by letting his psychic equilibrium be disoriented by chemical agencies that give him the sensation of experiencing tremendous things. Well, it is true that human beings sometimes have marvelous resources within themselves. It is also true that these resources are capable, ideally, of being released and made available to the man that harbors them and through him to others, and sometimes are so released. But it is not true that they can be released by hippie means.

It is only through effort, through doing, through action—never through passive experience—that man grows creatively. It is only by volition and effort that he becomes fully aware of what he has in him of creativity and becomes capable of embodying it, of making it a part of himself, of communicating it to others. There is no pose more fraudulent—and students would do well to remember this when they look at each other—than that of the individual who pretends to have been exalted and rendered more impressive by his communion with some sort of inner voice whose revelations he is unable to describe or to enact. And particularly is this pose fraudulent when the means he has chosen to render himself susceptible to this alleged revelation is the deliberate disorientation of his own psychic system; for it may be said with surety that any artificial intervention of this sort—into the infinitely delicate balance that nature created in the form of man's psychic makeup—produces its own revenge, takes its own toll, proceeds at the cost of the true creative faculties and weakens rather than strengthens.

The second error I see in the outlook of these people is the belief in the possibility and validity of a total permissiveness. They are misjudging, here, the innermost nature of man's estate. There is not, and cannot be, such a thing as total freedom. The normal needs and frailties of the body, not to mention the elementary demands of the soul itself, would rule that out if nothing else did. But beyond that, any freedom *from* something implies a freedom to something. And because our reality is a complex one, in which conflicts of values are never absent, there can be no advance toward any particular objective, not even the pursuit of pleasure, that does not imply the sacrifice of other possible objectives. Freedom, for this reason, is definable only in terms of the obligations and restraints and sacrifices it accepts. It exists, as a concept, only in relationship to something else which is by definition its opposite; and that means commitment, duty, self-restraint.

Every great artist has known this. Every great philosopher has recognized it. It has lain at the basis of Judaic-Christian teaching. Tell me what framework of discipline you are prepared to accept, and I will attempt to tell you what freedom might mean for you. But if you tell me that you are prepared to accept no framework of discipline at all, then I will tell you, as Dostoevski told his readers, that you are destined to become the most unfree of men; for freedom begins only with the humble acceptance of membership in, and subordination to, a natural order of things, and it grows only with struggle, and self-discipline, and faith.

To shun the cruelty and corruption of this world is one thing. It is not always unjustifiable. Not everyone is made to endure these things. There is something to be said for the cultivation, by the right people, and in the right way, of the virtues of detachment, of withdrawal, of unworldliness, of innocence and purity, if you will. That, as a phase of life, is just what Wilson was talking about. In an earlier age, those who are now the flower children and the hippies would perhaps have entered monastic life or scholarly life or both. But there, be it noted, they would very definitely have accepted a framework of discipline, and it would normally have been a very strict one. If it was a monastic order, their lives would have been devoted to the service of God and of other men, not of themselves and their senses. If it was the world of scholarship, their lives would have been devoted to the pursuit of truth, which never comes easily or without discipline and sacrifice. They would have accepted an obligation to cultivate order, not chaos; cleanliness, not filth; self-abnegation, not self-indulgence; health, not demoralization.

Now I have indicated that I pity these people, and in general I do. But sometimes I find it hard to pity them, because they themselves are sometimes so pitiless. There is, in this cultivation of an absolute freedom, and above all in the very self-destructiveness with which it often expresses itself, a selfishness, a hardheartedness, a callousness, an irresponsibility, an indifference to the feelings of others, that is its own condemnation. No one ever destroys just himself alone. Such is the network of intimacy in which every one of us is somehow embraced, that whoever destroys himself destroys to some extent others as well. Many of these people prattle about the principle of love; but their behavior betrays this principle in the most elementary way. Love—and by that I mean the receiving of love as well as the bestowal of it—is itself an obligation, and as such is incompatible with the quest for a perfect freedom. Just the cruelty to parents alone, which is implicit in much of this behavior, is destructive of the purest and most creative form of love that does exist or could exist in this mortal state.

And one would like to warn these young people that in distancing themselves so recklessly not only from the wisdom but from the feelings of parents, they are hacking at their own underpinnings—and even those of people as yet unborn. There could be no greater illusion than the belief that one can treat one's parents unfeelingly and with contempt and yet expect that one's own children will some day treat one otherwise; for such people break the golden chain of affection that binds the generations and gives continuity and meaning to life.

One cannot, therefore, on looking at these young people in all the glory of their defiant rags and hairdos, always just say, with tears in one's eyes: "There goes a tragically wayward youth, striving romantically to document his rebellion against the hypocrisies of the age." One has sometimes to say, and not without indignation: "There goes a perverted and willful and stony-hearted youth by whose destructiveness we are all, in the end, to be damaged and diminished."

These people also pose a problem in the quality of their citizenship. One thing they all seem to have in common—the angry ones as well as the quiet ones—is a complete rejection of, or indifference to, the political system of this country. The quiet ones turn their backs upon it, as though it did not concern them. The angry ones reject it by implication, insofar as they refuse to recognize the validity of its workings or to respect the discipline which, as a system of authority, it unavoidably entails.

I think there is a real error or misunderstanding here. If you accept a democratic system, this means that you are prepared to put up with those of its workings, legislative or administrative, with which you do not agree as well as with those that meet with your concurrence. This willingness to accept, in principle, the workings of a system based on the will of the majority, even when you yourself are in the minority, is simply the essence of democracy. Without it there could be no system of representative self-government at all. When you attempt to alter the workings of the system by means of violence or civil disobedience, this, it seems to me, can have only one of two implications: either you do not believe in democracy at all and consider that society ought to be governed by enlightened minorities such as the one to which you, of course, belong; or you consider that the present system is so imperfect that it is not truly representative, that it no longer serves adequately as a vehicle for the will of the majority, and that this leaves to the unsatisfied no adequate means of self-expression other than the primitive one of calling attention to themselves and their emotions by mass demonstrations and mass defiance of established authority. It is surely the latter of these two implications which we must read from the overwhelming majority of the demonstrations that have recently taken place.

I would submit that if you find a system inadequate, it is not enough simply to demonstrate indignation and anger over individual workings of it, such as the persistence of the Vietnam war, or individual situations it tolerates or fails to correct, such as the condition of the Negroes in our great cities. If one finds these conditions intolerable, and if one considers that they reflect no adequate expression either of the will of the majority or of that respect for the rights of minorities which is no less essential to the success of any democratic system, then one places upon one's self, it seems to me, the obligation of saying in what way this political system should be modified, or what should be established in the place of it, to assure that its workings would bear a better relationship to people's needs and people's feelings.

If the student left had a program of constitutional amendment or political reform—if it had proposals for the constructive adaptation of this political system to the needs of our age—if it was *this* that it was agitating for, and if its agitation took the form of reasoned argument and discussion, or even peaceful demonstration accompanied by reasoned argument and discussion—then many of us, I am sure, could view its protests with respect, and we would not shirk the obligation either to speak up in defense of institutions and national practices which we have tolerated all our lives, or to join these young people in the quest for better ones.

But when we are confronted only with violence for violence's sake, and with attempts to frighten or intimidate an administration into doing things for which it can itself see neither the rationale nor the electoral mandate; when we are offered, as the only argument for change, the fact that a number of people are themselves very angry and excited; and when we are presented with a violent objection to what exists, unaccompanied by any constructive concept of what, ideally, ought to exist in its place—then we of my generation can only recognize that such behavior bears a disconcerting resemblance to phenomena we have witnessed within our own time in the origins of totalitarianism in other countries, and then we have no choice but to rally to the defense of a public authority with which we may not be in agreement but which is the only one we've got and with which, in some form or another, we cannot conceivably dispense. People should bear in mind that if this—namely noise, violence and lawlessness—is the way they are going to put their case, then many of us who are no happier than they are about some of the policies that arouse their indignation will have no choice but to place ourselves on the other side of the barricades.

These observations reflect a serious doubt whether civil disobedience has any place in a democratic society. But there is one objection I know will be offered to this view. Some people, who accept our political system, believe that they have a right to disregard it and to violate the laws that have flowed from it so long as they are prepared, as a matter of conscience, to accept the penalties established for such behavior.

I am sorry; I cannot agree. The violation of law is not, in the moral and philosophic sense, a privilege that lies offered for sale with a given price tag, like an object in a supermarket, available to anyone who has the price and is willing to pay for it. It is not like the privilege of breaking crockery in a tent at the county fair for a quarter a shot. Respect for the law is not an obligation which is exhausted or obliterated by willingness to accept the penalty for breaking it.

To hold otherwise would be to place the privilege of lawbreaking preferentially in the hands of the affluent, to make respect for law a commercial proposition rather than a civic duty and to deny any authority of law independent of the sanctions established against its violation. It would then be all right for a man to create false fire alarms or frivolously to pull the emergency cord on the train, or to do any number of other things that endangered or inconvenienced other people, provided only he was prepared to accept the penalties of so doing. Surely, lawlessness and civil disobedience cannot be condoned or tolerated on this ground; and those of us who care for the good order of society have no choice but to resist attempts at its violation, when this is their only justification.

Now, being myself a father, I am only too well aware that people of my generation cannot absolve ourselves of a heavy responsibility for the state of mind in which these young people find themselves. We are obliged to recognize here, in the myopia and the crudities of *their* extremism, the reflection of our own failings: our faintheartedness and in some instances our weariness, our apathy in the face of great and obvious evils.

I am also aware that, while their methods may not be the right ones, and while their discontent may suffer in its effectiveness from the concentration on negative goals, the degree of their concern over the present state of our country and the dangers implicit in certain of its involvements is by no means exaggerated. This is a time in our national life more serious, more menacing, more crucial, than any I have ever experienced or ever hoped to experience. Not since the civil conflict of a century ago has this country, as I see it, been in such great danger; and the most excruciating aspect of this tragic state of affairs is that so much of this danger comes so largely from within, where we are giving it relatively little official attention, and so little of it comes, relatively speaking, from the swamps and jungles of Southeast Asia into which we are pouring our treasure of young blood and physical resources.

For these reasons, I do not mean to make light of the intensity of feeling by which this student left is seized. Nor do I mean to imply that people like myself can view this discontent from some sort of smug Olympian detachment, as though it were not our responsibility, as though it were not in part our own ugly and decadent face that we see in this distorted mirror. None of us could have any justification for attempting to enter into communication with these people if we did not recognize, along with the justification for their unhappiness, our own responsibility in the creation of it, and if we did not accompany our appeal to them with a profession of readiness to join them, where they want us to, in the attempt to find better answers to many of these problems.

I am well aware that in approaching them in this way and in taking issue as I have with elements of their outlook and their behavior, it is primarily myself that I have committed, not them. I know that behind all the extremisms—all the philosophical errors, all the egocentricities and all the oddities of dress and deportment—we have to do here with troubled and often pathetically appealing people, acting, however wisely or unwisely, out of sincerity and idealism, out of the unwillingness to accept a meaningless life and a purposeless society.

Well, this is not the life, and not the sort of society, that many of us would like to leave behind us in this country when our work is done.

How wonderful it would be, I sometimes think to myself, if we and they —experience on the one hand, strength and enthusiasm on the other— could join forces.

THE SEARCH FOR REFORM

> *"For it is in the ideal of a community of concerned persons who share a common interest in the life of the mind and the quality of human experience that the genius of the university lies."*

HAROLD TAYLOR

STUDENTS AS TEACHERS
Harold Taylor

College administrators who appear to be preoccupied with rigid traditions, with grades, course units, professional status, the lecture system, etc., have been under attack for providing too few opportunities for creative teaching and learning. Harold Taylor, former president of Sarah Lawrence College and author of *The World as Teacher* and *Art and the Intellect,* joins the attack and proposes that students become more directly involved in teaching each other: "What is needed is a conception of teaching and learning which reaches back into the undergraduate student body and considers undergraduate and graduate students as members of one community, capable of teaching each other."

When a university sets out to reform its educational program in direct collaboration with students, the quality of teaching and learning is immediately affected. In the first place, the academic departments have to be much more careful in making appointments to the faculty exclusively on the basis of publication records and academic reputation. Inability to teach, or even disinterest in teaching, then becomes a potential source of embarrassment to the administration and to the departmental chairmen and their advisory committees. Too much concern with academic prestige and research ability, for even a limited period of time, means that soon there are not enough good teachers to go around, not enough scholars who enjoy working with students, or, what is worse for the departmental interest, not enough students to fill the classes and therefore not enough appointments available to sustain the size and position of the department in the university structure.

On the positive side, the academic faculty, when it collaborates with students in the development of courses and educational policy, has the very great advantage of working within its own disciplines with students whose talents and motivation in these fields begin to flourish at a higher level, both in teaching and in learning. Among the cooperating students, a far greater proportion than before becomes interested in working at an even higher level, with intellectual capacities of a broader range because of the experience they have had in their beginning courses and projects. The faculty thus finds itself with a breeding ground for future teaching and research talent and for the development of intellectual interests directly related to their own.

As for policy-making and government in student affairs, a great deal of this can be better arranged by students than by faculty members and administrative officers. The experimental colleges, particularly Antioch, Goddard, and Sarah Lawrence, have given students responsibilities in student affairs which in other colleges are handled entirely by college staff, and have found that not only the policy-making but the administration works in ways which call upon resources in students which would otherwise remain undeveloped. By bringing the students actively into the administration itself, the administrative problems of college life confront the students directly, and refute the idea that anyone who is an administrator belongs to the enemy camp.

The Sarah Lawrence pattern is one in which the Student Council not only has the power of deciding on the rules for the student community, from dormitory hours to chartering organizations, but the responsibility for administering their own rules through a council of vice-presidents of the student houses. In the case of student legislation which in the view of the administration or faculty is unwise or misguided, the opportunity exists for a reconsideration in a joint committee of elected faculty members, elected students, and administration. The joint committee holds the power of ultimate decision in matters of college policy in general. An appeal could of course be made beyond that body to the board of trustees, but to make such an appeal would mean to admit the failure of the very system which brings the students into a position of responsibility for their own college.

In view of the time and energy absorbed by the administration of student affairs by students, it is also necessary to consider that factor in planning a student schedule of education in the college, and in some cases to relieve a student of course work during a given semester or college year, and to pay a stipend for the services rendered to the community. When the educational program is arranged in such a way that the experience of organizing education on behalf of others is a genuine opportunity for the student, he may learn more from that kind of responsibility over a limited period of time than he would in the formal studies which would otherwise occupy him.

This is especially true of those who intend to become teachers or to enter one of the professions where the ability to organize oneself and to develop programs of use to others is a necessary corollary to whatever scholarship and learning one may possess in the field. The experience in personal relationships, in sustaining the delicate lines of connection which flow between persons and groups who are working in voluntary ways to achieve a common end, is a very important one for students in the entire field of the human services and the arts. The student of theater who has not learned to collaborate with others in the work of the theater, and who has not learned what is involved on the practical side in putting a production on the stage, is in the same position as a student who has not learned to do what has to be done when any useful human enterprise involving cooperative effort is set in motion.

[II]

This brings me to another matter basic to the reconstruction of the learning-teaching system, the matter of graduate students and their role in teaching. Their present status as teaching assistants to professors is a function of the lecture system and all its parts, not the result of an examination of how education may best be conducted through the talents which students of all kinds can bring to the teaching system. It is now a truism to say that in most cases in the big universities the graduate students provide one of the few opportunities for personal contact by the undergraduates with the teaching faculty. The rest is a matter of sitting in lectures. The graduate students know this, and are fully aware of the dependence of the present economic and cultural structure of the university on their work in teaching. At many universities they have organized Graduate Student Unions both to advance their economic interests and to influence educational policy. Their ranks contain some of the most intelligent, imaginative, and energetic educators the country has ever seen. The fact that they do not yet possess teaching credentials and higher degrees cannot disguise the fact that they are already functioning as teachers, regardless of faculty status—teachers who are working under wraps by the status they now occupy.

What is true of the graduate schools is true of the whole educational system and the society at large. Everywhere the idea of specified and certified professional and vocational skills, only available for public use after certified institutional training progrms, has taken hold of the country's institutional life. It has substituted itself for the idea that anyone who can demonstrate in action the quality of what he knows and what he can do has no need of diplomas and credentials in order to do it. Except in the case of brain surgeons and a limited range of professional talents, the certification is unjustified.

A move away from the pattern of the credential society is essential as the first step toward breaking down the barriers to the full use of all human talent, certified or uncertified. Psychiatric aides, for example, who spend more time with patients than anyone in the mental hospital staff and who have a serious degree of influence on the progress of the patients' recovery, should be given the recognition and responsibility that comes with their function. So should teachers' aides, student assistants in child-care centers, community volunteers, community workers without formal education. Once the obvious fact is recognized that education is an amalgam of influences and not simply a transaction between academic professionals and pupils who appear before them, the way is open for the full use of human resources of all kinds within the schools, the colleges, and the universities.

The students who have organized store-front colleges and street academies have already recognized the ability of ordinary people, without certificates and formal training, both to teach and to learn. Among those recruited by the students as tutors for their projects are high school drop-outs, mothers of children, automobile mechanics, former convicts, college professors. Others at the University of North Carolina and elsewhere have organized "poor people's universities" and in one instance have developed a category of university professor whom they call "poor professors," which, although open to wide misinterpretation, refers to poor people in the community who come to college classes in the humanities and social sciences to talk about social issues and realities from their position in the middle of poverty.

In the case of teachers like David Riesman, in whose undergraduate courses graduate assistants are given an opportunity to collaborate directly both in the teaching and in the educational planning, there is no particular status problem, since Riesman and others like him deal with the assistants as intellectual and teaching colleagues, not as hired hands to carry out tasks for which professors have no time or inclination. But in the system as a whole the graduate assistant, whose maturity of outlook and practical teaching experience qualify him as a full-fledged teacher, finds himself in the absurd situation of acting as a handy man when he should be recognized as a major element in the conduct of university instruction.

There is no need to repeat again the account of how this situation is related to failures of graduate education in general, and the lack of connection between the requirements for the doctoral degree and the preparation of students for teaching assignments in the colleges and universities. What is needed is a conception of teaching and learning which reaches back into the undergraduate student body and considers undergraduates and graduate students as members of one community, capable of teaching each other. There are many juniors and seniors in the colleges and universities whose gifts as teachers and educational leaders are presently ignored, and, were a different attitude to the curriculum and its operation taken by the university, could become a major element in the improvement of undergraduate learning.

I have already referred to the organic unity of undergraduates and graduate students within the civil rights and activist groups, and their intellectual and practical collaboration in educational and political projects without regard to age level or academic status. There is no reason why that kind of collaboration cannot be made a regular part of the teaching system. It requires only the initiative of the faculty to set it in motion, with or without an educational plan for the whole university. A faculty member is free to call upon individual members of his undergraduate classes, both those in the present classes and those whose work in previous classes recommended itself to their teachers, to act as seminar and discussion leaders, tutors, organizers, and aides in educational planning and teaching.

A budget should be provided to allow a teacher or group of teachers to appoint undergraduates with teaching talent who had previously worked within particular courses, with the students invited to reduce their course schedule in a given semester in order to give teaching assistance as aides in a course, with a stipend to match. Freshmen entering the university could be given the advantage of choosing a student adviser from among those appointed to such a student staff; the staff could organize a seminar and tutorial plan by which the freshmen could become involved in the discussion and clarification of the problems of becoming educated at the university. This simply pushes to a larger dimension the informal advising system which already exists among students, but which at present bears the handicap of not being part of a serious effort to give the entering student a chance to find his bearings and to establish a sense of colleagueship with students more advanced than himself in the educational system.

There are many in the ranks of the graduate students who have earned the right to teach students of their own, and who could supply the basic resources for the teaching staff of the freshman and sophomore years, as well as in the upper division. If they were invited to collaborate with the faculty in planning seminars and programs, this could replace the lecture system with one more in keeping with the needs of the undergraduates. Whenever lectures were needed, these could be supplied by calling together a number of the individual seminars into one class for a joint session to be addressed by a lecturer chosen for the particular contribution he could make to the problems under consideration in the seminars. Collaboration among the seminar teachers would be possible, not only in this way, but in many others. Individual students could combine their talents in symposia to be presented to a group of the seminars; outside visitors from the community, the faculty, and the graduate-student roster could also be included.

This would entail a different kind of organization within the graduate divisions themselves. In a given semester, as part of the master of arts or doctoral degree program, a student would spend the whole of his time, with an appropriate stipend, in the work of an undergraduate seminar, with the seminar materials and supervision of undergraduate projects considered as an integral part of the work of the graduate student in developing his own body of knowledge within his chosen field. There is no more effective way of organizing such a body of knowledge of one's own than by teaching it. The rationale for the semester or year of work of a graduate student as teacher is not simply that it would give the future college professor experience in teaching as a necessary component of his preparation, but that it would deepen his scholarship and his intellectual resources by the process of discovering what it was he had learned which was useful to others in the culture.

The rationale could also be extended to the undergraduate curriculum, where, in connection with work in psychology, anthropology, literature, sociology, physics, biology, or mathematics, the students would be asked, as part of their regular work, to volunteer for tutoring assignments with children or with high school students in areas and subjects where help was needed and in which the undergraduate had competence.

When the entire educational system is seen in terms of its interconnections through teaching and learning, not as a series of interlocking social and cultural agencies separated from each other by bureaucratic rules and testing devices, the stream of conciousness which runs from the child to the adolescent to the young adult and beyond then becomes the most vital and important thing about it. Links between one consciousness and another become the crucial matter, not the discontinuities and separations which the institutions make within themselves and among each other. The continuity of experience between the internal life of the school and college and the life of the society becomes a natural educational concept, with broad implications for the union of talents found within the educational institution and the need for these talents for education in the community. The curriculum of the college is then joined to the reality of the society, and through their union the student can learn to locate himself in the wider world and to act upon it. It is this continuity in consciousness which gives the basis for planning the internal life of the university so that at every point the students are linked to others, and education for students becomes the series of influences and experiences through which they teach and are taught.

[III]

How then do we proceed, finally, to accomplish the reforms? Where do we take hold? Who makes the next moves?

It will be clear from what I have been saying up to now that my view is that the moves must be collaborative; they must be made by the faculty, the administration, and the students together. I would add that it does not matter who moves first, as long as the students are centrally involved in what is done. The students can become involved by invitation of the faculty or the administration, by their own initiative, by a new curriculum, by the student's natural attachment to a student organization which is itself involved in educational reform. But in the last analysis, it is the responsibility of the university of which they are a part to find ways of creating the involvement by the structure of the internal life of the college.

The movement in reform can therefore start at any point, without the necessity of another faculty report, by simply taking seriously the proposition already stated that the best place to start a reform movement to improve a student's education is directly in the area of his intellectual life as this is lived at the university—that is, in the courses, on the campus, with his teachers.

The simplest way to set in motion a reform movement which starts in the working areas of the student's intellectual life is to take the educational questions one year at a time, that is, to set a group of interested faculty members and students to work on rethinking the freshman year, with some relation between their work and that of another group considering how the freshman year develops into the sophomore year. This would be linked to plans for the junior and senior years, with students drawn into the planning from each of the years in view of the recency of their experience and the degree of their talent and interest. In the case of the freshman year, many of the universities have their only connection with the high schools through the admissions office, in the review of transcripts and sometimes interviews with candidates. In some cases, the universities invite high school students to come to the campus for a day's visit, or they show films in the high schools and before community groups of football games or documentaries about the university. In other cases, in connection with some of the new programs for the relatively unprepared entrants, summer sessions are arranged to get the new students ready for entry in the fall.

An extension of the idea of linking each year of education with its preceding one, and the idea of involving students in the university curriculum, would entail the appointment of students, with an appropriate stipend, not merely to the faculty admissions committee, but to a student admissions staff drawn from a list of students recommended by the faculty. These students could visit local high schools, possibly taking a sabbatical leave during the first semester of the sophomore or junior year; they could visit high school classes, talk to the students and teachers there, and lead discussions of the courses and programs presently available to freshman students, and of other ones which the high school students would like to see organized in view of what they have already learned in high school and what they would most like to do when they first enter the university.

From the body of material collected by the student-traveller and reports made to the student-faculty committee on the freshman year, ideas for patterns of study and programs could be developed for the entering freshmen, each of whom could be asked to prepare for himself a study plan, or general outline of courses and their content, to be included among other materials presented as qualification for admission. Or the applicants could be asked to join with other students in the high school who were applying for admission, and to organize groups among themselves, on the basis of common interests, to develop ideas for projects and areas of study in which they would like to work during their freshman year at the university.

A program of this kind would have a direct effect in stimulating some new educational thinking among students and teachers in the high school about what to do with the junior and senior years aside from carrying out the obligatory academic exercises necessary to meet the present admissions requirements. There could emerge from this an internal curriculum in the high school through which the students, in order to improve their qualifications for admission to the university, could work with elementary and junior high school students as tutors and assistant teachers. Again, the rationale, as in the case of the graduate students, is that the best way to learn how to organize one's own education is to learn how to help others with theirs.

This could then serve a double purpose for the university. It would give to the faculty members who were planning the freshman year some fresh and interesting material for use in developing the freshman curriculum. It would help the admissions office to select the most promising students for admission, not exclusively in terms of their grades, rank in class, and academic credits, but by reference to the level of their intellectual interests and capacities, their talent for self-education, their potential contribution to the student community, their potential ability as teachers, community workers, artists, educational aides, and reformers once they arrived at the university.

The student appointee to the staff of the admissions office and the admissions committee, working with the committee on the freshman year, could review the study plans of high school students, along with the other admissions material from the applicants, some of which would be coming from students in the schools he had visited and whom he would know. From that material the student staff member could present ideas to the committee on the freshman year for various kinds of grouping within fields of study, distributing the freshmen throughout the university in terms of their interests, and organizing the teaching program around them.

One of the assignments for the entering freshmen could be to a seminar of the kind I have already suggested, similar to the exploratory courses taught at Sarah Lawrence by the faculty, to which freshmen are assigned on the basis of the account they have given of their past education and study plans in the admissions materials submitted to the college. The purpose of the exploratory course at Sarah Lawrence is to give a central place in the freshman year to each student, a place where, with whatever help and advice is needed from the teacher of the course, the student can explore the methods and materials for learning in an area of his interest and can raise a variety of questions on topics of concern, ranging from problems in handling the college life to issues of college policy or public affairs.

This kind of seminar provides the common intellectual experience for which the curriculum-makers have been in search, along with a sense of identification with the university, by the directly personal way in which the freshman seminar conducts its business, and the possibility of coming to know intimately and in the setting of a university class other students with similar interests and similar problems. In our experience at Sarah Lawrence, the exploratory course gave to each student a place to begin, a set of intellectual companions, and a central person in the faculty to whom one could go for advice and help on any matter connected with the experience of being in college.

When graduate students and upperclassmen are involved in advising and teaching this kind of freshman seminar, and sophomores and others are involved in the work of the admissions committee and the development of the freshman year, they create a completely new style of educational thinking. They bring to their colleagues in the faculty a wealth of empirical knowledge about students, and educational thinking can proceed on the basis of that knowledge rather than on generalizations about the student as an abstraction. They break down the barriers which separate the academic faculty from the student body, and introduce the idea of the learning-teaching community to replace the concept of the manufactured curriculum taught by hired hands.

They also produce a way of bridging the gap between the administration and the students, by carrying out some of the administrative tasks in cooperation with the administrators. In the case of the student members of the admissions staff, for example, there is no reason why such students should not correspond with high school applicants about their study plans, and prepare mimeographed material which would be useful to the high school student in understanding what would be expected of him when he comes to the university, and what he could expect to find available to him once he arrives there. Entering students can then learn to identify the university with its student body and not simply with its officials and their official pronouncements.

The same kind of approach through student-faculty planning can be taken to the sophomore year, with the returning sophomores asked to prepare preliminary study plans for themselves during the spring of the freshman year. Student members of the student-faculty committee staff could work during the summertime on the collation of the student plans into general outlines of possible courses, projects, and study groups, for use by the faculty in preparing the sophomore course offerings. In the case of the junior and senior years, when most students want to work in a major field, something approximating the student Council of Majors recommended by the Berkeley Commission on University Governance could be organized to work with the departments in making plans for courses in special fields of study.

Liberal allowances of choice could be made for students not yet ready for a full commitment to a specialized field; their programs could include a wider spread of courses, independent study under the supervision of graduate students, or work on a student research team with similar supervision. Not only would this keep the departments in touch with the changing needs of their clientele, but it would give them the benefit of many new ideas for undergraduate course offerings and different forms of organization, while linking their graduate students to the problems of the scholar-teacher.

In this way, from the freshman to the senior year and beyond, a new and sizeable internal network of student teachers and policymakers would be created on a university-wide scale. There would then be a basis for a far greater cohesion of interest in the student body as a whole and a wealth of opportunity for the undergraduates to combine forces among themselves in creating their own education and in finding close associates and colleagues who shared their interests. Out of that network can come the formal structure of student involvement in basic university policy questions, by elections from the student body, by nominations from both the students and faculty for appointments of students to the faculty bodies, administrative committees, and staff of the university. Through the existence of this internal structure, the primary elements of a true community of learning would have been assembled to carry out the tasks in which it is the business of that community to engage itself.

[IV]

The task of reform in education and society has no end, but only new beginnings. Reform goes on, planned or unplanned, in one way or another way, usually at a pace many years behind the need, by the efforts of those few who cannot be satisfied with what they find, and look for better ways, and by the necessities of historical change which keep pressing upon all institutions and testing their capacity for alteration and survival.

This is the first age in which so many untamed and unmanageable necessities have been pressing all at once, and the first age in which the historical circumstances have combined to produce a younger generation so fully aware of those circumstances. In other times it was possible to say that that is the way things go in the universities. The students enter and leave, the society changes and moves on, the universities stay at the quiet center, giving the mind its due, keeping the ideals of civilization alive.

It is clear that this is no longer a possible attitude, although the necessity for the quiet center continues to exist, and the protection of the ideals of civilization was never more urgent or necessary. The difference now is that the university is already engaged with the necessities and must act to engage itself with them now, on its own terms, without the time to speculate, but only time to confront. The society will not stand still, even to be studied and observed. It insists on acting.

In this situation of the university, once more the students are its greatest allies, and if some of them have declared themselves to be its enemies, let them be met by those in the universities who know and can teach that the real enemy of the university is ignorance, force, and violence, and that the way to overcome these is by knowledge, a passion for justice, and a commitment to truth.

For it is in the ideal of a community of concerned persons who share a common interest in the life of the mind and the quality of human experience that the genius of the university lies. The rest is a matter of how that community can best be constructed by the best efforts of all concerned. There is nobility and strength in the lovely old words "fraternity," "equality," "liberty and justice for all"—and the university is the place where these words can become names for the living experience of those within its environs. Unless the reality of that experience is to be found there, it is unlikely to be found in the larger world. Unless students learn through what they do there that equality is a two-edged sword, that fraternity means giving part of oneself away, that liberty is an affectionate state of mind, and that justice in a democracy is willingness to be faithful in action to agreed-upon principles, all the protest, controversy, radical action, and appeal to the big abstractions of moral enthusiasm will come to nothing but a continual attrition of the very ideals of which the young are in search.

That is why education and the university must both be redefined so that they may become instruments through which the influence of persons on each other may act to secure the elevation of spirit and quality of life which it is the purpose of all education to induce. The university should be a place where students help their teachers to teach them, where teachers help their students to learn, where administrators help both to accomplish what they have come together to do. That is why the role of the students must also be redefined, in order to make clear to them and to all others that students *are* the foundation of the university, that when everything else is taken away, as in fact it can be—the government contracts, the isolated research institutes, the alumni bodies, the services to industry, the travelling faculty, the organization men— what is left are persons working together to learn and to teach.

Learning and teaching in this sense have to do with the totality of human conduct, in which the conduct of the affairs of the mind is by turns political, social, public, private, intellectual, emotional, external, internal, and, in the last analysis, personal. Otherwise conduct has no meaning, the human act is stripped of motivation, empty of content, lacking in truth.

The education of students, therefore, means nothing less than their personal involvement in the conduct of the affairs of the mind. An equality of position in the polity of the community is a necessary condition of their involvement; otherwise they are playing a game the necessity for whose rules they never learn to understand—the commitment to play is never completely made. What the world needs above all is a large and increasing supply of incorruptibles, men and women who have learned to act in the interest of mankind, who are capable of noble action as an outcome of unpremeditated thought, and are capable of clarity of thought as a natural and intuitive result of their experience in thinking and in acting. It is the responsibility of the university so to arrange its affairs that the experience of its students in thinking and acting can teach them what it means to serve mankind and what it means to honor the intellect.

PART THREE

BLACK AND WHITE IN AMERICA

During the 1950's and 1960's, the conflict between the races emerged as one of the central issues of our time—perhaps the most important issue facing Americans in the twentieth century. America has had a long, and not very admirable, history of poor race relations: the American Indians have been the victims of white racism ever since their land was taken over, and, more recently, the Mexican-Americans have suffered from the prejudices of racial injustice and intolerance. But throughout the history of our country, racial hatred has been most strongly directed against those who were first brought to this land in 1619 to serve as slaves, the blacks. With riots in our cities, conflicts in our neighborhoods, tensions in our schools, America is now paying the debt for the centuries of hypocrisy which enabled her people to proclaim liberty and justice for all, while meaning liberty and justice for whites only.

The conflict between the races has resulted in tensions that are threatening to poison nearly every area of our national life. These tensions have often broken out into violence, wrecking delicate relationships, breaking up neighborhoods, destroying parts of our cities. One of the largest outbreaks of violence occurred in our cities during the summer of 1967. Following these civil disorders, President Johnson appointed a commission to discover the causes of the rioting and destruction. Within a few months the commission delivered its report, finding that "white racism is essentially responsible for the explosive mixture which has been accumulating in our cities since the end of World War II." While the findings of this commission have been disputed by many, including Jeffrey Hart in his essay, "Violence in America: The Negro in the City," it cannot be denied that racism still exists. The lesson of burning cities and slain citizens, of continued injustice and continued inequality—though taught so often in the past two decades—has not yet been learned. How we can exist in America, together and equal, still stands as one of our greatest problems, and presents one of the greatest challenges of the 1970's.

In the 1950's and early 1960's, the civil rights movement seemed to offer the most effective tool for combating racism; those supporting it believed that through nonviolent means they could convince their fellow Americans that freedom, justice, and equality should be shared by all men. The movement was not without its accomplishments: it was instrumental in stirring the conscience of the nation, and it changed the lives of many who were supporting it, as Alice Walker in "The Civil Rights Movement: What Good Was It?" so effectively describes. But, while achieving some of its goals, the civil rights movement was unable to move quickly enough to bring about the reforms which impatient blacks were justifiably demanding. Many blacks, disillusioned by the feeble attempts at integration, were demanding separation—separation with equal rights and equal power. This new demand for power and for the recognition of a separate black culture forced an even greater wedge between blacks and whites, so that at the end of the decade the polarization between the races seemed to be even greater than at its beginning.

The term "black power" has thus increasingly supplanted the cry for civil rights as a means for bringing about racial justice. In "Black Power: Its Need and Substance," Stokely Carmichael and Charles Hamilton define this term and discuss the kind of meaning it now has for some blacks. But the black power movement, like the civil rights movement, has met with much opposition. There are many blacks who do not share Carmichael and Hamilton's views, still believing that their aims can be achieved through less militant means. There are also many whites who resent any show of power or any initative on the part of those whom they have suppressed for so long. Finally, there are those, such as Christopher Lasch, who criticize the black power movement on a more sophisticated level, being disturbed by the militants' lack of adequate programs for the use of their power, and by the lack of a proper sense of responsibility, which they believe should accompany that power.

Power is one way to achieve one's goals; education is another. In the late 1960's, power was exerted to provide better educational opportunities for blacks, whose education has been systematically suppressed since their youth. On many campuses black studies programs were established, responding to the desire for a greater knowledge of black history and black culture. These programs have fulfilled a real need, and have enabled many blacks to gain a sense of identity and a greater pride in themselves, as DeVere Pentony points out in "The Case for Black Studies." But the programs have also been criticized by some who argue that blacks should concentrate on economic elevation rather than on spiritual or cultural enrichment, warning that a degree in black studies is poor preparation for participation in a complex, multiracial society.

Black power and black studies are only two approaches among the many that will likely be tried during the years ahead in an attempt to solve our racial problems. It is quite clear that these two approaches will not be enough. It is also clear that the solutions to our racial problems cannot come entirely from the blacks; all Americans must avoid living by the clichés of racial prejudice and must seek to eradicate the causes of a racism that is destroying our national life like a cancer.

Racism is therefore an issue affecting every American. How we deal with the problems created by our racial differences will largely determine whether the 1970's will be volatile or peaceful; whether we will see the emergence of the brotherhood of men; or whether we will be seeped in further conflict and turmoil. our hatreds increased, our cities burned, our spirits sapped. The problems of race matter to every one of us because we cannot expect to live humane lives, lives of dignity and decency, in a strife-torn country where two societies—separate and unequal—continue to exist.

THE PROBLEM

> *"Our nation is moving toward two societies, one black, one white—separate and unequal."*
>
> from the *Report of the National Advisory Commission on Civil Disorders*

WHITE MAN IN HARLEM
Peter Schrag

In an attempt to penetrate the black world, a white man goes to Harlem, which he believes "has become the forge of cultural and political styles and attitudes that shape Negro and white life everywhere in America." Peter Schrag is editor of *Change*, a magazine devoted to the problems of higher education, and the author of *Voices in the Classroom* and *Village School Downtown*.

Every white man is a stranger in Harlem. But any one of us who remains there too long or goes too often also becomes a stranger to his own place and perhaps to himself, a man unhinged, wondering now if Harlem is real or just the creature of a literary imagination, wondering again if anything else is real or if the rest of the world is the dream, and its inhabitants the dreamers.

For more than a year I have been making the crossing: downtown-uptown, uptown-downtown, and from the cool commuter trains of the New York Central to the intensity of 125th Street, traversing a psychic barrier that has no parallel in ordinary transformations of awareness. No matter how often it is done, each crossing makes one a racial alien whose skin betrays his mind. After two days in the ghetto I begin to feel as though the commuters on the White Plains local are a race apart, a distant culture. And each return to Harlem is a reminder of another estrangement, the white man in the black town, fearful and uncertain, trying to determine how—and if—any of his brothers and predecessors managed, under similar circumstances, to remain untouched.

To believe that Harlem really exists is to learn the horror of being white in contemporary America. I am not speaking here of guilt, or of the uncertainties produced by the varied responses of the black men and women one encounters: How much is guile and con, how much rage, how much envy or affection? How much is sheer disdain for a white man also become invisible? Talk about three hundred years of slavery and oppression doesn't stir—in me—any feeling of racial culpability. I want to be honored with a personal indictment, and perhaps have earned it, but if an angry man attacks me on some black street, it will be the absurd murder of someone who is being tried but does not yet feel convicted.

I came trying to understand the community and what it teaches its children and adults, and have learned a great deal, but I still don't understand, and feel now that I probably never shall. Yet I have come to terms with Harlem, and in doing so I discover that the place has become part of the furniture of my consciousness, become part of me. I have the rage without the suffering that would establish my right to have it. I assume that this is not unique; there must be hundreds of whites who have become psychic or racial nomads in this country; you meet them on the periphery of community-action programs and in tutoring centers, survivors of a civil rights movement working diligently to demonstrate loyalty to a cause which has a growing desire to declare them superfluous.

The horror derives from the fact that insofar as race defines any set of social problems in America, the action, vitality, and initiative—and hence the freedom—are black. What this means, I think, is that black power has not only established itself as an idea, but that it has already begun to turn the psychic tables on the whites. Liberal intellectuals have always had a tenuous kinship with my commuters, rarely identified with television heroes, and have certainly ceased to regard the history of Western civilization as an uninterrupted chronicle of ascending triumphs. In some respects, surely, they are as alien to white culture as the black kids who have so little common ground with the official world. Yet I think that what scares the liberals most is the real possibility that black power has begun to steal their virulence and courage. (That is, of course, also what scares them about student revolts.) They are supposed to be the initiators, the critics, the cranks. The blacks are forcing them into that—for them—most revolting of positions: defense of the Establishment.

Harlem is the source. Certainly it is a black ghetto like many others, and surely it is neither the largest nor the worst (whatever that means) among them. Detroit and Watts have demonstrated that sociological statistics and community programs devised by political officials are sorry indicators of good and bad in ghetto conditions. (Those conditions are, in many cases, defined by the attitudes and practices of the world outside. I doubt if Harlem would be regarded as a slum in Calcutta.) Nonetheless, Harlem is *it*. Harlem is the capital, the spiritual home of black men, even if they never left the plantation. "Harlem," wrote Harold Cruse in *The Crisis of the Negro Intellectual,* "is the black world's key community for historical, political, economic, cultural and/or ethnic reasons. The trouble is that Harlem has never been adequately analyzed in such terms. The demand often heard—'Break up the Harlem ghetto!'" (as a hated symbol of segregation)—represents nothing but the romantic and empty wail of politically insolvent integrationists, who fear ghetto riots only more than they fear the responsibilities of political and economic power that lie in the Harlem potential . . ." Harlem had (and to some extent still has) a culture that now flows into the mainstream. The jazz has gone downtown, the old Savoy has long disappeared, replaced by a supermarket. Langston Hughes is dead; Ralph Ellison lives on the West Side and belongs to the Century Club; James Baldwin, not long ago described as being "as angry as a man can get," has a million-dollar book contract. And if you want to see Nina or Ella or Harry Belafonte, your chances are better at the Persian Room than at the Apollo on 125th Street.

Still, Harlem is the source. It has provided America with its social vocabulary, its musical idiom, with a worldly self-awareness beyond the ebullient cliches of history. In its fusion of Southern and urban modes, in its distillation of suffering and the consciousness of suffering, in its ducts to New York's literary and intellectual sensibilities, it has become the forge of cultural and political styles and attitudes that shape Negro —and white—life everywhere in America. Harlem has begun to restore humility to affluence, humanity to arrogance. It threatens to take American life out of its polyethylene sterility, to introduce to it the tragic, the absurd, the imponderable. For the first time we are beginning to suspect that suffering is not a problem but a condition.

Harlem has no beginning or end. It has been said that Harlem starts in Alabama and Trinidad, and that it extends to the suburbs of Los An-

geles and the jungles of Vietnam. Part of what makes it peculiar to New
Yorkers is not Negro but Southern; part of what makes it confusing is
not black but American. There are Mississippi whites who have felt more
at home on Lenox Avenue than native New York liberals who live just
a few blocks away. Columbia University, separated from the black community by a narrow park, topographical elevation, and some real estate
maneuvers, is more distant than Yoknapatawpha County. Harlem's religion, its penchant for high life, and its violence germinated in the black
soil of the South, not on the pavements of the city.

In many respects it is not a place at all, certainly not a community,
despite the rhetoric of those militants who like to talk of what "the
community wants." More than anything it is a state of mind, and we
have all become its carriers. The American panic about crime in the
streets, about urban riots, indicates that one no longer has to go there to
be there. Harlem's uncertainty about itself—about whether it wants to
be in or out, whether it will be violent or docile, whether there is value
in being middle class—is also my uncertainty. Although I don't know
what I would like it to be, it has become too much part of me to leave
it alone. One can penetrate through layers of romance about black culture and statistics of deprivation and arrive at a blank wall whose only
escape is bias. Because Harlem is America, part of its mounting anger
can be attributed to *its* inability to escape, and to the fact that much of
its nationalistic liturgy won't serve as anything but a temporary incanta-
tion against white devils. We are, in short, prisoners together, each defining himself by the other, neither of us complete by himself.

The problem of Harlem is, immediately, the problem of cacoph-
ony, of filtering sound from noise, of distinguishing the Aesopian from
the sociological, of separating passion from propaganda. Every conversation, every street scene, every sidewalk pitchman throws up a cosmos,
angry, sycophantic, conspiratorial, insulting, amusing, style against
style, rhythm against rhythm: Muslims in brocaded caps, men in tur-
quoise pants and orange shirts, women in rhinestone slacks, children
dodging traffic to fly kites, playing basketball with peach baskets hung
on the fire escapes, souped-up checker games in the playgrounds, leaf-
lets, *Muhammad Speaks,* CORE, Urban League, numbers, the Su-
premes and James Brown and Aretha Franklin from the record store
loudspeakers, Brother Lewis Michaud in the back of his African nationalist bookstore, telling how "the politicians pacify, the preachers
sanctify, and the white man crucifies."

The preachers and the spiritualists grow rank—Madam Martha and
Sister Marie, Bishops of the World, prophets, healers, pitchmen—
rhetoricians of the gospel, sellers of indulgences, tough-talking Mau
Maus, foghorned mamas, pushers and pushed, a jungle of organizations
and committees, sects and movements. In the gothic novel one would

make his way through these peripheries to some dark heart, an inner secret, but here there is no secret, and that, in itself, is Harlem's most intimate possession.

Harlem is a collection—layers, networks, labyrinths—the dark alley of the American spirit—and to an outsider it is just as confounding as the Casbah or the Sicilian village. In part it suffers from sociological pollution—a territory covered by the muddy tracks of welfare investigators, professors, journalists, counting heads, making notes, asking questions, seeking symptoms and cures of a disease that draws its poison from other places and other roots. The basic statistics are simple, and we can all recite them: 300,000 souls, give or take a few thousands who bob below the vision of the census, a fourth of them without jobs, with broken families, poor education, poor housing, poor health—but they obfuscate more than they clarify because they flatten complexity and variety into a useless average. Despite the growing anger, despite the put-ons, one can still feel accepted, can be received into homes and hear stories of ambitions and struggles, can attend meetings and services, yet never get more than a fragmentary map of the community, a view through a hole in the ice.

The block, not the neighborhood, defines, for most people, the limits of place and belonging. The woman who has lived for a decade on 119th Street will never move—if she has a choice—because, as she tells you, "Here I feel safe." She will defend that block; any change imposed by the outside is likely to be for the worse. When urban renewal comes, it not only puts human beings out of familiar surroundings, it also destroys sources of strength and familiarity, old associations, and established patterns of life. The junkies and winos move to the next block; new protective habits must be developed. Every child in Harlem masters the streets and alleys of his neighborhood, knows every store and often every resident. "When I was a kid," said a Harlem teacher, "I could walk around my neighborhood blindfolded."

Within such settings there develops a local leadership—block leadership—that never registers on the radar screens of the outside world. These are the people who take care of the kids next door, raise money for the funeral or to ship the body down South, and who staff the networks of neighborhood councils, parents organizations, and protest committees that lace every precinct. There are no questions that one can ask of them. What they can communicate we already know. What we should learn they cannot tell us. Where they are lame we are blind. For them black power is beside the point. There is, after all, nothing else; there never has been. Certainly they have not survived on white justice, or even on white charity.

It is a place of environs and styles—in fashion, in speech, in architecture—but one of its central facts, it seems to me, is style itself

—a thing done with grace and flourish—Willie Mays catching a fly ball, an elegant riff on the trumpet, an outfit that stops the show. It is the curious impression that, for its size and poverty, Harlem seems to be full of establishments that rent tuxedos. On Upper Fifth Avenue it is a woman in a green pants suit, green shoes, and black derby hat walking a poodle, and two blocks away, in the playground at 142nd and Lenox, it is the beat and speed of a checker game, one of several surrounded by spectators, where the *click, click, click* of the jumping pieces plays a counterpoint to the separate monologues of the players. "Now what you want me to do?" *Click, click.* "Now what you want me to do?" *Click, click.* "I'll take care of that one later." *Click, click, click.* A double jump, *click, click,* answered by a triple jump, *click, click, click* and "Crown me!"

The style of Harlem is in the pride young boys develop in their toughness, in their ability to withstand pain without complaint, in the joy and laughter of children, in the mastery of the hustler, and in the uninhibited phrase-making of a street orator. "Around here," said a young resident, "they got guys that can sell you anything, and if they got nothin' to sell, they'll try to sell you nothin'. They have this con; they learned it from the masters. I remember a guy who was trying to sell a man a miff—a miff, now what the hell is that? Why there ain't no such thing. Why the hell doesn't General Motors hire these con men to sell cars? They've got the best experience in the world."

Style, I suspect, is one of the ultimate defenses against the all-too-insistent brutality of discrimination and disregard. Sharp clothes, if they serve no other purpose, make poverty bearable, may symbolize a small beachhead on the shores of affluence. For all of us, the automobile talks back to boredom and emptiness, promises escape, even if it never delivers. More important, however, Harlem is a repository of style and taste, not only in music and dance, but in clothes and *canapés* and floral arrangements. As a slave and servant, the American Negro learned the style of the aristocrat long before he learned to be middle class; he thus became, and to some extent still remains, the carrier of elegance and refinement in America. To claim this too stridently is to lay oneself open to accusations of romance from Marxist judges of social welfare. Yet surely we still live in a time when black maids and handymen, with all their aches and superstitions, often rescue suburban housewives by turning their domestic kitsch to culture.

If there is any continuity here—the sort of continuity that can be discerned by white eyes—it is in the interface between Soul and civilization. Each, it seems to me, is at war with itself, but each, more significantly, is at war with the other. Soul, finally, is anti-civilization, uncompromising passion, human instinct and experience before they have been subjugated and disciplined. Civilization is repressive, foreign, a white man's trick. Each of us, as Freud made clear, struggles with those issues, but Harlem—and the black revolt everywhere else—has given them new life and has extended their dimensions from the psychological to the political. Soul is not merely music or style or a form of black brotherhood; it is human reality uncontaminated by social demand and sociological strategy. Soul is, simultaneously, the dream of life before the fall—supremely American, the vision of the new man in a virgin land, free of the corruptions of the old world—*and* a statement of depths of experience and feeling that only fellow sufferers can understand. Either way, it stands apart from civilized convention, from civilization itself, questioning, challenging, demanding.

The struggle is not merely internal, though I suspect that anyone carrying a Molotov cocktail after the murder of Martin Luther King must have experienced it; it is also a contest between groups, styles of life, and varieties of commitment. "Everybody around here," said a young member of CORE, "is looking. The gutter types want to be grassroots types, the grassroots types want to be middle class, and the middle class wants to be white." There is a continuity between the bottom and the mainstream, but there is also resistance—Africanism, Black Awareness, schools of Swahili and a whole demonology cataloguing the deviltry of the white man. Speak to any three groups and you get three different versions of the universe, each of them certified to be The Real Black View. Nonetheless, they share what most of us have achieved only in the loftier reaches of rhetoric—an attempt to come to terms with an urban life for which America has yet to conceive a point of view.

If all this suggests that I regard Harlem as an exotic place, or that I ignore its shabbiness, its agonies, or its powerful middle-class ambitions, let me set the matter straight. Harlem is too American to be exempt from any of that; its anger does not derive from its other worldliness: We are not dealing with Indian mystics or medieval saints, but with American dreamers denied their frontier. The growing rage only makes sense in the context of hypocritical invitations and frustrated ambition. In cutting through to the bedrock of racism, it was inevitable that, as Eldridge Cleaver has said, leadership would eventually shift from the house niggers to the field niggers, from those whose position derived from a relationship with the master to those who had neither influence nor access to the established seats of power.

This means that, in the long run, the rhetoric will become more reliable, less manipulative, and, at the same time, harder to take. The test for the militants—the field niggers—will be in their ability to channel and control the violence of the community. That violence is not new, but, as Fanon and Malcolm X have pointed out, it was always directed against other victims of the oppressor's brutality, blacks killing blacks, turning their rage against each other, sparing the exploiter, and giving him new ground to assert his superiority. The leadership of nonviolence was buried with Martin Luther King. There is no one else left, except the young militants. For them, the problem is whether they can control their own neighborhoods or whether we will all be dealing with a mob.

Norman Mailer has written that the militant Negro "does not want equality any longer, he wants superiority, and he wants it because he feels he is in fact superior. And there is some justice on his side for believing it." Mailer continues:

Sufficiently fortunate to be alienated from the benefits of American civilization, the Negro seems to have been better able to keep his health. It would take a liberal with a psychotic sense of moderation to claim that whites and Negroes have equally healthy bodies; the Negroes know they have become on the average physically superior, and this *against all the logic of America's medical civilization*—the Negroes get less good food ostensibly, no vitamins, a paucity of antibiotics, less medical care, less fresh air, less light and sanitation in living quarters. Let us quit the list— it is parallel to another list one could make of educational opportunities vs. actual culture (which is to say—real awareness of one's milieu). The Negro's relatively low rate of literacy seems to be in inverse relation to his philosophical capacity to have a comprehensive vision of his life, a large remark whose only support is existential—let us brood, brothers, on the superior cool of the Negro in public places. For the cool comes from a comprehensive vision, a relaxation before the dangers of life, a readiness to meet death, philosophy or amusement at any turn.

Unless Mailer is referring to the smallest of minorities, he is not describing the people I have met and interviewed: housewives and block leaders trying to keep the junkies off the street and the cops honest; bankers promoting economic development; teachers talking about jobs and education and housing; community organizers checking food prices in supermarkets and installment interest rates on junk furniture. Harlem is not merely a reproach to the mainstream, a product of its atrocities, but also an affirmation. The private middle-class housing developments of Lenox Terrace and Riverbend, the elegance of the Stanford White houses on Strivers Row, the brownstones on Sugar Hill near City College make it abundantly clear that one part of militancy is a loud rap on the door to affluence. There are too many people who want in, who have college ambitions for their children, and who have become gymnasts on the exercise bars of the middle class to make Harlem exotic or to make Mailer's assertion acceptable.

What makes Mailer's statement notable is not what it says about black men but about whites, about the experience of being a white man in Harlem. We are no longer living in white America but in a country infiltrated by moral guerrillas demanding acceptance of our common fallibility. I know of no way that an ordinary white man can come to understand Harlem other than to understand the repressed and conflicting passions that he shares with its inhabitants. This is more than saying the Negro problem is a white problem, or that Harlem's resolution depends on Scarsdale. It is, rather, to confront those parts of our own lives that are unlivable, to see our own empty spaces. The problem is not the suburban community, but the suburban heart.

As a political philosophy, black power is, finally, a simple idea that smacks of nothing so much as Calhoun's doctrine of the concurrent majority. Where Calhoun wanted political parity for a minority of antebellum slave states, the black militant wants it for the Negro ghetto. But black power contains a moral component that makes it more than a political strategy. One of the most obvious and striking things about Harlem is the visible decay of the rural culture—religion, school, even family—that gave Negro life its tenuous stability in the South. What survives is the Jeffersonian reproach to urban brutality, and what grows from it is a search for an urban ethic beyond politics and welfare. The black militant scolds the white establishment in the tone and cadences of the black mammy, but what he demands is the kind of compensation that has value only if it hurts. The solution for Harlem is not the diversion of surplus wealth or an annual Saturday afternoon paint job, but shared suffering. In some way we must all learn to die for our sins. And to live and laugh again, too.

THE WHITE RACE AND ITS HEROES
Eldridge Cleaver

Until recently white Americans have only had a "white image" of their country, which, according to Eldridge Cleaver, has been a false image, full of distortions and contradictions. In this essay, however, he finds some hope for America in the youth who have begun to reject their white heroes and are abandoning the "American Way of Life." Cleaver was the first Minister of Information for the Black Panthers; he is now living abroad after allegedly violating his parole in California. A frequent contributor to *Ramparts,* he is the author of *Post Prison Writings and Speeches* and *Soul on Ice.*

White people cannot, in the generality, be taken as models of how to live. Rather, the white man is himself in sore need of new standards, which will release him from his confusion and place him once again in fruitful communion with the depths of his own being.

James Baldwin, *The Fire Next Time*

Right from the go, let me make one thing absolutely clear: I am not now, nor have I ever been, a white man. Nor, I hasten to add, am I now a Black Muslim—although I used to be. But I *am* an Ofay Watcher, a member of that unchartered, amorphous league which has members on all continents and the islands of the seas. Ofay Watchers Anonymous, we might be called, because we exist concealed in the shadows wherever colored people have known oppression by whites, by white enslavers, colonizers, imperialists, and neo-colonialists.

Did it irritate you, compatriot, for me to string those epithets out like that? Tolerate me. My intention was not necessarily to sprinkle salt over anyone's wounds. I did it primarily to relieve a certain pressure on my brain. Do you cop that? If not, then we're in trouble, because we Ofay Watchers have a pronounced tendency to slip into that mood. If it is bothersome to you, it is quite a task for me because not too long ago it was my way of life to preach, as ardently as I could, that the white race is a race of devils, created by their maker to do evil, and make evil appear as good; that the white race is the natural, unchangeable enemy of the black man, who is the original man, owner, maker, cream of the planet Earth; that the white race was soon to be destroyed by Allah, and that the black man would then inherit the earth, which has always, in fact, been his.

I have, so to speak, washed my hands in the blood of the martyr, Malcolm X, whose retreat from the precipice of madness created new room for others to turn about in, and I am now caught up in that tiny space, attempting a maneuver of my own. Having renounced the teachings of Elijah Muhammad, I find that a rebirth does not follow automatically, of its own accord, that a void is left in one's vision, and this void seeks constantly to obliterate itself by pulling one back to one's former outlook. I have tried a tentative compromise by adopting a select vocabulary, so that now when I see the whites of *their* eyes, instead of saying "devil" or "beast" I say "imperialist" or "colonialist," and everyone seems to be happier.

In silence, we have spent our years watching the ofays, trying to understand them, on the principle that you have a better chance coping with the known than with the unknown. Some of us have been, and some still are, interested in learning whether it is *ultimately* possible to live in the same territory with people who seem so disagreeable to live with; still others want to get as far away from ofays as possible. What we share in common is the desire to break the ofays' power over us.

At times of fundamental social change, such as the era in which we live, it is easy to be deceived by the onrush of events, beguiled by the craving for social stability into mistaking transitory phenomena for enduring reality. The strength and permanence of "white backlash" in America is just such an illusion. However much this rear-guard action might seem to grow in strength, the initiative, and the future, rest with those whites and blacks who have liberated themselves from the master/slave syndrome. And these are to be found mainly among the youth.

Over the past twelve years there has surfaced a political conflict between the generations that is deeper, even, than the struggle between the races. Its first dramatic manifestation was within the ranks of the Negro people, when college students in the South, fed up with Uncle Tom's hat-in-hand approach to revolution, threw off the yoke of the NAACP. When these students initiated the first sit-ins, their spirit spread like a raging fire across the nation, and the technique of non-violent direct action, constantly refined and honed into a sharp cutting tool, swiftly matured. The older Negro "leaders," who are now all die-hard advocates of this tactic, scolded the students for sitting-in. The students rained down contempt upon their hoary heads. In the pre-sit-in days, these conservative leaders had always succeeded in putting down insurgent elements among the Negro people. (A measure of their power, prior to the students' rebellion, is shown by their success in isolating such great black men as the late W. E. B. DuBois and Paul Robeson, when these stalwarts, refusing to bite their tongues, lost favor with the U.S. government by their unstinting efforts to link up the Negro revolution with national liberation movements around the world.)

The "Negro leaders," and the whites who depended upon them to control their people, were outraged by the impudence of the students. Calling for a moratorium on student initiative, they were greeted instead by an encore of sit-ins, and retired to their ivory towers to contemplate the new phenomenon. Others, less prudent because held on a tighter leash by the whites, had their careers brought to an abrupt end because they thought they could lead a black/white backlash against the students, only to find themselves in a kind of Bay of Pigs. Negro college presidents, who expelled students from all-Negro colleges in an attempt to quash the demonstrations, ended up losing their jobs; the victorious students would no longer allow them to preside over the campuses. The spontaneous protests on southern campuses over the repressive measures of their college administrations were an earnest of the Free Speech upheaval which years later was to shake the UC campus at Berkeley. In countless ways, the rebellion of the black students served as catalyst for the brewing revolt of the whites.

What has suddenly happened is that the white race has lost its heroes. Worse, its heroes have been revealed as villains and its greatest heroes as the arch-villains. The new generations of whites, appalled by the sanguine and despicable record carved over the face of the globe by their race in the last five hundred years, are rejecting the panoply of white heroes, whose heroism consisted in erecting the inglorious edifice of colonialism and imperialism; heroes whose careers rested on a system of foreign and domestic exploitation, rooted in the myth of white supremacy and the manifest destiny of the white race. The emerging shape of a new world order, and the requisites for survival in such a world, are fostering in young whites a new outlook. They recoil in shame from the spectacle of cowboys and pioneers—their heroic forefathers whose exploits filled earlier generations with pride—galloping across a movie screen shooting down Indians like Coke bottles. Even Winston Churchill, who is looked upon by older whites as perhaps the greatest hero of the twentieth century—even he, because of the system of which he was a creature and which he served, is an arch-villain in the eyes of the young white rebels.

At the close of World War Two, national liberation movements in the colonized world picked up new momentum and audacity, seeking to cash in on the democratic promises made by the Allies during the war. The Atlantic Charter, signed by President Roosevelt and Prime Minister Churchill in 1941, affirming "the right of all people to choose the form of government under which they may live," established the principle, although it took years of postwar struggle to give this piece of rhetoric even the appearance of reality. And just as world revolution has prompted the oppressed to re-evaluate their self-image in terms of the changing conditions, to slough off the servile attitudes inculcated by long years of subordination, the same dynamics of change have prompted the white people of the world to re-evaluate their self-image as well, to disabuse themselves of the Master Race psychology developed over centuries of imperial hegemony.

It is among the white youth of the world that the greatest change is taking place. It is they who are experiencing the great psychic pain of waking into consciousness to find their inherited heroes turned by events into villains. Communication and understanding between the older and younger generations of whites has entered a crisis. The elders, who, in the tradition of privileged classes or races, genuinely do not understand the youth, trapped by old ways of thinking and blind to the future, have only just begun to be vexed—because the youth have only just begun to rebel. So thoroughgoing is the revolution in the psyches of white youth that the traditional tolerance which every older generation has found it necessary to display is quickly exhausted, leaving a gulf of fear, hostility, mutual misunderstanding, and contempt.

The rebellion of the oppressed peoples of the world, along with the Negro revolution in America, have opened the way to a new evaluation of history, a re-examination of the role played by the white race since the beginning of European expansion. The positive achievements are also there in the record, and future generations will applaud them. But there can be no applause now, not while the master still holds the whip

in his hand! Not even the master's own children can find it possible to
applaud him—he cannot even applaud himself! The negative rings too
loudly. Slave-catchers, slaveowners, murderers, butchers, invaders,
oppressors—the white heroes have acquired new names. The great
white statesmen whom school children are taught to revere are revealed
as the architects of systems of human exploitation and slavery. Religious leaders are exposed as condoners and justifiers of all these evil
deeds. Schoolteachers and college professors are seen as a clique of
brainwashers and whitewashers.

The white youth of today are coming to see, intuitively, that to escape the onus of the history their fathers made they must face and
admit the moral truth concerning the works of their fathers. That such
venerated figures as George Washington and Thomas Jefferson owned
hundreds of black slaves, that all of the Presidents up to Lincoln presided over a slave state, and that every President since Lincoln connived
politically and cynically with the issues affecting the human rights and
general welfare of the broad masses of the American people—these
facts weigh heavily upon the hearts of these young people.

The elders do not like to give these youngsters credit for being able
to understand what is going on and what has gone on. When speaking
of juvenile delinquency, or the rebellious attitude of today's youth, the
elders employ a glib rhetoric. They speak of the "alienation of youth,"
the desire of the young to be independent, the problems of "the father
image" and "the mother image" and their effect upon growing children
who lack sound models upon which to pattern themselves. But they consider it bad form to connect the problems of the youth with the central
event of our era—the national liberation movements abroad and the
Negro revolution at home. The foundations of authority have been
blasted to bits in America because the whole society has been indicted,
tried, and convicted of injustice. To the youth, the elders are Ugly
Americans; to the elders, the youth have gone mad.

The rebellion of the white youth has gone through four broadly discernible stages. First there was an initial recoiling away, a rejection of
the conformity which America expected, and had always received,
sooner or later, from its youth. The disaffected youth were refusing to
participate in the system, having discovered that America, far from
helping the underdog, was up to its ears in the mud trying to hold the
dog down. Because of the publicity and self-advertisements of the more
vocal rebels, this period has come to be known as the beatnik era, although not all of the youth affected by these changes thought of themselves as beatniks. The howl of the beatniks and their scathing, outraged
denunciation of the system—characterized by Ginsberg as Moloch, a
bloodthirsty Semitic deity to which the ancient tribes sacrificed their
firstborn children—was a serious, irrevocable declaration of war. It is

revealing that the elders looked upon the beatniks as mere obscene misfits who were too lazy to take baths and too stingy to buy a haircut. The
elders had eyes but couldn't see, ears but couldn't hear—not even when
the message came through as clearly as in this remarkable passage from
Jack Kerouac's *On the Road:*

> At lilac evening I walked with every muscle aching among the lights of
> 27th and Welton in the Denver colored section, wishing I were a Negro,
> feeling that the best the white world had offered was not enough ecstasy for
> me, not enough life, joy, kicks, darkness, music, not enough night. I wished
> I were a Denver Mexican, or even a poor overworked Jap, anything but
> what I so drearily was, a "white man" disillusioned. All my life I'd had
> white ambitions. . . . I passed the dark porches of Mexican and Negro
> homes; soft voices were there, occasionally the dusky knee of some mysteri-
> ous sensuous gal; the dark faces of the men behind rose arbors. Little chil-
> dren sat like sages in ancient rocking chairs.

The second stage arrived when these young people, having decided emphatically that the world, and particularly the U.S.A., was unacceptable
to them in its present form, began an active search for roles they could
play in changing the society. If many of these young people were content to lay up in their cool beat pads, smoking pot and listening to jazz
in a perpetual orgy of esoteric bliss, there were others, less crushed by
the system, who recognized the need for positive action. Moloch could
not ask for anything more than to have its disaffected victims withdraw
into safe, passive, apolitical little nonparticipatory islands, in an economy less and less able to provide jobs for the growing pool of unemployed. If all the unemployed had followed the lead of the beatniks,
Moloch would gladly have legalized the use of euphoric drugs and marijuana, passed out free jazz albums and sleeping bags, to all those willing
to sign affidavits promising to remain "beat." The non-beat disenchanted white youth were attracted magnetically to the Negro revolution, which had begun to take on a mass, insurrectionary tone. But they
had difficulty understanding their relationship to the Negro, and what
role "whites" could play in a "Negro revolution." For the time being
they watched the Negro activists from afar.

The third stage, which is rapidly drawing to a close, emerged when
white youth started joining Negro demonstrations in large numbers. The
presence of whites among the demonstrators emboldened the Negro
leaders and allowed them to use tactics they never would have been able
to employ with all-black troops. The racist conscience of America is
such that murder does not register as murder, really, unless the victim is
white. And it was only when the newspapers and magazines started
carrying pictures and stories of white demonstrators being beaten and
maimed by mobs and police that the public began to protest. Negroes
have become so used to this double standard that they, too, react differently to the death of a white. When white freedom riders were brutal-

ized along with blacks, a sigh of relief went up from the black masses, because the blacks knew that white blood is the coin of freedom in a land where for four hundred years black blood has been shed unremarked and with impunity. America has never truly been outraged by the murder of a black man, woman, or child. White politicians may, if Negroes are aroused by a particular murder, say with their lips what they know with their minds they should feel with their hearts—but don't.

It is a measure of what the Negro feels that when the two white and one black civil rights workers were murdered in Mississippi in 1964, the event was welcomed by Negroes on a level of understanding beyond and deeper than the grief they felt for the victims and their families. This welcoming of violence and death to whites can almost be heard— indeed it can be heard—in the inevitable words, oft repeated by Negroes, that those whites, and blacks, do not die in vain. So it was with Mrs. Viola Liuzzo. And much of the anger which Negroes felt toward Martin Luther King during the Battle of Selma stemmed from the fact that he denied history a great moment, never to be recaptured, when he turned tail on the Edmund Pettus Bridge and refused to all those whites behind him what they had traveled thousands of miles to receive. If the police had turned them back by force, all those nuns, priests, rabbis, preachers, and distinguished ladies and gentlemen old and young—as they had done the Negroes a week earlier—the violence and brutality of the system would have been ruthlessly exposed. Or if, seeing King determined to lead them on to Montgomery, the troopers had stepped aside to avoid precisely the confrontation that Washington would not have tolerated, it would have signaled the capitulation of the militant white South. As it turned out, the March on Montgomery was a show of somewhat dim luster, stage-managed by the Establishment. But by this time the young whites were already active participants in the Negro revolution. In fact they had begun to transform it into something broader, with the potential of encompassing the whole of America in a radical reordering of society.

The fourth stage, now in its infancy, sees these white youth taking the initiative, using techniques learned in the Negro struggle to attack problems in the general society. The classic example of this new energy in action was the student battle on the UC campus at Berkeley, California —the Free Speech Movement. Leading the revolt were veterans of the civil rights movement, some of whom spent time on the firing line in the wilderness of Mississippi/Alabama. Flowing from the same momentum were student demonstrations against U.S. interference in the internal affairs of Vietnam, Cuba, the Dominican Republic, and the Congo and U.S. aid to apartheid in South Africa. The students even aroused the intellectual community to actions and positions unthinkable a few years ago: witness the teach-ins. But their revolt is deeper than single-issue protest. The characteristics of the white rebels which most alarm their elders—the long hair, the new dances, their love for Negro music, their use of marijuana, their mystical attitude toward sex—are all tools of their rebellion. They have turned these tools against the totalitarian fabric of American society—and they mean to change it.

From the beginning, America has been a schizophrenic nation. Its two conflicting images of itself were never reconciled, because never before has the survival of its most cherished myths made a reconciliation mandatory. Once before, during the bitter struggle between North and South climaxed by the Civil War, the two images of America came into conflict, although whites North and South scarcely understood it. The image of America held by its most alienated citizens was advanced neither by the North nor by the South; it was perhaps best expressed by Frederick Douglass, who was born into slavery in 1817, escaped to the North, and became the greatest leader-spokesman for the blacks of his era. In words that can still, years later, arouse an audience of black Americans, Frederick Douglass delivered, in 1852, a scorching indictment in his Fourth of July oration in Rochester:

What to the American slave is your Fourth of July? I answer: a day that reveals to him, more than all other days in the year, the gross injustice and cruelty to which he is the constant victim. To him your celebration is a sham; your boasted liberty, an unholy licence; your national greatness, swelling vanity; your sounds of rejoicing are empty and heartless; your denunciation of tyrants, brass-fronted impudence; your shouts of liberty and equality, hollow mockery; your prayers and hymns, your sermons and thanksgivings, with all your religious parade and solemnity, are, to him, more bombast, fraud, deception, impiety and hypocrisy—a thin veil to cover up crimes which would disgrace a nation of savages. . . .

You boast of your love of liberty, your superior civilization, and your pure Christianity, while the whole political power of the nation (as embodied in the two great political parties) is solemnly pledged to support and perpetuate the enslavement of three millions of your countrymen. You hurl your anathemas at the crown-headed tyrants of Russia and Austria and pride yourselves on your democratic institutions, while you yourselves consent to be the mere *tools* and *bodyguards* of the tyrants of Virginia and Carolina.

You invite to your shores fugitives of oppression from abroad, honor them with banquets, greet them with ovations, cheer them, toast them, salute them, protect them, and pour out your money to them like water; but the fugitive from your own land you advertise, hunt, arrest, shoot, and kill. You glory in your refinement and your universal education; yet you maintain a system as barbarous and dreadful as ever stained the character of a nation —a system begun in avarice, supported in pride, and perpetuated in cruelty.

You shed tears over fallen Hungary, and make the sad story of her wrongs the theme of your poets, statesmen and orators, till your gallant sons are ready to fly to arms to vindicate her cause against the oppressor; but, in regard to the ten thousand wrongs of the American slave, you would enforce the strictest silence, and would hail him as an enemy of the nation who dares to make these wrongs the subject of public discourse!

This most alienated view of America was preached by the Abolitionists, and by Harriet Beecher Stowe in her *Uncle Tom's Cabin*. But such a view of America was too distasteful to receive wide attention, and serious debate about America's image and her reality was engaged in only on the fringes of society. Even when confronted with overwhelming evidence to the contrary, most white Americans have found it possible, after steadying their rattled nerves, to settle comfortably back into their vaunted belief that America is dedicated to the proposition that all men are created equal and endowed by their Creator with certain inalienable rights—life, liberty and the pursuit of happiness. With the Constitution for a rudder and the Declaration of Independence as its guiding star, the ship of state is sailing always toward a brighter vision of freedom and justice for all.

Because there is no common ground between these two contradictory images of America, they had to be kept apart. But the moment the blacks were let into the white world—let out of the voiceless and faceless cages of their ghettos, singing, walking, talking, dancing, writing, and orating *their* image of America and of Americans—the white world was suddenly challenged to match its practice to its preachments. And this is why those whites who abandon the *white* image of America and adopt the *black* are greeted with such unmitigated hostility by their elders.

For all these years whites have been taught to believe in the myth they preached, while Negroes have had to face the bitter reality of what America practiced. But without the lies and distortions, white Americans would not have been able to do the things they have done. When whites are forced to look honestly upon the objective proof of their deeds, the cement of mendacity holding white society together swiftly disintegrates. On the other hand, the core of the black world's vision remains intact, and in fact begins to expand and spread into the psychological territory vacated by the non-viable white lies, i.e., into the minds of young whites. It is remarkable how the system worked for so many years, how the majority of whites remained effectively unaware of any contradiction between their view of the world and that world itself. The mechanism by which this was rendered possible requires examination at this point.

Let us recall that the white man, in order to justify slavery and, later on, to justify segregation, elaborated a complex, all-pervasive myth which at one time classified the black man as a subhuman beast of burden. The myth was progressively modified, gradually elevating the blacks on the scale of evolution, following their slowly changing status, until the plateau of separate-but-equal was reached at the close of the nineteenth century. During slavery, the black was seen as a mindless Super-masculine Menial. Forced to do the backbreaking work, he was conceived in terms of his ability to do such work—"field niggers," etc. The white man administered the plantation, doing all the thinking, exercising omnipotent power over the slaves. He had little difficulty dissociating himself from the black slaves, and he could not conceive of their positions being reversed or even reversible.

Blacks and whites being conceived as mutually exclusive types, those attributes imputed to the blacks could not also be imputed to the whites —at least not in equal degree—without blurring the line separating the races. These images were based upon the social function of the two races, the work they performed. The ideal white man was one who knew how to use his head, who knew how to manage and control things and get things done. Those whites who were not in a position to perform these functions nevertheless aspired to them. The ideal black man was one who did exactly as he was told, and did it efficiently and cheerfully. "Slaves," said Frederick Douglass, "are generally expected to sing as well as to work." As the black man's position and function became more varied, the images of white and black, having become stereotypes, lagged behind.

The separate-but-equal doctrine was promulgated by the Supreme Court in 1896. It had the same purpose domestically as the Open Door Policy toward China in the international arena: to stabilize a situation and subordinate a nonwhite population so that racist exploiters could manipulate those people according to their own selfish interests. These doctrines were foisted off as *the epitome of enlightened justice, the highest expression of morality*. Sanctified by religion, justified by philosophy and legalized by the Supreme Court, separate-but-equal was enforced by day by agencies of the law, and by the KKK & Co. under cover of night. Booker T. Washington, the Martin Luther King of his day, accepted separate-but-equal in the name of all Negroes. W. E. B. DuBois denounced it.

Separate-but-equal marked the last stage of the white man's flight into cultural neurosis, and the beginning of the black man's frantic striving to assert his humanity and equalize his position with the white. Blacks ventured into all fields of endeavor to which they could gain entrance. Their goal was to present in all fields a performance that would equal or surpass that of the whites. It was long axiomatic among blacks that a black had to be twice as competent as a white in any field in order to win grudging recognition from the whites. This produced a pathological motivation in the blacks to equal or surpass the whites, and a pathological motivation in the whites to maintain a distance from the blacks. This is the rack on which black and white Americans receive their delicious torture! At first there was the color bar, flatly denying the blacks entrance to certain spheres of activity. When this no longer worked, and blacks invaded sector after sector of American life and economy, the whites evolved other methods of keeping their distance. The illusion of the Negro's inferior nature had to be maintained.

One device evolved by the whites was to tab whatever the blacks did with the prefix "Negro." We had *Negro* literature, *Negro* athletes, *Negro* music, *Negro* doctors, *Negro* politicians, *Negro* workers. The malignant ingeniousness of this device is that although it accurately describes an objective biological fact—or, at least, a sociological fact in America—it concealed the paramount psychological fact: that to the white mind, prefixing anything with "Negro" automatically consigned it to an inferior category. A well-known example of the white necessity to deny due credit to blacks is in the realm of music. White musicians were famous for going to Harlem and other Negro cultural centers literally to steal the black man's music, carrying it back across the color line into the Great White World and passing off the watered-down loot as their own original creations. Blacks, meanwhile, were ridiculed as *Negro* musicians playing inferior coon music.

The Negro revolution at home and national liberation movements abroad have unceremoniously shattered the world of fantasy in which the whites have been living. It is painful that many do not yet see that their fantasy world has been rendered uninhabitable in the last half of the twentieth century. But it is away from this world that the white youth of today are turning. The "paper tiger" hero, James Bond, offering the whites a triumphant image of themselves, is saying what many whites want desperately to hear reaffirmed: *I am still the White Man, lord of the land, licensed to kill, and the world is still an empire at my feet.* James Bond feeds on that secret little anxiety, the psychological white backlash, felt in some degree by most whites alive. It is exasperating to see little brown men and little yellow men from the mysterious Orient, and the opaque black men of Africa (to say nothing of these impudent American Negroes!) who come to the UN and talk smart to us, who are scurrying all over *our* globe in their strange modes of dress— much as if they were new, unpleasant arrivals from another planet. Many whites believe in their ulcers that it is only a matter of time before the Marines get the signal to round up these truants and put them back securely in their cages. But it is away from this fantasy world that the white youth of today are turning.

In the world revolution now under way, the initiative rests with people of color. That growing numbers of white youth are repudiating their heritage of blood and taking people of color as their heroes and models is a tribute not only to their insight but to the resilience of the human spirit. For today the heroes of the initiative are people not usually thought of as white: Fidel Castro, Che Guevara, Kwame Nkrumah,

Mao Tse-tung, Gamal Abdel Nasser, Robert F. Williams, Malcom X, Ben Bella, John Lewis, Martin Luther King, Jr., Robert Parris Moses, Ho Chi Minh, Stokely Carmichael, W. E. B. DuBois, James Forman, Chou En-lai.

The white youth of today have begun to react to the fact that the "American Way of Life" is a fossil of history. What do they care if their old baldheaded and crew-cut elders don't dig their caveman mops? They couldn't care less about the old, stiffassed honkies who don't like their new dances: Frug, Monkey, Jerk, Swim, Watusi. All they know is that it feels good to swing to way-out body-rhythms instead of drag-assing across the dance floor like zombies to the dead beat of mind-smothered Mickey Mouse music. Is it any wonder that the youth have lost all respect for their elders, for law and order, when for as long as they can remember all they've witnessed is a monumental bickering over the Negro's place in American society and the right of people around the world to be left alone by outside powers? They have witnessed the law, both domestic and international, being spat upon by those who do not like its terms. Is it any wonder, then, that they feel justified, by sitting-in and freedom riding, in breaking laws made by lawless men? Old funny-styled, zipper-mouthed political night riders know nothing but to haul out an investigating committee *to look into the disturbance* to find the cause of the unrest among the youth. Look into a mirror! The cause is you, Mr. and Mrs. Yesterday, you with your forked tongues.

A young white today cannot help but recoil from the base deeds of his people. On every side, on every continent, he sees racial arrogance, savage brutality toward the conquered and subjugated people, genocide; he sees the human cargo of the slave trade; he sees the systematic extermination of American Indians; he sees the civilized nations of Europe fighting in imperial depravity over the lands of other people—and over possession of the very people themselves. There seems to be no end to the ghastly deeds of which his people are guilty. GUILTY. The slaughter of the Jews by the Germans, the dropping of atomic bombs on the Japanese people—these deeds weigh heavily upon the prostrate souls and tumultuous consciences of the white youth. The white heroes, their hands dripping with blood, are dead.

The young whites know that the colored people of the world, Afro-Americans included, do not seek revenge for their suffering. They seek the same things the white rebel wants: an end to war and exploitation. Black and white, the young rebels are free people, free in a way that Americans have never been before in the history of their country. And they are outraged.

There is in America today a generation of white youth that is truly worthy of a black man's respect, and this is a rare event in the foul annals of American history. From the beginning of the contact between blacks and whites, there has been very little reason for a black man to respect a white, with such exceptions as John Brown and others lesser known. But respect commands itself and it can neither be given nor withheld when it is due. If a man like Malcom X could change and repudiate racism, if I myself and other former Muslims can change, if young whites can change, then there is hope for America. It was certainly strange to find myself, while steeped in the doctrine that all whites were devils by nature, commanded by the heart to applaud and acknowledge respect for these young whites—despite the fact that they are descendants of the masters and I the descendant of slave. The sins of the fathers are visited upon the heads of the children—but only if the children continue in the evil deeds of the fathers.

FROM THE REPORT OF THE NATIONAL ADVISORY COMMISSION ON CIVIL DISORDERS

In an attempt to discover the causes of the social disorders during the summer of 1967 and to understand their meaning, President Johnson appointed an advisory commission headed by Otto Kerner, then Governor of Illinois. After making its study, the Kerner Commission concluded that the United States is "moving toward two societies, one black, one white—separate and unequal." The commission placed the responsibility for this division on white racism. Following are excerpts from the Introduction and Chapter 4 ("The Basic Causes") of the commission report, which was issued in March, 1968.

FROM INTRODUCTION

The summer of 1967 again brought racial disorders to American cities, and with them shock, fear and bewilderment to the nation.

The worst came during a two-week period in July, first in Newark and then in Detroit. Each set off a chain reaction in neighboring communities.

On July 28, 1967, the President of the United States established this Commission and directed us to answer three basic questions:

What happened?

Why did it happen?

What can be done to prevent it from happening again?

To respond to these questions, we have undertaken a broad range of studies and investigations. We have visited the riot cities; we have heard many witnesses; we have sought the counsel of experts across the country.

This is our basic conclusion: Our nation is moving toward two societies, one black, one white—separate and unequal.

Reaction to last summer's disorders has quickened the movement and

From "Introduction" and "Why Did It Happen" from *Report of the National Advisory Commission on Civil Disorders,* March 1968.

deepened the division. Discrimination and segregation have long permeated much of American life; they now threaten the future of every American.

This deepening racial division is not inevitable. The movement apart can be reversed. Choice is still possible. Our principal task is to define that choice and to press for a national resolution.

To pursue our present course will involve the continuing polarization of the American community and, ultimately, the destruction of basic democratic values.

The alternative is not blind repression or capitulation to lawlessness. It is the realization of common opportunities for all within a single society.

This alternative will require a commitment to national action—compassionate, massive and sustained, backed by the resources of the most powerful and the richest nation on this earth. From every American it will require new attitudes, new understanding, and, above all, new will.

The vital needs of the nation must be met; hard choices must be made, and, if necessary, new taxes enacted.

Violence cannot build a better society. Disruption and disorder nourish repression, not justice. They strike at the freedom of every citizen. The community cannot——it will not—tolerate coercion and mob rule.

Violence and destruction must be ended—in the streets of the ghetto and in the lives of people.

Segregation and poverty have created in the racial ghetto a destructive environment totally unknown to most white Americans.

What white Americans have never fully understood—but what the Negro can never forget—is that white society is deeply implicated in the ghetto. White institutions created it, white institutions maintain it, and white society condones it.

It is time now to turn with all the purpose at our command to the major unfinished business of this nation. It is time to adopt strategies for action that will produce quick and visible progress. It is time to make good the promises of American democracy to all citizens—urban and rural, white and black, Spanish-surname, American Indian, and every minority group.

Our recommendations embrace three basic principles:

To mount programs on a scale equal to the dimension of the problems:

To aim these programs for high impact in the immediate future in order to close the gap between promise and performance;

To undertake new initiatives and experiments that can change the system of failure and frustration that now dominates the ghetto and weakens our society.

These programs will require unprecendented levels of funding and performance, but they neither probe deeper nor demand more than the problems which called them forth. There can be no higher priority for national action and no higher claim on the nation's conscience.

We issue this Report now, four months before the date called for by the President. Much remains that can be learned. Continued study is essential.

As Commissioners we have worked together with a sense of the greatest urgency and have sought to compose whatever differences exist among us. Some differences remain. But the gravity of the problem and the pressing need for action are too clear to allow further delay in the issuance of this Report.

FROM CHAPTER 4 / THE BASIC CAUSES

We have seen what happened. Why did it happen?

In addressing this question we shift our focus from the local to the national scene, from the particular events of the summer of 1967 to the factors within the society at large which have brought about the sudden violent mood of so many urban Negroes.

The record before this Commission reveals that the causes of recent racial disorders are imbedded in a massive tangle of issues and circumstances—social, economic, political, and psychological—which arise out of the historical pattern of Negro-white relations in America.

These factors are both complex and interacting; they vary significantly in their effect from city to city and from year to year; and the consequences of one disorder, generating new grievances and new demands, become the causes of the next. It is this which creates the "thicket of tension, conflicting evidence and extreme opinions" cited by the President.

Despite these complexities, certain fundamental matters are clear. Of these, the most fundamental is the racial attitude and behavior of white Americans toward black Americans. Race prejudice has shaped our history decisively in the past; it now threatens to do so again. White racism is essentially responsible for the explosive mixture which has been accumulating in our cities since the end of World War II. At the base of this mixture are three of the most bitter fruits of white racial attitudes:

Pervasive discrimination and segregation. The first is surely the continuing exclusion of great numbers of Negroes from the benefits of economic progress through discrimination in employment and education, and their enforced confinement in segregated housing and schools. The corrosive and degrading effects of this condition and the attitudes that underlie it are the source of the deepest bitterness and at the center of the problem of racial disorder.

Black migration and white exodus. The second is the massive and growing concentration of impoverished Negroes in our major cities resulting from Negro migration from the rural South, rapid population growth and the continuing movement of the white middle-class to the suburbs. The consequence is a greatly increased burden on the already depleted resources of cities, creating a growing crisis of deteriorating facilities and services and unmet human needs.

Black ghettos. Third, in the teeming racial ghettos, segregation and poverty have intersected to destroy opportunity and hope and to enforce failure. The ghettos too often mean men and women without jobs, families without men, and schools where children are processed instead of educated, until they return to the street—to crime, to narcotics, to dependency on welfare, and to bitterness and resentment against society in general and white society in particular.

These three forces have converged on the inner city in recent years and on the people who inhabit it. At the same time, most whites and many Negroes outside the ghetto have prospered to a degree unparalleled in the history of civilization. Through television—the universal appliance in the ghetto—and the other media of mass communications, this affluence has been endlessly flaunted before the eyes of the Negro poor and the jobless ghetto youth.

As Americans, most Negro citizens carry within themselves two basic aspirations of our society. They seek to share in both the material resources of our system and its intangible benefits—dignity, respect and acceptance. Outside the ghetto many have succeeded in achieving a decent standard of life, and in developing the inner resources which give life meaning and direction. Within the ghetto, however, it is rare that either aspiration is achieved.

Yet these facts alone—fundamental as they are—cannot be said to have caused the disorders. Other and more immediate factors help explain why these events happened now.

Recently, three powerful ingredients have begun to catalyze the mixture.

Frustrated hopes. The expectations aroused by the great judicial and legislative victories of the civil rights movement have led to frustration, hostility and cynicism in the face of the persistent gap between promise and fulfillment. The dramatic struggle for equal rights in the South has sensitized Northern Negroes to the economic inequalities reflected in the deprivations of ghetto life.

Legitimation of violence. A climate that tends toward the approval and encouragement of violence as a form of protest has been created by white terrorism directed against nonviolent protest, including instances of abuse and even murder of some civil rights workers in the South; by the open defiance of law and federal authority by state and local officials resisting desegregation; and by some protest groups engaging in civil disobedience who turn their backs on nonviolence, go beyond the

Constitutionally protected rights of petition and free assembly, and resort to violence to attempt to compel alteration of laws and policies with which they disagree. This condition has been reinforced by a general erosion of respect for authority in American society and reduced effectiveness of social standards and community restraints on violence and crime. This in turn has largely resulted from rapid urbanization and the dramatic reduction in the average age of the total population.

Powerlessness. Finally, many Negroes have come to believe that they are being exploited politically and economically by the white "power structure." Negroes, like people in poverty everywhere, in fact lack the channels of communication, influence and appeal that traditionally have been available to ethnic minorities within the city and which enabled them—unburdened by color—to scale the walls of the white ghettos in an earlier era. The frustrations of powerlessness have led some to the conviction that there is no effective alternative to violence as a means of expression and redress, as a way of "moving the system." More generally, the result is alienation and hostility toward the institutions of law and government and the white society which controls them. This is reflected in the reach toward racial consciousness and solidarity reflected in the slogan "Black Power."

These facts have combined to inspire a new mood among Negroes, particularly among the young. Self-esteem and enhanced racial pride are replacing apathy and submission to "the system." Moreover, Negro youth, who make up over half of the ghetto population, share the growing sense of alienation felt by many white youth in our country. Thus, their role in recent civil disorders reflects not only a shared sense of deprivation and victimization by white society but also the rising incidence of disruptive conduct by a segment of American youth throughout the society.

Incitement and encouragement of violence. These conditions have created a volatile mixture of attitudes and beliefs which needs only a spark to ignite mass violence. Strident appeals to violence, first heard from white racists, were echoed and reinforced last summer in the inflammatory rhetoric of black racists and militants. Throughout the year, extremists crisscrossed the country preaching a doctrine of black power and violence. Their rhetoric was widely reported in the mass media; it was echoed by local "militants" and organizations; it became the ugly background noise of the violent summer.

We cannot measure with any precision the influence of these organizations and individuals in the ghetto, but we think it clear that the intolerable and unconscionable encouragement of violence heightened tensions, created a mood of acceptance and an expectation of violence, and thus contributed to the eruption of the disorders last summer.

The Police. It is the convergence of all these factors that makes the role of the police so difficult and so significant. Almost invariably the incident that ignites disorder arises from police action. Harlem, Watts, Newark and Detroit—all the major outbursts of recent years—were precipitated by routine arrests of Negroes for minor offenses by white police.

But the police are not merely the spark. In discharge of their obligation to maintain order and insure public safety in the disruptive conditions of ghetto life, they are inevitably involved in sharper and more frequent conflicts with ghetto residents than with the residents of other areas. Thus, to many Negroes police have come to symbolize white power, white racism and white repression. And the fact is that many police do reflect and express these white attitudes. The atmosphere of hostility and cynicism is reinforced by a widespread perception among Negroes of the existence of police brutality and corruption, and of a "double standard" of justice and protection—one for Negroes and one for whites.

To this point, we have attempted only to identify the prime components of the "explosive mixture." In the chapters that follow we seek to analyze them in the perspective of history. Their meaning, however, is already clear:

In the summer of 1967, we have seen in our cities a chain reaction of racial violence. If we are heedless, we shall none of us escape the consequences.

VIOLENCE IN AMERICA:
THE NEGRO IN THE CITY
Jeffrey Hart

Not all Americans agreed with the findings of the Kerner Commission. In this essay Jeffrey Hart, Professor of English at Dartmouth and a frequent contributor to the *National Review*, refutes the charge of the commission that white racism is the root cause of our racial problems.

In recent months Americans have been subjected to an escalating series of news stories, articles, books and reports dealing with Negro-white relations. We are given to understand that our cities are shortly to be burned down. We are told that a "second Civil War" is imminent or has already started. One day we hear that an extremist orator in New York has urged Negroes to arm themselves in preparation for a "hunting season" in which whites will be the quarry; the next day a fanatic in De-

From *National Review*, Vol. XX, No. 24 (June 18, 1968). Reprinted by permission of *National Review*, 150 East 35th Street, New York, New York 10016.

troit announces plans to establish a black enclave consisting of two or three Southern states, and enclave which would be backed by atomically-armed Chinese submarines. We read that American Negro athletes may boycott the Olympics over the inclusion of South Africa—though they have, so far, experienced no principled qualms over competing against Russians, North Koreans or teams representing the East European tyrannies. And recently the President's Commission on Civil Disorders has blamed the entire problem on white "racism"—thus retrospectively excusing the destruction that has already occurred, and giving a kind of moral blank check to the potential rioters of the future. The Commission in effect has blamed everyone for the riots but those who rioted.

The ordinary citizen may well feel that he is living in the midst of widespread madness on the racial question, may well feel that where race is concerned the normal rules of observation and of reason are suddenly suspended. Nor does the madness seem confined to America. Thus England has been condemned as "racist" by World Opinion for limiting the immigration of Asians from Kenya; but not a word has been breathed about the Kenyan racism which makes conditions there so intolerable for them that they want to leave for England. Thus, again, World Opinion sees nothing grotesque in tirades delivered against South Africa by, of all countries, the Soviet Union—which has been persecuting Christians ruthlessly for fifty years.

It seems to me that nothing is more important with regard to racial problems than to remove the whole discussion from the atmosphere of fantasy and illogic. If we are to get anywhere at all we must de-escalate the rhetoric, take a toughly realistic look at the problems we face and propose reasonable solutions where solutions in fact are possible. We must clear away a number of myths, sacred to some but myths nevertheless, and so finally damaging to all.

First of all, however, it must be made perfectly clear to all that the civil order will be maintained. "There is no grievance," said Abraham Lincoln, "that is a fit object of redress by mob law." Any citizen has a fundamental right to have his store or his home protected. Providing such protection is one of the basic tasks of government and indeed a main reason for its existence. A government unwilling to do what is necessary to enforce the law and to maintain order deserves to be replaced. Unfortunately it is true that these tasks have been made more difficult in recent years by an erosion of concern for law and public order—an erosion often assisted by persons who should know better. A few years ago, for example, Adlai Stevenson remarked to a college audience that breaking the law in a good cause was all very well, and that the leadership of the country would soon very likely pass to those who had done some time in jail. Others, from Martin Luther King to Dr.

Spock—whether in good cause or bad is not really relevant—have been remarkably casual with respect to perfectly valid laws, simply breaking them rather than working to have them changed by the ordinary democratic methods. At the very highest level, some decisions of the Supreme Court have smacked more of judicial will than legal reason. We have, moreover, grown all too accustomed to so-called demonstrations, on the campus and elsewhere, which casually violate the rights of others. A demonstrator blocking a passage or helping to tie up a thoroughfare is actually employing a form of violence, and too often the rights of his victim have been forgotten or ignored. Such essentially frivolous attitudes toward the very bases of public order have done much to create an atmosphere in which violence and anarchy become more likely. It seems clear today that we must make a deliberate and sustained effort to return to our laws their former primacy, and the first step will be to enforce them strictly.

II

The report of the President's Commission stresses white racism as the root cause of the Negroes' problems. This is a spectacular charge. Naturally it has attracted widespread notice, and the authors of the report have been praised for their courage in making it. The key question, however, has not been pressed: Is the charge true? My own view is that it is false, and further, that among the nations of the world America is in fact one to which the charge of racism is least appropriately applied. The charge of racism is in fact very much at odds with the best analyses of the problem that have appeared recently. The American reality is more complex than such blanket diagnoses suggest.

First of all, it has been shown that at the higher educational levels, disadvantages due to discrimination have rapidly disappeared, more rapidly, indeed, than often was the case for previous immigrant minorities. (And the large migration of Negroes to Northern cities during the post World War II period justifies the description of them as a new minority there.) Today the demand for Negro college graduates is greater than the supply; more places in colleges, law schools, and medical schools are available than qualified Negro applicants to fill them; more places are available in corporations, banks, and so forth than trained applicants for them. One social scientist summarizes the situation this way: "A shortage of skills and educational qualities may now be a much greater block to Negro advancement that a shortage of available jobs." At the level in question, at any rate, the problem does not look like one of racism but rather like the lag to be expected when a group with a predominantly agricultural background attempts to adjust to urban conditions and new goals. Are we to suppose that the modern technology which produced an agricultural revolution and so pushed ten million Negroes into Northern cities was "racism"? We need to remind ourselves that previous groups took at least three generations to make the advance from manual labor to proportional representation in the white collar jobs and in the professions. The sharp rise in the last fifteen years in the number of Negroes holding clerical jobs suggests that a similar rise will take place in the next generation in the professional category. Furthermore, there is abundant evidence that resistance to Negroes on the less advanced levels is really a class objection rather than a race objection—the reaction to a felt difference in behavior and in value structure. At every level, however, whether high or low, education proves to be the key. Job equality depends upon qualifications, and they, in turn, depend upon education. Yet the improvement of Negro education faces a number of obstacles, some of which are formidable.

Part of the difficulty surrounding discussion of the Negroes flows from a failure to recognize certain plain truths about the nature of American society. Indeed, the whole stress on integration as a primary goal is based on the myth that America is a completely homogeneous country, whereas to a significant extent America is a nation of distinctive groups. According to the myth, successive immigrant groups gradually melted into the population and became indistinguishable from the rest. The reality is more complex, and in fact more interesting. In their well-known study *Beyond the Melting Pot* the sociologists Nathan Glazer and Daniel Moynihan point out that though an immigrant group is *changed* by its American experience it does not on that account cease to be recognizable: the groups are given structure and solidarity through interest, family, and fellow-feeling; they produce distinctive institutions and associations; they vote differently; many have their own neighborhoods; they have different attitudes toward education, sex, religion; they are "in many essential ways as different from one another as their grandfathers had been." The weakness of the program aimed at total Negro integration is that it attempts to impose on the whole area of Negro-white relations a novel and abstract pattern which has not been followed by the other historic American groups. It is for this reason that laws designed to achieve integration have been so largely ineffective; at the same time, the insistence upon integration as the primary goal, as in the report of the President's Commission, creates expectations which are continually frustrated, and the frustration leads to bitterness. "Time alone," writes Nathan Glazer, "does not dissolve the groups if they are not close to the Anglo-Saxon center. Color marks off a group regardless of time; and perhaps most significantly, the 'majority' group, to which assimilation should occur, has taken on the character of an ethnic group." No one really believes that Negroes will cease to be a distinctive group, and integration therefore should be redefined to mean *"integration into the pattern of American group experience,"* that larger

pattern which involves work-save-study-earn-rise. The obstacles which
exist to integration into this pattern must be dealt with, and some of
them are peculiarly formidable. But integration in other terms does not
seem to be a practical possibility.

The preoccupation with integration, indeed, has probably distracted
us from paying close enough attention to the real problems. The entire
discussion of integration has a peculiar, not to say ideological, character. For example, if, as alleged, it is bad for Negro children to attend
predominantly Negro schools, why then is it not bad for white children
as well to attend such schools? The so-called flight to the suburbs by
white parents need not be evidence of racism, as often charged. Responsible parents want their children to attend schools in which learning is
not made more difficult than necessary. Nor is there any evidence that
benefits have in fact resulted from attempts to achieve "racial balance"
in the classroom. If legislation is based upon illusions, it will create
rather than solve problems. For example the bussing of children to
achieve racial balance in classrooms may only serve to erode ties to
neighborhood and local community, ties which in any case are undesira-
bly tenuous in modern society.

III

The real problems of the Negroes have less to do with Negro-white relations than with the relationship of Negroes to one another, and it is to
these real problems that the Negroes, together with other Americans,
can most valuably direct attention.

A number of important differences exist between Negroes and other
American ethnic groups. Social scientists have pointed out that Negroes
have not developed a comparable degree of group solidarity, and that
this failure is an important factor in retarding advancement. Comparing
Negroes with Puerto Ricans in New York, Nathan Glazer makes this
pertinent observation: "It is interesting to note some contrasts between
Negro and Puerto Rican employment patterns. Negroes and Puerto Ricans both work in sizable numbers in hotels. Puerto Ricans entered
after Negroes, and it is not likely that they face less discrimination. Yet
many more Puerto Ricans than Negroes are employed in the hotel industry. The same thing holds in branches of the garment industry. Perhaps the difference can be ascribed in part to the relative weakness of
clan and extended family feeling among the Negroes. One Puerto Rican
may be quicker to bring in another, and there seems to be more of a
tendency for family and related groups to work together." With the single and important exception of the Negro churches, Negroes have failed
to develop those associations and institutions which have played such a
vital role in the advancement of other groups. Other groups have pa-
tronized their own shops and businesses, family and extended family
have provided "little pools for ethnic businessmen to tap"; but Negroes

have been much more atomistic, less aware of the need to advance as a group, less aware that the fortunes of one are connected with the fortunes of all. One serious consequence has been the failure of Negro business to develop satisfactorily, and business, historically, has proved the effective road to advancement for the various ethnic groups. The development of businesses, indeed, is more than an economic matter. The local businessman develops know-how which can be transmitted to other members of the group; he has access to credit and experience in managing it; he may be influential in local politics; and he is part of a network of jobs related to his enterprise. The Chinese restaurant buys its food supplies from a Chinese distributor, uses a Chinese laundry, hires Chinese help. The Italian who owns a grocery store gives a break to a friend or a relative who is working his way up as a salesman. As Glazer points out, the astonishing and telling fact is that Chinese income from Chinese owned businesses is, in proportion to their numbers, 45 times as great as the income of Negroes from Negro-owned businesses.

Another serious obstacle to Negro advancement has been the chronic instability of the Negro family. At the present time about a quarter of urban Negro families are headed by women; the rate of Negro illegitimacy is fourteen or fifteen times that of whites; as a result, more Negro children than white live apart from parents, or in overcrowded homes, or among strangers, lodgers, etc. We do not know with assurance the effects of these circumstances on the children, but we cannot doubt that they adversely affect the performance of the Negro child in school, and, therefore, later on in the society at large. As Glazer observes of the Negro boy growing up under such conditions, it is "understandable that his knowledge of the adult world should be weak and uncertain, that his aspirations should be unrealistic, and that his own self-image should be unsure and impaired."

The atomistic character of the Negro group, its failure to develop satisfactorily its own economic institutions, and the instability of the Negro family, are the most important obstacles to Negro advancement at the present time, and because of them low status tends to become self-perpetuating. "Poverty, high fertility, high rates of illegitimacy, widespread family disorganization, and similar conditions that hold lower class Negroes down could continue for decades after the influences originally responsible for them were virtually eliminated." So write Leonard Broom and Norval Glenn in a sociological work on the American Negro. The result has been, as we have seen, that unlike other groups the Negroes are not ready to take advantage of the opportunities that open up.

What, then, can be done by the Negroes and by those who wish them well? The expenditure of money undirected by intelligence is pointless. And anyone can propose spending money. If the recommendation of two billion a month is hailed as sagacity, one might easily earn a reputation for genius by recommending six billion. The prospects at the present time, however, are best understood in the light of actuality, and of history. Those who have studied the problem most closely tell us that, historically, the Negroes have gone through three broad phases since emancipation. After the Civil War there was a period of submission and accommodation. The condition of the Negro actually seems to have reached a low ebb during the Eighties and Nineties of the last century, at least as measured by the evidence of health standards and death rates. The first half of this century witnessed an increasing migration of Negroes to Northern and Western cities, accompanied by increasing restiveness. Beginning in the 1950s, the Negroes passed into the phase of demonstration and protest. This last phase, it is important to know, reflected an advance in over-all condition, an advance in white-collar work, skilled and semi-skilled employment, and purchasing power. The initiative in the demonstrations, beginning in 1954, in fact came from college students and from middle-class Negroes. The demonstrations did not arise out of hopelessness, but from ambitions that had been stimulated by advances already made. Even riots, recent studies show, can be motivated by improving circumstances. "Our studies strongly suggest," reports a Detroit social scientist, "that the rioters were a well-employed group making an average of some $115 to $120 a week, a group which felt that it had substantially improved its status in the community during the past three to five years." Asked to explain why such people would riot, he concluded: "The closer the distance becomes between the lower and the middle class, the more militant and aggressive and assertive the lower class becomes."

But the protest and demonstration phase of the Negro experience in America has surely reached the point of diminishing returns. Virtually all legal barriers to Negro advancement have been eliminated, and the problems that remain are, as we have seen, particularly recalcitrant. Negro energies, it seems clear, should be turned inward to the problems of the Negro community, rather than directed outward toward confrontations with the rest of society. Negro energies should be invested in improving the Negro condition rather than wasted in self-defeating expressions of resentment. Demonstrations and riots may be emotionally gratifying to some, and it is true that serious day-to-day work provides no comparable outlet for hostility. Yet the solution of hard core problems is not likely to be sudden or spectacular. Here is the conclusion reached by Glazer and Moynihan in *Beyond the Melting Pot:*

[The] important tasks, necessary ones on the agenda of American Negroes, are shirked and ignored. These are tasks that conceivably no one but Negroes can do. It is probable that no investment of public and private agencies on delinquency and crime prevention programs will equal the return from an investment by Negro-led and Negro-financed agencies. It is probable that no offensive on the public school system to improve the educational results among Negroes will equal what may be gained from an equivalent investment by Negro-led and Negro-financed groups.

"If anything can be done," they conclude, "it is likely that Negro agencies will be far more effective than public agencies and those of white Protestants." It would be an excellent thing if politicians, Negro leaders, and Presidential commissions would learn something from the tone employed by these responsible students of the Negro problem, from their restraint, from their unwillingness to hold out excessive hope for spectacular results, and their continence in proposing remedies. Some problems are complicated and recalcitrant enough to admit of no immediate solution; such problems cannot be solved but only endured, and the person who does not discipline his expectations will be disciplined by actuality.

There are, however, some things the rest of society can do to promote the advance of the Negroes. Improvement, integration into the larger American pattern, depends upon the growth of a Negro middle class, and a consequent increase in family stability. The key here is improved education. Yet improvements here will not come easily. The available evidence indicates that even the Negro first-grader, if he comes from a culturally deficient background, may be too far behind his white classmates ever to catch up. Naturally, no attempt to fabricate a substitute for a satisfactory family environment is likely to be wholly successful. And yet preschool nursery programs, to which children would be admitted as early as practicable, could offer training in standard English and in personal discipline and could foster attitudes conducive to a good performance in the classroom later on. If such preschool programs enabled the Negro child to derive more benefit from his regular schooling the eventual economies in relief and in welfare costs might offset the initial expenditure. Other measures might well help in the area of education. Negro diligence is hampered in school by a widespread belief that higher education will not be rewarded by openings in white collar jobs and in the professions. If such a belief once was justified, it no longer is, and intensive counseling should be able to correct it. We have seen that the Negro community has largely failed to develop the kind of solidarity and group pride possessed by other ethnic groups. It may be that school and community programs in Negro history, culture and literature, in America and, particularly, in Africa, can strengthen the Negro's self-image and make for greater solidarity with the community to which he belongs. There is no reason why such programs should not be encouraged.

It is particularly important that the Negroes develop a business class. Until now, their failure to do so has been striking, and we have seen that one reason for the failure was a lack of group solidarity. In addition, the competitive weaknesses of Negro businesses has made them a greater credit risk than their white equivalents. They have a higher failure-rate, tend to be smaller and less efficient, and those who run them have not had a tradition of business know-how to draw upon. Yet it is important that Negroes come to own the businesses, especially those operating in Negro neighborhoods. Property, after all, tends to produce responsibility and dignity. Assistance to this end could well take the form of state insurance for loans extended to qualified Negro businessmen, or potential businessmen, for capital investment. The private sector could also do much here. Perhaps civic minded businessmen in the various fields could set up committees for the purpose of advising Negroes who are initiating enterprises.

There is one area in which a major occupational breakthrough does not depend upon a vast improvement in education. In the skilled trades, restrictive union practices have too often effectively excluded Negroes. Yet these restrictive practices are largely retrograde in an expanding economy in which positions could be opened up without threatening white jobs. Unions have long memories, but it seems about time that they recovered from a Depression psychology. This would seem one of the most appropriate places to apply legislative pressure. Opening up skilled positions would have an important effect in curbing Negro restiveness. Negro males who have completed high school but not attended college differ more in occupational status from their white equivalents than Negroes at any other level.

Other measures are important as well. Negroes should be encouraged to enter the urban police forces, and Negro policemen and Negro officers should have primary responsibility in Negro neighborhoods. The impact of minimum wage laws deserves special scrutiny. We need not wonder why so many Negro teen-agers are on the streets during the summer when we consider the effect such laws are likely to have on the neighborhood small businessman. In many cities, the subject of rent control is politically explosive. Yet these same cities invariably suffer from an acute shortage of decent housing. There seems little reason to doubt that rent control discourages building; that this in turn produces the shortage; and that shortage of supply, as always, and inevitably, leads to indifference and negligence on the part of the landlord.

All these measures, and others, will be of use. Yet we cannot expect spectacular results in the short run. The advance of the Negroes, like the advance of other groups, will come mainly, if at all, through the efforts of the group itself. And while we are discussing the Negroes, it would be well for us to remember that the problem of urban violence is by no means exclusively a Negro problem. Beyond the specific problems of the Negroes looms a larger and more pervasive problem which seemingly is connected with the very conditions of modern urban existence.

We have pointed to the weakness of the Negro family and to the atomistic character of the Negro community. Yet the white family is often no rock of Gibraltar, and all too many affluent middle-class white children give themselves over to pot, pill, and protest. We hear much of Negro violence. But at every level of the society an increasing number of people are empty and violent, depraved and irresponsible. Those all too modern murderers in Truman Capote's *In Cold Blood* were not Negroes.

THE SOLUTION: BLACK POWER OR BLACK STUDIES?

"The adoption of the concept of Black Power is one of the most legitimate and healthy developments in American politics and race relations in our time."

STOKELY CARMICHAEL AND CHARLES HAMILTON

THE CIVIL RIGHTS MOVEMENT: WHAT GOOD WAS IT?
Alice Walker

In the 1950's and early 1960's many Americans believed that the civil rights movement would offer the solutions to most of our racial problems. But the slowness of social change caused numerous blacks to abandon their nonviolent stance and turn to militancy and separatism. The claim was often heard that the civil rights movement had accomplished nothing. Alice Walker—a young, black woman born in 1944—disputes that claim. Though the civil rights movement may be dead, she finds that it accomplished much: it gave blacks a new sense of freedom and a new sense of history; it developed pride and courage, provided hope and heroes, and made blacks fight harder than ever before for life.

Someone said recently to an old black lady from Mississippi, whose legs had been badly mangled by local police who arrested her for "disturbing the peace," that the civil rights movement was dead, and asked, since it was dead, what she thought about it. The old lady replied, hobbling out of his presence on her cane, that the civil rights movement was like herself, "if it's dead, it shore ain't ready to lay down!"

This old lady is a legendary freedom fighter in her small town in the

From *The American Scholar*, Vol. XXXVI, No. 4 (Autumn 1967). Copyright © 1967 by the United Chapters of Phi Beta Kappa. Reprinted by permission of the author and the publisher.

Delta. She has been severely mistreated for insisting on her rights as an American citizen. She has been beaten for singing movement songs, placed in solitary confinement in prisons for talking about freedom, and placed on bread and water for praying aloud to God for her jailers' deliverance. For such a woman the civil rights movement will never be over as long as her skin is black. It also will never be over for twenty million others with the same "affliction," for whom the movement can never "lay down," no matter how it is killed by the press and made dead and buried by the white American public. As long as one black American survives, the struggle for equality with other Americans must also survive. This is a debt we owe to those blameless hostages we leave to the future, our children.

Still, white liberals and deserting civil rights sponsors are quick to justify their disaffection from the movement by claiming that it is all over. "And since it is over," they will ask, "would someone kindly tell me what has been gained by it?" They then list statistics supposedly showing how much more advanced segregation is now than ten years ago—in schools, housing, jobs. They point to a gain in conservative politicians during the last few years. They speak of ghetto riots and of the recent survey that shows that most policemen are admittedly too anti-Negro to do their jobs in ghetto areas fairly and effectively. They speak of every area that has been touched by the civil rights movement as somehow or other going to pieces.

They rarely talk, however, about human attitudes among Negroes that have undergone terrific changes just during the past seven to ten years (not to mention all those years when there was a movement and only the Negroes knew about it). They seldom speak of changes in personal lives because of the influence of people in the movement. They see general failure and few, if any, individual gains.

They do not understand what it is that keeps the movement from "laying down" and Negroes from reverting to their former *silent* second-class status. They have apparently never stopped to wonder why it is always the white man—on his radio and in his newspaper and on his television—who says that the movement is dead. If a Negro were audacious enough to make such a claim, his fellows might hanker to see him shot. The movement is dead to the white man because it no longer interests him. And it no longer interests him because he can afford to be uninterested: he does not have to live by it, with it, or for it, as Negroes must. He can take a rest from the news of beatings, killings and arrests that reach him from North and South—if his skin is white. Negroes cannot now and will never be able to take a rest from the injustices that plague them for they—not the white man—are the target.

Perhaps it is naïve to be thankful that the movement "saved" a large number of individuals and gave them something to live for, even if it did not provide them with everything they wanted. (Materially, it provided them with precious little that they wanted.) When a movement awakens people to the possibilities of life, it seems unfair to frustrate them by then denying what they had thought was offered. But what was offered? What was promised? What was it all about? What good did it do? Would it have been better, as some have suggested, to leave the Negro people as they were, unawakened, unallied with one another, unhopeful about what to expect for their children in some future world?

I do not think so. If knowledge of my condition is all the freedom I get from a "freedom movement," it is better than unawareness, forgottenness and hopelessness, the existence that is like the existence of a beast. Man only truly lives by knowing, otherwise he simply performs, copying the daily habits of others, but conceiving nothing of his creative possibilities as a man, and accepting someone else's superiority and his own misery.

When we are children, growing up in our parents' care, we await the spark from the outside world. Sometimes our parents provide it—if we are lucky—sometimes it comes from another source far from home. We sit, paralyzed, surrounded by our anxiety and dread, hoping we will not have to grow up into the narrow world and ways we see about us. We are hungry for a life that turns us on; we yearn for a knowledge of living that will save us from our innocuous lives that resemble death. We look for signs in every strange event; we search for heroes in every unknown face.

It was just six years ago that I began to be alive. I had, of course, been living before—for I am now twenty-three—but I did not really know it. And I did not know it because nobody told me that I—a pensive, yearning, typical high-school senior, but Negro—existed in the minds of others as I existed in my own. Until that time my mind was locked apart from the outer contours and complexion of my body as if it and the body were strangers. The mind possessed both thought and spirit—I wanted to be an author or a scientist—which the color of the body denied. I had never seen myself and existed as a statistic exists, or as a phantom. In the white world I walked, less real to them than a shadow; and being young and well-hidden among the slums, among people who also did not exist—either in books or in films or in the government of their own lives—I waited to be called to life. And, by a miracle, I was called.

There was a commotion in our house that night in 1960. We had managed to buy our first television set. It was battered and overpriced, but my mother had gotten used to watching the afternoon soap operas at the house where she worked as maid, and nothing could satisfy her on days when she did not work but a continuation of her "stories." So she pinched pennies and bought a set.

I remained listless throughout her "stories," tales of pregnancy, abortion, hypocrisy, infidelity and alcoholism. All these men and women were white and lived in houses with servants, long staircases that they floated down, patios where liquor was served four times a day to "relax" them. But my mother, with her swollen feet eased out of her shoes, her heavy body relaxed in our only comfortable chair, watched each movement of the smartly coiffed women, heard each word, pounced upon each innuendo and inflection, and for the duration of these "stories" she saw herself as one of them. She placed herself in every scene she saw, with her braided hair turned blonde, her two hundred pounds compressed into a sleek size seven dress, her rough dark skin smooth and *white*. Her husband became dark and handsome, talented, witty, urbane, charming. And when she turned to look at my father sitting near her in his sweat shirt with his smelly feet raised on the bed to "air," there was always a tragic look of surprise on her face. Then she would sigh and go out to the kitchen looking lost and unsure of herself. My mother, a truly great woman—who raised eight children of her own and half a dozen of the neighbors' without a single complaint—was convinced that she did not exist compared to "them." She subordinated her soul to theirs and became a faithful and timid supporter of the "Beautiful White People." Once she asked me, in a moment of vicarious pride and despair, if I didn't think that "they" were "jest naturally smarter, prettier, better." My mother asked this; a woman who never got rid of any of her children, never cheated on my father, was never a hypocrite if she could help it, and never even tasted liquor. She could not even bring herself to blame "them" for making her believe what they wanted her to believe: that if she did not look like them, think like them, be sophisticated and corrupt-for-comfort's-sake like them, she was a nobody. Black was not a color on my mother, it was a shield that made her invisible. The heart that beat out its life in the great shadow cast by the American white people never knew that it was really "good."

Of course, the people who wrote the soap opera scripts always made the Negro maids in them steadfast, trusty and wise in a home-remedial sort of way; but my mother, a maid for nearly forty years, never once identified herself with the scarcely glimpsed black servant's face beneath the ruffled cap. Like everyone else, in her daydreams at least, she thought she was free.

Six years ago, after half-heartedly watching my mother's soap operas and wondering whether there wasn't something more to be asked of life, the civil rights movement came into my life. Like a good omen for the future, the face of Dr. Martin Luther King, Jr., was the first black face I saw on our new television screen. And, as in a fairy tale, my soul was stirred by the meaning for me of his mission—at the time he was being rather ignominiously dumped into a police van for having led a protest march in Alabama—and I fell in love with the sober and determined face of the movement. The singing of "We Shall Overcome"—that song betrayed by nonbelievers in it—rang for the first time in my ears. The influence that my mother's soap operas might have had on me became impossible. The life of Dr. King, seeming bigger and more miraculous than the man himself, because of all he had done and suffered, offered a pattern of strength and sincerity I felt I could trust. He had suffered much because of his simple belief in nonviolence, love and brotherhood. Perhaps the majority of men could not be reached through these beliefs, but because Dr. King kept trying to reach them in spite of danger to himself and his family, I saw in him the hero for whom I had waited so long.

What Dr. King promised was not a ranch-style house and an acre of manicured lawn for every black man, but jail and finally freedom. He did not promise two cars for every family, but the courage one day for all families everywhere to walk without shame and unafraid on their own feet. He did not say that one day it will be us chasing prospective buyers out of our prosperous well-kept neighborhoods, or in other ways exhibiting our snobbery and ignorance as all other ethnic groups before us have done; what he said was that we had a right to live anywhere in this country we chose, and a right to a meaningful well-paying job to provide us with the upkeep of our homes. He did not say we had to become carbon copies of the white American middle-class; but he did say we had the right to become whatever we wanted to become.

Because of the movement, because of an awakened faith in the newness and imagination of the human spirit, because of "black and white together"—for the first time in our history in some human relationship on and off TV—because of the beatings, the arrests, the hell of battle during the past years, I have fought harder for my life and for a chance to be myself, to be something more than a shadow or a number, than I have ever done before in my life. Before there had seemed to be no real reason for struggling beyond the effort for daily bread. Now there was a chance at that other that Jesus meant when He said we could not live by bread alone.

I have fought and kicked and fasted and prayed and cursed and cried myself to the point of existing. It has been like being born again, literally. Just "knowing" has meant everything to me. Knowing has pushed me out into the world, into college, into places, into people.

Part of what existence means to me is knowing the difference between what I am now and what I was then. It is being capable of looking after myself intellectually as well as financially. It is being able to tell when I am being wronged and by whom. It means being awake to protect myself and the ones I love. It means being a part of the world community, and being *alert* to which part it is that I have joined, and knowing how to change to another part if that part does not suit me. To know is to exist; to exist is to be involved, to move about, to see the world with my own eyes. This, at least, the movement has given me.

The hippies and other nihilists would have me believe that it is all the same whether the people in Mississippi have a movement behind them or not. Once they have their rights, they say, they will run all over themselves trying to be just like everybody else. They will be well-fed, complacent about things of the spirit, emotionless, and without that marvelous humanity and "soul" that the movement has seen them practice time and time again. What has the movement done, they ask, with the few people it has supposedly helped? Got them white-collar jobs, moved them into standardized ranch houses in white neighborhoods, given them intellectual accents to go with their nondescript gray flannel suits? "What are these people now?" they ask. And then they answer themselves, "Nothings!"

I would find this reasoning—which I have heard many, many times, from hippies and nonhippies alike—amusing, if I did not also consider it serious. For I think it is a delusion, a copout, an excuse to disassociate themselves from a world in which they feel too little has been changed or gained. The real question, however, it appears to me, is not whether poor people will adopt the middle-class mentality once they are well-fed, rather, it is whether they will ever be well-fed enough to be able to choose whatever mentality they think will suit them. The lack of a movement did not keep my mother from *wishing* herself bourgeois in her daydreams.

There is widespread starvation in Mississippi. In my own state of Georgia there are more hungry families than Lester Maddox would like to admit—or even see fed. I went to school with children who ate red dirt. The movement has prodded and pushed some liberal senators into pressuring the government for food so that the hungry may eat. Food stamps that were two dollars and out of the reach of many families not long ago have been reduced to fifty cents. The price is still out of the reach of some families, and the government, it seems to a lot of people, could spare enough free food to feed its own people. It angers people in the movement that it does not; they point to the billions in wheat we send free each year to countries abroad. Their government's slowness while people are hungry, its unwillingness to believe that there are Americans starving, its stingy cutting of the price of food stamps, make many civil rights workers throw up their hands in disgust. But they do not give up. They do not withdraw into the world of psychedelia. They apply what pressure they can to make the government give away food to hungry people. They do not plan so far ahead in their disillusionment with society that they can see these starving families buying identical ranch-style houses and sending their snobbish children to Bryn Mawr and Yale. They take first things first and try to get them fed.

They do not consider it their business, in any case, to say what kind of life the people they help must lead. How one lives is, after all, one of the rights left to the individual—when and if he has opportunity to choose. It is not the prerogative of the middle class to determine what is worthy of aspiration.

There is also every possibility that the middle-class people of tomorrow will turn out ever so much better than those of today. I even know some middle-class people of today who are not *all* bad. Often, thank God, what monkey sees, monkey *avoids* doing at all costs. So it may be, concerning what is deepest in him, with the Negro.

I think there are so few Negro hippies today because middle-class Negroes, although well-fed, are not careless. They are required by the treacherous world they live in to be clearly aware of whoever or whatever might be trying to do them in. They are middle-class in money and position, but they cannot afford to be middle-class in complacency. They distrust the hippie movement because they know that it can do nothing for Negroes as a group but "love" them, which is what all paternalists claim to do. And since the only way Negroes can survive (which they cannot do, unfortunately, on love alone) is with the support of the group, they are wisely wary and stay away.

A white writer tried recently to explain that the reason for the relatively few Negro hippies is that Negroes have built up a "super-cool" that cracks under LSD and makes them have a "bad trip." What this writer doesn't guess at is that Negroes are needing drugs less than ever these days for any kind of trip. While the hippies are "tripping," Negroes are going after power, which is so much more important to their survival and their children's survival than LSD and pot.

Everyone would be surprised if the Israelis ignored the Arabs and took up "tripping" and pot smoking. In this country we are the Israelis. Everybody who can do so would like to forget this, of course. But for us to forget it for a minute would be fatal. "We Shall Overcome" is just a song to most Americans, *but we must do it*. Or die.

What good was the civil rights movement? If it had just given this country Dr. King, a leader of conscience for once in our lifetime, it would have been enough. If it had just taken black eyes off white television stories, it would have been enough. If it had fed one starving child, it would have been enough.

If the civil rights movement is "dead," and if it gave us nothing else, it gave us each other forever. It gave some of us bread, some of us shelter, some of us knowledge and pride, all of us comfort. It gave us our children, our husbands, our brothers, our fathers, as men reborn and with a purpose for living. It broke the pattern of black servitude in this country. It shattered the phony "promise" of white soap operas that sucked away so many pitiful lives. It gave us history and men far greater than Presidents. It gave us heroes, selfless men of courage and strength, for our little boys to follow. It gave us hope for tomorrow. It called us to life.

Because we live, it can never die.

BLACK POWER: ITS NEED AND SUBSTANCE
Stokely Carmichael and Charles V. Hamilton

A militant black leader and a black historian define the concept of black power and assert the need for blacks to unite and organize. Their goal is to build and strengthen the black community, for they fear that the present drive for integration "means that black people must give up their identity, deny their heritage." Born in Trinidad in 1941, Stokely Carmichael has long been active in the movement for greater black power and influence; he was once head of the Student Non-Violent Coordinating Committee. Charles Hamilton is Professor of Political Science at Roosevelt University.

"To carve out a place for itself in the politico-social order," V. O. Key, Jr. wrote in *Politics, Parties and Pressure Groups,* "a new group may have to fight for reorientation of many of the values of the old order" (p. 57). This is especially true when that group is composed of black people in the American society—a society that has for centuries deliberately and systematically excluded them from political participation. Black people in the United States must raise hard questions, questions which challenge the very nature of the society itself: its long-standing values, beliefs and institutions.

To do this, we must first redefine ourselves. Our basic need is to reclaim our history and our identity from what must be called cultural terrorism, from the depredation of self-justifying white guilt. We shall have to struggle for the right to create our own terms through which to define ourselves and our relationship to the society, and to have these terms recognized. This is the first necessity of a free people, and the first right that any oppressor must suspend.

In *Politics Among Nations,* Hans Morgenthau defined political power as "the psychological control over the minds of men" (p. 29). This control includes the attempt by the oppressor to have *his* definitions, *his* historical descriptions, *accepted* by the oppressed. This was true in Africa no less than in the United States. To black Africans, the word

"Uhuru" means "freedom," but they had to fight the white colonizers for the right to use the term. The recorded history of this country's dealings with red and black men offers other examples. In the wars between the white settlers and the "Indians," a battle won by the Cavalry was described as a "victory." The "Indians'" triumphs, however, were "massacres." (The American colonists were not unaware of the need to define their acts in their own terms. They labeled their fight against England a "revolution"; the English attempted to demean it by calling it "insubordination" or "riotous.")

The historical period following Reconstruction in the South after the Civil War has been called by many historians the period of Redemption, implying that the bigoted southern slave societies were "redeemed" from the hands of "reckless and irresponsible" black rulers. Professor John Hope Franklin's *Reconstruction* or Dr. W. E. B. DuBois' *Black Reconstruction* should be sufficient to dispel inaccurate historical notions, but the larger society persists in its own self-serving accounts. Thus black people came to be depicted as "lazy," "apathetic," "dumb," "shiftless," "good-timers." Just as red men had to be recorded as "savages" to justify the white man's theft of their land, so black men had to be vilified in order to justify their continued oppression. Those who have the right to define are the masters of the situation. Lewis Carroll understood this:

> "When I use a word," Humpty Dumpty said in a rather scornful tone, "it means just what I choose it to mean—neither more nor less."
> "The question is," said Alice, "Whether you *can* make words mean so many different things."
> "The question is," said Humpty Dumpty, "which is to be master—that's all." [1]

Today, the American educational system continues to reinforce the entrenched values of the society through the use of words. Few people in this country question that this is "the land of the free and the home of the brave." They have had these words drummed into them from childhood. Few people question that this is the "Great Society" or that this country is fighting "Communist aggression" around the world. We mouth these things over and over, and they become truisms not to be questioned. In a similar way, black people have been saddled with epithets.

"Integration" is another current example of a word which has been defined according to the way white Americans see it. To many of them, it means black men wanting to marry white daughters; it means "race mixing"—implying bed or dance partners. To black people, it has meant a way to improve their lives—economically and politically. But

---

[1] Lewis Carroll, *Through the Looking Glass.*

the predominant white definition has stuck in the minds of too many people.

Black people must redefine themselves, and only *they* can do that. Throughout this country, vast segments of the black communities are beginning to recognize the need to assert their own definitions, to reclaim their history, their culture; to create their own sense of community and togetherness. There is a growing resentment of the word "Negro," for example, because this term is the invention of our oppressor; it is *his* image of us that he describes. Many blacks are now calling themselves African-Americans, Afro-Americans or black people because that is *our* image of ourselves. When we begin to define our own image, the stereotypes—that is, lies—that our oppressor has developed will begin in the white community and end there. The black community will have a positive image of itself that *it* has created. This means we will no longer call ourselves lazy, apathetic, dumb, good-timers, shiftless, etc. Those are words used by white America to define us. If we accept these adjectives, as some of us have in the past, then we see ourselves only in a negative way, precisely the way white America wants us to see ourselves. Our incentive is broken and our will to fight is surrendered. From now on we shall view ourselves as African-Americans and as black people who are in fact energetic, determined, intelligent, beautiful and peace-loving.

There is a terminology and ethos peculiar to the black community of which black people are beginning to be no longer ashamed. Black communities are the only large segments of this society where people refer to each other as brother—soul-brother, soul-sister. Some people may look upon this as *ersatz,* as make-believe, but it is not that. It is real. It is a growing sense of community. It is a growing realization that black Americans have a common bond not only among themselves, but with their African brothers. In *Black Man's Burden,* John O. Killens described his trip to ten African countries as follows:

Everywhere I went people called me brother. . . . "Welcome, American brother." It was a good feeling for me, to be in Africa. To walk in a land for the first time in your entire life knowing within yourself that your color would not be held against you. No black man ever knows this in America [p. 160].

More and more black Americans are developing this feeling. They are becoming aware that they have a history which pre-dates their forced introduction to this country. African-American history means a long history beginning on the continent of Africa, a history not taught in the standard textbooks of this country. It is absolutely essential that black people know this history, that they know their roots, that they develop an awareness of their cultural heritage. Too long have they been kept in submission by being told that they had no culture, no manifest heritage, before they landed on the slave auction blocks in this country. If black people are to know themselves as a vibrant, valiant people, they must know their roots. And they will soon learn that the Hollywood image of man-eating cannibals waiting for, and waiting on, the Great White Hunter is a lie.

With redefinition will come a clearer notion of the role black Americans can play in this world. This role will emerge clearly out of the unique, common experiences of Afro-Asians. Killens concludes:

> I believe furthermore that the American Negro can be the bridge between the West and Africa-Asia. We black Americans can serve as a bridge to mutual understanding. The one thing we black Americans have in common with the other colored peoples of the world is that we have all felt the cruel and ruthless heel of white supremacy. We have all been "niggerized" on one level or another. And all of us are determined to "deniggerize" the earth. To rid the world of "niggers" is the Black Man's Burden, human reconstruction is the grand objective [p. 176].

Only when black people fully develop this sense of community, of themselves, can they begin to deal effectively with the problems of racism in *this* country. This is what we mean by a new consciousness; this is the vital first step.

The next step is what we shall call the process of political modernization—a process which must take place if the society is to be rid of racism. "Political modernization" includes many things, but we mean by it three major concepts: (1) questioning old values and institutions of the society; (2) searching for new and different forms of political structure to solve political and economic problems; and (3) broadening the base of political participation to include more people in the decision-making process. These notions (we shall take up each in turn) are central to our thinking throughout this book and to contemporary American history as a whole. As David Apter wrote in *The Politics of Modernization,* ". . . the struggle to modernize is what has given meaning to our generation. It tests our cherished institutions and our beliefs. . . . So compelling a force has it become that we are forced to ask new questions of our own institutions. Each country, whether modernized or modernizing, stands in both judgment and fear of the results. Our own society is no exception (p. 2).

The values of this society support a racist system; we find it incongruous to ask black people to adopt and support most of those values. We also reject the assumption that the basic institutions of this society must be preserved. The goal of black people must *not* be to assimilate into middle-class America, for that class—as a whole—is without a viable conscience as regards humanity. The values of the middle class

permit the perpetuation of the ravages of the black community. The values of that class are based on material aggrandizement, not the expansion of humanity. The values of that class ultimately support cloistered
little closed societies tucked away neatly in tree-lined suburbia. The values of that class do *not* lead to the creation of an open society. That
class *mouths* its preference for a free, competitive society, while at the
same time forcefully and even viciously denying to black people as a
group the opportunity to compete.

We are not unmindful of other descriptions of the social utility of the
middle class. Banfield and Wilson, in *City Politics,* concluded:

> The departure of the middle class from the central city is important in
> other ways. . . . The middle class supplies a social and political leavening in
> the life of a city. Middle-class people demand good schools and integrity in
> government. They support churches, lodges, parent-teacher associations,
> scout troops, better-housing committees, art galleries, and operas. It is the
> middle class, in short, that asserts a conception of the public interest. Now
> its activity is increasingly concentrated in the suburbs [p. 14].

But this same middle class manifests a sense of superior group position
in regard to race. This class wants "good government" for *themselves;* it
wants good schools *for its children.* At the same time, many of its members sneak into the black community by day, exploit it, and take the
money home to their middle-class communities at night to support their
operas and art galleries and comfortable homes. When not actually robbing, they will fight off the handful of more affluent black people who
seek to move in; when they approve or even seek token integration, it
applies only to black people like themselves—as "white" as possible.
This class is the backbone of institutional racism in this country.

Thus we reject the goal of assimilation into middle-class America because the values of that class are in themselves anti-humanist and because that class as a social force perpetuates racism. We must face the
fact that, in the past, what we have called the movement has not really
questioned the middle-class values and institutions of this country. If
anything, it has accepted those values and institutions without fully realizing their racist nature. Reorientation means an emphasis on the dignity of man, not on the sanctity of property. It means the creation of a
society where human misery and poverty are repugnant to that society,
not an indication of laziness or lack of initiative. The creation of new
values means the establishment of a society based, as Killens expresses
it in *Black Man's Burden,* on "free people," not "free enterprise" (p.
167). To do this means to modernize—*indeed, to civilize*—this country.

Supporting the old values are old political and economic structures;
these must also be "modernized." We should at this point distinguish

between "structures" and "system." By system, we have in mind the entire American complex of basic institutions, values, beliefs, etc. By structures, we mean the specific institutions (political parties, interest groups, bureaucratic administrations) which exist to conduct the business of that system. Obviously, the first is broader than the second. Also, the second assumes the legitimacy of the first. Our view is that, given the illegitimacy of the system, we cannot then proceed to transform that system with existing structures.

The two major political parties in this country have become non-viable entities for the legitimate representation of the real needs of masses —especially blacks—in this country. Walter Lippmann raised the same point in his syndicated column of December 8, 1966. He pointed out that the party system in the United States developed before our society became as technologically complex as it is now. He says that the ways in which men live and define themselves are changing radically. Old ideological issues, once the subject of passionate controversy, Lippmann argues, are of little interest today. He asks whether the great urban complexes—which are rapidly becoming the centers of black population in the U.S.—can be run with the same systems and ideas that derive from a time when America was a country of small villages and farms. While not addressing himself directly to the question of race, Lippmann raises a major question about our political institutions; and the crisis of race in America may be its major symptom.

Black people have seen the city planning commissions, the urban renewal commissions, the boards of education and the police departments fail to speak to their needs in a meaningful way. We must devise new structures, new institutions to replace those forms or to make them responsive. There is nothing sacred or inevitable about old institutions; the focus must be on people, not forms.

Existing structures and established ways of doing things have a way of perpetuating themselves and for this reason, the modernizing process will be difficult. Therefore, timidity in calling into question the boards of education or the police departments will not do. They must be challenged forcefully and clearly. If this means the creation of parallel community institutions, then that must be the solution. If this means that black parents must gain control over the operation of the schools in the black community, then that must be the solution. The search for new forms means the search for institutions that will, for once, make decisions in the interest of black people. It means, for example, a building inspection department that neither winks at violations of building codes by absentee slumlords nor imposes meaningless fines which permit them to continue their exploitation of the black community.

Essential to the modernization of structures is a broadened base of political participation. More and more people must become politically sensitive and active (we have already seen this happening in some areas of the South). People must no longer be tied, by small incentives or handouts, to a corrupting and corruptible white machine. Black people will choose their own leaders and hold those leaders responsible to *them*. A broadened base means an end to the condition described by James Wilson in *Negro Politics,* whereby "Negroes tended to be the objects rather than the subjects of civic action. Things are often done for, or about, or to, or because of Negroes, but they are less frequently done *by* Negroes" (p. 133). Broadening the base of political participation, then, has as much to do with the quality of black participation as with the quantity. We are fully aware that the black vote, especially in the North, has been pulled out of white pockets and "delivered" whenever it was in the interest of white politicians to do so. That vote must no longer be controllable by those who have neither the interests nor the demonstrated concern of black people in mind.

As the base broadens, as more and more black people become activated, they will perceive more clearly the special disadvantages heaped upon them as a group. They will perceive that the larger society is growing more affluent while the black society is retrogressing, as daily life and mounting statistics clearly show (see Chapters I and VIII). V. O. Key describes what often happens next, in *Politics, Parties and Pressure Groups:* "A factor of great significance in the setting off of political movements is an abrupt change for the worse in the status of one group relative to that of other groups in society. . . . A rapid change for the worse . . . in the relative status of any group . . . is likely to precipitate political action" (p. 24). Black people will become increasingly active as they notice that their retrogressive status exists in large measure because of values and institutions arraigned against them. They will begin to stress and strain and call the entire system into question. Political modernization will be in motion. We believe that it is now in motion. One form of that motion is Black Power.

The adoption of the concept of Black Power is one of the most legitimate and healthy developments in American politics and race relations in our time. The concept of Black Power speaks to all the needs mentioned in this chapter. It is a call for black people in this country to unite, to recognize their heritage, to build a sense of community. It is a call for black people to begin to define their own goals, to lead their own organizations and to support those organizations. It is a call to reject the racist institutions and values of this society.

The concept of Black Power rests on a fundamental premise: *Before a group can enter the open society, it must first close ranks.* By this we mean that group solidarity is necessary before a group can operate effectively from a bargaining position of strength in a pluralistic society. Traditionally, each new ethnic group in this society has found the route to social and political viability through the organization of its own institutions with which to represent its needs within the larger society. Studies in voting behavior specifically, and political behavior generally, have made it clear that politically the American pot has not melted. Italians vote for Rubino over O'Brien; Irish for Murphy over Goldberg, etc. This phenomenon may seem distasteful to some, but it has been and remains today a central fact of the American political system. There are other examples of ways in which groups in the society have remembered their roots and used this effectively in the political arena. Theodore Sorensen describes the politics of foreign aid during the Kennedy Administration in his book *Kennedy:*

> No powerful constituencies or interest groups backed foreign aid. The Marshall Plan at least had appealed to Americans who traced their roots to the Western European nations aided. But there were few voters who identified with India, Colombia or Tanganyika [p. 351].

The extent to which black Americans can and do "trace their roots" to Africa, to that extent will they be able to be more effective on the political scene.

A white reporter set forth this point in other terms when he made the following observation about white Mississippi's manipulation of the anti-poverty program:

> The war on poverty has been predicated on the notion that there is such a thing as a community which can be defined geographically and mobilized for a collective effort to help the poor. This theory has no relationship to reality in the deep South. In every Mississippi county there are two communities. Despite all the pious platitudes of the moderates on both sides, these two communities habitually see their interests in terms of conflict rather than cooperation. Only when the Negro community can muster enough political, economic and professional strength to compete on somewhat equal terms, will Negroes believe in the possibility of true cooperation and whites accept its necessity. En route to integration, the Negro community needs to develop a greater independence—a chance to run its own affairs and not cave in whenever "the man" barks—or so it seems to me, and to most of the knowledgeable people with whom I talked in Mississippi. To OEO, this judgment may sound like black nationalism. . . .[1]

The point is obvious: black people must lead and run their own organizations. Only black people can convey the revolutionary idea—and it is a revolutionary idea—that black people are able to do things themselves. Only they can help create in the community an aroused and continuing black consciousness that will provide the basis for political strength. In the past, white allies have often furthered white supremacy

[1] Christopher Jencks, "Accommodating Whites: A New Look at Mississippi," *The New Republic* (April 16, 1966).

without the whites involved realizing it, or even wanting to do so. Black people must come together and do things for themselves. They must achieve self-identity and self-determination in order to have their daily needs met.

Black Power means, for example, that in Lowndes County, Alabama, a black sheriff can end police brutality. A black tax assessor and tax collector and county board of revenue can lay, collect, and channel tax monies for the building of better roads and schools serving black people. In such areas as Lowndes, where black people have a majority, they will attempt to use power to exercise control. This is what they seek: control. When black people lack a majority, Black Power means proper representation and sharing of control. It means the creation of power bases, of strength, from which black people can press to change local or nation-wide patterns of oppression—instead of from weakness.

It does not mean *merely* putting black faces into office. Black visibility is not Black Power. Most of the black politicians around the country today are not examples of Black Power. The power must be that of a community, and emanate from there. The black politicians must start from there. The black politicians must stop being representatives of "downtown" machines, whatever the cost might be in terms of lost patronage and holiday handouts.

Black Power recognizes—it must recognize—the ethnic basis of American politics as well as the power-oriented nature of American politics. Black Power therefore calls for black people to consolidate behind their own, so that they can bargain from a position of strength. But while we endorse the *procedure* of group solidarity and identity for the purpose of attaining certain goals in the body politic, this does not mean that black people should strive for the same kind of rewards (i.e., end results) obtained by the white society. The ultimate values and goals are not domination or exploitation of other groups, but rather an effective share in the total power of the society.

Nevertheless, some observers have labeled those who advocate Black Power as racists; they have said that the call for self-identification and self-determination is "racism in reverse" or "black supremacy." This is a deliberate and absurd lie. There is no analogy—by any stretch of definition or imagination—between the advocates of Black Power and white racists. Racism is not merely exclusion on the basis of race but exclusion for the purpose of subjugating or maintaining subjugation. The goal of the racists is to keep black people on the bottom, arbitrarily and dictatorially, as they have done in this country for over three hundred years. The goal of black self-determination and black self-identity—Black Power—is full participation in the decision-making processes affecting the lives of black people, and recognition of the virtues in themselves as black people. The black people of this country have not lynched whites, bombed their churches, murdered their children and manipulated laws and institutions to maintain oppression. White racists have. Congressional laws, one after the other, have not been necessary to stop black people from oppressing others and denying others the full enjoyment of their rights. White racists have made such laws necessary. The goal of Black Power is positive and functional to a free and viable society. No white racist can make this claim.

A great deal of public attention and press space was devoted to the hysterical accusation of "black racism" when the call for Black Power was first sounded. A national committee of influential black churchmen affiliated with the National Council of Churches, despite their obvious respectability and responsibility, had to resort to a paid advertisement to articulate their position, while anyone yapping "black racism" made front-page news. In their statement, published in the *New York Times* of July 31, 1966, the churchmen said:

We, an informal group of Negro churchmen in America, are deeply disturbed about the crisis brought upon our country by historic distortions of important human realities in the controversy about "black power." What we see shining through the variety of rhetoric is not anything new but the same old problem of power and race which has faced our beloved country since 1619.

. . . The conscience of black men is corrupted because having no power to implement the demands of conscience, the concern for justice in the absence of justice becomes a chaotic self-surrender. Powerlessness breeds a race of beggars. We are faced with a situation where powerless conscience meets conscienceless power, threatening the very foundations of our Nation.

We deplore the overt violence of riots, but we feel it is more important to focus on the real sources of these eruptions. These sources may be abetted inside the Ghetto, but their basic cause lies in the silent and covert violence which white middle class America inflicts upon the victims of the inner city.

. . . In short, the failure of American leaders to use American power to create equal opportunity *in life* as well as *law,* this is the real problem and not the anguished cry for black power.

. . . Without the capacity to participate with power, i.e., to have some organized political and economic strength to really influence people with whom one interacts, integration is not meaningful.

. . . America has asked its Negro citizens to fight for opportunity as *individuals,* whereas at certain points in our history what we have needed most has been opportunity for the *whole group,* not just for selected and approved Negroes.

. . . We must not apologize for the existence of this form of group power, for we have been oppressed as a group and not as individuals. We will not find our way out of that oppression until both we and America accept the need for Negro Americans, as well as for Jews, Italians, Poles, and white Anglo-Saxon Protestants, among others, to have and to wield group power.

It is a commentary on the fundamentally racist nature of this society that the concept of group strength for black people must be articulated —not to mention defended. No other group would submit to being led by others. Italians do not run the Anti-Defamation League of B'nai B'rith. Irish do not chair Christopher Columbus Societies. Yet when black people call for black-run and all-black organizations, they are immediately classed in a category with the Ku Klux Klan. This is interesting and ironic, but by no means surprising: the society does not expect black people to be able to take care of their business, and there are many who prefer it precisely that way.

In the end, we cannot and shall not offer any guarantees that Black Power, if achieved, would be non-racist. No one can predict human behavior. Social change always has unanticipated consequences. If black racism is what the larger society fears, we cannot help them. We can only state what we hope will be the result, given the fact that the present situation is unacceptable and that we have no real alternative but to work for Black Power. The final truth is that the white society is not entitled to reassurances, even if it were possible to offer them.

We have outlined the meaning and goals of Black Power; we have also discussed one major thing which it is not. There are others of greater importance. The advocates of Black Power reject the old slogans and meaningless rhetoric of previous years in the civil rights struggle. The language of yesterday is indeed irrelevant: progress, non-violence, integration, fear of "white backlash," coalition. Let us look at the rhetoric and see why these terms must be set aside or redefined.

One of the tragedies of the struggle against racism is that up to this point there has been no national organization which could speak to the growing militancy of young black people in the urban ghettos and the black-belt South. There has been only a "civil rights" movement, whose tone of voice was adapted to an audience of middle-class whites. It served as a sort of buffer zone between that audience and angry young blacks. It claimed to speak for the needs of a community, but it did not speak in the tone of that community. None of its so-called leaders could go into a rioting community and be listened to. In a sense, the blame must be shared—along with the mass media—by those leaders for what happened in Watts, Harlem, Chicago, Cleveland and other places. Each time the black people in those cities saw Dr. Martin Luther King get slapped they became angry. When they saw little black girls bombed to death *in a church* and civil rights workers ambushed and murdered, they were angrier; and when nothing happened, they were steaming mad. We had nothing to offer that they could see, except to go out and be beaten again. We helped to build their frustration.

We had only the old language of love and suffering. And in most places—that is, from the liberals and middle class—we got back the old language of patience and progress. The civil rights leaders were saying to the country: "Look, you guys are supposed to be nice guys, and we are only going to do what we are supposed to do. Why do you beat us up? Why don't you give us what we ask? Why don't you straighten yourselves out?" For the masses of black people, this language resulted in virtually nothing. In fact, their objective day-to-day condition worsened. The unemployment rate among black people increased while that among whites declined. Housing conditions in the black communities deteriorated. Schools in the black ghettos continued to plod along on outmoded techniques, inadequate curricula, and with all too many tired and indifferent teachers. Meanwhile, the President picked up the refrain of "We Shall Overcome" while the Congress passed civil rights law after civil rights law, only to have them effectively nullified by deliberately weak enforcement. "Progress is being made," we were told.

Such language, along with admonitions to remain non-violent and fear the white backlash, convinced some that that course was the *only* course to follow. It misled some into believing that a black minority could bow its head and get whipped into a meaningful position of power. The very notion is absurd. The white society devised the language, adopted the rules and had the black community narcotized into believing that that language and those rules were, in fact, relevant. The black community was told time and again how *other* immigrants finally won *acceptance:* that is, by following the Protestant Ethic of Work and Achievement. They worked hard; therefore, they achieved. We were not told that it was by building Irish Power, Italian Power, Polish Power or Jewish Power that these groups got themselves together and operated from positions of strength. We were not told that "the American dream" wasn't designed for black people. That while today, to whites, the dream may *seem* to include black people, it cannot do so by the very nature of this nation's political and economic system, which imposes institutional racism on the black masses if not upon every individual black. A notable comment on that "dream" was made by Dr. Percy Julian, the black scientist and director of the Julian Research Institute in Chicago, a man for whom the dream seems to have come true. While not subscribing to "black power" as he understood it, Dr. Julian clearly understood the basis for it: "The false concept of basic Negro inferiority is one of the curses that still lingers. It is a problem created by the white man. Our children just no longer are going to accept the patience we were taught by our generation. We were taught a pretty little lie— excel and the whole world lies open before you. *I obeyed the injunction and found it to be wishful thinking."* (Authors' italics) [2]

A key phrase in our buffer-zone days was non-violence. For years it has been thought that black people would not literally fight for their

[2] *The New York Times* (April 30, 1967), p. 30.

lives. Why this has been so is not entirely clear; neither the larger society nor black people are noted for passivity. The notion apparently stems from the years of marches and demonstrations and sit-ins where black people did not strike back and the violence always came from white mobs. There are many who still sincerely believe in that approach. From our viewpoint, rampaging white mobs and white night-riders must be made to understand that their days of free head-whipping are over. Black people should and must fight back. Nothing more quickly repels someone bent on destroying you than the unequivocal message: "O.K., fool, make your move, and run the same risk I run—of dying."

When the concept of Black Power is set forth, many people immediately conjure up notions of violence. The country's reaction to the Deacons for Defense and Justice, which originated in Louisiana, is instructive. Here is a group which realized that the "law" and law enforcement agencies would not protect people, so they had to do it themselves. If a nation fails to protect its citizens, then that nation cannot condemn those who take up the task themselves. The Deacons and all other blacks who resort to self-defense represent a simple answer to a simple question: what man would not defend his family and home from attack?

But this frightened some white people, because they knew that black people would now fight back. They knew that this was precisely what *they* would have long since done if *they* were subjected to the injustices and oppression heaped on blacks. Those of us who advocate Black Power are quite clear in our own minds that a "non-violent" approach to civil rights is an approach black people cannot afford and a luxury white people do not deserve. It is crystal clear to us—and it must become so with the white society—*that there can be no social order without social justice.* White people must be made to understand that they must stop messing with black people, or the blacks *will* fight back!

Next, we must deal with the term "integration." According to its advocates, social justice will be accomplished by "integrating the Negro into the mainstream institutions of the society from which he has been traditionally excluded." This concept is based on the assumption that there is nothing of value in the black community and that little of value could be created among black people. The thing to do is siphon off the "acceptable" black people into the surrounding middle-class white community.

The goals of integrationists are middle-class goals, articulated primarily by a small group of Negroes with middle-class aspirations or status. Their kind of integration has meant that a few blacks "make it," leaving the black community, sapping it of leadership potential and know-how. As we noted in Chapter I, those token Negroes—absorbed into a white mass—are of no value to the remaining black masses. They become meaningless show-pieces for a conscience-soothed white society.

Such people will state that they would prefer to be treated "only as individuals, not as Negroes"; that they "are not and should not be preoccupied with race." This is a totally unrealistic position. In the first place, black people have not suffered as individuals but as members of a group; therefore, their liberation lies in group action. This is why SNCC—and the concept of Black Power—affirms that helping *individual* black people to solve their problems on an *individual* basis does little to alleviate the mass of black people. Secondly, while color blindness *may* be a sound goal ultimately, we must realize that race is an overwhelming fact of life in this historical period. There is no black man in this country who can live "simply as a man." His blackness is an ever-present fact of this racist society, whether he recognizes it or not. It is unlikely that this or the next generation will witness the time when race will no longer be relevant in the conduct of public affairs and in public policy decision-making. To realize this and to attempt to deal with it does not make one a racist or overly preoccupied with race; it puts one in the forefront of a significant *struggle*. If there is no intense struggle today, there will be no meaningful results tomorrow.

"Integration" as a goal today speaks to the problem of blackness not only in an unrealistic way but also in a despicable way. It is based on complete acceptance of the fact that in order to have a decent house or education, black people must move into a white neighborhood or send their children to a white school. This reinforces, among both black and white, the idea that "white" is automatically superior and "black" is by definition inferior. For this reason, "integration" is a subterfuge for the maintenance of white supremacy. It allows the nation to focus on a handful of Southern black children who get into white schools at a great price, and to ignore the ninety-four percent who are left in unimproved all-black schools. Such situations will not change until black people become equal in a way that means something, and integration ceases to be a one-way street. Then integration does not mean draining skills and energies from the black ghetto into white neighborhoods. To sprinkle black children among white pupils in outlying schools is at best a stop-gap measure. The goal is not to take black children out of the black community and expose them to white middle-class values; the goal is to build and strengthen the black community.

"Integration" also means that black people must give up their identity, deny their heritage. We recall the conclusion of Killian and Grigg: "At the present time, integration as a solution to the race problem demands that the Negro foreswear his identity as a Negro." The fact is that integration, as traditionally articulated, would abolish the black community. The fact is that what must be abolished is not the black community, but the dependent colonial status that has been inflicted upon it.

The racial and cultural personality of the black community must be preserved and that community must win its freedom while preserving its cultural integrity. Integrity includes a pride—in the sense of self-acceptance, not chauvinism—in being black, in the historical attainments and contributions of black people. No person can be healthy, complete and mature if he must deny a part of himself; this is what "integration" has required thus far. This is the essential difference between integration as it is currently practiced and the concept of Black Power.

The idea of cultural integrity is so obvious that it seems almost simple-minded to spell things out at this length. Yet millions of Americans resist such truths when they are applied to black people. Again, that resistance is a comment on the fundamental racism in the society. Irish Catholics took care of their own first without a lot of apology for doing so, without any dubious language from timid leadership about guarding against "backlash." Everyone understood it to be a perfectly legitimate procedure. Of course, there would be "backlash." Organization begets counterorganization, but this was no reason to defer.

The so-called white backlash against black people is something else: the embedded traditions of institutional racism being brought into the open and calling forth overt manifestations of individual racism. In the summer of 1966, when the protest marches into Cicero, Illinois, began, the black people knew they were not allowed to live in Cicero and the white people knew it. When blacks began to demand the right to live in homes in that town, the whites simply reminded them of the status quo. Some people called this "backlash." It was, in fact, racism defending itself. In the black community, this is called "White folks showing their color." It is ludicrous to blame black people for what is simply an overt manifestation of white racism. Dr. Martin Luther King stated clearly that the protest marches were not the cause of the racism but merely exposed a long-term cancerous condition in the society.

We come now to the rhetoric of coalition as part of the traditional approach to ending racism: the concept of the civil rights movement as a kind of liaison between the powerful white community and a dependent black community. "Coalition" involves the whole question of how one approaches politics and political alliances. It is so basic to an understanding of Black Power that we will devote an entire chapter to the subject.

THE TROUBLE WITH BLACK POWER
Christopher Lasch

In this essay Christopher Lasch, Professor of History at Northwestern University and author of *The New Radicalism* and *Agony of the American Left,* criticizes the black power movement, and particularly two of its spokesmen, Stokely Carmichael and Charles Hamilton, for not fully considering the nature and the implications of the power they seek. Lasch finds the black power movement abounding in contradictions and suffering from a lack of concrete, realistic proposals.

"In the place of a matured social vision there will always be those who will gladly substitute the catastrophic and glorious act of martyrdom and self-immolation for a cause."

Harold Cruse, *The Crisis of the Negro Intellectual*

Whatever else "Black Power" means, the slogan itself indicates that the movement for racial equality has entered a new phase. Even those who argue that the change is largely rhetorical or that Black Power merely complements the struggle for "civil rights" would presumably not deny that "Black Power" articulates, at the very least, a new sense of urgency, if not a sense of impending crisis. Together with last summer's riots, it challenges the belief, until recently widespread, that the United States is making substantial progress toward racial justice and that it is only a matter of time and further effort before the color line is effectively obliterated.

Now even the opponents of Black Power issue warnings of apocalypse. "We shall overcome" no longer expresses the spirit of the struggle. Race war seems a more likely prospect. The Negro movement itself is splitting along racial lines. In the form in which it existed until 1963 or 1964, the civil rights movement is dead: this is not a conjecture but a historical fact. Whether the movement can be revived in some other form, or whether it will give way to something completely different, remains to be seen. Meanwhile time seems to be working on the side of an imminent disaster.

What has changed? Why did the civil rights movement which seemed so confident and successful at the time of the Washington march in 1963, falter until now it seems to have reached the point of collapse? Why has "Black Power" displaced "freedom" as the rallying-point of Negro militancy?

There are several reasons for this change. The most obvious is that the apparent victories of the civil rights coalition have not brought about any discernible changes in the lives of most Negroes, at least not in the North. Virtually all the recent books and articles on Black Power acknowledge this failure or insist on it, depending on the point of view. Charles E. Fager's *White Reflections on Black Power,* for example, analyzes in detail the Civil Rights Act of 1964—the major legislative achievement of the civil rights coalition—and shows how the act has been systematically subverted in the South, title by title, and how, in the North, many of its provisions (such as voting safeguards and desegregation of public accommodations) were irrelevant to begin with. The inadequacy of civil rights legislation is not difficult to grasp. Even the most superficial accounts of the summer's riots see the connection between hopes raised by civil rights agitation and the Negroes' disappointing realization that this agitation, whatever its apparent successes, has nevertheless failed to relieve the tangible miseries of ghetto life.

Not only have the civil rights laws proved to be intrinsically weaker and more limited in their application than they seemed at the time they were passed, but the unexpectedly bitter resistance to civil rights, particularly in the North, has made it difficult to implement even these limited gains, let alone to win new struggles for open housing, an end to de facto segregation, and equal employment. Northern segregationists may not be strong enough to elect Mrs. Hicks mayor of Boston, but they can delay open housing indefinitely, it would seem, in Milwaukee as well as in every other Northern city—even those which have nominally adopted open housing. Everywhere in the North civil rights agitation, instead of breaking down barriers as expected, has met a wall of resistance. If anything, Negroes have made more gains in the South than in the North. The strategy of the civil rights movement, resting implicitly on the premise that the North was more enlightened than the South, was unprepared for the resistance it has encountered in the North.

The shifting focus of the struggle from the South to the North thus has contributed both to the weakening of the civil rights movement and to the emergence of Black Power. The implications of this change of scene go beyond what is immediately evident—that federal troops, for instance, appear on the side of the Negroes in Little Rock, whereas in Detroit they are the enemy. The civil rights movement in the South was the product of a set of conditions which is not likely to be repeated in the North: federal efforts to "reconstruct" the South; the tendency of Northern liberals to express their distaste for American society vicariously by attacking racism in the South, rather than by confronting racism at home; the revival of Southern liberalism. Moreover, the civil rights movement, in its Southern phase, rested on the indigenous Negro subculture which has grown up since the Civil War under the peculiar conditions of Southern segregation—a culture separate and unequal but semiautonomous and therefore capable of giving its own distinctive character to the movement for legal and political equality.

E. Franklin Frazier once wrote that the Negro's "primary struggle" in America "has been to acquire a culture"—customs, values, and forms of expression which, transmitted from generation to generation, provide a people with a sense of its own integrity and collective identity. Under slavery, African forms of social organization, family life, religion, language, and even art disintegrated, leaving the slave neither an African nor an American but a man suspended, as Kenneth Stampp has said, "between two cultures," unable to participate in either. After the Civil War, Southern Negroes gradually developed institutions of their own, derived from American sources but adapted to their own needs, and therefore capable of giving the Negro community the beginnings at least of cohesiveness and collective self-discipline. The Negro church managed to impose strict standards of sexual morality, thereby making possible the emergence of stable families over which the father—not the mother, as under slavery—presided.

Stable families, in turn, furnished the continuity between generations without which Negroes could not even have begun their slow and painful self-advancement—the accumulation of talent, skills, and leadership which by the 1950s had progressed to the point where Southern Negroes, together with their liberal allies, could launch an attack against segregation. The prominence of the Negro church in their struggle showed the degree to which the civil rights movement was rooted in the peculiar conditions of Negro life in the South—conditions which had made the church the central institution of the Negro subculture. Even radicals like Charles M. Sherrod of SNCC who condemned the passivity of the Negro church realized that "no one working in the South can expect to 'beat the box' if he assumes . . . that one does not need the church as it exists."

The breakdown of the Southern Negro subculture in the North has recreated one of the conditions that existed under slavery, that of dangling between two cultures. Unlike other rural people who have migrated over the last hundred and forty years to the cities of the North, Southern Negroes have not been able to transplant their rural way of life even with modifications. The church decays; the family reverts to the matricentric pattern. The schools, which are segregated but at the same time controlled by white people, hold up middle-class norms to which black children are expected to conform; if they fail they are written off as "unteachable." Meanwhile the mass media flood the ghetto with images of affluence, which Negroes absorb without absorbing the ethic of disciplined self-denial and postponement of gratification that has traditionally been a central component of the materialist ethic.

In the South, the Negro church implanted an ethic of patience, suffering, and endurance. As in many peasant or precapitalist societies, this kind of religion proved surprisingly conducive—once endurance was divorced from passive resignation—to effective political action. But the ethic of endurance, which is generally found among oppressed peoples in backward societies, cannot survive exposure to modern materialism. It gives way to an ethic of accumulation. Or, if real opportunities for accumulation do not exist, it gives way to hedonism, opportunism, cynicism, violence, and self-hatred—the characteristics of what Oscar Lewis calls the culture of poverty.

Lewis writes:

The culture of poverty is a relatively thin culture. . . . It does not provide much support or long-range satisfaction and its encouragement of mistrust tends to magnify helplessness and isolation. Indeed, the poverty of culture is one of the crucial aspects of the culture of poverty.

These observations rest on Lewis's studies of the ghettos of Mexico City and of the Puerto Rican ghettos of San Juan and New York, where the breakdown of traditional peasant cultures has created a distinctive type of culture which comes close to being no culture at all. Something of the same thing has happened to the Negro in the North; and this helps to explain what Frazier meant when he said that the Negro's primary struggle in America had been "to acquire a culture."

This analysis in turn makes it possible to see why nationalist sects like the Nation of Islam, which have never made much headway in the South, find the Northern ghetto a fertile soil; while the civil rights movement, on the other hand, has become progressively weaker as the focus of the Negroes' struggle shifts from the South to the North. The civil rights movement does not address itself to the question of how Negroes are to acquire a culture, or to the consequences of their failure to do so. It addresses itself to legal inequalities. In so far as it implies a cultural program of any kind, the civil rights strategy proposes to integrate Negroes into the culture which already surrounds them.

Now the real objection to this is not the one so often given by the advocates of Black Power—that Negroes have nothing to gain from integrating into a culture dominated by materialist values. Since most Negroes have already absorbed those values, this is a frivolous argument—especially so since it seems to imply that there is something virtuous and ennobling about poverty. What the assimilationist argument does overlook is that the civil rights movement owes its own existence, in part, to the rise of a Negro subculture in the South, and that the absence of a comparable culture in the ghetto changes the whole character of the Negro problem in the North. American history seems to show that a group cannot achieve "integration"—that is, equality—

without first developing institutions which express and create a sense of its own distinctiveness. That is why black nationalism, which attempts to fill the cultural vacuum of the ghetto, has had a continuing attraction for Negroes, and why, even during the period of its eclipse in the Thirties, Forties, and Fifties, nationalism won converts among the most despised and degraded elements of the Negro community in spite of the low repute in which it was held by Negro leaders.

Nationalist sects like the Black Muslims, the Black Jews, and the Moorish Temple Science movement speak to the wretchedness of the ghetto, particularly to the wretchedness of the ghetto male, in a way that the civil rights movement does not. Thus while the free and easy sexual life of the ghetto may excite the envy of outsiders, the Black Muslims correctly see it as a disrupting influence and preach a strict, "puritanical" sexual ethic. In a society in which women dominate the family and the church, the Muslims stress the role of the male as provider and protector. "Protect your women!" strikes at the heart of the humiliation of the Negro male. Similarly, the Muslims attack the hedonism of the ghetto. "Stop wasting your money!" says Elijah Muhammad. ". . . Stop spending money for tobacco, dope, cigarettes, whiskey, fine clothes, fine automobiles, expensive rugs and carpets, idleness, sport and gambling. . . . If you must have a car, buy the low-priced car." Those who see in the Black Muslims no more than "the hate that hate produced" mistake the character of this movement, which joins to the mythology of racial glorification a practical program of moral rehabilitation. As Lawrence L. Tyler has noted (*Phylon,* Spring 1966), the Muslim style of life is "both mystical and practical," and it is the combination of the two that "has definitely provided an escape from degradation for lower-class Negroes." If anyone doubts this, he should consider the Muslims' well-documented success in redeeming, where others have failed, drug pushers, addicts, pimps, criminals of every type, the dregs of the slums. In subjecting them to a harsh, uncompromising, and admittedly authoritarian discipline, the Black Muslims and other sects have organized people who have not been organized by nonviolence, which presupposes an existing self-respect and a sense of community, or by any other form of Negro politics or religion.

Black Power represents, among other things, a revival of Negro-American nationalism and therefore cannot be regarded simply as a response to recent events. Black Power has secularized the separatist impulse which has usually (though not always) manifested itself in religious forms. Without necessarily abandoning the myth of the Negroes as a chosen people, the new-style nationalists have secularized this myth by identifying the American Negroes—whom many of them continue to regard as in some sense Negroes of the diaspora—not with "the Asian Black Nation and the tribe of Shabazz," as in Black Muslim theology, but with the contemporary struggle against colonialism in the third world. Where earlier nationalist movements, both secular and religious, envisioned physical separation from America and reunion with Islam or with Africa, many of the younger nationalists propose to fight it out here in America, by revolutionary means if necessary, and to establish—what? a black America? an America in which black people can survive as a separate "nation"? an integrated America?

Here the new-style nationalism begins to reveal underlying ambiguities which make one wonder whether it can properly be called nationalist at all. Older varieties of black nationalism—Garveyism, DuBois's Pan-Africanism, the Nation of Islam—whatever their own ambiguities, consistently sought escape from America, either to Africa, to some part of America which might be set aside for black people, or to some other part of the world. The new-style nationalists, however, view their movement as a revolution against American "colonialism" and thereby embark on a line of analysis which leads to conclusions that are not always consistent with the premise that American Negroes constitute a "nation."

Clearly, the rhetoric of Black Power owes more to Frantz Fanon and to Che Guevara than it owes to Marcus Garvey or DuBois, let alone to Elijah Muhammad. Last August, Stokely Carmichael presented himself to the congress of the Organization of Latin American Solidarity in Havana as a conscious revolutionary. Claiming to speak for the black people of the United States, he is reported to have said:

We greet you as comrades because it becomes increasingly clear to us each day that we share with you a common struggle; we have a common enemy. Our enemy is white Western imperialist society; our struggle is to overthrow the system which feeds itself and expands itself through the economic and cultural exploitation of non-white, non-Western peoples. We speak with you, comrades, because we wish to make clear that we understand that our destinies are inter-twined.

The advocates of Black Power, it should be noted, do not have a monopoly on this type of rhetoric or on the political analysis, or lack of it, which it implies. The New Left in general more and more identifies itself with Castro, Guevara, Régis Debray, and Ho Chi Minh; many of the new radicals speak of "guerrilla warfare" against "colonialism" at home; and in fact they see the black militants, as the black militants see themselves, as the revolutionary vanguard of violent social change. The congruence of the rhetoric of Black Power with the ideology of the more demented sections of the white Left suggests that Black Power is more than a revival of Negro-American nationalism, just as it is more than a response to the collapse of the civil rights movement in the

North. Black Power is itself, in part, a manifestation of the New Left. It shares with the white Left not only the language of romantic anarchism but several other features as well, none of them (it must be said) conducive to its success—a pronounced distrust of people over thirty, a sense of powerlessness and despair, for which the revolutionary rhetoric serves to compensate, and a tendency to substitute rhetoric for political analysis and defiant gestures for political action. Even as they seek to disentangle themselves from the white Left, of which they are understandably contemptuous, black militants continue to share some of its worst features, the very tendencies that may indeed be destroying what strength the New Left, during its brief career, has managed to accumulate. The more these tendencies come to dominate Black Power itself, the gloomier, presumably, will be the outlook for its future.

Because Black Power has many sources, it abounds in contradictions. On the one hand Black Power derives from a tradition of Negro separatism, self-discipline, and self-help, advocating traditional "nationalist" measures ranging from cooperative businesses to proposals for complete separation. On the other hand, some of the spokesmen for Black Power contemplate guerrilla warfare against American "colonialism." In general, CORE is closer to the first position, SNCC to the second. But the ambiguity of Black Power derives from the fact that both positions frequently coexist—as in *Black Power,* the new book by Stokely Carmichael and Charles V. Hamilton, chairman of the political science department at Roosevelt University.

This book is disappointing, first of all because it makes so few concrete proposals for action, and these seem hardly revolutionary in nature: black control of black schools, black-owned businesses, and the like. Carmichael and Hamilton talk vaguely of a "major reorientation of the society" and of "the necessarily total revamping of the society" (expressions they use interchangeably) as the "central goal" of Black Power, and they urge black people not to enter coalitions with groups not similarly committed to sweeping change. But they never explain why their program demands such changes, or indeed why it would be likely to bring them about.

In order to deal with this question, one would have to discuss the relation of the ghetto to the rest of American society. To what extent does American society *depend* on the ghetto? It is undoubtedly true, as the advocates of Black Power maintain, that there is no immediate prospect that the ghettos will disappear. But it is still not clear whether the ghettos in their present state of inferiority and dependence are in some sense necessary for the functioning of American society—that is, whether powerful interests have a stake in perpetuating them—or whether they persist because American society can get along so well without black people that there is no motive either to integrate them by getting rid of the ghettos or to allow the ghettos to govern themselves. In other words, what interests have a stake in maintaining the present state of affairs? Does the welfare of General Motors depend on keeping the ghetto in a state of dependence? Would self-determination for the ghetto threaten General Motors? Carmichael and Hamilton urge black people to force white merchants out of the ghetto and to replace them with black businesses, but it is not clear why this program, aimed at businesses which themselves occupy a marginal place in American corporate capitalism, would demand or lead to a "total revamping of the society."

On this point the critics of Black Power raise what appears to be a telling objection, which can be met only by clarifying the Black Power position beyond anything Carmichael and Hamilton have done here. In a recent article in *Dissent* ("The Pathos of Black Power," January–February 1967), Paul Feldman writes:

A separatist black economy—unless it were to be no more than a carbon copy of the poverty that already prevails—would need black steel, black automobiles, black refrigerators. And for that, Negroes would have to take control of General Motors and US Steel: hardly an immediate prospect, and utter fantasy as long as Carmichael proposes to "go it alone."

But a related criticism of Black Power, that it merely proposes to substitute for white storekeepers black storekeepers who would then continue to exploit the ghetto in the same ways, seems to me to miss the point, since advocates of Black Power propose to replace white businesses with black *cooperatives*. In this respect Black Power does challenge capitalism, at least in principle; but the question remains whether a program aimed at small businessmen effectively confronts capitalism at any very sensitive point.

Still, small businessmen, whatever their importance outside, are a sensitive issue in the ghetto and getting rid of them might do wonders for Negro morale. Not only that, but Negro cooperatives would help to reduce the flow of capital out of the ghetto, contributing thereby, if only modestly, to the accumulation of capital as well as providing employment. A "separatist black economy" is not really what Black Power seems to point to, any more than it points to exploitive Negro shopkeepers in place of white ones. "In the end," Feldman writes, "the militant-sounding proposals for a build-it-yourself black economy (a black economy, alas, without capital) remind one of . . . precisely those white moderates who preach self-help to the Negroes." But Black Power envisions (or seems to envision) *collective* self-help, which is not the same thing as individualist petty capitalism on the one hand, or, on the other hand, a separate black economy.

Black Power proposes, or seems to propose, that Negroes do for themselves what other ethnic groups, faced with somewhat similar conditions, have done—advance themselves not as individuals but as groups conscious of their own special interests and identity. The Irish advanced themselves by making politics their own special business, the Italians by making a business of crime. In both cases, the regular avenues of individual self-advancement were effectively closed, forcing ethnic minorities to improvise extra-legal institutions—the political machine in the one case, crime syndicates in the other. These were defined as illegitimate and resisted by the rest of society, but they were finally absorbed after protracted struggles. Those who urge Negroes to advance themselves through the regular channels of personal mobility ignore the experience of earlier minorities in America, the relevance of which is obscured both by the tendency to view the history of immigration as a triumph of assimilation and by the individualism which persistently blinds Americans to the importance of collective action, and therefore to most of history.

Carmichael and Hamilton mention the parallel with other ethnic groups, but only in passing, and without noticing that this analogy undermines the analogy with colonial people which they draw at the beginning of the book and wherever else their militant rhetoric appears to demand it. They observe, correctly, that on the evidence of ethnic voting "the American pot has not melted," politically at least, and they recognize that "traditionally, each new ethnic group in this society has found the route to social and political viability through the organization of its own institutions." But they do not explain how this analysis of the Negro's situation squares with the argument that "black people in this country form a colony and it is not in the interest of the colonial power to liberate them."

Quite apart from this inconsistency, the ethnic parallel, whether or not it finally proves useful, needs to be systematically explored. Did the struggles of other minorities contribute to a "major reorientation of the society"? Not if a "major reorientation" is equivalent to the "complete revision" of American institutions, which is the precondition, according to Carmichael and Hamilton, of black liberation. Perhaps the analogy is therefore misleading and should be abandoned. On the other hand, it may be that the special institutions created by other nationalities in America—like Tammany and the Mafia—do in fact represent "major reorientations," even though they fall somewhat short of a "total revamping" or "complete revision" of society. Perhaps it is confusing to think of "major reorientations" as synonymous with "complete revisions," particularly when the nature of the changes proposed remains so indeterminate. In that case it is the colonial analogy that should be dropped, as contributing to the confusion.

Black Power contains many other examples of sloppy analysis and the failure to pursue any line of reasoning through to its consequences. Basic questions are left in doubt. Is the Negro issue a class issue, a race issue, or a "national" (ethnic) issue? Treating it as a class issue—as the authors appear to do when they write that the "only coalition which seems acceptable to us," in the long run, is "a coalition of poor blacks and poor whites"—further weakens the ethnic analogy and blurs the concept of black people as a "nation"—the essential premise, one would think, of "Black Power."

. . . The pendulum swings back and forth between nationalism and integrationism, but as with so many discussions among American intellectuals, the discussion never seems to progress to a higher level of analysis. Today, riots, armed self-defense, conflicts over control of ghetto schools, efforts of CORE to move Negroes into cooperative communities in the South, and other uncoordinated actions, signify a reawakening of something that can loosely be called nationalism; but they express not a new synthesis but varying degrees of disenchantment with integration. The advocates of Black Power have so far failed to show why their brand of nationalism comes any closer than its predecessors to providing a long-range strategy not for escaping from America but for changing it. The dilemma remains; more than ever it needs to become the object of critical analysis.

In the meantime, will events wait for analysis? Immediate crises confront us, and there is no time, it seems, for long-range solutions, no time for reflection. Should we all take to the streets, then, as Andrew Kopkind recommends? In critical times militancy may appear to be the only authentic politics. But the very gravity of the crisis makes it all the more imperative that radicals try to formulate at least a provisional theory which will serve them as a guide to tactics in the immediate future as well as to long-range questions of strategy. Without such a perspective, militancy will carry the day by default; then, quickly exhausting itself, it will give way to another cycle of disillusionment, cynicism, and hopelessness.

THE CASE FOR BLACK STUDIES

DeVere Pentony

In the past few years many colleges and universities have instituted black studies programs in response to student demands. Other schools have resisted such demands, fearing that hastily organized courses would not meet

From the *Atlantic Monthly,* Vol. 223 (April 1969). Copyright © 1969, by The Atlantic Monthly Company, Boston, Mass. Reprinted by permission of De Vere Pentony.

the standards set in the traditional academic program. In this essay DeVere Pentony, Dean of the School of Behavioral and Social Sciences at San Francisco State College, makes a case for black studies. He argues that "the time is now for higher education to show that it can disenthrall itself and become relevant to the problems of social change highlighted by the call for black studies."

The history of the development of various American groups into an integrated culture is a complex story, but there is one simple fact that seems germane to the problems of black-white integration in the United States. This obvious fact is that almost every immigrant group with the major exception of the blacks came to these shores because they wanted to come. America was to be the land of opportunity, the land where the rigidities for social mobility would be relaxed, and the land where a man could be free. That these expectations were not quickly fulfilled is a cloudy part of the political and social history of the United States, but in retrospect the members of most of these groups, the Irish, the Germans, the Dutch, the Scotch, the Italians now view the story of their ethnic past in the United States as a reasonably successful one.

No similar memories have been available to the black man and woman. Brought to this country in chains, torn from family and tribal past, physically and psychologically enslaved, taught by lash and example to be subservient, forced to suffer indignities to their basic humanity, and instantly categorized by the accident of color, black people have all too often found the American dream a nightmare. Instead of joining the dominant culture, many have learned to exist in the psychologically bewildering atmosphere neither slave nor free. That they have survived at all is tribute to their magnificent resiliency and basic toughness; but that some carry with them a heavy baggage of hate and rage is not surprising.

While many whites in America have congratulated themselves upon the progress toward freedom and equality that has recently been made, a number of black intellectuals are eloquently questioning whether, indeed, meaningful progress has been made. Perhaps blacks are all too familiar with the ability of white people to dash black hopes for freedom and dignity on rocks of intransigence and patience. Witness the rise and fall of hope in the story of black men in America: in the aftermath of the Civil War they were told that they were freed from slavery only to find that they were not free—not free to be treated as individuals, not free to eat, or sleep, or live, or go to school, or drink from the same fountain, or ride the same conveyance, or enjoy the same political and economic privileges as people of "white" skin. And when in the twentieth century they had their hopes raised by long overdue court decisions and civil rights legislation finally demanding integration, these hopes were once again shattered as blacks found that significant segments of the white culture often lagged far behind the basic justice of these acts.

This has led some of the black community to question whether integration was not just another scheme to preserve the dominance of the whites, seducing blacks to give up their black identities and to copy the speech, manner, hair, dress, and style of the whites, and to accept the myths, heroes, and historical judgment of white America without reciprocity or without appreciation of, or respect for, black experience. Moreover, this estimate has been coupled with the hunch that in any significant way, only the "talented tenth" of the black community could really hope to overcome the monetary, social, and psychological barriers to true integration with whites. The remaining 90 percent would, therefore, be left in poverty and psychological degradation, doomed to an almost motiveless, hopeless existence, forever on the dole, forever caught in hate of self and of others. Thus has been posed a transcendent dilemma for the black man and woman: to succeed in the white world is to fail, to overcome the outrageous obstacles thrown in their way by white society seems partially to deny their black experience. Above all, to integrate on an individual basis in a society that makes this increasingly possible for the fortunate may well mean an exodus of the talented tenth from the black community, with the consequent decimation of the ranks of potential leaders whose commitment to the whole community could help set their people free.

Seen in this light, the demand for black studies is a call for black leadership. The argument is that if there is to be an exodus from the land of physical and psychological bondage, an informed and dedicated leadership is needed to help bring about individual and group pride and a sense of cohesive community. To accomplish this, black people, like all people, need to know that they are not alone. They need to know that their ancestors were not just slaves laboring under the white man's sun but that their lineage can be traced to important kingdoms and significant civilizations. They need to be familiar with the black man's contribution to the arts and sciences. They need to know of black heroes and of the noble deeds of black men. They need to know that black, too, is beautiful, and that under the African sky people are at proud ease with their blackness. In historical perspective they need to know the whole story of white oppression and of the struggles of some blacks, and some whites too, to overcome that oppression. They need to find sympathetic encouragement to move successfully into the socioeconomic arenas of American life.

To help fulfill all these needs, the contention is, a black studies effort must be launched. At the beginning, it must be staffed by black faculty, who must have the time and resources to prepare a solid curriculum for college students and to get the new knowledge and new perspectives into the community as quickly as possible. In a situation somewhat similar to the tremendous efforts at adult education in some of the less developed societies, the advocates of black studies press to get on with the urgent tasks.

It is in this context that a basic challenge is made to many of the traditional values of the college or university. Important critical questions arise: Will black studies be merely an exchange of old lies for new myths? Is it the work of the college to provide an ideological underpinning for social movement? Will the traditional search for the truth be subordinated to the goal of building a particular group identity? Is the ideal of the brotherhood of all men to be sacrificed to the brotherhood of some men and the hatred of others? Can the college teach group solidarity for some groups and not for others? Will the results of separatist studies be a heightening of group tensions and a reactive enlarging of the forces of racism? Will standards of excellence for students and faculty alike be cast aside in the interest of meeting student and community needs? Will anti-intellectualism run rampant? Will constitutional and other legal provisions be violated by this new version of "separate if not equal"?

A REMEDY FOR WHITE STUDIES

It seems clear that the advocates of a black studies program see it as a remedy for "white studies" programs that they have been subjected to all their lives and as a way to bring pride, dignity, and community to black people. They are questioning the relevance of the style and content of education designed to meet the needs and expectations of the dominant white culture, and some seem to be suggesting that the life-styles and ways of perceiving the world in much of the black community are sufficiently different to justify a new, almost bicultural approach to educating the members of the community who are at once a part of, yet apart from, the general American culture. While they hope that this effort will range over the whole educational experience from childhood through adulthood, they seem to view the college or university as the place where talents can be gathered and resources mobilized to provide intellectual leadership and academic respectability to their efforts. The college is to be the place for the writing of books, the providing of information, and the training of students to help with the critical tasks. It is to be one of the testing grounds for the idea that black people need to have control of their own destiny.

But what of the outcome? There is obvious concern that efforts to focus on blackness as one of the answers to white racism will result in an equally virulent black racism. Black "nationalism," with its glorifying of the black ingroup, may have powerful meaning only when it focuses on the hate object of whiteness. Indeed, it is painfully true that whites through their words and deeds over many generations have provided the black nationalists with all the bitter evidence they need for building a negative nationalism based mainly on hatred and rage. Thus we should expect that a significant ingredient in constructing black unity and group dignity would be an antiwhiteness.

Increasingly, the black intellectual is drawing a colonial analogy to the situation of the black community in the United States. Like people in the colonized lands of Asia, Africa, and Latin America, some black men look at their rather systematic exclusion from first-class citizenship in the United States as a close parallel to the exploitation and subjugation perpetrated by those who shouldered the "white man's burden" during the high tide of imperialism. Thus the focus on black culture and black history is to prepare the black community to be as free and proud as anyone in the newly emerging states. And the outcome of that may be the growth of the self-confidence and sense of personal dignity that pave the way for an easier integration into a common culture on the basis of feelings of real equality.

While it would be foolish to deny that ugly and self-defeating racism may be the fruits of the black studies movement, we should not forget that a sense of deep compassion and intense concern for all humanity has often shone through the rage and hate of such prophets of the movement as Malcolm X, Stokely Carmichael, and W. E. B. Dubois. Whether that hopeful strain of compassion and human concern will gain the upper hand in the days that lie ahead may well depend on the degree of understanding and tenderness with which the white community is able to react to these efforts.

There is the possibility that an emphasis on blackness, black dignity, black contributions, and black history will provide whites with new perspectives about the black man and woman. In turn, these new perspectives may indicate what clues of behavior and guides to proper responsiveness are necessary to enable whites to relate to blacks in something other than a patronizing or deprecating fashion. Through black studies there may be opportunities for whites to enrich their understanding of the black man and thus, perhaps, to help build more meaningful bridges of mutual respect and obligation. Moreover, if the truth can make blacks free and open, it may also free the whites from their ignorant stereotypes of the black man and his culture. Unfortunately, it may also be possible for those who teach black studies to reinforce those stereotypes by aping the worst features of the white society and becoming merely a mirror image of that aspect of white society that is insensitive and inhuman.

STANDARDS AND SCHOLARSHIP

Will accepted standards and scholarship be maintained in the black studies program? When any new program is proposed, a question of this sort is certainly appropriate for members of the academic community. However, it is an extremely difficult one to answer for a black studies program or for any other new program. All that can be safely said is that the pressures for respectable scholarly performance and for recognized achievements will be at least as great for black studies as for any other new program.

In the performance and evaluation of students, we can probably expect the same ferment over learning, grading, and evaluative practices that perturbs the rest of the academic world. But academicians who are pushing the black studies idea give no indication that they will be content with a half-hearted, sloppy, shoddy intellectual effort on the part of themselves or their students. Indeed, one of the underlying assumptions of black studies seems to be that students who become involved in it will become highly motivated toward academic success not only in black studies but in the rest of the curriculum as well. Out of the black studies experience are to come black students, committed, socially aware, ambitious, devoted to the welfare of black people, and equipped for helping the black community assume its rightful place in American society. These are high ambitions which are not likely to be fulfilled immediately by a black studies program, but which deserve to be given the same benefit of doubt and the same opportunities for growth by trial and error that most new programs are given.

Will black studies scholars manipulate data, bias their studies, and create towering myths which bear little resemblance to the shifting realities of human existence? The answer is difficult to assess.

In one respect the quest for pristine outside objectivity may miss the point. A distinguished philosopher has argued that the search for intergroup accommodation must be based upon what he terms the discovery of the normative inner order—that is, the values, assumptions, and world views or images of various societies or cultures. It may be that one of the most important roles that the black scholar can play is to share in the discovery and articulation of this normative inner order of the black community, with the possible result of improving the chances for mutually beneficial black-white interaction.

In this process we should expect that there will be black professors who profess a certain "ideology" just as white professors do. We can even expect a case for racial superiority of blacks, but surely this is not a reason for opposing black studies. To do so on those grounds would be analogous to opposing the teaching of biology because a certain biologist has attempted to make a case for a black inferiority based on some of his genetic investigations, or of economics because certain economists continue to adhere to pre-Keynesian economic principles.

Moreover, the ideology argument may mean no more than that black scholars will attempt to emphasize common assumptions about American society from the perspective of the black experience. But this kind of "indoctrination" is not essentially different from what is found, for example, in many college textbooks in American government which rest on some value-laden assumptions about the American political system. A more serious charge would be that black professors may insist that their students follow some "party line" as they examine the various facets of the black situation. But students are not as gullible as we sometimes imagine and are generally quite capable of resisting efforts at indoctrination.

Closely allied to the questions of standards and scholarship are questions of curriculum. What is an appropriate beginning curriculum for a black studies effort? The unspoken consensus seems to be that an area studies program should dig as deeply as possible into the history, the culture, the language, the politics, the economics, the geography, the literature, the arts, the life-styles, and the world views of the people in the area concerned. How this is all put together in a way that students will understand and benefit from is a significant organizing problem for all area studies programs, including black studies. But it would be foolish to expect those problems to be creatively attacked before a working faculty is on the scene. The first efforts to establish a satisfactory curriculum in black studies will be experimental in many ways and as such subject to more rapid change than our established curricula.

ARE BLACK STUDIES LEGAL AND PROPER?

The question of legality of a black studies program requires examination. Like the closely related area studies program, the curriculum would seem to face no legal questions from federal or state law. However, it is in the realm of staffing and student access that the most serious questions arise. For example, can tests of color be applied for hiring faculty members in the black studies program? Posed in this sharp way, the answer to the question is probably no. The equal protection of the laws section of the United States Constitution and various state legal requirements about nondiscrimination in employment could very likely be interpreted to preclude the hiring of faculty simply because they are black. However, if the qualifications for hiring are put on a broader experiential basis than color alone, then the questions and answers may change. Already factors of ethnic background and experience play a role in hiring at the colleges and universities in the United States. While this is particularly obvious in the hiring of teachers in foreign languages and literature—note, for example, the number of people teaching

Chinese language and literature who are Chinese—ethnic background has often been considered in other aspects of area studies and other programs from the Peace Corps to social work.

The question of hiring black faculty is probably not a legal question at all. Rather the critical focal point for the black studies program would seem to be, on the one hand, whether the particular experiences gained from a black ethnic background tend to make the faculty member a better scholar and teacher or, on the other hand, whether the ethnic emotional involvement will permit a useful scholarly detachment in the evaluation and presentation of data. Completely satisfactory answers to this dilemma are not likely to be found. A short-run solution to the dilemma may rest on the ability of black studies programs to attract black faculty with a passion for the truth as well as an emotional identification with the subject of blackness, and on the certainty that nonblack scholars will continue to view, comment upon, and analyze the black experience in various parts of the academic community. Enough flexibility and openness should exist for students majoring in black studies to encounter the views of nonblack scholars. Similarly, the educational experiences of the rest of the academic community would undoubtedly be enriched by the participation of black studies faculty in the general intellectual life of the college. It would be tragic if the black studies faculty were to be prevented from commentary on the general questions of man in society by their own preoccupation with black studies. Few would argue that the infusion of an increasing number of black faculty into the academic community is not desirable. The black studies program would speed the process and provide the black community with incentives and opportunities for greater participation in the education of youth. The institutions of higher education cannot rely on narrow legal interpretation and conventional dogmas as trustworthy guidelines to hiring faculty in programs like black studies.

A second serious question about the legality of the black studies program is the question of student access to it. Can an academic institution worthy of the name deny access to any of its academic programs on the basis of color or ethnic background? The answer is no. Here the legal answer and the moral answer would seem to reinforce one another. If one of the purposes of the black studies program is to tell it as it really is, then the message should go out to students regardless of color even though it is likely to have a particular additional value to the black student. The college cannot be a place where knowledge is developed and subjects taught in semi-secret. Just as any college contracting to the government for secret research would be open to serious charges of violation of the traditional ethics of scholarship, so would any academic program that excluded students solely on the basis of ethnic background raise serious questions of propriety and legality.

However, even in this connection a dilemma remains. As anyone who has participated in an area program in a Peace Corps training effort knows, the things that can be easily said about one's own culture and about another culture tend to be modified when there are members of another culture in attendance. It seems to become more difficult to tell it "as it really is" or at least as it "really is perceived" when the outsiders are in. This is a significant problem that will have to be faced by the black studies program. The fortunate thing about many of those who are advocating black studies is that they want to tell it as it really is to anyone who will listen. They have been shielding their feelings, perceptions, and analyses so long that it will probably be refreshing for them to speak honestly with nonblack students as well as blacks. Nonetheless, they may feel that the first efforts to get their programs established will be so overrun by well-meaning whites anxious to gain new perspectives that black students will not have access to the courses.

In practice, the problem may not be so great, especially since courses about various ethnic communities will continue to be offered in the existing departments, with even the possibility of exchange of faculty on occasion. Nonetheless, the colleges must make every effort within the budgetary limitations imposed upon them to accommodate as many students as possible. No black student who enters the college should be denied an opportunity to take black studies courses; neither, of course, should he be forced to do so. In this connection, the attractiveness of the course offerings to whites as well as blacks may be important in the effort to sustain enrollments in a fledgling program, and thus help provide the necessary resources which are closely tied to the level of student demand for courses. So, the question of student access seems to be not so much a question of legality as of the availability of faculty and other resources.

A sometime country lawyer once said: "The dogmas of the quiet past are inadequate to the stormy present. The occasion is piled high with difficulty, and we must rise to the occasion. As our case is new, so we must think anew and act anew. We must disenthrall ourselves, and then we shall save the country" (Abraham Lincoln). The time is now for higher education to show that it can disenthrall itself and become relevant to the problems of social change highlighted by the call for black studies. If a black studies program serves only to awaken whites to the desperate need to change themselves, it will have been worth the effort.

THE NEW BLACK MYTHS
Peter Schrag

Is the Negro an American or an African, heir of a separate culture, or the most indigenous of citizens? Is his experience significant for its uniqueness or its universality? Will black studies really benefit him? Peter Schrag (see also p. 165), editor of *Change* magazine, raises these questions in his essay. In finding answers, he warns us to stay away from the old clichés.

The rush is on. Come and get it: Afro-Americanism, black studies, the Negro heritage. From Harvard to Ocean Hill, from Duke to Madison Avenue, they are trying, as they say, to restore the Negro to his rightful place in American history and culture; black (and white) intellectuals, scholars, teachers, politicians, hustlers busy with black restoration. The spirit is upon them, the writers and publishers, the polemicists and pushers, and the implications are enormous. But the richest soil is education, the schools and colleges, and the processes of growing up in which they're involved.

The academy is an obvious mark because it is an accessible purveyor of culture, because it tends to be guilt-ridden anyway, and because it has apparently failed black children not only in its practice but in its mythology. The school was supposed to offer—had claimed it could offer—equality, democracy, and opportunity. Instead what it provided was selectivity; it selected people in, and selected them out. By and large, black people were selected out, not because the school was independently discriminatory, but because it offered and gave what the society asked. When finally we looked inside the little black box—the mystique of education and advancement, the mystique of academic standards and professionalism—it turned out to be empty. If teachers and schools knew anything about teaching anybody (which is an open question) they plainly knew little about teaching people who did not already belong to the middle class or who refused to conform to its culture.

Black restoration was not invented inside the schools, but the intellectuals have taken it up, the students are promoting it, and the academics are debating it. Moreover, it is—for better or worse—accessible to every amateur. The line between history and mythology is indefinite, but where the first is at least theoretically subject to disciplinary standards, the latter is not. Any number can play.

Black studies can have just as much legitimacy as anything else; if Harvard has a program on East Asia or Latin America, why not Africa? If American Negro experience has been left out of American history courses—as it has—then surely it should be restored. But the significance of black restoration—even aside from its separatist extremities (the establishment of an independent black state in America, for example)—has greater and more ambiguous implications. Is the American Negro, by whatever name, an American or an African, the heir of a separate culture, or the most indigenous of citizens? Is fiction or music produced by American Negroes uniquely a product of black experience or of an "African heritage," or is it, like all art, dependent on styles and materials from every conceivable source and tradition? Is there white art and black art in America, or just art? Is the Negro experience on this continent more significant for its uniqueness or for its human universality? "I am proud to be black," writes the sixth-grade kid in Harlem. "Say it loud: 'I am proud.' " Here it is, a response to a pile of clichés and labels, a response that may mean something, or that may be just another cliché, this one more vicious because it promised more.

For three hundred years one of the black man's problems in America has been growing up—to be a man but not a white man, to be a woman but not a chattel, to be black and visible as a complete human being. The hackneyed descriptions of self-hate and childishness may be partly the fantasy of intellectuals who are shocked that Negroes don't behave like college professors, yet clearly the price of admission to the white world has been self-denial and the willingness to play one of the stock parts by which the white world justified its own discrimination. Little Black Sambo, Uncle Tom, Uppity Nigger, House Nigger, Bourgeois Black, the urban poor. And in school the culturally deprived, the disruptive child, "black but *bright.*" Clearly all Americans have had similar problems—to grow up, to establish an adult identity on one's own terms. But it is, nonetheless, a special problem for anyone born black, and it has, in recent years, been magnified—even glorified—by the growing consciousness of the subtleties of polite discrimination.

"Each generation," wrote the Negro psychiatrists William H. Grier and Price M. Cobbs, "grows up alone." The past, it is said, exists, but it has been erased from memory, devalued, lost, and denied—denied often by the most well-meaning and liberal of Americans. Is a black man anything but a white man incomplete? Other ethnic groups seem to have the armament of a unique history and tradition—or simply the tradition of the "West"—to carry them into the mainstream. In a sense the Negro has always been in that mainstream—as a slave and servant who knew the master better than the master knew himself—but always as a Negro who could never quite aspire to full citizenship as a valid social protagonist. He was often the carrier of the culture, or even its creator: in music, in patterns of speech, in the cadences of a whole region that resented his blood but talked more of his language than it ever cared to admit. Here was the waiter who determined the appropriate status of the guests and placed them at tables according to *his* assessment of *their* merits; here was the maid who knew the secrets of the household, its triumphs and scandals; there the musician who gave his art and style to generations of white performers but never, until recently, shared in the recognition. Here was a whole race that had walked through all the rooms of the white culture but had never been allowed through the front door. The problem for the Negro was that his culture and his life became too much mainstream, that it was hard to distinguish what he had done and what he had absorbed, but that it was always easy to distinguish *him* by the color of his skin.

James Baldwin once referred to himself as a "bastard of the West." There was no full citizenship—and no recognized tradition—for the black man in America, yet there was no other place to go either.

When I followed the line of my past [Baldwin wrote] I did not find myself in Europe but in Africa. And this meant that in some subtle way, in a really profound way, I brought to Shakespeare, Bach, Rembrandt, to the stones of Paris, to the cathedral of Chartres, and to the Empire State Building, a special attitude. These were not really my creations, they did not contain my history; I might search in them in vain forever for any reflection of myself. I was an interloper; this was not my heritage. At the same time I had no other heritage which I could possibly hope to use—I had certainly been unfitted for the jungle or the tribe. I would have to appropriate these white centuries, I would have to make them mine—I would have to accept my special attitude, my special place in this scheme—otherwise I would have no place in any scheme. . . .

Baldwin's problem was, and still is, the problem of every black person in America—and certainly of every black child in school. Was there a way to succeed in America without denying one's own blackness, to make it *regardless* of (not in spite of) one's negritude? Was there a black identity beyond the limited roles that the official world allowed? One could always hustle the world, could con it, or adopt some form of Tomism, but was there a way of really making it without pretending that one was white?

Almost every black writer in America has been preoccupied with this question, yet until recently it remained in the realm of literature. It was something that came from the imagination, and therefore wasn't quite real. Perhaps such a problem doesn't in fact exist until someone can invent a language—an imaginative form—to describe it. In this sense, then, it always remains a literary problem and the response, whether it is a child's poem or a professional's novel, is a rhetorical response. Nonetheless, the literature, and the vast amount of derivative material coming from the mimeograph machines, are expressing a new set of attitudes, giving shape to a new style of personal and political behavior, and shaping the content and practices of education. There are reasons for what that child in Harlem wrote, for the fact that there are public schools teaching Swahili, and that Malcolm X is an appropriate figure for public school commemoration.

In the past decade, perception of the Negro problem has moved in two directions: on the one hand, it has become pop sociology; on the other, it has been incorporated into a new mythology. The first is the rhetoric of the matriarchal family, the lack of father figures, the passion for a "relevant curriculum"; the second, the growth of a world of African culture, black pride, and black power. Preston Wilcox, who has been an intellectual spokesman for the black school movement (and is now chairman of the Association of Afro-American Educators), recently declared:

The surge to restore the Black community in intellectual, psychological, physical, social, economic, and political terms is taking place in the form of a cultural revolution at the doorstep of the traditional Little Red Schoolhouse from which Black Americans have been planfully excluded. This culturally radical effort forces one to view the Black Restoration Movement as a nation-building activity—a process designed to build into the instinct and habit systems of Black people a need to view the many pieces of the struggle as a single conceptual response to white America's design to turn Black people away from their African heritage—and their historic charge to *figuratively* return to Africa to join in the liberation struggle of Black people around the world.

Examine the language: Black Restoration, nation-building activity, the figurative return to Africa. With the exception of Marcus Garvey and his African nationalists, no American has ever talked this way before. Black Americans are not to invent an identity, or to regard themselves as complete Americans and fight for a place within the prevailing culture, they are to restore, to return, to reclaim the things that America has taken away.

The compelling central figure in this drama is not the bourgeois manager negotiating with the Establishment for more jobs or for a civil-rights law, nor even a Christian martyr, but a street fighter, a hustler, a high-style liver who masters the adversities on his own terms, the man who synthesizes new meaning from familiar experience. Martin Luther King still wins the polls as "a great Negro leader," but it is the gut fighters who command the imagination. King was the ultimate Southern preacher, the man who used traditional materials—the cadencies of the prayer meeting, the imperatives of the Christian witness, the moral confrontation—and improvised a new style. Suffering promised salvation even to the oppressor. His style was Baptist, Southern, and rural. The new figures are urban. They begin as compromised individuals, men who have not simply been victimized as Negroes, but who have, often joyously, participated in the underworld of the ghetto. Men like Eldridge Cleaver, Claude Brown, and Malcolm X may never become mythic heroes, but their experiences on the city streets, however untypical, are now closer to home than those of the Southern plantation. (For certain intellectuals, black and white, they may also be a way of identifying with—and romanticizing—the poor.)

The prophetic hero is Malcolm X, the man who solved the riddle of blackness, and—apparently—grew up. Other Americans had come from the depths of the common black experience, had been corrupted by the white culture, and had risen above it. Malcolm did not invent the new cosmology—black power, black is beautiful, think black—or the mystique of Africanism. As he tells it in the *Autobiography,* it was all revealed to him, first in prison, and later on a visit to Mecca. But it was Malcolm who delivered it to the world, who spread the gospel:

"You don't even know who you are," Reginald [his brother] had said. "You don't even know, the white devil has hidden it from you, that you are of a race of people of ancient civilizations, and riches in gold and kings. You don't even know your true family name, you wouldn't recognize your true language if you heard it. You have been cut off by the devil white man from all true knowledge of your own kind. You have been a victim of the evil of the devil white man ever since he murdered and raped and stole from your native land in the seeds of your forefathers. . . ."

All these revelations amounted to a religious experience, a transformation that he likened to the experience of St. Paul hearing the voice of Christ on the road to Damascus. What Malcolm heard was a coherent legend—a myth of plunder and conspiracy—that matched any classic tale of creation. The story came from Elijah Muhammad, the patriarch of the Muslims, whose servant Malcolm later became. According to the story, which runs for three pages in Malcolm's *Autobiography,* the first humans were black, among them the tribe of Shabazz from "which America's Negroes, so-called, descend." Among them was born a mad scientist named Mr. Yacub who was exiled with his followers. In his hatred toward Allah, Mr. Yacub created a white devil race which enslaved black men and turned what "had been a peaceful heaven on earth into a hell by quarreling and fighting." The story prophesied that this race would rule the earth for six thousand years and would then destroy itself. At that time the nonwhite people would rise again. That time was now at hand.

Malcolm eventually broke with Muhammad, and he repudiated the devil theory, but the story symbolizes the sense of racial theft that enrages the black teachers and intellectuals who are articulating the objectives of black schools and black culture. If Ben Franklin and Horatio

Alger symbolized the mythology of the traditional American school—the school of hard work crowned by worldly success—Malcolm is coming to share with them a rhetorical and symbolic role in the ghetto school run by blacks. The significance of the mythology is not in its blackness, and certainly not in its disdain for hard work—Malcolm was as much of a Puritan as any Yankee schoolmarm—but in its apparent capacity to organize ghetto experience against the bankrupt claims of the official system. As a symbolic representation—a fantasy and a projection—it provides a rationale for the pursuit of African history and culture, for African dress and hair styles, and for the passionate search for history and tradition. If much of that history has to be created or magnified, if petty chiefs are being elevated into great kings, if obscure tinkerers are growing into great scientists, that does not fully obviate the validity of the myth or the needs it fulfills. Rather it enhances them. Every travesty of scholarship conducted in the name of African culture reflects a corresponding travesty in the name of American history and civilization.

At the heart of that mythology, however, lies a naïve faith in some sort of collective identity, and in the magical transformation that will produce it. That faith grows partly out of intimidation—intimidation, that is, by the self-congratulatory declarations of groups which have made it—and partly out of the bewilderment of a misunderstood and largely illusory failure. It assumes, for example, that the Negro is not an American, is, indeed, not much of anything, a sort of cultural savage who was stripped of his inheritance and given little in return. In its most primitive form—in its blackest versions—the myth depicts the white man as a thief who stole everything he has, whose economic and political power was achieved at the expense of the Negro. The Negro, in other words, was not merely a slave in America, he was the prime source of the white man's wealth. But in seeking to emulate other ethnic groups, even the sophisticated black nationalist who knows economic history better than to ascribe all American wealth to slavery —even he remains the victim of the white man's sociology. The Jews made it—according to the current notion—because they came to America with cultural traditions and an ethnic cohesiveness that provided identity and a basis for collective action. The Negro in this vision is still an immigrant; he, too, will make it by reclaiming his immigrant's baggage and starting the process of acculturation all over again. By going back, back, back into some sort of primordial past, into the African kingdoms, to ancient Egypt, even to the beginnings of human life (which, we are now told, can be placed in Africa), the Negro will find himself and achieve the power to be personally and socially effective.

This is confusion confounded. Malcolm never shed his innocent's belief that in some Eastern or African state, in some distant land, men had achieved the ability to live together in harmony without friction or exploitation. His narrative of the royal treatment he received from Arabian sheiks and African politicians is the story of a hustler pushing the golden elixir, a hipster's version of the promised land. In his exotic descriptions of his pilgrimage to the East, there is never a suggestion that Arabia is still a feudal state which exploits its underclass as ruthlessly as any society on earth and whose record of slavery is unmatched in human history. For Malcolm, the Middle East was a blessed society of mutual respect, racial brotherhood, and personal dignity, and American civilization was feudal and corrupt.

The American myth has, in effect, been turned inside out, but it is still the American myth. Malcolm, in his last years, shed his Muslim preoccupations and his mystical racism. But he never resolved his ambiguities about American values. Nor did he fully come to understand either his own Americanism or what it means to be an American Negro. Every black Peace Corps volunteer in Senegal or Tanzania has discovered that in every respect that matters he is not an African come home, but an American abroad. The nationalist still imagines that he can will himself into an African, and that by so doing, he can become what in nineteenth-century romantic thought was described as the American Adam, the new man, free from the corruptions of the old world (then Europe, now America), who, in a new Eden (then America, now a country still to be imagined) could build a world untainted by sin. The African mythology, rather than affirming the Negro's American identity, rather than glorifying it, wants to strip him of it.

The black drive for recognition and the pressure for the institution of black forms—African and American—is riven with inconsistencies and ambiguities. It wants to send the American Negro on two symbolic transatlantic voyages when he probably has no need to make even one. At the same time it is divided between the urge to foster an indigenous Afro-American culture and its passion to give Negroes the power and possibilities to control Western institutions, technology, and culture. To deny anyone the opportunity to learn Swahili may well be parochial or even racist; but to demand—in the name of black power—that Swahili be taught is to ask a luxury that few people—white or black—can afford. This is not to say that the search for the black past and for the legitimate recognition of the black present is worthless. It means only that it is misdirected and still too much subject to the implications of white supremacy.

What the nationalists want to do with the schools is simply to replace white boredom with black. They have, of course, every right to ask for it. It is no more damaging to fall asleep over Benjamin Banneker, Crispus Attucks, and the kingdoms of the Nile than it is over Thomas Edison, Sam Adams, and the tariff of 1820. But in doing it the nationalists are confusing symbol and substance and aping those forms and styles that constitute the weakest elements of the existing system. In one breath they have declared the prevailing American myth a sham; in the next they have adopted it, colored it black, and labeled it good. Scratch African nationalism just a little bit, and it comes out American: puritanical, messianic, and bourgeois. Deep inside him, Malcolm was a cross between the Ben Franklin of hard work and thrift, the George F. Babbitt who knew that it paid to advertise, and the Calvinistic moralist decrying the decline in values. Without knowing it, Malcolm, too, was a bastard of the West. A school run largely on his ultimate premises—and there are not likely to be many—would make any Yankee schoolmaster proud.

Which is not to denigrate the idea of black power, only to redefine and liberate it from the pursuit of a false ethnic model. A disproportionate number of Negro intellectuals—and black militants—are bemused by Jews. Because the entire mythology of urban education and ethnic cohesiveness is saturated with Jewish examples, and because in New York the schools are predominantly Jewish, that bemusement is understandable. The Jews used the schools, why shouldn't the Negro? The Jews have Israel, why shouldn't the Negroes have Africa? If the Jews relied on their old-world culture to propel them into the mainstream of America, why not the Negroes? The American Negro, in other words, is supposed to turn himself into an African so that he can become a Jew and thereby transform himself into a WASP.

It may well be true that the Jews were more successful than most ethnic groups in using the schools to gain advancement. Yet clearly that success—of whatever degree—was based on the character of the cultural content of Jewish tradition and not simply the existence of a culture. To the extent that they succeeded in the public schools, the Jews —and especially the European Jews—were superbly matched to the demands and style of their teachers and curriculum. The tradition of education, and the respect for teachers and learning was, in most instances, reinforced by the sense of mercantile values. Both coincided with the values and aspirations of the schools. The Jews were qualified bourgeois clients for bourgeois education. That those schools also happened to be Protestant—with "nondenominational" prayers and hymns and Protestant teachers—merely reinforced ethnic and religious cohesiveness and provided enough discrimination to motivate the recruits.

Most other immigrant groups did not use the schools for advancement into the mainstream. Irish or Italian power was exercised through the Church, the political ward, and a vast array of semi- or non-skilled political or commercial occupations, some of them of doubtful legality. Neither the Italians nor the Irish brought any great passion for intellectual attainment. Most of the Italians were southern villagers among whom there was no ideology of change. "Intellectual curiosity and originality were ridiculed or suppressed," wrote Nathan Glazer in *Beyond the Melting Pot.* " 'Do not make your child better than you are,' runs a south Italian proverb." And while the Irish dutifully sent their children to school (often to parochial school), they rarely expected the school to do much more than enforce standards of discipline, order, and morality.

The historical precedents for black power are, therefore, not educational but political; ethnic pride and cohesiveness manifested themselves in political activity or in social and commercial associations, but they were antithetical to the educational practices and mythology of the schools. Even when the schools recognized ethnic distinctions, they usually did so in terms of condescending clichés: Italian grocers, Chinese laundries, Jewish tailors, and all the rest. In many instances, the best the schools ever did for any real display of cultural individuality was to treat it as quaint, and the frequent result was that children of immigrant parents were embarrassed by the customs and manners of their elders.

Black power, despite its mythological overtones, is more like Irish or Italian power than Jewish power. Though its prime objective in the cities includes the schools, the most immediate results are likely to be political and not educational. What it contains in educational or cultural theory—leaving aside its African mystique—is not very far from the mainstream. At the same time, restoration of some form of political ward system (which, after all, is what local control resembles) may be the most effective route of entry into the mainstream.The schools and social services generally (welfare, social work, poverty programs) are the major growth areas in the social economy today.

The claims of black or community power for school control are, needless to say, perfectly legitimate, not because they necessarily promise educational superiority, but because in the American political tradition public institutions are presumably controlled by the people they serve. When a black community leader declares that a particular public school is "our school," he is speaking as an American, not as an educational theorist. To oppose colonialism, after all, is not necessarily to be an African. "We are," said a Negro who was demonstrating for local control, "like Boston Tea Party Indians."

What the black experience can bring to the classroom and to the educational process (in black schools as well as white) is its own passion, its own humanity, its own techniques for survival in a society that threatens increasingly to make every individual invisible. There is no necessity to make a virtue of suffering, or to romanticize the glories of Negro survival under brutalizing conditions. The image of the ubiquitous plantation revolutionary—every man a Nat Turner—is as sentimental as the mythology of the happy slave. Stereotypes, it seems always tend to breed countertypes. Nonetheless, there is hardly any argument against the assertion—the fact—that the Negro's life in America and his accumulated experience and passions represent something that demands recognition, something that this society and especially its schools desperately needs.

The trouble with the conventional school is not its failure to credit the achievements of "great Negroes"—one sees their pictures pinned to every wallboard of every black school in America: King, Thurgood Marshall, Dr. Charles Drew, William H. Hastie, Baldwin—but its failure to recognize the cultural and social importance of the Negro experience. The pictures on the wall (or the names in the book) affirm that a bunch of black guys, given a chance, can do as well as whites in the white man's game. And surely this is important. But perhaps it is equally important—more important—to indicate that some whites, if they work hard at it, are almost as good as blacks as jazz musicians, dancers, athletes, and human beings; that, indeed, there are whites who believe as fervently in justice as blacks. Which is to say that the schools might begin to consider the question of whether the many things to which they now pay only lip service may not be of greater value than the things they actually practice and reward. Where is the school that regards the arts, music, literature on a par with formalized and routinized operations of the three R's, and that upholds the graces of civilized life—good food, good stories, personal and moral courage, and political and legal justice—with the rhetoric of petty bourgeois life: thrift, punctuality, conformity? In this respect, it is not the bourgeois character of the schools that can and should be altered, but their pettiness. What they lack is the sense of high purpose. They suffer, in short, from an historic innocence. Yes, they are out of place, but they are also out of time and out of mind. They exist in a middle world like prisons, police stations, and penal colonies—are, in a sense, part of a world that is neither black nor white, neither modern and technological, nor traditional and humane. If they are irrelevant to the Negro, it is not simply because they are missing the peculiar idiom of the ghetto, because they deal in white picket fences and green lawns while their pupils know only tenements and asphalt. It is because they don't deal in the fundamentals of life at all: birth, death, love, violence, passion; because they don't recognize the morality or the brevity of human existence; because, in their passion for fundamentals they miss the elemental: the tragic, the heroic, the beautiful, the ugly. And it is in these things that the Negro and his experience may have far more to ask, far more to contribute.

That man [wrote Baldwin] who is forced each day to snatch his manhood, his dignity, out of the fire of human cruelty that rages to destroy it, knows if he survives his effort, and even if he does not survive it, something about himself and human life that no school on earth—and indeed, no church—can teach.

And indeed, these cannot be taught, they can only be learned, yet clearly they can be part of the ethos in which schools and teachers operate. The schools can recognize that singing the blues is not an aberration, but a universal condition.

PART FOUR

SCIENCE AND THE IMPACT OF TECHNOLOGY

Everyone recognizes the most publicized problems directly or indirectly related to science and technology: nuclear war, the population explosion (partially a result of modern medical and agricultural sciences), pollution of the biosphere, the biological revolution. Since science and technology touch every aspect of our culture, it is not surprising that the articles and issues in Part Four also pertain to the matters discussed in the previous parts of this book.

The youth movement, for example, seldom seems united except when it opposes the most negative aspects of technology: napalm, defoliants, mace, and other nefarious gadgetry of modern warfare. Then too, youth's attraction to the Peace Corp and Vista or to communes and "dropping out" is often a reaction against the inhumanity and standardization indirectly accompanying a technological revolution which gives each person many identification numbers and cards, but which also minimizes his individuality.

The implications of scientific and technological innovations also relate to matters of education and race. Note Mark Rudd's language when he attacks higher education:

> . . . the purpose of universities like Berkeley and Columbia is to train the technicians who will administer our society. . . . Within this university factory, students are manipulated and channeled, stripped of creativity and energy, ready at the end of the assembly line to take their places in death-like offices of still more educational factories.

What students want from colleges is more personal treatment and less "pure research," more relevant courses and fewer televised lectures. These desires cannot be satisfactorily met by increasing the automated services that universities too often think of as significant improvements in the educational process.

Even racial tensions have been exacerbated by developments within the areas of science and technology. The two societies toward which America is moving, according to the Kerner Commission, can be differentiated in terms of the education, vocational opportunity, and justice available in each, or in terms of the products of a technological and affluent culture available in each—air conditioners, garbage disposals, electronic security devices, etc. Black Americans resent being deprived of these technological amenities just as much as they resent poor education and injustice. Also, when mechanization causes industries and unions to reduce their work forces, the workers with least seniority, which often means men from minority groups, lose their jobs first. In this way, the technological revolution, which has created so many jobs for white Americans, reduces the vocational opportunities of blacks and puts a premium on quality education, a commodity still unavailable to many black Americans.

When advocates of change discuss youth culture, education, or race, they often simplify the issues with a slogan: a person is either a part of the old or the new order, a part of the problem or of the solution. But science and technology are simultaneously part of the problem and part of the solution. If science and technology created the possibility that man will destroy himself in nuclear war, they also produce the devices that make arms control feasible. And only science and its application can prevent the population explosion, feed and educate extra billions of people, depollute the air and water, recycle our wastes, and even, according to Martin Shubik, preserve our democratic institutions in an overpopulated future. Science and technology pose both a threat and a promise, and the essays in Part Four point out this dual nature of the subject.

We cannot survey all of the problems associated with science and technology. Yet the first article—Herman Kahn and Anthony J. Wiener's "The Next Thirty-three Years: A Framework for Speculation"—with its numerous predictions, provides a good background for any speculation on how thoroughly science and technology might revolutionize our lives. Innovations such as chemical stimulation of memory, permanent cosmetological changes, and gene modification promise to eliminate many tensions; but they also portend a world foreseen by Orwell and Huxley in which people look, think, and act alike. With such possibilities in the future, it is understandable that many of the essays ask with Wilbur H. Ferry, "Must We Rewrite the Constitution to Control Technology?"

Interestingly, none of the authors doubt the inexorable quality of research and experimentation. Even after Hiroshima and the Van Allen Belt, some scientists and technologists still maintain that whatever is knowable and doable must be pursued. Because the scientific community does not regulate its own research, most of the authors in this section implicitly agree with Murray Bookshin's "Toward an Ecological Solution," that scientific and technological matters are finally decided by the political process. In this sense, the average citizen is not only the revolution, as Abbie Hoffman says, but also the space program, pollution control, and the biological revolution—topics which receive specific attention in Part Four.

Freeman Dyson, for instance, contributes a glowing estimation of the short- and long-term benefits to be derived from space flights. This prominent scientist believes that the empirical knowledge that we gain will be extensive, but less important than its philosophical implications. In contrast, the statements by Ralph David Abernathy and Lewis Mumford in "The Moon Program: Prize or Lunacy," contend that exploration of outer space will not improve man's earthly existence. Rather, it may heighten existing problems by using money needed for social problems, or by encouraging the development of more sophisticated military devices. This division of opinion over the desirability of our space program will be repeated throughout the 1970's in Congress and on the political campaign trails.

There is much less apparent controversy over efforts to control pollution. Yet, as Lord Ritchie-Calder shows in "Polluting the Environment," tampering with the biosphere continues amidst all the unanimous utterances about saving the environment. Likewise, as the essay by Martin Shubik indicates, the biological, managerial, and communication revolutions are likely to accelerate, although no one can safely predict the positive or negative results. Facing these changes, many readers will agree with Wilbur H. Ferry that our institutions and perhaps even our constitution need to be updated in order to cope with the power of a science-military-industrial-governmental complex; but not so many readers will accept Murray Bookchin's contention that capitalism is the most pervasive polluter of man's mind and environment.

Science and technology appear in this part of this book because the problems associated with them repeat the issues directly or indirectly raised by the work as a whole. Change seems to be the constant quality of our times. Will the changes in education and race relations be evolutionary or revolutionary? Will the youth culture develop into a viable alternative to the standard culture or degenerate into a marginal life style? Whatever the answers, these changes in ways of living will proceed slowly. For instance, the initial court decision on integration came in the middle 1950's, yet the solution to successful school integration still eludes us. Changes and innovations in science and technology, on the other hand, seem to have a greater immediacy and finality. A man lands on the moon, a heart-transplant is performed, the biological code is deciphered. The deed is done, and science races on toward newer discoveries, leaving other institutions to interpret and cope with an altered world.

LIFE IN THE FUTURE

> *". . . the coming generation will be the last generation to*
> *seize control over technology before technology has ir-*
> *reversibly seized control over it. A generation is not much*
> *time, but it is some time. . . ."*

> ROBERT L. HEILBRONER
> (IN "Must We Rewrite the Constitution
> to Control Technology?")

THE NEXT THIRTY-THREE YEARS: A FRAMEWORK
FOR SPECULATION
Herman Kahn and Anthony J. Wiener

The "likely innovations" in the following list serve as a background for the question implicit in Part Four: does technology solve more problems than it creates? Some of the innovations have the potential to dissolve the tensions discussed in this book. Number 44, postponement of aging, provides one means of bridging the generation gap; number 58, chemical methods of improving learning, would decrease problems of college eligibility and standards; and number 49, "permanent" cosmetological changes, could be the final answer to racial conflict. Yet everyone who has read Orwell and Huxley can see the totalitarian potential of these innovations. Herman Kahn is a noted defense analyst, founder of the Hudson Institute, and author of such provocative books as *On Thermonuclear War, Thinking About the Unthinkable,* and, with Anthony J. Wiener, *The Year 2000.*

One Hundred Technical Innovations Likely
in the Next Thirty-Three Years

1. Multiple applications of lasers and masers for sensing, measuring, communicating, cutting, heating, welding, power transmission, illumination, destructive (defensive), and other purposes
2. Extremely high-strength or high-temperature structural materials
3. New or improved super-performance fabrics (papers, fibers, and plastics)
4. New or improved materials for equipment and appliances (plastics, glasses, alloys, ceramics, intermetallics, and cermets)

From *Daedalus,* journal of the American Academy of Arts and Sciences, Boston, Massachusetts, Vol. XCVI, No. 3 (Summer 1967). Reprinted by permission.

5. New airborne vehicles (ground-effect machines, VTOL and STOL, superhelicopters, giant supersonic jets)

6. Extensive commercial application of shaped charges

7. More reliable and longer-range weather forecasting

8. Intensive or extensive expansion of tropical agriculture and forestry.

9. New sources of power for fixed installations (for example, magnetohydrodynamic, thermionic, and thermoelectric, radioactive)

10. New sources of power for ground transportation (storage-battery, fuel-cell propulsion or support by electromagnetic fields, jet engine, turbine)

11. Extensive and intensive world-wide use of high-altitude cameras for mapping, prospecting, census, land use, and geological investigations

12. New methods of water transportation (large submarines, flexible and special-purpose "container ships," more extensive use of large automated single-purpose bulk cargo ships)

13. Major reduction in hereditary and congenital defects

14. Extensive use of cyborg techniques (mechanical aids or substitutes for human organs, sense, limbs)

15. New techniques for preserving or improving the environment

16. Relatively effective appetite and weight control

17. New techniques in adult education

18. New improved plants and animals

19. Human "hibernation" for short periods (hours or days) for medical purposes

20. Inexpensive "one of a kind" design and procurement through use of computerized analysis and automated production

21. Controlled super-effective relaxation and sleep

22. More sophisticated architectural engineering (geodesic domes, thin shells, pressurized skins, esoteric materials)

23. New or improved uses of the oceans (mining, extraction of minerals, controlled "farming," source of energy)

24. Three-dimensional photography, illustrations, movies, and television

25. Automated or more mechanized housekeeping and home maintenance

26. Widespread use of nuclear reactors for power

27. Use of nuclear explosives for excavation and mining, generation of power, creation of high-temperature/high-pressure environments, or for a source of neutrons or other radiation

28. General use of automation and cybernation in management and production

29. Extensive and intensive centralization (or automatic interconnec-

tion) of current and past personal and business information in high speed data processors

30. Other new and possibly pervasive techniques for surveillance, monitoring, and control of individuals and organizations
31. Some control of weather or climate
32. Other (permanent or temporary) changes or experiments with the over-all environment (for example, the "permanent" increase in C-14 and temporary creation of other radioactivity by nuclear explosions, the increasing generation of CO, in that atmosphere, projects Starfire, West Ford, Storm Fury, and so forth)
33. New and more reliable "educational" and propaganda techniques for affecting human behavior—public and private
34. Practical use of direct electronic communication with and stimulation of the brain
35. Human hibernation for relatively extensive periods (months to years)
36. Cheap and widely available or excessively destructive central war weapons and weapons systems
37. New and relatively effective counterinsurgency techniques (and perhaps also insurgency techniques)
38. New kinds of very cheap, convenient, and reliable birth-control techniques
39. New, more varied, and more reliable drugs for control of fatigue, relaxation, alertness, mood, personality, perceptions, and fantasies
40. Capability to choose the sex of unborn children
41. Improved capability to "change" sex
42. Other genetic control or influence over the "basic constitution" of an individual
43. New techniques in the education of children
44. General and substantial increase in life expectancy, postponement of aging, and limited rejuvenation
45. Generally acceptable and competitive synthetic foods and beverages (carbohydrates, fats, proteins, enzymes, vitamins, coffee, tea, cocoa, liquor)
46. "High quality" medical care for underdeveloped areas (for example, use of referral hospitals, broad-spectrum antibiotics, artificial blood plasma)
47. Design and extensive use of responsive and super-controlled environments for private and public use (for pleasurable, educational, and vocational purposes)
48. "Nonharmful" methods of "overindulging"
49. Simple techniques for extensive and "permanent" cosmetological changes (features, "figures," perhaps complexion, skin color, even physique)

50. More extensive use of transplantation of human organs
51. Permanent manned statellite and lunar installations—interplanetary travel.
52. Application of space life systems or similar techniques to terrestrial installations
53. Permanent inhabited undersea installations and perhaps even colonies
54. Automated grocery and department stores
55. Extensive use of robots and machines "slaved" to humans
56. New uses of underground tunnels for private and public transportation
57. Automated universal (real time) credit, audit, and banking systems
58. Chemical methods for improved memory and learning
59. Greater use of underground buildings
60. New and improved materials and equipment for buildings and interiors (variable transmission glass, heating and cooling by thermoelectric effect, electroluminescent and phosphorescent lighting)
61. Widespread use of cryogenics
62. Improved chemical control of some mental illness and some aspects of senility
63. Mechanical and chemical methods for improving human analytical ability more or less directly
64. Inexpensive and rapid techniques for making tunnels and underground cavities in earth or rock
65. Major improvements in earth moving and construction equipment generally
66. New techniques for keeping physically fit or acquiring physical skills
67. Commercial extraction of oil from shale
68. Recoverable boosters for economic space launching
69. Individual flying platforms
70. Simple inexpensive video recording and playing
71. Inexpensive high-capacity, world-wide, regional, and local (home and business) communication (using satellites, lasers, light pipes and so forth)
72. Practical home and business use of "wired" video communication for both telephone and television (possibly including retrieval of taped material from libraries or other sources) and rapid transmission and reception of facsimiles (possibly including news, library material, commercial announcements, instantaneous mail delivery, other printouts)
73. Practical large-scale desalinization

74. Pervasive business use of computers for the storage, processing and retrieval of information
75. Shared-time (public and interconnected) computers generally available to home and business on a metered basis
76. Other widespread use of computers for intellectual and professional assistance (translation, teaching, literary research, medical diagnosis, traffic control, crime detection, computation, design, analysis, and, to some degree, as a general intellectual collaborator)
77. General availability of inexpensive transuranic and other esoteric elements
78. Space defense systems
79. Inexpensive and reasonably effective ground-based ballistic missile defense
80. Very low-cost buildings for home and business use
81. Personal "pagers" (perhaps even two-way pocket phones) and other personal electronic equipment for communication, computing, and data-processing)
82. Direct broadcasts from satellites to home receivers
83. Inexpensive (less than $20), long-lasting, very small, battery-operated television receivers
84. Home computers to "run" the household and communicate with outside world
85. Maintenance-free, long-life electronic and other equipment
86. Home education via video and computerized and programmed learning
87. Programmed dreams
88. Inexpensive (less than 1 cent a page) rapid, high-quality black and white reproduction; followed by colored, highly detailed photography reproduction
89. Widespread use of improved fluid amplifiers
90. Conference television (both closed-circuit and public communication systems)
91. Flexible penology without necessarily using prisons (by use of modern methods of surveillance, monitoring, and control)
92. Common use of individual power source for lights, appliances, and machines
93. Inexpensive world-wide transportation of humans and cargo
94. Inexpensive road-free (and facility-free) transportation
95. New methods for teaching languages rapidly
96. Extensive genetic control for plants and animals
97. New biological and chemical methods to identify, trace, incapacitate, or annoy people for police and military uses

98. New and possibly very simple methods for lethal biological and chemical warfare
99. Artificial moons and other methods of lighting large areas at night
100. Extensive use of "biological processes" in the extraction and processing of minerals

MUST WE REWRITE THE CONSTITUTION TO CONTROL TECHNOLOGY?

Wilbur H. Ferry

"Technology is the American theology, promising salvation by material works," according to Wilbur H. Ferry. It is another false god, a force which subtracts "as much or more from the sum of human welfare" as it adds. Ferry also argues that major alterations in basic American institutions may be necessary if we are to control technology, instead of being controlled by it. If we once wrote a constitution to protect the individual from the powers of the state, why should not we rewrite it to protect the individual from the even greater powers of an unchecked technology? The author, an associate of the Center for the Study of Democratic Institutions, has written many books and articles on American political and economic systems.

I shall argue here the proposition that the regulation of technology is the most important intellectual and political task on the American agenda.

I do not say that technology *will* be regulated, only that it *should* be.

My thesis is unpopular. It rests on the growing evidence that technology is subtracting as much or more from the sum of human welfare as it is adding. We are substituting a technological environment for a natural environment. It is therefore desirable to ask whether we understand the conditions of the new as well as we do those of the old, and whether we are prepared to do what may be necessary to see that this new environment is made suitable to men.

Until now, industrial man has only marginally and with reluctance undertaken to direct his ingenuity to his own welfare. It is a possibility merely—not a probability—that he will become wise enough to commit himself fully to that goal. For today the infatuation with science and technology is bottomless.

Here is where all the trouble begins—in the American confidence that technology is ultimately the medicine for all ills. This infatuation

From *Saturday Review*, March 2, 1968.   Saturday Review, Inc. Reprinted by permission of the author and the publisher.

may, indeed, be so profound as to undercut everything of an optimistic tone that follows. Technology is the American theology, promising salvation by material works.

I shall argue that technology is merely a collection of means, some of them praiseworthy, others contemptible and inhumane. There is a growing list of things we *can* do that we *must not* do. My view is that toxic and tonic potentialities are mingled in technology and that our most challenging task is to sort them out.

A few cautionary words are in order.

First, I am aware of the distinctions between science and technology but intend to disregard them because the boundary between science and technology is as dim and confused as that between China and India. Besides, it is impossible to speak of public regulation of technology while according the mother-lode, science, a privileged sanctuary. At the same time, it must be granted that the scientists have been more conscientious than the technologists in appraising their contributions and often warning the community of the consequences of scientific discovery.

Next, I shall use everyday examples. Some will therefore consider my examples superficial. But it appears to me to be better to illustrate the case by situations about which there is considerable general knowledge. I shall rely on well known contemporary instances of technological development chiefly to show the contrast between their popular aspects, including popular ideas about control, and those less well known side effects that in the long run threaten to cancel out promised benefits.

The first point to be made is that technology can no longer be taken for granted. It must be thought about, not merely produced, celebrated, and accepted in all its manifestations as an irrepressible and essentially benign human phenomenon. The treason of the clerks can be observed in many forms, but there is no area in which intellectuals have been more remiss than in their failure to comprehend technology and assign it its proper place in humane society. With many honorable exceptions —I give special recognition to Lewis Mumford, who for forty years has been warning against the castration of spirit by technique—the attitude of the physical scientists may be summarized in advice once proffered to me, "Quit worrying about the new scientific-technical world and get with it!" And the disposition of the social scientists, when they notice technology at all, is to suggest ways of adjusting human beings to its requirements. Kenneth Keniston says in *The Uncommitted:* "We have developed complex institutions to assure (technology's) persistence and acceleration (and we) seldom seek to limit its effects."

We are here near the core of the issue. Technology is not just another historical development, taking its place with political parties, religious establishments, mass communications, household economy, and other chapters of the human story. Unlike the growth of those institutions, its growth has been quick and recent, attaining in many cases exponential velocities. Federal expenditure for research and development in 1940 was $74,000,000—less than 1 per cent of total government spending. In 1966 it was $16 billion—15 per cent of federal spending. This is not history in the old sense, but instant history. Technology has a career of its own, so far not much subject to the political guidance and restraints imposed on other enormously powerful institutions.

This is why technology must be classed as a mystery and why the lack of interest of the intellectuals must be condemned. A mystery is something not understood. Intellectuals are in charge of demystification. Public veneration is the lot of most mysteries, and technology is no exception. We can scarcely blame statesmen for bumbling and fumbling with this phenomenon, for no one has properly explained it to them. We can scarcely rebuke the public for its uncritical adoration, for it knows only what it is told, and most of the information comes now from the high priests and acolytes of technology's temples. They are enraptured by the pursuit of what they most often call truth, but what in fact is often obscene curiosity, as when much of a nation's technological quest is for larger and more vicious ways of killing—the situation today.

There is an anology between the rise of modern economics and that of the new technology that one would have thought intellectuals would be especially eager to examine. Technological development today is in the enshrined position in political-economic theory that was accorded to economic development in the nineteenth and early twentieth centuries. Unguided and self-directed technology is the free market all over again. The arguments justifying *laissez faire* were little different from those justifying unrestrained technology. The arguments in both cases are either highly suspect or invalid. The free market dwindles in real importance, though the myth remains durable enough. But we know now that the economic machine needs to be managed if it is not to falter and behave eccentrically and needlessly injure people. That we have not yet conquered the political art of economic management only shows how arduous and thought-demanding a process it is, and why we should get after the equivalent task in technology at once.

Quite a lot of imaginative writing has been done about the world to come, whether that world develops from the technological tendencies already evident or is reconstructed after a nuclear war. This future-casting used to be known as Utopian writing. Utopias today are out of fashion, at least among novelists and poets, who are always the best guides to the future. With only two exceptions, the novels I have read tell of countries that no one here would care to live in for five minutes.

The conditions imagined are everywhere the same. High technology rules. Efficiency is the universal watchword. Everything works. All decisions are made rationally, with the rationality of the machines. Humans, poor folk, are the objects of the exercise, never the subjects. They are watched and manipulated, directed, and fitted in. The stubborn few in whom ancient juices of feeling and justice flow are exiled to Mars or to the moon. Those who know *how* are the ones who run things; a dictator who knows *all* reigns over all; and this dictator is not infrequently a machine, or—more properly—a system of procedures. I need go no further, for almost everyone is familiar with Orwell's *1984*.

I proceed to examples of the benign and malignant capacities of technology. I am aware that many will find unacceptable my treatment of technology as a semi-autonomous force. These critics say that *tonic* and *toxic* are words to apply to human beings, to ignorant or wise statesmen, to thoughtless or conscientious engineers, to greedy or well-intentioned entrepreneurs. To holders of this viewpoint, there is no intrinsic flaw or benefit or value in technology itself. But I hope to demonstrate that technology has an ineluctable persistence of its own, beyond the reach of all familiar arguments based on the power structure.

My first example is privacy, today a goner, killed by technology. We are still in the early days of electronic eavesdropping, itself an offshoot of communications research, and at first celebrated as a shortcut to crime control. But now no office, schoolhouse, or bedroom is any longer safe from intrusions. A good many people, including Senators, casino operators, felons, and executives on holiday with their secretaries have been made conscious of possible bugs in their cocktail olives and automobiles as well as in their telephones. A good many others were aroused when it was disclosed some time ago that the FBI possesses the fingerprints of tens of millions of citizens. What are we to think of the proposal for a National Data Center, which will have the capacity and perhaps the responsibility to collect every last bit of information concerning every citizen? Not only tax records, but police records, school grades, property and bank accounts, medical history, credit ratings, even responses to the Kinsey sexual behavior questionnaire.

To its credit, Congress has already taken a cautious look. A subcommittee of the House Committee on Government Operations took several hundred pages of testimony in the summer of 1966 on "The Computer and Invasion of Privacy." Referring to the programs designed to "help America" under the efficient guidance of the Data Center, Subcommittee Chairman Cornelius Gallagher said: "Such programs should not be at the cost of individual privacy. What we are looking for is a sense of balance. We do not want to deprive ourselves of the rewards of science; we simply want to make sure that human dignity and civil liberties remain intact. . . . Thought should be given to these questions now, before we awaken some morning in the future and find that . . . liberty as we know it has vanished."

Chairman Gallagher then said he did not doubt that some way of re-conciling the claims of efficiency and privacy would be found. To me, however, this is by no means a foregone conclusion. It ought to be against public policy to take any chance whatever with the little privacy remaining to Americans.

We have been reading a lot recently about the greatest intrusion on privacy yet dreamed up, in terms of numbers of people affected. I refer to the supersonic transport plane, a multibillion-dollar folly to which the nation is now apparently committed irrevocably. In a few years' time, the sonic boom of the SST will daily and nightly waken sleepers; worsen the condition of the sick; frighten tens of millions; induce neuroses; and cause property damage beyond estimate.

At least three European countries are considering putting the travel-ing thunderclap of the sonic boom on the forbidden list by passing leg-islation which would prevent SSTs from flying over their territories. The position of these countries on this issue is people first, machines second.

The idea has been wafted about by the Federal Aviation Authority of the United States—which has been more than ordinarily slippery on the issue of the SST—that we will spend the billions required for SST but forbid its use overland in this country. I don't believe it for a mo-ment. Overland flight is where the big profits are to be made. If, as seems to be the case, SSTs will be built here, there can be no doubt that tens of millions of Americans will be subjected to sonic boombardment.

The doctrine of the United States is that whatever can be done must be done; otherwise, the United States will fall behind in the technologi-cal race. That is the thesis. Therefore, if the SST can be built, it must be built. This technological imperative is bolstered by dozens of irrele-vant arguments in support of SST. It is said that other nations will gather the glory and profit and jobs resulting from SST manufacture. American manufacture of SST will help the balance of payments. These arguments are as popular as they are off the mark. Against them are many equally valid.

It has not occurred to many that the argument should be about the superiority of SST, all things considered, as a means of getting from here to there. It should be about the benefits to the thousands and the disbenefits to the millions. The pursuit of super-speed is being con-ducted by experts who might better be working to make present avia-tion supersafe. The socially necessary tasks to which these nimble minds might be turned are uncountable if we should take seriously the propo-sition that people must come first, machines second.

The deep irony is that we, the taxpayers, are paying for this unprecedented attack on ourselves. The unalterable fact is that the pri-vacy and right to quiet of millions of Americans will shortly be sacrificed to an undertaking that thereby becomes fundamentally senseless. Their welfare goes down before the desires of a few hundred or thousand people who may ultimately be able to get from Los Angeles to New York in half the present time.

When SST proponents are asked to justify the assault on the bodies and minds of human beings, the customary answer is, "They'll get used to it." Some technologists, however, are more direct. Speaking of the sonic boom, Engineer Charles T. Leonard gives this prescription: "A greatly more tolerant populace than is presently assumed to be the case . . . may well become mandatory if the SST is to realize its full potential."

It may turn out this way: We may be compelled to become tolerant of every and all techniques—but at what human expense we may not appreciate for generations. Silicosis among miners was not discovered until long after they had become used to dust-laden mineshafts. Neurophysiologists warn that the growing din of modern life is already making us deaf, and ravaging sensibilities and nervous systems. This is part of the price already being exacted by technology; and with SST we are choosing, as a nation, to raise the price enormously.

"Choosing" is perhaps the wrong word, although authority for the SST has been tentatively granted by Congress. And a silly Senate has recently authorized a further $143 million in development funds—at the exact time it was reducing expenditures on programs for people. But it is not a true choice, for reasons already given. Congress, lacking the understanding of the evils of technology because of the slackness of the intellectuals, merely has been swept along in the technological madness.

That public servants can act with good sense and foresight when informed about the impact of technology is illustrated by the City Council of Santa Barbara. Responding to incessant boombarding of that quiet city, the council recently passed an anti-boom ordinance.

In only one case, that of atomic energy, has this country had enough imagination about results to put a stiff bridle on technology. The Atomic Energy Commission came into being partly because of the lethal potentialities of the new force and partly because of a few leaders—mainly scientists—were able to convince Congress that this cosmic threat should never be a military monopoly.

The ineffectuality of efforts toward smog control in the last twenty years is instructive. In the first few years, not enough was known to do anything about it. Air pollution was considered an unavoidable evil of modern life, as the ear pollution of the SST is now said to be by its proponents. For the last ten years the air pollution problem has been clearly identified, yet there is as much smog as ever, or more. Federal, state, county, and city governments all are working on the control of air pollution, so it is idle to say that public attention is lacking. We gain little yardage by declaiming against the automobile and petroleum interests, though assuredly their products are the main source of the garbage-laden air. Technology is the villain.

The fact that so much of the smog control effort is going into scrubbing the atmosphere obscures the real scope of the problem. For instance, Frank Stead, in *Cry California,* says that the way to deal with it is "to serve legal notice that after 1980 no gasoline-powered motor vehicles will be permitted to operate in California." So far, so good. The non-emission-producing automobile would be a clear gain for urban areas, and not only for California. At the moment, the automobile industry is making piteous sounds about giving up the gasoline engine, explaining week after week how costly and difficult it is going to be to produce a substitute.

Now, it is hard to think that a new kind of automobile is an insuperable technical challenge to a nation that can dock ships in space. Designing a fume-free car would seem a far more worthy objective for government research than placing a man on the moon or re-creating the deadly plague, another of our bloodiest technical preoccupations. Yet the absurdly small sums allocated for federal research in new motor car design show how serious we are about alternatives.

We must not, incidentally, be misled by the optimistic publicity now being emitted by auto and petroleum industry centers. The dean of smog-studiers, Professor A. J. Haagen-Smit of Caltech, says, "I have yet to see a smog control plan that gives me any confidence we will some day have reasonably clean air."

Mr. Stead says little about the larger question, that of the entire transportation technology. He has hold of a very sharp technical thorn, but it is only one of a large cluster. Suppose, for instance, a way were found to dissipate the atmospheric peculiarities that lead to air pollution. Replacing internal combustion by electricity may lower the incidence of emphysema and eye trouble. By itself, however, it will do nothing about the equally troubling questions of urban congestion and dedication of more and more land, rural and urban, to asphalt. Not a little of the furor in Watts arose from lack of inexpensive transportation to jobs and recreation. One will say, "What about rapid transit?" The answer is, yes, of course, but still that is not the resolution, as the situations of those cities with well-developed transit systems attest. Buses, subways, and commuter trains may only compound the misery, as any visitor to New York will be able to testify.

What is needed is a firm grasp on the technology itself, and an equally clear conviction of the primacy of men, women, and children in all the calculations. This is a resounding prescription, and I regret to admit that I am more clear about ultimate steps than I am about how to do what needs to be done in the near future.

I am convinced only that political institutions and theory developed in other times for other conditions offer little hope. We now have, by courtesy of the 89th U.S. Congress, a Department of Transportation whose task is, in the words of President Johnson, "to untangle, to coordinate, and to build the national transportation system that America is deserving of." Under what authority, and by what means?

The mind wanders to the lengths of asking what would happen if the new department might one day soon feel itself compelled to limit by fiat the manufacture of cars and trucks; to coerce car owners by tax or otherwise to use public transportation; to close state and city borders to visitors approaching by car; to tear up rather than to build freeways, garages, bridges, and tunnels.

I turn to my final example of technological invasion. American business executives a half dozen years ago wakened to the existence of a multibillion-dollar market—education. It was hard to ignore. Today's real growth industry is education. The $4 billion we spent on it at the end of World War II has grown to $50 billion plus—an annual rate of increase of more than 12 per cent. New corporate marriages have been hastily arranged. Large hardware companies wed large software companies. The object is profits, not education, although the public relations experts have got together on a prothalamion designed to convey the notion that these new matrimonial arrangements aim basically at the welfare of the educational enterprise, from the grades to the graduate schools. As always, the central claim is efficiency. Mass education, it is said, requires mass production methods. The result is already discernible, and may be called technication. The central image of technication is the student at the console of a computer.

Our educational purposes have never been very clear. Technication may compel removal of the ambiguities and establishment of straightforward aims. But who will undertake this task? How shall we assure that the result is the betterment of children and not the convenience of machines? Are we really all that crazy about efficiency, or what we are told is efficiency? Already, tests are being devised that can be applied and graded by machines, thereby getting the cart squarely in front of the horse. I am not pressing the panic button but the one next to it. I am not denying that certain advantages to education are offered by the new technology. I'm repeating that tonic and toxic technology are here mixed in unknown proportions.

The forces of technication are already infiltrating our grade schools, encountering little resistance. Once again we are in the area of narrow choices. How shall we distinguish between what helps and what hurts? I know that education has suffered from lack of research for years, and that much of what is projected may well modernize anachronistic practices. We have no standards as to what shall be admitted, what rejected.

The temptations to rely unquestioningly on technology are very great. The possibilities that are said to be inherent in the new gadgetry are dazzling. We are told that the high costs of technication will bar widespread use for a long while. This is what was said of television in the early days.

The perils are manifest. One of them lies in adopting the totally wrong notion that an educational system can be thought of in terms like those of a factory for producing steel plate or buttons. Another peril is to that indefinable relation between teacher and taught: Dare we think of it as a mere holdover from another world, as subject to the junkpile as the horse-drawn fire engine has been? A third peril is that the ends of education, already a near-forgotten topic, will be gobbled up by the means.

Webster College President Jacqueline Grennan speaks for education, not technication, when she asks for the development "not of one voice of democracy but of the voices of democracy." The great need, she says, "is to enable an individual to find his own voice, to speak with it, to stand by it. . . . Learning is not essentially expository but essentially exploratory."

Technication means standardization. The history of factories shows the benefits and limits of standardization. Factories are fine for producing things, but their record with people is terrible. We cannot expect to hear the voices of democracy emerging from education factories; we can hear only the chorus. Technication, as Robert M. Hutchins observes, will "dehumanize a process the aim of which is humanization."

The effect on the taught is crucial. The rebellion at Berkeley centered on the indifference of multiversity's mechanism to the personal needs of the students. When the protesters pinned IBM cards to their jackets—an act duplicated on campuses throughout the land—they were declaring against impersonality and standardization; and it cannot be said too often that impersonality and standardization are the very hallmarks of technology.

I have offered not-very-penetrating illustrations of the way technology is raising conspicuous questions about the social and personal welfare of Americans. Behind all these matters, as I remarked at the outset, are dangerous convictions that science and technology provide the panacea for all ailments. It is curious that this conviction should be so widespread, for life today for most people appears to be more puzzling and unsatisfactory and beset with unresolved difficulties than ever before. For most people—but not, I suppose, for the scientists and technologists, the priesthood of the modern theology that is more and more ruling the land, and from whose ingenious devices and fateful decisions we must find a way to make effective appeal.

One must nevertheless be grateful to those few members of the sanhedrin who keep pointing out the dangers as the nation turns doubtful corners. Dr. Murray Gell-Mann of the California Institute of Technology says that "society must give new direction to technology, diverting it from applications that yield higher productive efficiency and into areas that yield greater human satisfaction. . . ." Carl Kaysen of the Institute for Advanced Studies at Princeton emphasizes that government institutions are no longer equal to the job of guiding the uses of technology.

Scientists and technologists are the indubitable agents of a new order. I wish to include the social scientists, for whose contributions to the technological puzzle I could find no space in this paper. Whether the political and social purpose of the nation ought to be set by these agents is the question. The answer to the question is no. We need to assign to their proper place the services of scientists and technologists. The sovereignty of the people must be reestablished. Rules must be written and regulations imposed. The writing must be done by statesmen and philosophers consciously intent on the general welfare, with the engineers and researchers summoned from their caves to help in the doing when they are needed.

How specifically to cope? How to regulate? Answers are beginning to filter through. Not many years ago it was considered regressive and ludditish even to suggest the need for control of technology. Now a general agreement is emerging that something must be done. But on what scale, and by whom?

E. J. Mishan, the British economist, calls for "amenity rights" to be vested in every person. He says, "Men [should] be invested by law with property rights in privacy, quiet, and clear air—simple things, but for many indispensable to the enjoyment of life." The burden would be on those offending against these amenities to drop or mend their practices, or pay damages to victims. Mishan's argument is scholarly and attractive, though scarcely spacious enough for the problems of a federal industrial state of the size of the United States. It does not seem likely that we can maintain our amenities by threat of tort suits against the manifold and mysterious agents, public and private, that are the "enemy."

The most comprehensive and thoughtful approach to the problem of regulation is that of U.S. Congressman Emilio Q. Daddario, chairman of the House Subcommittee on Science, Research, and Development. Representative Daddario starts with the necessity for "technological assessment," which he characterizes as urgent. It will amount to a persisting study of cause-effect relationships, alternatives, remedies. Representative Daddario does not speak of tonic and toxic, but of desirable, undesirable, and uncertain effects.

The subcommittee's study is only beginning, but it is based on some of the convictions that animated the writing of this article. Thus, the introduction to the first Congressional volume on technological assessment speaks of the dawning awareness of "the difficulties and dangers which applied science may carry in its genes" and of "the search for effective means to counter them."

It would be unfair to summarize the scope and method of this promising document in a sentence or two. I must leave it to those interested to look further into a first-rate beginning. It is too early to guess whether Congressman Daddario's group will come out where I do on this matter, but it seems unlikely. The subcommittee will probably come out for certain statutory additions to the present political organization as the proper way to turn back or harness technique's invading forces. There is ample precedent.

We can regard the panoply of administrative agencies and the corpus of administrative law as early efforts in this direction. They have not been very effective in directing technical development to the common good, although I do not wish to minimize the accomplishments of these agencies in other ways. Perhaps they have so far prevented technology from getting wholly out of hand. But it is very clear from examples like the communications satellites that our statutory means for containing technology are insufficient.

America is not so much an affluent as a technical society; this is the essence of the dilemma. The basic way to get at it, in my judgment, would be through a revision of the Constitution of the United States. If technology is indeed the main conundrum of American life, as the achieving of a more perfect union was the principal conundrum 175 years ago, it follows that the role and control of technology would have to be the chief preoccupation of the new founding fathers.

Up to now the attitude has been to keep hands off technological development until its effects are plainly menacing. Public authority usually has stepped in only after damage almost beyond repair has been done: in the form of ruined lakes, gummed-up rivers, spoilt cities and countrysides, armless and legless babies, psychic and physical damage to human beings beyond estimate. The measures that seem to me urgently needed to deal with the swiftly expanding repertoire of toxic technology go much further than I believe would be regarded as Constitutional.

What is required is not merely extensive police power to inhibit the technically disastrous, but legislative and administrative authority to *direct* technology in positive ways: the power to encourage as well as forbid, to slow down as well as speed up, to plan and initiate as well as to oversee developments that are now mainly determined by private forces for private advantage.

Others argue that I go too far in calling for wholesale revision of our basic charter. They may be right. Some of these critics believe that Constitutional amendment will do, and that what is needed is, in effect, reconsideration of the Bill of Rights, to see that it is stretched to cover the novel situations produced by technology. This is a persuasive approach, and I would be content as a starter to see how far Constitutional amendments might take us in protecting privacy and individual rights against the intrusions of technique.

But I also think that such an effort would soon disclose that technology is too vast, too pervasive to be dealt with in this way. The question is not only that of American rights, but of international relations as well, as Comsat illustrates. Technology is already tilting the fundamental relationships of government, and we are only in the early stages. A new and heavy factor has entered the old system of checks and balances. Thus, my perception of the situation is that the Constitution has become outdated by technical advance and deals awkwardly and insufficiently with technology's results.

Other critics tell me that we are sliding into anarchy, and that we must suffer through a historical period in which we will just "get over" our technological preoccupations. But I do not face the prospect of anarchy very readily.

So that my suggestion of fundamental Constitutional revision is not dismissed as merely a wild gasp of exasperation, I draw attention to the institutions dominating today's American scene which were not even dimly foreseen by the Founding Fathers. I refer to immense corporations and trade unions; media of communication that span continent and globe; political parties; a central government of stupendous size and world-shattering capabilities; and a very un-Jeffersonian kind of man at the center of it all.

It seems to me, in face of these novelties, that it is not necessarily madness to have a close look at our basic instrument in order to determine its ability to cope with these utterly new conditions, and especially with the overbearing novelty of technique. Technology touches the person and the common life more intimately and often than does any government, federal or local; yet it is against the aggrandizement of government that we are constantly warned. Technology's scope and penetration places in the hands of its administrators gigantic capabilities for arbitrary power. It was this kind of power the Founding Fathers sought to diffuse and attenuate.

Constitutional direction of technology would mean planning on a scale and scope that is hard now to imagine. Planning means taking account, insofar as possible, of the possibilities of technique for welfare. It means working toward an integrated system, a brand-new idea in this nation.

I recognize all the dangers in these suggestions. But leaving technology to its own devices or to the selfish attentions of particular groups is a far more hazardous course. For it must not be forgotten that the enormous proliferation of technology is today being planned by private hands that lack the legitimacy to affect the commonwealth in such profound measure.

The wholesale banning of certain techniques becomes absolutely necessary when technical development can no longer help but only harm the human condition. Scientists Jerome Wiesner and Herbert York exemplify this dictum in its most excruciating aspect when they say:

> Both sides in the arms race are . . . confronted by the dilemma of steadily increasing military power and steadily decreasing national security. It is our considered professional judgment that *this dilemma has no technical solution.* . . . If the great powers continue to look for solutions in the area of science and technology only, the result will be to worsen the situation.

Though many lives are being wrecked, though the irrationality and human uselessness of much new technology is steadily becoming more evident, we are not yet over the edge. I close with Robert L. Heilbroner's estimate of the time available:

> . . . the coming generation will be the last generation to seize control over technology before technology has irreversibly seized control over it. A generation is not much time, but it is *some* time. . . .

INFORMATION, RATIONALITY, AND FREE CHOICE IN A FUTURE DEMOCRATIC SOCIETY
Martin Shubik

We have become so accustomed to dark prophecies about the future that Martin Shubik's contention—that the market and voting systems, and even concepts such as justice and freedom, may need to be altered or discarded in a superpopulated, highly-computerized world—is not completely surprising. Shubik, author of *Game Theory and Related Approaches to Social Behavior* and editor of *Essays in Mathematical Economics,* does not depreciate the technology that would partially produce these changes. He says that "if we wish to preserve even modified democratic values in a multi-billion-person society, then the computer, mass data processing and communications are absolute necessities."

Underlying the concepts of the free market and the democratic voting process are some implicit models of man both as a rational, informed

From *Daedalus,* journal of the American Academy of Arts and Sciences, Boston, Massachusetts, Vol. XCVI, No. 3 (Summer 1967). Reprinted by permission.

individual and as a decision-maker with an important freedom of choice. The rational utilitarian man, the Invisible Hand, and the democratic vote may be regarded as forming a trinity for an economic and political faith in a free-enterprise democracy.

Changes in society and in knowledge have caused us to question all of these concepts. The behavioral sciences, especially psychology and economics, and to some extent political science, sociology, and anthropology, have provided new tools with which one may examine them.

What are the economic and political values that a democratic society wishes to foster and preserve? What conditions must be imposed on institutions designed to obtain and maintain these values? What assumptions have been made implicitly or explicitly in current doctrines concerning the role and the nature of the individual?

Numbers, communication, the growing importance of joint property and services, as well as the speed of change in knowledge and information, force a reconsideration of our concepts. In terms of the democratic state and its citizens, we must re-examine power, equality, freedom of choice, ownership, centralization, "fair shares for all," "to each according to his needs, from each according to his ability," and many other appealing yet ill-defined words and slogans.

Both implicitly and explicitly much of our economic and political thought draws upon the peculiarly rationalistic basis of utilitarianism. Rational economic man in the economists' model is someone who knows what he wants, what his choices are, what his resources are. His value system is assumed to be well defined; his cool, consistent mind quickly and costlessly scans the myriads of alternatives facing him. His flawless discernment enables him to spy subtle differences in quality. He even calculates the value differences between the "giant economy size" and the regular pack. Many an economist realizes, however, that this is not so; that gaps in information exist; that *homo economicus* is not always certain of his desires. Yet it has been felt that the utilitarian model of the maximizing man with complete information is a good approximation. How good an approximation and of what are questions that remain to be answered. As technology grows, markets expand, and societies grow in size, the individual's share of the knowable decreases drastically. More and more the question becomes: How much should one pay for information the worth of which cannot be evaluated until it has been obtained?

Given clear preferences and complete knowledge, rational behavior amounts to following a consistent plan of action toward one's goals. The optimal program may be very complex, but it is well defined. Modern decision theory, economics, psychology, and game theory recognize, as a basic case, clearly motivated individual choice under conditions of complete information. It is also recognized that two unfortunate facts of life remove us from the relative simplicity of this basic case. The first concerns man as an information processor and the second the conflict of individual with group preferences.

Man lives in an environment about which his information is highly incomplete. Not only does he not know how to evaluate many of the alternatives facing him, he is not even aware of a considerable percentage of them. His perceptions are relatively limited; his powers of calculation and accuracy are less than those of a computer in many situations; his searching, data processing, and memory capacities are erratic. As the speed of transmission of stimuli and the volume of new stimuli increase, the limitations of the individual become more marked relative to society as a whole. *Per se* there is no indication that individual genius or perceptions have changed in an important manner for better or worse in the last few centuries, but the numbers of humans, the size of the body of knowledge, and the complexity of society have grown larger by orders of magnitude.

Perhaps the eighteenth and nineteenth centuries will go down as the brief interlude in which the growth of communications and knowledge relative to the size of population, speed of social and political change, and size of the total body of knowledge encouraged individualism and independence. By its very success, this brought about the tremendous need for and growth of knowledge reflected in the research monasteries, colleges of specialists, and cloisters of experts of the twentieth century's corporate society.

Dr. Johnson observed that there were two types of knowledge: knowing something oneself or knowing who knows it. In bureaucracies it is often said pejoratively that "it is not what you know but whom you know." Both of these observations are reasonable in terms of a world in which the gathering and evaluation of information is costly. As the number of individuals, things, and concepts grows, it becomes more and more difficult to maintain a constant relative level of information. The languages of signs, sounds, and motions provide us with methods of coding vast amounts of information in a compact manner. An experience shared can often be called to view at a glance by those who shared it. Yet even with our ingenuity for coding, the overload grows, especially if we wish to maintain values that stress individual men not as small component parts of the social intelligence, but as individuals.

If we believe that our political and economic values are based on the individual who understands principles, knows what the issues are, and has an important level of knowledge and understanding of his fellow citizens, then the twentieth and twenty-first centuries pose problems never posed before. Quantitative change has brought important qualitative distinctions. Specifically, how viable is the jury system for cases with technical evidence? How close must we move to formalizing concepts of statistical justice where the costs and time in the process, together with impersonal probabilities of being caught, become more important considerations than the case itself?

In spite of growth in communications, has there been any considerable change in the number of individuals that a person can get to know well? Since spatial distribution has changed, the individual may select his friends from a larger set. Yet regardless of the growth of modern science and the speeds of transportation, an evening with a friend, except for the transportation factor, will still call for the same amount of time to be expended in the twenty-first century as in the nineteenth. It has been suggested that 71 (5,040) citizens is the optimum size for the city state. Span of control literature suggests 7 as the largest span. George A. Miller's "magical number 7 ± 2" discusses the data-processing implications of this number.[1]

Taking a few crude calculations we observe that if half a day a year is needed to maintain contact with a relatively good friend, then there is an upper bound of seven hundred people with whom we could have much personal interaction. How many cases can the judge handle? How many patients can the psychiatrist treat? Is personal interaction becoming a luxury that modern mass society cannot afford, or are there new social forms and institutions that will foster and preserve it?

In voting do we have criteria other than a blind faith in the "stolid common sense of the yeomen"? The growth in the size of the electorate and in the numbers and complexities of issues is only exceeded by the torrents of writings in which the public may be buried if it so chooses. In the jungle of municipal politics, even the well-educated and relatively more articulate part of the population is woefully under-informed. At what point does a division of labor become a division of values and of social responsibilities?

The second fact of life that limits any simple view of individual rational men with freedom of choice, who wisely select actions so that their private welfare coincides with the public welfare, is that, given the preferences of all, market mechanisms and voting procedures will only succeed if very special conditions prevail (even assuming complete information). These conditions were indicated in writings from Adam Smith onwards. They call for certain technical properties to hold for the production processes in society; it is necessary to consider that the preferences of the individual are either completely independent of the welfare of others or subject to very strict limitations (such as being identical). Furthermore, the conditions go against intensive specialization, as many individuals are needed in all walks of life in order to avoid the

---

[1] George A. Miller, "The Magical Number Seven, Plus or Minus Two—Some Limits on Our Capacity for Processing Information," *Psychological Review,* Vol. 63, No. 2 (1956), pp. 81–97.

dangers of monopolization. It is doubtful that conditions for the smooth functioning of the price system were ever applicable to the majority of the economy of any society; in general, they do not hold. As the size of the population and cities grows and as modern communication and information technologies weld previously independent groups together, the chances for the conditions to hold become even more diminished.

The aggregation of individual wants and powers into social wants and powers is one of the central problems of political science, economics, and sociology. We are currently in the position where we need to, and may be able to, answer certain fundamental questions concerning the possibility of constructing institutions to satisfy desired properties for the relation between the individual and his society. In particular, we are at least able to formulate in several different ways concepts such as equality, centralization, and power, and to ask if it is at least logically possible to discover methods for making diverse aims of a society consistent. It is neither obvious nor true that there may be any institutions that enable our desires for decentralization, dispersion of power, and equality (or equity) of distribution to be simultaneously satisfied.

These casual comments should be taken merely as preliminary and somewhat disjointed notes calling for the rethinking of some of our models of political and economic man so that they fit the pattern of the uncertain decision-maker acting under severely restricted conditions of information embedded within a communication system upon which he is becoming increasingly more dependent. His freedom of scope is limited by the powers of others; as these powers become more numerous and technology permits quicker communication, his actions become more deeply intertwined with those of others. Given our view of man, and for the moment assuming no great biological changes, we need to explore the arithmetic of economics and politics for the restrictions on the societies of the future.

Where will we be in the year 2000 or 2100 is far more a problem in control and anticipation than in prediction. Man has succeeded so far because of his incredible flexibility and adaptability. Now that he has learned to control fantastic sources of energy and to create devices in the form of computers and communication equipment that promise to aid his intellectual and organizational abilities, his power to manipulate the future has grown tremendously.

Knowledge has grown, and our abilities to analyze have increased. Has there been a like increase in either individual or social wisdom? Additions to human power without like additions to wisdom could set up the conditions for the destruction of civilization. The case has not yet been proved in either direction. Whether this society will destroy itself or not cannot be answered even with the proliferation of modern weaponry.

We may not be able to specify sufficient conditions to guarantee the preservation of values and of man. It is possible, however, to consider some necessary conditions. These involve a thinking-through of a political economy for the modern world. We need to touch upon conceptual problems dealing with measurements and the logic of society's control of itself, and to re-examine both the values to be preserved in our society and the role of modern technology in the attainment of its goals.

Problems are often complex and cannot be explained in a few sentences. The market mechanism is not sufficient to solve the problems of optimum allocation in our society. The voting mechanism in combination with the price system may provide a way, though not necessarily an optimal one, for the achievement of society's goals. Our beliefs and desires may call for a preservation of both the market and voting mechanisms at the federal, state, municipal, and corporate levels. Nevertheless, many modifications are possible. The period from 1930 to the present can be characterized by a tremendous growth in the means and measures of economic control. National income accounting, input-output tables, gross national income figures, and other monetary measures came to the fore. The next thirty years must be characterized by the development of social statistics and measures for the control of the services and joint processes of society. What are the measures by which to judge the performance of the police, education, social services, justice, and so forth? Such measures will undoubtedly be complex and subject to dangerous misinterpretation. (For example, how are the police to be credited for crime prevention?) Because of the difficulties involved in constructing suitable measures, it may easily require decades of devising and revising the appropriate indices and processes for obtaining them.

Compulsory levels of sanitation and education are not regarded by any except a small minority as limitations on freedom. Does this also hold for the draft, Medicare, taxation, or fluoridation of the water supply? In the next few years, birth control and possibly even genetic control must be considered seriously. The nature of government for a multi-billion-person world (and, eventually, planetary system) is neither quantitatively nor qualitatively the same as that required for an isolated New England village. What freedoms do we intend to preserve? Perhaps it would be more accurate to ask: What new concepts of freedom do we intend to attach the old names to?

The purely academic economic, social, or political theorist may claim that we can scarcely define values, can hardly measure them and cannot compare them. Only the Philistine or the administrator faced with the problem dares to ask the question, "What price should we pay to increase the safety level for an astronaut?" In spite of themselves, the behavioral sciences have been forced to become applied sciences. Measurements have been and will be made that many claim are impossible.

Even the crudest approximation provides a guide for behavior where a decision *has* to be made.

The influence of the high-speed digital computer upon society cannot be underestimated. If we wish to preserve even modified democratic values in a multi-billion-person society, then the computer, mass data processing, and communications are absolute necessities. It must be stressed again that they are necessary, but not sufficient. Using an analogy from the ballet, as the set becomes more complex and the dancers more numerous, the choreography required to maintain a given level of co-ordination becomes far more refined and difficult. The computer and modern data processing provide the refinment—the means to treat individuals as individuals rather than as parts of a large aggregate.

The treatment of an individual as an individual will not be an unmixed blessing. Problems concerning the protection of privacy will be large. Once established, the universal identification number will mean a great release from the drudgery of having to use a dozen cards to establish one's credit rating. A computer check of central files could supply the individual with an extensive dossier whenever he needed it. It could, however, also supply the dossier to others unless appropriate checks on availability are established.

Devices on automobiles or other property may be invented in order to keep track of their use. This would enable societies to enforce tax schemes for the use of joint assets that are closely related to individual use—such as parking space and roads. Computers would do the accounting, meter reading, and billing. Once more we are confronted with questions concerning privacy. At what point do we wish to stop "Big Brother" from watching our every move?

Voting patterns could change by use of the "instant referendum." With the availability of a computer console as a standard consumer good as commonly available as a television set, it would be feasible to present the electorate with the opportunity to vote directly and immediately on a variety of issues. Not only could they be asked to vote, but they could be supplied with information by direct library interrogation prior to casting their vote.

Computer and other modern information technology can make it possible to preserve or even to extend the treatment by society of the individual as an individual. His own memory and internal data processing may not change, but information technology will increase by several orders of magnitude his ability to obtain information and to store and retrieve it externally.

The growth of numbers of people, amounts of knowledge, and speed of change in technology work against the individual being in a position to exercise free, reasonably well-informed, rational, individual choice concerning much of his destiny. The advent of computing and communications devices to aid both in the obtaining and analysis of information has provided the possibility of preserving and possibly extending the individual's freedom. Technology is necessary, but it is not enough. Sophisticated devices and sophisticated measures and methods for the co-ordination of behavior in a complex free society may call for a sophisticated society with sophisticated individual members. If we wish to preserve and extend our freedoms, to permit the growth of world population to tens of billions, to increase the world's standard of living, to explore and possibly colonize space, then the next changes may well have to be within ourselves.

MAN AND OUTER SPACE

"The best hope space exploration offers is that this colossal perversion of energy, thought and other precious human resources may awaken a spontaneous collective reaction sufficient to bring us down to earth again. Any square mile of inhabited earth has more significance for man's future than all the planets in our solar system . . ."

LEWIS MUMFORD

THE MOON PROGRAM: PRIZE OR LUNACY?
Newsweek

The four "opinion makers" polled by *Newsweek* are so prominent that they need no introduction. Likewise their views, which pertain to the priority assigned to scientific and technological goals, need little explanation. Their opinions are as divergent as their backgrounds and range from the scientist's hope that space exploration will provide the key to mankind's most important cosmological questions to the philosopher's fear that it will culminate the destructive tendencies of a power-oriented civilization.

(The moon not only stirs the tides and the hearts of lovers. It is the object of wide-ranging debate on the purpose, cost and desirability of going there. On the eve of Apollo 11, Newsweek asked a sampling of opinion makers their views of the new age man is entering:) [Editor of *Newsweek*]

ROBERT JASTROW, 43, physicist.

When the Apollo 11 crew lands on the moon, they will step out onto a poor piece of real estate, lacking air, probably lacking water, bombarded by lethal ultraviolet and cosmic rays, and almost certainly lifeless. The booty they bring back to earth will be a wheelbarrow full of rocks. From a scientific viewpoint, why are they making the trip?

The classic answer was given by Prof. Harold Urey, father of modern lunar science, who pointed out that the features that make the moon hostile to life also make the rocks on its surface uniquely valuable. The surface of the moon, he suggested, is timeless and unchanging; it carries the secret of the earth's past.

We suspect that the earth and the moon, along with the rest of the solar system, were formed 4.5 billion years ago. Sometime in the first billion years, life appeared on the earth's surface. Slowly, the fossil record indicates, living organisms climbed the ladder from simple to more advanced forms, until—perhaps a million years ago—the threshold of intelligence was crossed.

Earthbound creatures can never learn how it happened or what conditions led to the emergence of life, because the record of the critical first billion years has been wiped out here. The air and water that make our planet livable have worn down the oldest rocks and washed their remains into the oceans, while mountain-building activity has churned the surface, removing the remaining evidence. The years in which life began are blank pages in the earth's history.

This seemingly lifeless moon may tell us about the origin of life on the earth. The explanation of this paradox is connected with recent theories which suggest that the first creatures on the earth evolved spontaneously out of nonliving molecules. These molecules, immersed in the waters of the earth, collided ceaselessly; now and then the collisions linked small molecules—amino acids and nucleotides—into larger ones, proteins and DNA. This was the beginning of the evolution of life out of nonliving chemicals. Now, unless the basic molecules are immersed in water, they cannot move about, and cannot collide and stick together. Because today the surface of the moon is completely dry, all the nutritious elements of life might be spread out in abundance there, but still they could never unite to form the simplest living organisms.

But the moon may have had an abundance of water for a short time in its youth. Lunar Orbiter photographs reveal meandering channels, apparently cut out of the moon's surface by the flow of a liquid, that look very much like dried-out river beds on the earth. The source of the channel usually is an opening in the moon's surface out of which water, or some watery fluid, must have gushed. If water was ever present on the moon, on the surface or just beneath, chemical evolution could have taken the first steps along the path from nonlife to life in that brief watery period, and then been cut off midway in its passage across the threshold, as the water disappeared.

If this happened, the traces of those complex, half-living molecules will eventually be found in the samples of lunar rock to be brought back to earth by Apollo astronauts. Such molecules, lying between life and nonlife, will be nearly as important as the discovery of extraterrestrial life itself, because they will reveal a way in which life can appear on an earthlike planet.

By no means are all scientists optimistic about uncovering this richest prize of all. The expectation of discovery is based on Urey's "cold moon" theory—the idea that the moon either was formed cold, or cooled off shortly after its birth, and has never been the scene of the upheavals that the earth continuously suffers. The cold-moon scientists believe that parts of the moon's surface date back to the beginning of the solar system. In this cold storage even the astronauts' first footprint might last a million years.

Opposed to this view is the "hot moon" school, led by a number of eminent geologists who believe that the record of the first billion years, if it exists at all on the moon, lies deeply buried and will be difficult to read. The hot-moon scientists argue that the moon is like the earth, with a molten or partly molten interior, and a surface marked by volcanic upheavals and by floods of lava that have largely obliterated its past.

Cold-moon scientists see few volcanoes, if any, in lunar photographs; hot-moon scientists see many volcanoes—extinct as well as modern—in the same photographs. Cold-moon scientists offer proof that the lunar maria are ancient, possibly 4.5 billion years old; hot-moon scientists offer proof that the lunar seas are beds of relatively fresh lava, no more than 100 million years old. The evidence is strong on both sides, and contradictory. Attitudes are hardening as the day of the landing approaches.

This controversy is reminiscent of the great scientific arguments of the past. Like them, it centers on a technical issue but carries broad implications for cosmology and evolution—the origin of the universe, the origin of the solar system and the origin of life. Such subjects touch on the central problems of human existence: What am I? How did I get here? The uproar of the 1860s over Darwin's theory of evolution was of this kind. So was the cosmological quarrel between adherents of the big-bang and steady-state universes.

The resolution of this moon argument may ride with Apollo 11. A feeling of intense excitement grips the scientific community as we await the return of the priceless rocks. When that cargo arrives the NASA lab in Houston will become the focus of scientific curiosity. The rocks will be doled out—perhaps a thimbleful, perhaps less, never more than the minimum needed—cut, sliced, ground and examined nearly atom by atom. Possibly one such slice will reveal a "page" of earth's lost history.

RALPH DAVID ABERNATHY, 43, president of the Southern Christian Leadership Conference.

A society that can resolve to conquer space; to put man in a place where in ages past it was considered only God could reach; to appropriate vast billions; to systematically set about to discover the necessary scientific knowledge; that society deserves both our acclaim and our contempt.

It deserves acclaim for achievement and contempt for bizarre social values. For though it has had the capacity to meet extraordinary challenges, it has failed to use its ability to rid itself of the scourges of racism, poverty and war, all of which were brutally scarring the nation even as it mobilized for the assault on the solar system.

It is not hard to understand the drama and excitement of space exploration. Everyone must feel the thrilling exaltation of subduing the unknown and accomplishing the impossible of yesterday. But, why, in an allegedly cultured and civilized land, is it not exalted to conquer human misery, the decadence of racism, and the barbarism of war? Why is it less exciting to the human spirit to enlarge man by making him brother to his fellow man? There is more distance between the races of man than between the moon and the earth. To span the vastness of human space is ultimately more glorious than any other achievement. And to make that long, never accomplished journey will be of more benefit to all of humanity than a journey even to the most remote stars.

Finally, those who go, go only as the men they are. If their spirit is shriveled by inhumanity no conquests of science and the unknown will cure the insignificance of the travelers.

This is not an attack on the space adventure itself, it is an attack on the failure to do what else was required for man to be Man.

MARGARET MEAD, 67, anthropologist.

Human history has been characterized by the faulty translation of vision into actuality. With each advance man has been faced with new limitations—in their turn to be transcended. He has learned to heal but not to plan so that the population of the earth would be balanced. He has fashioned marvelous new objects but in doing so has strewn the earth with waste products. He has used his unique powers of imagination to transform his neighbors into prey or predator and fastened the practice of warfare on mankind.

Much that we did and failed to do in the past was done in ignorance and innocence. Today we can plead neither. We have just accomplished a spectacular feat in man's ability to invent, to construct, to work in unison, to combine heroism with responsibility and patience. But we are robbing our children of this moment of joy and wonder—man's birthright that has made this moment possible. When the first satellite went up it was the elders who were puzzled, more concerned with international competition than with the miracle of man in space, while the children were filled with hope and joy. Today it is the elders who are glimpsing again the pure wonder of their own childhood vision. But for the children the moment has been tarnished by their despair over the mounting crises here on earth. It is as if a man on the moon, like the Man in the Moon, were saying to those down below when entreated in the children's song to come down to them and help them: "I'll send my moonbeams, but I cannot go."

This can be a first step, not into space alone, but into the disciplined and courageous use of enhanced human powers for man, ennobled as he is today, as the first men step on the moon.

LEWIS MUMFORD, 73, philosopher.

When I was 18 I wrote the beginning of a one-act play, which opened with an ancient philosopher, seated before a wallsize television screen (not yet invented) watching a band of Supermen take off in a spacecraft, leaving less gifted Earthlings behind. That adolescent fantasy was not a peculiarly modern one; it had first come forth some 5,000 years ago when an Egyptian Pharaoh commanded the construction of a static space rocket, called a pyramid, to enable him after death to join his fellow deities, Atum-Re, the sun god, and Hat-hor, the moon goddess, in the sky.

Now I am that old philosopher, about to witness through television the first landing by men on the moon (a feat that the astronomer Johannes Kepler had already vividly pictured in 1609 in a little pamphlet, "Kepler's Dream"). My youthful scenario will be enacted, not by Pharaohs or Supermen, but by professionally brave military men, charged to forfeit their lives if necessary to achieve this extravagant feat of technological exhibitionism: a feat dedicated to the same malign military-political purposes that now endanger the very survival of the human race.

Though many now credulously believe that space travel will open up marvelous new possibilities, there are strong historic grounds for believing rather that this marks the fatal terminus of a process that has from the Pyramid Age on curbed human development. For it was then that the negative agents of power that have retarded and disrupted civiliza-

tion were institutionalized: slavery, mass military and industrial conscription, the ruthless exploitation of the weak by a weapons-command-
ing elite—all climaxed repeatedly by war, systematic destruction, and
random total extermination.

Under thin disguises, all these anti-human institutions exist today,
modernized and immensely magnified by the advances of technology.
Space exploration itself is strictly a military by-product; and without
pressure from the Pentagon and the Kremlin it would never have found
a place in any national budget.

The best hope space exploration offers is that this colossal perversion
of energy, thought and other precious human resources may awaken a
spontaneous collective reaction sufficient to bring us down to earth
again. Any square mile of inhabited earth has more significance for
man's future than all the planets in our solar system. It is not the outer-
most reaches of space, but the innermost recesses of the human soul
that now demand our most intense exploration and cultivation. Space
exploration, realistically appraised, is only a sophisticated effort to escape from human realities, promoted by Pyramid Age minds, utilizing
our advanced Nuclear Age technology, in order to fulfill their still
adolescent—or more correctly infantile—fantasies of exercising absolute power over nature and mankind. The prime task of our age is not
to conquer space but to overcome the institutionalized irrationalities
that have sacrificed the values of life to the expansion of power, in all
its demoralizing and dehumanizing forms.

HUMAN CONSEQUENCES OF THE EXPLORATION OF SPACE

Freeman Dyson

As he readily admits, Freeman Dyson's remarks on the manned-space program resemble science fiction. According to Dyson, colonization of space
will ease a technological problem such as pollution by removing polluting
industries into space. More importantly, colonization will ease the generation gap and racial tensions by providing a permanent open frontier for floating city-states where rebels, youths, racists, experimenters of all kinds, will
be free to establish their own societies—just as the immigrants to America
and Australia did. Behind these optimistic predictions rests the belief that
science and technology will provide mankind with the means to solve its
problems. Freeman Dyson is a physicist and a member of the Institute for
Advanced Study at Princeton University.

From *Man on the Moon,* edited by Eugene Rabinovitch and Richard S. Lewis.
© 1969 by Education Foundation for Nuclear Science, Basic Books, Inc., Publishers, New York.

When Columbus set sail into the Atlantic, he knew he was going to do something great, but he did not know what. This remark about Columbus is trite. It has been made a hundred times before by people discussing man's activities in space, yet it is the truest thing that can be said. In my personal view of the human situation, the exploration of space appears as the most hopeful feature of a dark landscape. Everything I say may well be as wrong and irrelevant as Columbus' reasons for sailing West. The important thing is that he did sail West and we do go into space. The true historical consequences of these events can only be known much later.

In recent months many thoughtful voices have been heard, questioning the wisdom of pursuing big space projects at a time when so many human problems remain unsolved on earth. Just now, when the direction of space activities after the Apollo missions is still to be decided, it is important for us to think seriously about the value of such enterprises. This article is an attempt to think ahead, to sketch a possible future for man in space. My intention is not to make my readers believe everything I say, but to provoke them into forming their own judgments, their own visions of human needs and purposes.

I do not think we need to have a generally agreed set of goals before we do anything ambitious. I do not believe that any philosopher-king or hierarchy of committees can dissolve the causes of human discord and give us a universally accepted order of priorities. On the contrary, I consider it natural and right that we shall continue to stumble ahead into space without really knowing why. The ultimate strength of the space program derives from the fact that it unites in a constructive effort a crowd of people who are in it for quite diverse reasons. I am in it partly because I am a scientist and am interested in astronomical problems. But many scientists are indifferent or hostile to the program, while I myself was enthusiastic about space travel long before I became a scientist.

THE HUMAN SIDE

I shall be expressing opinions about matters which are much more human than scientific. I shall put forward a point of view about the social problems of our time, problems which have little to do with science or with space. At the end I will argue that the exploration of space offers remedies to some of our social diseases, but my argument will remain on the level of literature rather than of science.

When I am discussing human affairs, I like to deal in individual people rather than in abstract principles. For this reason I find science fiction more helpful than sociology in suggesting probable futures. Like anybody who is concerned with the long-range future, I owe a great debt to the ideas of H. G. Wells. Wells was an unsuccessful biologist who became a successful novelist. He understood better than most of us the comedy of the individual human being, and yet he never lost sight of his biological background, of the human species emerging from dubious origins and groping its way to an even more dubious destiny. He was no physicist, and he never took space travel seriously, although he used it on occasion as a stage property for his stories. His visions of man's future are earthbound, pessimistic, and quite different from my vision as I shall describe it to you tonight. But I do not need to agree with Wells in detail in order to acknowledge the greatness of his influence. I take his contribution to human thought to be not the description of particular futures, but the awareness of the future as an object of intellectual study, having a depth and breadth as great as the study of the historic past. I am a child of Wells insofar as I cannot think of human destiny beyond the year 2000 as lying outside the scope of my responsibilities.

As an example of the sort of insight into human character that I find more illuminating than sociological analysis, let me mention the Artilleryman who appears briefly in Wells' "War of the Worlds." This is an insignificant man who becomes convinced, as civilization collapses around him, that he can keep everything under control. He has unlimited self-confidence and a fine flow of words, quite out of touch with reality. Recently I met a U.S. diplomat who serves in a country where our policies might charitably be described as being on the point of collapse. At first I wondered, "Now where have I met this man before?"—and then I remembered Wells' Artilleryman. If you listen carefully, you will hear the voice of the Artilleryman wherever human society is facing problems of overwhelming difficulty.

Another splendid example of Wells' insight is the General Intelligence Machine which appears in his story "When the Sleeper Wakes," written in 1899. It did not take much wisdom to foresee in 1899 a machine which would sit in somebody's living room and speak upon request, giving up-to-date news reports concerning the events of the day. Wells' insight is shown in the nature of the information which the machine provides. It puts out a continuous stream of advertising commercials and political propaganda, at such a level of imbecility that the characters in the story refer to it only by the name of "Babble Machine." To give the flavor of the thing, I quote directly from Wells: "Babble Machines of a peculiarly rancid tone filled the air with strenuous squealing and an idiotic slang, 'Skin your eyes and slide,' 'Gewhoop, bonanza,' 'Gollipers come and hark!'" I find it comforting, when the drivel put out by our contemporary Babble Machines drives me to fury or despair, to reflect that even the worst television commercials are not quite as bad as Wells imagined they would be.

FACTS OF LIFE

Let me give you a short list of facts which I regard as central to the human situation. Like Wells and other social analysts, I shall select my facts to make my theory plausible.

One fact of human life which is hard to ignore is nationalism. In all parts of the world nationalism is the strongest political force. In most places it is the only effective force making possible the organization of man's efforts for peace or war. Where nationalism is weak, as in Nigeria or Belgium, it is usually because a smaller political unit—a tribe or a province—has usurped the place of the nation in men's minds. The strength of nationalism in the world as a whole has steadily increased during recent centuries, and is probably still increasing.

Another obvious fact of life is race. The events of the last years have made it clear, if it was not clear before, that the problem of race runs deep in our society. No society with a substantial racial minority is free from problems. Some societies are more tolerant than others, but tolerance is fragile. For most of us it is pleasanter to live segregated than to face the frictions of racially mixed housing. In the pure-white English society into which I was born, having at that time no Negroes to worry about, we developed our famous class system instead. As a middle-class child, I was unable to communicate with most of the children of my neighborhood, since they were "Oiks" and spoke a different dialect.

A third fact of life is drugs. By this I mean not the harmless legal drugs like aspirin and penicillin, but the illegal ones, LSD, marijuana and so forth. Many people no doubt have more experience with these than I do, but at least I have not brought up a couple of teen-agers without realizing that drugs are an important part of the landscape. And it is clear to me that the existing drugs are only the first wave of an ever-increasing series of problems which may be included under the general heading of biological experimentation. As biochemistry advances there will be more varied drugs, illegally available, offering strange adventures to reckless young people. To make these legal will never be acceptable to anxious parents and neighbors; to make them illegal will never effectively stop their abuse. Later on, when biology and genetics have advanced a little further, even more serious problems of medical experimentation will arise. Our young people may be able to induce dreams and hallucinations in each other, programmed to order, by gadgetry feeding directly into the brain. What reality would be able to compete with this dream-world for their minds? Ultimately, perhaps a hundred years from now or perhaps sooner, humanity will be faced with the possibility of deliberate programming of the genetic make-up of children. Either a government using its paternalistic authority, or a group of individuals in defiance of authority, may cause children to be born differing radically from the norm in moral or intellectual power. Such experimentation may be of immense value from certain points of view. What a grand and terrible thing it would be to call into being a child with the endowments of Einstein or of Martin Luther King! And yet, which of our existing social institutions is strong enough to withstand the stresses that a generation of genetic experimentation would produce?

I have listed three disagreeable facts that confront the human species, the facts of nationalism, racism, and biological engineering. Under the heading of biological engineering I include the whole range of problems of which LSD gives us a foretaste. These three facts are usually regarded as separate problems, each to be handled as best we can in its own context. I shall instead concentrate attention on the features common to all three, and see if there is perhaps some underlying pattern.

PEOPLE IN SMALL GROUPS

I find the underlying pattern to be the propensity of human beings to function best in rather small groups. We are almost all familiar with the happiness that comes from a communal effort. Goethe has described it imperishably in the death scene of his "Faust." Our teen-agers are disoriented because they are no longer involved in the communal activities of family and village, sowing and harvesting, hedging and ditching.

Our pot-smoking teen-agers are unanimous in saying that the great thing about pot is not the drug itself but the comradeship which it creates. And to make the comradeship real, there must not only be a group of friends inside the circle but enemies outside, police and parents and authorities to be defied. Just as, in the old Yorkshire wool factory, the spirit among the workers was warm and intimate, not in spite of but because of their shared hostility to the mill-owner and his managers. This is human life the way it is: my son wearing his hair odiously long just because I dislike to be seen together with it in public, and we of the older generation fulfilling our duty as parents by keeping our hair short and marijuana illegal.

I believe the strength of nationalism and racism derives ultimately from the same source as the tension between the generations. We all have a psychological need to feel identified with a group, preferably not too large a group, with a common purpose and a common enemy. Countries like the United States are already far too big to fulfill this need satisfactorily. Small countries like Holland and Switzerland can generally handle social problems better than big ones. Nationalism is most triumphantly successful in countries which are both small and threatened, such as Finland, Israel, North Vietnam and Biafra.

GENETIC DRIFT

It is easy to theorize, as many paleontologists have theorized, that the human species has built-in instincts of tribal exclusiveness, frozen into our inheritance during the hundreds of thousands of years which our ancestors spent roaming in small nomadic bands. Such a theory is plausible as an explanation of present-day nationalism, racism and teen-age gang warfare, but I do not know whether it can ever be proved. For my purposes it is not important to decide whether exclusiveness is an inherited instinct or a culturally acquired characteristic. The important thing is that tribal exclusiveness exists in our species and has been essential to our rapid evolution.

Rapid evolution in any species depends largely on a phenomenon known as "genetic drift." Genetic drift is the random drifting of the average genetic make-up in a small inbreeding population. The speed of drift varies inversely with the square-root of the size of the breeding-group. The direction of drift is somewhat influenced by natural selection, but drift occurs even in the absence of selection. It seems to me incontestable that a group of apes could develop an aptitude for calculus, or symphonic music, or theological argument, only through genetic drift and not through natural selection. In fact all the things which we prize most in human culture, our appreciation of art, poetry, holiness and natural beauty, must be products of genetic drift.

I believe, though this is pure speculation, that genetic drift has been of decisive importance to human progress even in historic times. When we make a list of the most creative periods in human history, confining ourselves to the Christian-European tradition with which I am familiar, we think immediately of eighth-century Jerusalem, fifth-century Athens, and fourteenth-century Florence. In each case we have a city, hardly more than a village by modern standards, producing out of a small population within a hundred years an astonishing concentration of intellectual achievement. In each case the outburst of genius followed a long period during which the city existed with an even smaller population, rather isolated from its neighbors and quarreling with them incessantly. It seems to me plausible that the best recipe for human cultural progress would read roughly as follows: Take a hundred city-states, each with population between ten and a hundred thousand; let each one hate its neighbors sufficiently to prevent substantial interbreeding; encourage priestly and aristocratic caste systems to reduce still further the size of breeding units; introduce an occasional major war or plague to keep the populations small) let the mixture simmer for a thousand years, and maybe one of your hundred cities will be the new Florence, the new Athens, or the new Jerusalem.

FORCES OF TECHNOLOGY

So far I have presented the case for human divisiveness, for insularity, exclusiveness and intolerance. I want to make clear that these human qualities, however evil their consequences in our present society, are not easily to be eradicated. Throughout the long centuries of our prehistory and even until quite recently, these qualities have been beneficial to our species. In the self-sacrifice of a soldier, the fury of a mob, the loyalty to his friends of a teen-ager, the same qualities are still with us. We still function best in small groups.

Now we are all well aware that this is only half the story. We cannot go back to the Middle Ages or to classical Greece, even if we wished to. The idea of universal human brotherhood may still be remote for most of us. But against the historic forces of tribalism stand the three great forces of modern technology, the forces of weaponry, population growth, and pollution. We are in danger of exterminating ourselves with our hydrogen bombs and the still worse horrors with which biological engineering will soon provide us. We are in danger of exhausting our resources and ultimately reducing ourselves to a starvation diet through over-population. We are in danger of ruining all that is beautiful on this planet through our accumulations of poisonous mess. All three dangers demand that mankind unite. Each of them, and the problem of weapons above all, requires a worldwide authority to protect us from our own folly. Slowly and against stubborn resistance, practical necessities are driving us to forget our quarrels and accept peaceful coexistence with our enemies. For 24 years the nuclear physicists have been saying "One world, or none," and there is no reason to doubt that in the long run they are right. The Earth has grown too small for bickering tribes and city-states to exist on it. Our bombs are too big, our machines are too complicated, our smog and garbage are too pervasive to be left much longer in the hands of local authorities.

As far into the future as anyone can see, the dangers of modern technology will continue to grow and will threaten mankind on this planet with the choice of political union or death. Political union will inevitably mean some degree of political oppression, government by remote bureaucracy, over-centralization. We will be lucky if we can succeed in organizing a world government which does not degenerate into a world police state. But I believe the forces of tribalism and nationalism will for a long time remain strong enough to defeat attempts to impose world government. Men will prefer to live in filth with the threat of annihilation hanging over their heads, rather than allow foreigners to tax them.

Unfortunately the unifying force of technology, while not yet powerful enough to bind us into a world-wide brotherhood, is already quite strong enough to destroy the historic benefits which we once derived from tribalism.

THE HOPE OF SPACE

Now I come at last to the hopeful part of my message. I have presented a gloomy view of our human predicament. On the one hand, we are historically attuned to living in small exclusive groups, and we carry in us a stubborn disinclination to treat all men as our brothers. On the other hand, we live on a shrinking and vulnerable planet which our lack of foresight is rapidly turning into a slum. Never again on this planet will there be unoccupied land, cultural isolation, freedom from bureaucracy, freedom for people to get lost and be on their own. Never again on this planet. But how about somewhere else?

I believe in fact that space-travel does provide an answer to many of these grave human problems. The only question in my mind is "When?" Many of you may consider it ridiculous to think of space as a way out of our difficulties, when the existing space program, such as it is, is being rapidly cut down, precisely because it appears to have nothing to offer to the solution of social problems. It is of course true that the existing space program has nothing to offer. If one believes in space as a major factor in human affairs, one must take a very long view.

A SHARP DISTINCTION

To avoid misunderstanding, I would like to emphasize again that I am making a sharp distinction between human affairs and scientific affairs. The existing space program consists of two very unequal parts, the scientific program using unmanned vehicles and absorbing about one-tenth of the money, and the unscientific program including manned flights and taking nine-tenths of the money. The scientific program has already been of immense value to science. In the next two decades, if the economy axe has not chopped it to pieces, the scientific space program should be able to settle the question of the existence of life on Mars, and I cannot think of any question in the whole of science more important than that. In the long run the discovery of alien life would undoubtedly have human as well as scientific consequences, but I do not include these in my discussion. I am looking for consequences of space travel that affect the mass of my fellow citizens and not merely my academic colleagues. The unscientific part of the existing space program affects the public more directly but only superficially. It is in essence an international sporting event with the whole world as spectators. I am a supporter of the manned space program for reasons which I will presently explain, but I do not pretend that it yet offers benefits commensurate with its cost, either to science or to the general public.

How long it will take for space travel to become socially important is mainly a matter of economics, a field in which I have no competence. I will only put forward a few tentative remarks to suggest that the time should be measured in decades rather than in centuries. There is a prevalent view among the educated public that space travel is necessarily and permanently so expensive that it can never be made available to large masses of people. I believe this view to be incorrect. An interesting analysis of the economics of our existing space operations was made by Theodore Taylor ("Propulsion of Space Vehicles" in Marshak, "Perspectives in Modern Physics," Interscience, 1966). He calculated the cost of running a commercial jet-plane service from New York to Los Angeles under the following ground rules: (1) There shall be no more than one flight per month. (2) The airplane shall be thrown away after each flight. (3) The entire costs of Kennedy and Los Angeles airports shall be covered by the freight charges. Under these rules, which are the rules governing our present space program, the cost of freight between New York and Los Angeles is comparable to the cost of putting freight into orbit. The point of this calculation is that the economies of commercial airline operations are economies of scale and of efficient organization. There is no basic physical or engineering reason why it should be enormously cheaper to fly to Los Angeles than to fly into orbit.

I will not go here into a technical discussion of the problems of space propulsion. In order to make space travel cheap we need two things. The first is a reliable vehicle, preferably an air-breather, which can take off from an airport, fly itself directly into orbit, re-enter and land, and be ready to repeat the operation day after day. The second is a massive volume of traffic and a correspondingly massive sale of tickets. I believe the second of these requirements will be met automatically within a few decades after the first is achieved. There are formidable technical problems involved in producing the re-usable orbital vehicle, but I do not believe the problems are permanently insoluble. Few people in the existing space program have worked on these problems, because the policy has been to do things fast rather than cheaply. The present cut-back may in fact encourage more long-range work on cheaper vehicles. I hesitate to make numerical predictions, but it may help to make my remarks meaningful if I state my actual expectations for the time-scale of these developments. I expect that sometime between 50 and 100 years from now we will have space travel with a volume of traffic and a cost to the passengers comparable with our present intercontinental jet flights. This prediction has the great advantage that if the reality exceeds my hopes I may be here to enjoy it, whereas, if I am proved wrong the other way, I will never know it.

THE BENEFITS

I will not say more about the economic aspects of space travel. The technical problems can be solved only by long and hard work, not by philosophical discourse. I am here discussing the problems of goals and purpose. Why should so many people want to rush around in space? And what good will it all do?

First I should like to make clear that I do not envisage emigration from Earth as solving the problem of the population explosion. Emigrants will always be a small minority, like the Spanish conquistadores rather than the Irish peasants of the Hungry Forties. Those who stay on Earth must solve their population problems, one way or another. Those who emigrate will have only postponed theirs.

I conceive the expansion of mankind into space to confer benefits on us in three main respects. (I am still ignoring entirely the scientific benefits and speaking only of social benefits.) The three benefits I will call garbage disposal, invulnerability and the open frontier, in what I consider to be increasing order of importance.

If humanity were to be forever confined to Earth, the problem of pollution could hardly be solved without an enforced economic stagnation. Many industrial processes are inherently messy, and the sum-total of industrial processes threatens to heat the Earth's biosphere to an intolerable extent within a century or two at present rates of economic growth. If cheap space transportation were available, it would become socially desirable and probably economically advantageous to move many of the messier industries into space. The solar wind is a magnificent garbage-disposal system, sweeping any dispersed matter in the solar system into the outer darkness where it will never be seen again. Prime candidates for the move upstairs would be the nuclear reactor and processing industries with their very large radioactive waste and thermal pollution problems.

The migration of industry into space need not be directed by a grandiose governmental plan. It would probably occur spontaneously as a result of economic pressures, if polluting industries were forced to pay for the privilege of remaining on Earth the actual cost of their pollutions. I foresee a time, a few centuries from now, when the bulk of heavy industry is space-borne, with the majority of mining operations perhaps transferred to the moon, and the Earth preserved for the enjoyment of its inhabitants as a green and pleasant land.

IF WE ARE LUCKY

If the problem of garbage disposal for an Earth-bound humanity is difficult, the problem of invulnerability is essentially insoluble. How can we expect to go on living forever on this exposed planetary surface, armed with deadly weapons which year by year grow more numerous and more widely dispersed? The only way to make the Earth safe from these weapons would be to establish a supra-national monopoly of military force, and even such a monopoly would not give us permanent security. The guardians of the monopoly would be men with their own national loyalties, and there would always be danger that the monopoly would break up in ruinous civil war, as happened on a smaller scale in 1861. We can hope to survive in a world bristling with hydrogen bombs for a few centuries, if we are lucky. But I believe we have small chance of surviving 10,000 years if we stay stuck to this planet. We are too many eggs in too small a basket.

The emigration into distant parts of the solar system of a substantial number of people would make our species as a whole invulnerable. A nuclear holocaust on Earth would still be an unspeakable tragedy, and might still wipe out 99 per cent of our numbers. But the one per cent who had dispersed themselves could not be wiped out simultaneously by any man-made catastrophe, and they would remain to carry on the promise of our destiny. Perhaps some of them would also come back to repopulate the Earth, after the radioactivity had cooled off. I at least find it a consoling thought that the human race will one day be invulnerable, that we have only to survive this awkward period of a century or two between the discovery of nuclear weapons and the large-scale expansion of our habitat, and then we shall be masters of our fate, freed from the threat of permanent extinction.

THE OPEN FRONTIER

The third and to my mind deepest benefit which space offers to mankind is the recovery of an open frontier. At this point we come back to the question: Where will all these people go when they set out in their latter-day Mayflowers? It is conventional in science fiction to think of going to planets, to Mars in particular. But I do not think planets will play the major role in man's future. For one thing, they are mostly uninhabitable. For another thing, even if they are habitable they will not increase our living-space very much. If we succeed in colonizing Mars, Mars will soon resemble the Earth, complete with parking lots, income tax forms, and all the rest of it. It will not be possible to hide on Mars any more than on Earth.

I believe the real future of man in space lies far away from planets, in isolated city-states floating in the void, perhaps attached to an inconspicuous asteroid or perhaps to a comet. Comets are especially important. It is believed that between a billion and 10 billion comets exist on the outer fringes of the solar system, loosely attached to the sun and only very rarely passing close to it. Each of these comets is a mine of biologically useful materials, carbon, nitrogen and water. Together they provide a thousand times as much living space as the planets. Above all they provide an open frontier, a place to hide and to disappear without trace, beyond the reach of snooping policemen and bureaucrats.

This vision of comet-hopping emigrants, streaming outward like the covered wagons on the Santa Fe Trail, is perhaps absurdly romantic or fanciful. Maybe it will never happen the way I imagine it. But I am convinced that something more or less along these lines will ultimately happen. Space is huge enough, so that somewhere in its vastness there will always be a place for rebels and outlaws. Near to the sun, space will belong to big governments and computerized industries. Outside, the open frontier will beckon as it has beckoned before, to persecuted minorities escaping from oppression, to religious fanatics, escaping from their neighbors, to recalcitrant teen-agers escaping from their parents, to lovers of solitude escaping from crowds. Perhaps most important of all for man's future, there will be groups of people setting out to find a place where they can be safe from prying eyes, free to experiment undisturbed with the creation of radically new types of human beings, surpassing us in mental capacities as we surpass the apes.

A HOPE FOR MAN

So I foresee that the ultimate benefit of space travel to man will be to make it possible for him once again to live as he lived throughout prehistoric time, in isolated small units. Once again his human qualities of clannish loyalty and exclusiveness will serve a constructive role, instead of being the chief dangers to his survival.

Men's tribal instincts will move back from the destructive channels of nationalism, racism and youthful alienation, and find satisfaction in the dangerous life of a frontier society. Genetic drift and diversification will again become important factors in human progress. Only in this way, I believe, can the basic dilemmas of our age, arising from the discordance between our tribal loyalties and the necessities of a world-wide technological civilization, be resolved. And when the angry young men and rebels and racists have again a frontier to which they can go, perhaps we timid and law-abiding citizens who choose to stay quietly down here on Earth will find it easier to live together in peace.

MAN AND HIS ENVIRONMENT

*"When the mad professor of fiction blows up his labora-
tory and then himself, that's O.K., but when scientists and
decision-makers act out of ignorance and pretend it is
knowledge, they are using the biosphere, the living space,
as an experimental laboratory. The whole world is put in
hazard."*

LORD RITCHIE-CALDER

POLLUTING THE ENVIRONMENT
Lord Ritchie-Calder

This essay surveys many varieties of pollution and concludes that science
and technology must not be allowed to experiment as freely in the future as
they have in the past. The results of atomic testing and of the Van Allen
Belt show that scientific investigations often have unforeseeable ecological
consequences, and the planet can no longer tolerate such tampering with its
delicate balance of life-sustaining forces. Lord Ritchie-Calder often writes on
ecological problems; he is the author of *The Inheritors, Living With the
Atom,* and *Common Sense About a Starving World.*

To hell with posterity! After all, what have the unborn ever done for
us? Nothing. Did they, with sweat and misery, make the Industrial Revolution possible? Did they go down into the carboniferous forests of
millions of years ago to bring up coal to make wealth and see nine-
tenths of the carbon belched out as chimney soot? Did they drive the
plows that broke the plains to release the dust that the buffalo had
trampled and fertilized for centuries? Did they have to broil in steel
plants to make the machines and see the pickling acids poured into the
sweet waters of rivers and lakes? Did they have to labor to cut down the
tall timbers to make homesteads and provide newsprint for the Sunday
comics and the celluloid for Hollywood spectaculars, leaving the hills
naked to the eroding rains and winds? Did they have the ingenuity to
drill down into the Paleozoic seas to bring up the oil to feed the inter-
nal-combustion engines so that their exhausts could create smog? Did

From *Center Magazine*, Vol. II, No. 3 (May 1969). Reprinted by permission of
the Center for the Study of Democratic Institutions in Santa Barbara, California.

they have the guts to man rigs out at sea so that boreholes could probe for oil in the offshore fissures of the San Andreas Fault? Did they endure the agony and the odium of the atom bomb and spray the biosphere with radioactive fallout? All that the people yet unborn have done is to wait and let us make the mistakes. To hell with posterity! That, too, can be arranged. As Shelley wrote: "Hell is a city much like London, a populous and smoky city."

At a conference held at Princeton, New Jersey, at the end of 1968, Professor Kingsley Davis, one of the greatest authorities on urban development, took the role of hell's realtor. The prospectus he offered from his latest survey of world cities was hair-raising. He showed that thirty-eight per cent of the world's population is already living in what are defined as "urban places." Over one-fifth of the world's population is living in cities of a hundred thousand or more. Over 375,000,000 people are living in cities of a million and over. On present trends it will take only fifteen years for half the world's population to be living in cities, and in fifty-five years everyone will be urbanized.

Davis foresaw that within the lifetime of a child born today, on present rates of population increase, there will be fifteen billion people to be fed and housed—over four times as many as now. The whole human species will be living in cities of a million and over and the biggest city will have 1,300,000,000 inhabitants. Yes, 1.3 billion. That is 186 times as many as there are in Greater London today.

In his forebodings of Dystopia (with a "y" as in dyspepsia, but it could just as properly be "Dis," after the ruler of the Underworld), Doxiades has warned about the disorderly growth of cities, oozing into each other like confluent ulcers. He has given us Ecumenopolis—World City. The East Side of Ecumenopolis would have as its Main Street the Eurasian Highway, stretching from Glasgow to Bangkok, with the Channel tunnel as an underpass and a built-up area all the way. West Side, divided not by railroad tracks but by the Atlantic, is already emerging (or, rather, merging) in the United States. There is talk, and evidence, of "Boswash," the urban development of a built-up area from Boston to Washington. On the Pacific Coast, with Los Angeles already sprawling into the desert, the realtor's garden cities, briskly reënforced by industrial estates, are slurring into one another and presently will stretch all the way from San Diego to San Francisco. The Main Street of Sansan will be Route 101. This is insanity. We do not need a crystal ball to foresee what David and Doxiades are predicting—we can see it through smog-colored spectacles; we can smell it seventy years away because it is in our nostrils today; a blind man can see what is coming.

Are these trends inevitable? They are unless we do something about them. I have given up predicting and have taken to prognosis. There is a very important difference. Prediction is based on the projection of trends. Experts plan for the trends and thus confirm them. They regard warnings as instructions. For example, while I was lecturing in that horror city of Calcutta, where three-quarters of the population live in shacks without running water or sewage disposal, and, in the monsoon season, wade through their own floating excrement, I warned that within twenty-five years there would be in India at least five cities, each with populations of over sixty million, ten times bigger than Calcutta. I was warning against the drift into the great conurbations now going on, which has been encouraged by ill-conceived policies of industrialization. I was warning against imitating the German Ruhr, the British Black Country, and America's Pittsburgh. I was arguing for "population dams," for decentralized development based on the villages, which make up the traditional cultural and social pattern of India. These "dams" would prevent the flash floods of population into overpopulated areas. I was *warning,* but they accepted the prediction and ignored the warning. Soon thereafter I learned that an American university had been given a contract to make a feasibility study for a city of sixty million people north of Bombay. When enthusiasts get busy on a feasibility study, they invariably find that it is feasible. When they get to their drawing boards they have a whale of a time. They design skyscrapers above ground and subterranean tenements below ground. They work out minimal requirements of air and hence how much breathing space a family can survive in. They design "living-units," hutches for battery-fed people who are stacked together like kindergarten blocks. They provide water and regulate the sewage on the now well-established cost-efficiency principles of factory-farming. And then they finish up convinced that this is the most economical way of housing people. I thought I had scotched the idea by making representations through influential Indian friends. I asked them, among other things, how many mental hospitals they were planning to take care of the millions who would surely go mad under such conditions. But I have heard rumors that the planners are so slide-rule happy they are planning a city for six hundred million.

Prognosis is something else again. An intelligent doctor, having diagnosed the symptoms and examined the patient's condition, does not say (except in soap operas): "You have six months to live." He says: "Frankly, your condition is serious. Unless you do so-and-so, and unless I do so-and-so, it is bound to deteriorate." The operative phrase is "do so-and-so." One does not have to plan *for* trends; if they are socially undesirable our duty is to plan *away* from them, and treat the symptoms before they become malignant.

A multiplying population multiplies the problems. The prospect of a world of fifteen billion people is intimidating. Three-quarters of the world's present population is inadequately fed—hundreds of millions are not getting the food necessary for well-being. So it is not just a question of quadrupling the present food supply; it means six to eight times that to take care of present deficiencies. It is not a matter of numbers, either; it is the *rate* of increase that mops up any improvements. Nor is it just a question of housing but of clothing and material satisfactions—automobiles, televisions, and the rest. That means greater inroads on natural resources, the steady destruction of amenities, and the conflict of interest between those who want oil and those who want oil-free beaches, or between those who want to get from here to there on wider and wider roads and those whose homes are going to collapse in mud slides because of the making of those roads. Lewis Mumford has suggested that civilization really began with the making of containers—cans, non-returnable bottles, cartons, plastic bags, none of which can be redigested by nature. Every sneeze accounts for a personal tissue. Multiply that by fifteen billion.

Environmental pollution is partly rapacity and partly a conflict of interest between the individual, multimillions of individuals, and the commonweal; but largely, in our generation, it is the exaggerated effects of specialization with no sense of ecology, i.e. the balance of nature. Claude Bernard, the French physiologist admonished his colleagues over a century ago: "True science teaches us to doubt and in ignorance to refrain." Ecologists feel their way with a detector through a minefield of doubts. Specialists, cocksure of their own facts, push ahead, regardless of others.

Behind the sky-high fences of military secrecy, the physicists produced the atomic bomb—just a bigger explosion—without taking into account the biological effects of radiation. Prime Minister Attlee, who consented to the dropping of the bomb on Hiroshima, later said that no one, not Churchill, nor members of the British Cabinet, nor he himself, knew of the possible genetic effects of the blast. "If the scientists knew, they never told us." Twenty years before, Hermann Muller had shown the genetic effects of radiation and had been awarded the Nobel Prize, but he was a biologist and security treated this weapon as a physicist's bomb. In the peacetime bomb-testing, when everyone was alerted to the biological risk, we were told that the fallout of radioactive materials could be localized in the testing grounds. The radioactive dust on The Lucky Dragon, which was fishing well beyond the proscribed area, disproved that. Nevertheless, when it was decided to explode the H-bomb the assurance about localization was blandly repeated. The H-bomb would punch a hole into the stratosphere and the radioactive gases would dissipate. One of those gases is radioactive krypton, which decays into radioactive strontium, a particulate. Somebody must have known that but nobody worried unduly because it would happen above the troposphere, which might be described as the roof of the weather system. What was definitely overlooked was the fact that the troposphere is not continuous. There is the equatorial troposphere and the polar troposphere and they overlap. The radioactive strontium came back through the transom and was spread all over the world by the climatic jet streams to be deposited as rain. The result is that there is radiostrontium (which did not exist in nature) in the bones of every young person who was growing up during the bomb-testing—every young person, everywhere in the world. It may be medically insignificant but it is the brandmark of the Atomic Age generation and a reminder of the mistakes of their elders.

When the mad professor of fiction blows up his laboratory and then himself, that's O.K., but when scientists and decision-makers act out of ignorance and pretend it is knowledge, they are using the biosphere, the living space, as an experimental laboratory. The whole world is put in hazard. And they do it even when they are told not to. During the International Geophysical Year, the Van Allen Belt was discovered. The Van Allen Belt is a region of magnetic phenomena. Immediately the bright boys decided to carry out an experiment and explode a hydrogen bomb in the Belt to see if they could produce an artifical aurora. The colorful draperies, the luminous skirts of the aurora, are caused by drawing cosmic particles magnetically through the rare gases of the upper atmosphere. It is called ionization and is like passing electrons through the vacuum tubes of our familiar neon lighting. It was called the Rainbow Bomb. Every responsible scientist in cosmology, radio-astronomy, and physics of the atmosphere protested against this tampering with a system we did not understand. They exploded their bomb. They got their pyrotechnics. We still do not know the price we may have to pay for this artificial magnetic disturbance.

We could blame the freakish weather on the Rainbow Bomb but, in our ignorance, we could not sustain the indictment. Anyway, there are so many other things happening that could be responsible. We can look with misgiving on the tracks in the sky—the white tails of the jet aircraft and the exhausts of space rockets. These are introducing into the climatic system new factors, the effects of which are immensurable. The triggering of rain clouds depends upon the water vapor having a toehold, a nucleus, on which to form. That is how artificial precipitation, so-called rainmaking, is produced. So the jets, crisscrossing the weather system, playing tic-tac-toe, can produce a man-made change of climate.

On the longer term, we can see even more drastic effects from the many activities of *Homo insapiens,* Unthinking Man. In 1963, at the

United Nations Science and Technology Conference, we took stock of the several effects of industrialization on the total environment.

The atmosphere is not only the air which humans, animals, and plants breathe; it is the envelope which protects living things from harmful radiation from the sun and outer space. It is also the medium of climate, the winds and the rain. These are inseparable from the hydrosphere, including the oceans, which cover seven-tenths of the earth's surface with their currents and evaporation; and from the biosphere, with the vegetation and its transpiration and photosynthesis; and from the lithosphere, with its minerals, extracted for man's increasing needs. Millions of years ago the sun encouraged the growth of the primeval forests, which became our coal, and the life-growth in the Paleozoic seas, which became our oil. Those fossil-fuels, locked in the vaults through eons of time, and brought out by modern man and put back into the atmosphere from the chimney stacks and exhaust pipes of modern engineering.

This is an overplus on the natural carbon. About six billion tons of primeval carbon are mixed with the atmosphere every year. During the past century, in the process of industrialization, with its burning of fossil-fuels, more than four hundred billion tons of carbon have been artificially introduced into the atmosphere. The concentration in the air we breathe has been increased by approximately ten per cent; if all the known reserves of coal and oil were burned the concentration would be ten times greater.

This is something more than a public-health problem, more than a question of what goes into the lungs of the individual, more than a question of smog. The carbon cycle in nature is a self-adjusting mechanism. One school of scientific thought stresses that carbon monoxide can reduce solar radiation. Another school points out that an increase in carbon dioxide raises the temperature at the earth's surface. They are both right. Carbon dioxide, of course, is indispensable for plants and hence for the food cycle of creatures, including humans. It is the source of life. But a balance is maintained by excess carbon being absorbed by the seas. The excess is now taxing this absorption, and the effect on the heat balance of the earth can be significant because of what is known as "the greenhouse effect." A greenhouse lets in the sun's rays and retains the heat. Similarly, carbon dioxide, as a transparent diffusion, does likewise; it admits the radiant heat and keeps the convection heat close to the surface. It has been estimated that at the present rate of increase (those six billion tons a year) the mean annual temperature all over the world might increase by 5.8° F. in the next forty to fifty years.

Experts may argue about the time factor or about the effects, but certain things are observable not only in the industrialized Northern Hemisphere but also in the Southern Hemisphere. The ice of the north polar seas is thinning and shrinking. The seas, with their blanket of carbon dioxide, are changing their temperatures with the result that marine life is increasing and transpiring more carbon dioxide. With this combination, fish are migrating, even changing their latitudes. On land, glaciers are melting and the snow line is retreating. In Scandinavia, land which was perennially under snow and ice is thawing. Arrowheads of a thousand years ago, when the black earth was last exposed and when Eric the Red's Greenland was probably still green, have been found there. In the North American sub-Arctic a similar process is observable. Black earth has been exposed and retains the summer heat longer so that each year the effect moves farther north. The melting of the sea ice will not affect the sea level because the volume of floating ice is the same as the water it displaces, but the melting of the land's ice caps and glaciers, in which water is locked up, will introduce additional water to the oceans and raise the sea level. Rivers originating in glaciers and permanent snowfields (in the Himalayas, for instance) will increase their flow, and if the ice dams break the effects could be catastrophic. In this process, the patterns of rainfall will change, with increased precipitation in areas now arid and aridity in places now fertile. I am advising all my friends not to take ninety-nine-year leases on properties at present sea level.

The pollution of sweet-water lakes and rivers has increased so during the past twenty-five years that a Freedom from Thirst campaign is becoming as necessary as a Freedom from Hunger campaign. Again it is a conflict of motives and a conspiracy of ignorance. We can look at the obvious—the unprocessed urban sewage and the influx of industrial effluents. No one could possibly have believed that the Great Lakes in their immensity could ever be overwhelmed, or that Niagra Falls could lose its pristine clearness and fume like brown smoke, or that Lake Erie could become a cesspool. It did its best to oxidize the wastes from the steel plants by giving up its free oxygen until at last it surrendered and the anaerobic microörganisms took over. Of course, one can say that the mortuary smells of Lake Erie are not due to the pickling acids but to the dead fish.

The conflict of interests amounts to a dilemma. To insure that people shall be fed we apply our ingenuity in the form of artificial fertilizers, herbicides, pesticides, and insecticides. The runoff from the lands gets into the streams and rivers and distant oceans. DDT from the rivers of the United States has been found in the fauna of the Antarcitic, where no DDT has ever been allowed. The dilemma becomes agonizing in places like India, with its hungry millions. It is now believed that the new strains of Mexican grain and I.R.C. (International Rice Center in the Philippines) rice, with their high yields, will provide enough food for them, belly-filling if not nutritionally balanced. These strains, however, need plenty of water, constant irrigation, plenty of fertilizers to sustain the yields, and tons of pesticides because standardized pedigree plants are highly vulnerable to disease. This means that the production will be concentrated in the river systems, like the Gangeatic Plains, and the chemicals will drain into the rivers.

The glib answer to this sort of thing is "atomic energy." If there is enough energy and it is cheap enough, you can afford to turn rivers into sewers and lakes into cesspools. You can desalinate the seas. But, for the foreseeable future, that anergy will come from atomic fission, from the breaking down of the nucleus. The alternative, promised but undelivered, is thermonuclear energy—putting the H-bomb bomb into dungarees by controlling the fusion of hydrogen. Fusion does not produce waste products, fission does. And the more peaceful atomic reactors there are, the more radioactive waste there will be to dispose of. The really dangerous material has to be buried. The biggest disposal area in the world is at Hanford, Washington. It encloses a stretch of the Columbia River and a tract of country covering 650 square miles. There, a twentieth-century Giza, it has cost much more to bury live atoms than it cost to entomb all the mummies of all the Pyramid Kings of Egypt.

At Hanford, the live atoms are kept in tanks constructed of carbon steel, resting in a steel saucer to catch any leakage. These are enclosed in a reëforced concrete structure and the whole construction is buried in the ground with only the vents showing. In the steel sepulchers, each with a million-gallon capacity, the atoms are very much alive. Their radio-activity keeps the acids in the witches' brew boiling. In the bottom of the tanks the temperature is well above the boiling point of water. There has to be a cooling system, therefore, and it must be continuously maintained. In addition, the vapors generated in the tanks have to be condensed and scrubbed, otherwise a radioactive miasma would escape from the vents. Some of the elements in those high-level wastes will remain radioactive for at least 250,000 years. It is most unlikely that the tanks will endure as long as the Egyptian pyramids.

Radioactive wastes from atomic processing stations have to be transported to such burial grounds. By the year 2000, if the present practices continue, the number of six-ton tankers in transit at any given time would be well over three thousand and the amount of radioactice products in them would be 980,000,000 curies—that is a mighty number of curies to be roaming around in a populated country.

There are other ways of disposing of radioactive waste and there are safeguards against the hazards, but those safeguards have to be enforced and constant vigilance maintained. There are already those who say that the safety precautions in the atomic industry are excessive.

Polluting the environment has been sufficiently dramatized by events in recent years to show the price we have to pay for our recklessness. It is not just the destruction of natural beauty or the sacrifice of recreational amenities, which are crimes in themselves, but interference with the whole ecology—with the balance of nature on which persistence of life on this planet depends. We are so fascinated by the gimmicks and gadgetry of science and technology and are in such a hurry to exploit them that we do not count the consequences.

We have plenty of scientific knowledge but knowledge is not wisdom: wisdom is knowledge tempered by judgment. At the moment, the scientists, technologists, and industrialists are the judge and jury in their own assize. Statesmen, politicians, and administrators are ill-equipped to make judgments about the true values of discoveries or developments. On the contrary, they tend to encourage the crash programs to get quick answers—like the Manhattan Project, which turned the laboratory discovery of uranium fission into a cataclysmic bomb in six years; the Computer/Automation Revolution; the Space Program; and now the Bio-engineering Revolution, with its possibilities not only of spare-organ plumbing but of changing the nature of living things by gene manipulation. They blunder into a minefield of undetected ignorance, masquerading as science.

The present younger generation has an unhappy awareness of such matters. They were born into the Atomic Age, programmed into the Computer Age, rocketed into the Space Age, and are poised on the threshold of the Bio-engineering Age. They take all these marvels for granted, but they are also aware that the advances have reduced the world to a neighborhood and that we are all involved one with another in the risks as well as the opportunities. They see the mistakes writ large. They see their elders mucking about with *their* world and *their* future. That accounts for their profound unease, whatever forms their complaints may take. They are the spokesmen for posterity and are justified in their protest. But they do not have the explicit answers, either.

Somehow science and technology must conform to some kind of social responsibility. Together, they form the social and economic dynamic of our times. They are the pacesetters for politics and it is in the political frame of reference that answers must be found. There can never be any question of restraining or repressing natural curiosity, which is true science, but there is ample justification for evaluating and judging developmental science. The common good requires nothing less.

TOWARD AN ECOLOGICAL SOLUTION
Murray Bookchin

"The notion that man must dominate nature emerges directly from the domination of man by man." Using this premise, Murray Bookchin discusses an "ecological solution" in very political terms: "Propertied society, domina-

From *Ramparts*, Vol. 8, No. 11 (May 1970). Copyright 1970 Ramparts Magazine, Inc. Reprinted by permission of the Editors.

tion, hierarchy and the state, in all their forms, are utterly incompatible with the survival of the biosphere." Mr. Bookchin contends that restraints placed on science and technology will be unsuccessful in combating the ecological deterioration unless the controls result from a reconstruction of society. The author has written (using the pseudonym Lewis Herber) *Crisis in Our Cities.*

Popular alarm over environmental decay and pollution did not emerge for the first time merely in the late '60's, nor for that matter is it the unique response of the present century. Air pollution, water pollution, food adulteration and other environmental problems were public issues as far back as ancient times, when nations of environmental diseases were far more prevalent than they are today. All of these issues came to the surface again with the Industrial Revolution—a period which was marked by burgeoning cities, the growth of the factory system, and an unprecedented befouling and polluting of air and waterways.

Today the situation is changing drastically and at a tempo that portends a catastrophe for the entire world of life. What is not clearly understood in many popular discussions of the present ecological crisis is that the very nature of the issues has changed, that the decay of the environment is directly tied to the decay of the existing social structure. It is not simply certain malpractices or a given spectrum of poisonous agents that is at stake, but rather the very structure of modern agriculture, industry and the city. Consequently, environmental decay and ecological catastrophe cannot be averted merely by increased programs like "pollution control" which deal with sources rather than systems. To be commensurable to the problem, the solution must entail far-reaching revolutionary changes in society and in man's relation to man.

To understand the enormity of the ecological crisis and the sweeping transformation it requires, let us briefly revisit the "pollution problem" as it existed a few decades ago. During the 1930's, pollution was primarily a muckraking issue, a problem of exposé journalism typified by Kallet and Schlink's "100 Million Guinea Pigs."

This kind of muckraking literature still exists in abundance and finds an eager market among "consumers," that is to say, a public that seeks personal and legislative solutions to pollution problems. Its supreme pontiff is Ralph Nader, an energetic young man who has shrewdly combined traditional muckraking with a safe form of "New Left" activism. In reality, Nader's emphasis belongs to another historical era, for the magnitude of the pollution problem has expanded beyond the most exaggerated accounts of the '30's. The new pollutants are no longer "poisons" in the popular sense of the term; rather they belong to the problems of ecology, not merely pharmacology, and these do not lend themselves to legislative redress.

What now confronts us is not the predominantly specific, rapidly degradable poisons that alarmed an earlier generation, but long-lived carcinogenic and mutagenic agents, such as radioactive isotopes and chlorinated hydrocarbons. These agents become part of the very anatomy of the individual by entering his bone structure, tissues and fat deposits. Their dispersion is so global that they become part of the anatomy of the environment itself. They will be within us and around us for years to come, in many cases for generations to come. Their toxic effects are usually chronic rather than acute; the deadly and mutational effects they produce in the individual will not be seen until many years have passed. They are harmful not only in large quantities, but in trace amounts; as such, they are not detectable by human senses or even, in many cases, by conventional methods of analysis. They damage not only specific individuals but the human species as a whole and virtually all other forms of life.

No less alarming is the fact that we must drastically revise our traditional notions of what constitutes an environmental "pollutant." A few decades ago it would have been absurd to describe carbon dioxide and heat as "pollutants" in the customary sense of the term. Yet in both cases they may well rank among the most serious sources of future ecological imbalance and pose major threats to the viability of the planet. As a result of industrial and domestic combustion activities, the quantity of carbon dioxide in the atmosphere has increased by roughly 25 per cent in the past 100 years, a figure that may well double again by the end of the century. The famous "greenhouse effect," which increasing quantities of the gas is expected to produce, has already been widely discussed: eventually, it is supposed, the gas will inhibit the dissipation of the earth's heat into space, causing a rise in overall temperatures which will melt the polar ice caps and result in an inundation of vast coastal areas. Thermal pollution, the result mainly of warm water discharged by nuclear and conventional power plants, has disastrous effects on the ecology of lakes, rivers and estuaries. Increases in water temperature not only damage the physiological and reproductive activities of fish; they also promote the great blooms of algae that have become such formidable problems in waterways.

What is at stake in the ecological crisis we face today is the very capacity of the earth to sustain advanced forms of life. The crisis is being drawn together by massive increases in "typical" forms of air and water pollution; by a mounting accumulation of nondegradable wastes, lead residues, pesticide residues and toxic additives in food; by the expansion of cities into vast urban belts; by increasing stresses due to congestion, noise and mass living; by the wanton scarring of the earth as a result of mining operations, lumbering, and real estate speculation. The result of all this is that the earth within a few decades has been despoiled on a scale that is unprecedented in the entire history of human habitation on the planet.

Finally, the complexity and diversity of life which marked biological evolution over many millions of years is being replaced by a simpler, more synthetic and increasingly homogenized environment. Aside from any esthetic considerations, the elimination of this complexity and diversity may prove to be the most serious loss of all. Modern society is literally undoing the work of organic evolution. If this process continues unabated, the earth may be reduced to a level of biotic simplicity where humanity—whose welfare depends profoundly upon the complex food chains in the soil, on the land surface and in the oceans—will no longer be able to sustain itself as a viable animal species.

II

In recent years a type of biological "cold warrior" has emerged who tends to locate the ecological crisis in technology and population growth, thereby divesting it of its explosive social content. Out of this focus has emerged a new version of "original sin" in which tools and machines, reinforced by sexually irresponsible humans, ravage the earth in concert. Both technology and sexual irresponsibility, so the argument goes, must be curbed—if not voluntarily, then by the divine institution called the state.

The naivete of this approach would be risible were it not for its sinister implications. History has known of many different forms of tools and machines, some of which are patently harmful to human welfare and the natural world, others of which have clearly improved the condition of man and the ecology of an area. It would be absurd to place plows and mutagenic defoliants, weaving machines and automobiles, computers and moon rockets, under a common rubric. Worse, it would be grossly misleading to deal with these technologies in a social vacuum.

Technologies consist not only of the devices humans employ to mediate their relationship with the natural world, but also the attitudes associated with these devices. These attitudes are distinctly social products, the results of the social relationships humans establish with each other. What is clearly needed is not a mindless deprecation of technology as such, but rather a reordering and redevelopment of technologies according to ecologically sound principles. We need an eco-technology that will help harmonize society with the natural world.

The same over-simplification is evident in the neo-Malthusian alarm over population growth. The reduction of population growth to a mere ratio between birth rates and death rates obscures the many complex social factors that enter into both statistics. A rising or declining birth rate is not a simple biological datum, any more than is a rising or declining death rate. Both are subject to the influences of the economic status of the individual, the nature of family structure, the values of society, the status of women, the attitude toward children, the culture of the community, and so forth. A change in any single factor interacts with the remainder to produce the statistical data called "birth rate" and "death rate." Culled from such abstract ratios, population growth rates can easily be used to foster authoritarian controls and finally a totalitarian society, especially if neo-Malthusian propaganda and the failure of voluntary birth control are used as an excuse. In arguing that forcible measures of birth control and a calculated policy of indifference to hunger may eventually be necessary to stabilize world populations, the neo-Malthusians are already creating a climate of opinion that will make genocidal policies and authoritarian institutions socially acceptable.

It is supremely ironic that coercion, so clearly implicit in the neo-Malthusian outlook, has acquired a respected place in the public debate on ecology— for the roots of the ecological crisis lie precisely in the coercive basis of modern society. The notion that man must dominate nature emerges directly from the domination of man by man. The patriarchal family may have planted the seed of domination in the nuclear relations of humanity; the classical split between spirit and reality— indeed, mind and labor—may have nourished it; the anti-naturalistic bias of Christianity may have tended to its growth; but it was not until organic community relations, be they tribal, feudal or peasant in form, dissolved into market relationships that the planet itself was reduced to a resource for exploitation.

This centuries-long tendency finds its most exacerbating development in modern capitalism: a social order that is orchestrated entirely by the maxim "Production for the sake of production." Owing to its inherently competitive nature, bourgeois society not only pits humans against each other, but the mass of humanity against the natural world. Just as men are converted into commodities, so every aspect of nature is converted into a commodity, a resource to be manufactured and merchandised wantonly. Entire continental areas in turn are converted into factories, and cities into marketplaces. The liberal euphemisms for these unadorned terms are "growth," "industrial society" and "urban blight." By whatever language they are described, the phenomena have their roots in the domination of man by man.

As technology develops, the maxim "Production for the sake of production" finds its complement in "Consumption for the sake of consumption." The phrase "consumer society" completes the description of the present social order as an "industrial society." Needs are tailored by the mass media to create a public demand for utterly useless commodities, each carefully engineered to deteriorate after a predetermined period of time. The plundering of the human spirit by the marketplace is paralleled by the plundering of the earth by capital. The tendency of the liberal to identify the marketplace with human needs, and capital with technology, represents a calculated error that neutralizes the social thrust of the ecological crisis.

The strategic ratios in the ecological crisis are not the population rates of India but the production rates of the United States, a country that produces more than 50 per cent of the world's goods. Here, too, liberal euphemisms like "affluence" conceal the critical thrust of a blunt word like "waste." With a vast section of its industrial capacity committed to war production, the U.S. is literally trampling upon the earth and shredding ecological links that are vital to human survival. If current industrial projections prove to be accurate, the remaining 30 years of the century will witness a five-fold increase in electric power production, based mostly on nuclear fuels and coal. The colossal burden in radioactive wastes and other effluents that this increase will place on the natural ecology of the earth hardly needs description.

In shorter perspective, the problem is no less disquieting. Within the next five years, lumber production may increase an overall 20 per cent; the output of paper, five per cent annually; folding boxes, three per cent annually; metal cans, four to five per cent annually; plastics (which currently form one to two per cent of municipal wastes), seven per cent annually. Collectively, these industries account for the most serious pollutants in the environment. The utterly senseless nature of modern industry activity is perhaps best illustrated by the decline in returnable (and reusable) beer bottles from 54 billion bottles in 1960 to 26 billion today. Their place has been taken over by "one-way bottles" (a rise from 8 to 21 billion in the same period) and cans (an increase from 38 to 53 billion). The "one-way bottles" and cans, of course, pose tremendous problems in solid waste disposal, but they do sell better.

It may be that the planet, conceived as a lump of minerals, can support these mindless increases in the output of trash. The earth, conceived as a complex web of life, certainly cannot. The only question is, can the earth survive its looting long enough for man to replace the current destructive social system with a humanistic, ecologically oriented society.

The apocalyptic tone that marks so many ecological works over the past decade should not be taken lightly. We are witnessing the end of a world, although whether this world is a long-established social order or the earth as a living organism still remains in question. The ecological crisis, with its threat of human extinction, has developed appositely to the advance of technology, with its promise of abundance, leisure and material security. Both are converging toward a single focus: At a point where the very survival of man is being threatened, the possibility of removing him from the trammels of domination, material scarcity and toil has never been more promising. The very technology that has been used to plunder the planet can now be deployed, artfully and rationally, to make it flourish.

It is necessary to overcome not only bourgeois society but also the long legacy of propertied society: the patriarchal family, the city, the state—indeed, the historic splits that separated mind from sensuousness, individual from society, town from country, work from play, man from nature. The spirit of spontaneity and diversity that permeates the ecological outlook toward the natural world must now be directed toward revolutionary change and utopian reconstruction in the social world. Propertied society, domination, hierarchy and the state, in all their forms, are utterly incompatible with the survival of the biosphere. Either ecology action is revolutionary action or it is nothing at all. Any attempt to reform a social order that by its very nature pits humanity against all the forces of life is a gross deception and serves merely as a safety valve for established institutions.

The application of ecological principles to social reconstruction, on the other hand, opens entirely new opportunities for imagination and creativity. The cities must be decentralized to serve the interests of both natural and social ecology. Urban gigantism is devastating not only to the land, the air, the waterways and the local climate, but to the human spirit. Having reached its limits in the megalopolis—an urban sprawl that can best be described as the "non-city"—the city must be replaced by a multitude of diversified, well-rounded communities, each scaled to human dimensions and to the carrying capacity of its ecosystem. Technology, in turn, must be placed in the service of meaningful human needs, its output gauged to permit a careful recycling of wastes into the environment.

With the community and its technology sculptured to human scale, it should be possible to establish new, diversified energy patterns: the combined use of solar power, wind power and a judicious use of fossil and nuclear fuels. In this decentralized society, a new sense of tribalism, of face-to-face relations, can be expected to replace the bureaucratic institutions of propertied society and the state. The earth would be shared communally, in a new spirit of harmony between man and man and between man and nature.

In the early years of the 19th century, this image of a new, free and stateless society was at best a distant vision, a humanistic ideal which revolutionaries described as communism or anarchism, and their opponents as utopia. As the one century passed into its successor, the advance of technology increasingly brought this vision into the realm of possibility. The ecological crisis of the late 20th century has now turned the possibility of its early decades into a dire necessity. Not only is humanity more prepared for the realization of this vision than at any time in history—a fact intuited by the tribalism of the youth culture—but upon its realization depends the very existence of humanity in the remaining years ahead.

Perhaps the most important message of Marx a century ago was the concept that humanity must develop the means of survival in order to live. Today, the development of a flexible, open-ended technology has reversed this concept completely. We stand on the brink of a post-scarcity society, a society that can finally remove material want and domination from the human condition. Perhaps the most important message of ecology is the concept that man must master the conditions of life in order to survive.

During the May–June uprising of 1968, the French students sensed the new equation in human affairs when they inscribed the demand: "Be realistic! Do the impossible!" To this demand, the young Americans who face the next century can add the more solemn injunction: "If we don't do the impossible, we shall be faced with the unthinkable."

PART FIVE

WOMEN'S LIBERATION

> *"Freud to the contrary, anatomy is not destiny, at least not for more than nine months at a time."*
>
> GLORIA STEINEM

> *"And this is one of the most important things the feminist movement can accomplish: to make people whole again, to enable us all to develop all parts of ourselves and not to have to worry about being 'feminine' or 'masculine.' Then we will be able to be human."*
>
> "THE NEW FEMINISM"

This decade promises new life styles, new education, new race relations, and new technology. Affected by and affecting these changes will be a "new woman"—if advocates of Women's Liberation are right. In 1920 women won the right to vote; since then they have served such causes as civil rights and population control. In the 1970's they seem ready to work for Women's Liberation—a broad, far-reaching movement embracing many schemes, ranging all the way from abortion reform to daycare centers to sexual apartheid. What the radical feminist and her moderate sister share primarily, however, is a longing for roles and opportunities equal to those enjoyed by men. Fortunately for women in their search for new roles, models are already available as replacements or alternatives for the old stereotypes of Mother, Housewife, and Secretary. While advertisements for Barbie Doll still instruct little girls that cheerleading and proms, clothes and dates are the proper concerns for a junior miss, today's headlines present to teenagers and matrons the images of Angela Davis, Bernadette Devlin, and Margaret Mead, all of whom have proven that women need not be passive spectators in a "man's world." In the past, according to Kate Millett, woman's image was created by man to perpetuate his domination of her. What the Women's Liberation movement offers, then, is a new self-made image—or at least a choice among several images.

Stereotyping of women has, unfortunately, been all too common. As Leslie Fiedler has pointed out, literary portraits of women in American fiction have always been polarized, with few realistic female characters to bridge the gap between "Fair Maiden" and "Dark Lady." The same situation exists in real life. Not many housewives see themselves as Girl Scout or Femme Fatale. And even the new images available—activists, career woman, liberated woman—may seem remote from the life of child-burdened, temporarily employed Mrs. America. The difficulty in finding a rewarding role is one of the motivations driving women into the Women's Liberation movement. Once there, women find that their cause is extremely diverse, as the names of its publicized organizations suggest: they range from the rather conventional NOW (National Organization for Women), founded by Betty Friedan, to the radical WITCH (Woman's International Terrorist Conspiracy from Hell). Ultimately such organizations will create many new possibilities and roles for women, but their more immediate goals are to redress some specific sources of discontent among women.

As in many protest movements, the most tangible goals of today's feminists are economic. They want free child-care centers, compensation for their household chores, low-cost abortions. But most importantly they want equal pay for equal work. Women perform many of the same jobs that men do. Yet the median salary for women working full-time is only 58% of that for men. While 23% of working men make over $10,000 a year, only 3% of the working women exceed that figure. Not only do women get paid less, they also have fewer opportunities for the more interesting jobs. Women have escaped from the kitchen, but they still face repression in the office, the airplane, and the hospital. Men are the executives, the pilots, the doctors; women, the secretaries, stewardesses, nurses. To remedy these problems, women demand enforcement of federal laws against job discriminations based on sex. They also seek changes in educational practices, so that children will be directed into vocations on the basis of ability, not biology.

Another goal of some feminists is an alteration of such basic institutions as courtship, marriage, and the family. Most people sympathize with women's efforts to gain equal economic and educational opportunities. The feminists' proposals concerning sexual relationships and child care, however, are less likely to receive wide support at this time. Some of the extreme measures devised by the extreme fringe of the liberation movement can be implied from the titles of journals such as *No More Fun and Games* and *Up from Under*. One spokeswoman, Ti-Grace Atkinson, argues for the elimination of marriage and the establishment of communal child care; another, Anne Koedt, goes even farther and, in "The Myth of the Vaginal Orgasm," denies the necessity of men for attaining sexual satisfaction.

Of course, most women desire less radical modifications in family management and sexual relationships. Marriage is still the goal for the average woman, but she is less likely to think of it as a career and more likely to expect her husband to share domestic duties. As women work more outside of the home, men will probably have to work more inside.

If many women want equality in their marriages, some also want to revolutionize romance. As Gloria Steinem pointed out in a recently published interview with Hugh Hefner, *Playboy* doesn't know everything about what women want from men. Nor does Dr. Reuben know everything about sex. The sexual revolution, one of Hefner's favorite causes, helped to free women and men from Puritanical concepts about sin and sex (although sexual behavior patterns among Americans have actually changed only slightly since the 1920's). But feminists now claim that the revolution only accentuated the woman-as-object image which fills girlie magazines and X-rated films. In a related area, Helen Gurley Brown admits that That Cosmopolitan Girl works hard at being beautiful and seductive. But many liberated women scoff at such concern with appearances and the body. Women from Abby Rockefeller (who advises her followers to wear pants and flat heels for self-protection) to Mamma Cass and Barbra Streisand are saying, in their own ways, that females don't need fashionable clothes, classic features, and spectacular figures to be attractive. Plain and ugly men rarely feel the need to falsify their appearance; women want the same tolerance extended to them. Most importantly, women want to be loved for more than their appearance and for longer than their youth.

When discussing the legitimacy of such demands, feminists constantly compare their cause to the black's struggle for equality. According to Kate Millett's book, *Sexual Politics,* women were the first "minority" and continue to suffer minority-class status, even though they account for 51% of the American population. Women talk of being "exploited" and "enslaved" by men. They claim that education takes little notice of "her" story in *history.* Consequently women are in the same position that Negroes occupied prior to the Black Power movement: they suffer from an identity crisis, which often manifests itself in self-hatred (a commonly heard opinion is that women can't get along with one another) and identification with the dominant group, the men. Even the same kind of jokes link the female and the black movements: "I have nothing against feminists, but I wouldn't want my son to marry one." Finally, as the name "NOW" implies, women, like blacks, want freedom and equality today, not tomorrow.

Critics of Women's Liberation are quick to point out a dissimilarity between these movements. Biologically, there are no appreciable differences between the races that matter. The same can not be said about the differences between the sexes. Opponents such as Kate Millett and Lionel Tiger debate how important the biological differences are in determining cultural concepts of feminine and masculine roles. The question that feminists have to answer usually takes a standard form: Is anatomy destiny? Women admit that the answer is "Yes" during pregnancy; they deny that it should be so at other times. They resent the male chauvinism that justifies menial, inferior status on anatomical and biological grounds.

The first two essays in Part Five, by staff members of the *Ladies' Home Journal,* expand on the issues raised above and survey the scope and limitations of the new feminism. They are followed by a pair of essays which present the opposing views of two of today's leading sexual patriots, Kate Millett and Lionel Tiger. The concluding article gives an optimistic prediction of what the world might be like if the new woman has her way. Gloria Steinem does not foresee a time when women are superior and men supine. The image which she offers is not that of woman as Boss, but woman as Partner. When that image gains currency, both women and men will be liberated.

FROM "THE NEW FEMINISM"
The Ladies' Home Journal

The anonymous nature of this piece seems to contradict a major goal of the Women's Liberation movement: a more accurate appraisal of woman's actual and potential contributions to society. But the small groups of women who wrote these sections for an issue of *The Ladies' Home Journal* probably felt that by effacing themselves they could better represent all American women, who, according to feminists, are rarely seen individually, but usually in terms of anonymous stereotypes: the Girlfriend, the Mother, the Mother-in-Law. They discuss the major issues which bind the female revolution: equality in the office and classroom; recognition in the kitchen; liberation in the bedroom. Their comments are frank; their demands reasonable. But beyond the specific issues they raise, their article is a rallying cry: Women, unite!

WOMEN AND WORK

Just what is it that men have that we envy? The freedom, the right, the encouragement, the *responsibility* to go outside the home and work for a living. We want that responsibility—because we believe that the social rewards for holding down a job are critical to one's sense of dignity and self-worth. Some of the rewards are obvious, like the paycheck at the end of the week (your own paycheck, not an allowance), the paid vacations, the holidays, the pensions—all those rights hard won by working men, we want them, too! Also the chance to develop new skills, the chance to make *more* money, the satisfaction and appreciation that come when a difficult task is well done.

But there is another value to outside work that is equally important —the social interaction that occurs on a job. The housewife's biggest problem is loneliness; she lives in her own little ghetto, often with no-body to talk to all day long but her children. So we talk to ourselves, we talk to some tradespeople, we talk to a neighbor, and we watch TV soap operas. But what are our men doing? Whether or not they are working at a job they like—and, admittedly, most work is dull and repetitive—*men are working with other adult human beings,* talking to them, communicating about the job or about a ball game, joking, grip-ing, laughing, eating lunch together, sometimes traveling, being adults together on a job that society says is the only "real" work—and proves it by paying them for it.

Well, here we are, talking about work as if it is a privilege when we know it is first and foremost an economic necessity. Did you know that 42 percent of all women already work outside the home? That's 29 mil-lion working women, sisters! We women make up 38 percent of the total work force in this country. Three out of five of those of us who work are married with children. And nearly all of us work because we need the money.

One of the myths about wives who work is that they are working merely to "supplement" their husband's income, "helping out" in order to buy some "luxuries." Nonsense! This myth that women don't *have* to work to support themselves and their families is a powerful weapon used to keep our salaries low. But what are people paid for? They are paid for the labor they perform, not for the number of people they have to support. It goes without saying that there should be equal pay for equal work. But the U.S. Department of Commerce statistics show that women earn an average of $3,000 a year less than men for performing exactly the same work.

Not only are women paid less for equal work, they are passed over for on-the-job training and for promotions to supervisory positions— with the argument, "You don't need more money." Then there is the deliberate practice of hiring women on a part-time basis—which denies them health insurance, paid vacations, sick leave, profit sharing, retire-ment benefits and tenure. Management saves untold millions of dollars because only part of the work force must be granted these fringe bene-fits.

And think of the jobs that aren't open to women at all. You can bet that if the job commands a better salary it has a "for men only" tag at-tached to it. Why is there something inherently "feminine" about secre-tarial work? In the middle of the 19th century, nearly all clerical work was performed by men. Later, when the typewriter was introduced, it was considered "too complex" a machine for women to handle. (When men discovered that typing was drudgery, they graciously dropped the

Smith-Coronas in our laps.) Is there something inherently "masculine" about being a doctor? In the Soviet Union, for example, 75 percent of all doctors are women.

In our culture, the so-called "feminine" jobs are nurse, secretary, elementary school teacher, librarian, airline stewardess, etc. The opportunities for advancement in these fields, and the top salaries, are limited. Of course, these are the fields that women are encouraged to enter. In the corresponding "masculine" jobs, doctor, business manager and executive, school administrator, head librarian and pilot, etc., the job opportunities and salary scales are completely different. The lowest pay for these "men's" jobs may be far higher than the top pay for the corresponding "women's" job.

Women are kept from better-paying jobs by many methods. The first is by out-and-out sex segregation that is actually a part of the law. This is the way it works: Several states have so-called "protective" laws on the books. These laws were enacted during the early part of this century when working conditions, particularly in factories, were hazardous and fatiguing to both men and women. The "protective" laws limit the number of hours a woman can work and the maximum weight she is permitted to lift (it varies from 15 to 35 pounds). Some states, in the name of chivalry, also prohibit women from night work. These laws effectively bar all women from being considered for certain jobs, *no matter what an individual woman's capacities or wishes may be.* A women can be turned down for a job requiring her to occasionally lift an object weighing 30 pounds even though she is quite accustomed to picking up and carrying a 30-pound child. Last year two women won separate law suits against large firms when they were "protected" out of jobs which required lifting 30 pounds of weight.

The case of Mrs. Ida Phillips may soon make Supreme Court history. Mrs. Phillips, now 36, lived in Orlando, Florida, with her husband, a truck mechanic, and their seven children. To help support her family, she worked as a waitress. "I've always had to work for a living," she says. "I was earning six dollars a day, including tips, waiting on table in Orlando. So I thought I would try to get a factory job. The hours would be more regular and there would be those company benefits. When you work as a waitress you never know what kinds of hours you're going to have to work, and business is really slow at certain seasons. Well, I tried the local factories and plants, but when they heard I had seven children they turned me down cold. Then one day in 1966, I saw an ad in the paper for one hundred assembly trainees at the Martin Marietta plant. The pay started at two dollars and twenty-five cents an hour."

Mrs. Phillips rushed over to Martin Marietta and was one of the first in line. When she filled out her employment application she wrote down that she had seven children and that the youngest, a two-year-old girl, was in a day nursery. "It never occurred to me not to be honest," she says. The Martin Marietta people refused to hire her. They said it was their policy not to hire women with pre-school-age children. Mrs. Phillips took her case to the Equal Employment Opportunities Commission and, finally, into the courts. She is suing Martin Marietta for back wages and damages.

The U.S. Supreme Court has agreed to hear her case this fall, and the Federal government has filed a brief on Mrs. Phillips' behalf. Mrs. Phillips still works as a waitress. "It's not just for myself that I'm doing this," she says, referring to her lawsuit, "it's for all mothers."

Another way in which women are kept from better jobs is by the perpetuation of a host of myths designed to make us believe in our own inferiority and incompetence. What is the real truth about women who work? Test your own knowledge by taking our "Working Women Quiz." Answer "true" or "false" to the following statements:

1. The children of women who work are often delinquents and do poorly in school.
2. The majority of working women are single.
3. Women have higher rates of absenteeism on the job than men.
4. Women change jobs more often than men.
5. White women earn more than nonwhite men.
6. Women are less capable than men of standing stress.
7. Women are basically more passive than men.
8. Women don't have the drive needed for success.
9. Women aren't as logical as men and can't handle abstract ideas.
10. Women cry when they don't get their way.

If you haven't already guessed, the answer to all of these questions is "false." Most working women are married, their absenteeism is about the same as men's, and they change jobs at about the same rate. The median annual wage for a white man is $7,164. Nonwhite men earn $4,528; white women earn $4,152, and nonwhite women earn $2,949. Women are capable of standing as much stress as men, and possibly more, according to some recent studies. Women are as aggressive or passive as men might be. Logic is sexless, and so is emotion. But when *you've* gone out to look for a job, have you had any of these 10 myths thrown at *you?* Or has the interviewer said, "We weren't considering a woman for this job"? Or: "I know you're competent, but are you really serious about a career"? Or: "We have nothing against women, it's just that our company has a 50-year tradition of hiring men for the job you want"? (A variation of this last excuse was actually used by the editor of *Newsweek* when 46 female researchers and secretaries employed at the magazine sued it because they were denied a chance to use their abilities at writers' jobs.)

The most vicious slander used against a woman who has become successful is that whisper, "She used her sex to get ahead; she slept her way to the top." Men have used *their* sex to keep themselves on top.

Women have been victims of a gigantic conspiracy. We were told that the way to get along in this male-dominated society was to be passive, sweet and utterly uncompetitive, whether we felt that way or not. We were told that we didn't have to figure out what to do with our individual lives because that would be taken care of with marriage. Our only "real" job in life would be to find the right man and then take good care of him and the children.

We must tear down the myths and the laws that chain us to the house or to low-paying jobs. We must begin to construct a new psychology, based on the principle of equality for all. We must demand that society take a fresh look at how things ought to be done. If the Martin Marietta plant, for instance, felt genuine concern for Ida Phillips' pre-school-age child, why didn't it set up a day care center on the premises for Mrs. Phillips' child and for all the pre-school-age children of all their employees, male and female? It is our belief that all large offices and factories should provide child care centers for their employees' small children, and that those centers should be under the control of the employees themselves. Until such time as we have free universal child care centers, we think that a mother who works should be able to take the full cost of child care and housekeeping off her income tax.

We are asking for options. We want the right to go out and get as good a job as a man can get. We want our men to share equally in those tasks that they have relegated to us in the name of "women's work"— child rearing and housekeeping.

Women, come out of the house! You have everything to gain!

SHOULD THIS MARRIAGE BE SAVED?

"Every morning my children and my husband leave the house, dressed and ready to spend the day outside. I am still in my nightgown, my teeth aren't brushed yet, and I have to go back to the breakfast dishes and the house. It makes me feel terrible, as if they were people but I am not."

This is the voice of Barbara, 33 years old, mother of three little girls, wife of a successful, independent businessman, as she told her story to a consciousness-raising session of a Woman's Liberation group.

"When I was a girl, I wanted to do something important. First I wanted to be an explorer, and then a scientist. Then I got other ideas. I wanted to—it certainly seems really ridiculous now—I wanted to be a Congresswoman or Senator. Senator Barbara from Illinois, can you imagine? Me, who can't even get dressed in the morning?

"My family got worried about all my crazy ideas. After a while, I stopped having those daydreams. I went to the state university, where I met my husband, Bill. He was very smart, ambitious and powerful. I couldn't believe he wanted to marry me. He was graduating, and he didn't want to wait for me to finish college; three years seemed too much. So, although I was a good student, I dropped out and got married. I was nineteen years old.

"Being married was fun at first, except that I didn't know what to do with myself during the day and I was too scared to go out and get a job. My husband didn't want me to, anyway. Then the children came along and we moved out to the suburbs, and since then it's been, well, you know what it's like, cooking and shopping and washing diapers and picking up kids and bringing them home and arranging everything for everybody, all that sort of thing.

"I never felt at ease as a housewife. It was as if I were an actress playing a role, a role I'm not very good at. Bill is making good money now. We go out a lot and have many friends. But it seems to me that I am never myself with these people, but just Bill's wife.

"At home he is very demanding. For example, he doesn't like the way laundries put starch in his shirts, so I have to iron them myself. He wants a gourmet dinner every night, so at five o'clock I make hot dogs and beans for the kids and at seven o'clock, veal *cordon bleu* with a dry white wine for me and Bill. He selects the wine, but I have to be sure it's perfectly chilled.

"We don't have sex very often; he doesn't seem to want it. But when he does, I know I have to make myself available. I used to want him all the time. Now I don't feel that way anymore. These days it seems as if we either fight or don't talk with each other at all. Last year I went to a psychiatrist. He intimated that I had hidden masculine drives. This frightened me so I never went back.

"Sometimes when I'm alone in the house I wander into the children's rooms and look at the piles of dirty underwear. I feel helpless and confused. I want to cry and can't decide which pile to pick up first. I ask myself, what shall I do with the rest of my life?"

If Barbara had told her story to a marriage counselor, perhaps to one of the counselors at the American Institute of Family Relations (which sponsors the "Can This Marriage Be Saved?" column in the JOURNAL), you may be sure the answer would have been yes. Barbara would probably have been advised to examine her career fantasies and to understand that they were just fantasies. The counselor would have shown her how to channel her strivings into acceptable forms—volunteer work, perhaps, or a part-time job. He would have pointed out that her hostility to Bill was largely unfair, stemming perhaps from her competitive feelings toward men. But he would also have advised Bill to take Barbara less for granted, to stop demanding a gourmet meal every night, to help her around the house, to show her that he understands her difficulties.

Perhaps Barbara and Bill would have saved their marriage. But they would not have changed its fundamental nature. They would not have changed Bill's status as breadwinner and effective head of the household. They would not have changed the fact of Barbara's economic dependence upon him, nor the idea, implicit in the marriage arrangement, that the man's career strivings are important and necessary, while the woman's work, aside from what she does to maintain the household and care for the children, is merely something to be fitted in at odd hours, something not very serious. Bill's needs and desires would still have been primary. *The major adjustments would have been Barbara's.*

Barbara, however, did not seek marital counseling. She attended Women's Liberation meetings and talked about her problems with women like herself. And when she talked, she did not ask herself, "Can My Marriage Be Saved?" She asked, instead, *"Should* My Marriage Be Saved?"

The answer turned out to be no. When Barbara reviewed her marriage, she discovered that the things Bill wanted from his life were in hopeless conflict with the things she wanted from hers. Barbara's rebellion against housework was not frivolous or childish. She hated it and therefore was right in refusing to accept it as her main work in life. Part-time jobs, education courses, or volunteer work were not the answer for her, although they might be for another woman.

Barbara wanted to be independent and was meant to be. It was this desire, suppressed and turned against herself, which had caused her depression and resentment. Barbara wanted to use her capacities to be somebody, not just somebody's wife. To say that her ambitions were "masculine" is to say that a woman should not have ambitions.

It is a truism of our culture, an idea so deeply ingrained as to be the subject of jokes, that marriage is a trap for a man. That it is far more truly a trap for a woman is something we have only recently begun to grasp. The subjugation of a woman is an integral part of the marriage arrangement, even of the extra-legal marriage arrangement. For marriage rests upon a class system in which the man represents the ruling (or superior) class; the woman, the subordinate (or inferior) class. The woman performs domestic service inside the home and raises the children in exchange for her bed and board, in exchange for economic and emotional security.

Every woman knows from girlhood that marriage and motherhood will be her main career, that if she has to work to support herself, she will be doing so because she has failed to find a man to support her. She knows that to develop her own skills with the drive and selfishness which are necessary to attain competence in the world outside the home will render her unfit for a career as wife, a career that demands more than anything else the capacity for subordinating the interests of self to the interests of others—the capacity for putting somebody else's needs first. The fact is that most women are unable to choose *not* to marry; society makes sure that in one way or another they are fit for nothing else. It is no accident that only 25 percent of the women in America are entirely self-supporting. And it is no accident that the decision to divorce, even to divorce a husband with whom she is miserable, is so terribly difficult for a woman who has been married most of her adult life.

"At first when I thought about leaving my husband," says Barbara, "I felt I just couldn't do it. When I think of a divorcee, I think of a nervous woman with a hard face and a shrill voice. Someone you don't want to ask for dinner, because she's not part of a couple. Someone who's always after your husband. Someone you think you should find a husband for.

"How would life be any better for me if I were divorced? I'd still have to do housework and take care of the children, but without even the little help I get from my husband. Get a job? What job? Where? I've never worked except for the summers when I was in school. I can't imagine what it would be like. I haven't developed any particular skills. Besides, the thought of getting up in the morning and going out to work, real work, frightens me. I don't think I'd be up to it.

"What about my children? It seems wrong to me to deprive them of a stable home, even if that is a cliché.

"Divorce means you have to put yourself back on the marketplace again, to fix yourself up to catch another husband. Divorce means nobody wants you. It means lawyers and fights and custody agreements.

"The loneliness, how could I face it? Those awful nights by yourself with only the kids or maybe another woman for company. It takes a lot of courage to go anywhere as a single woman these days. Just the way waiters look at you in a restaurant if you haven't got a male escort makes me want to crawl back to my own house and home and husband, no matter how awful the situation there is."

Barbara did get a divorce, although it took her several years to reach that point. While she was still married, she went to a school and got a degree in political science. She is now employed as a researcher on a sociology project at a nearby college. Her job is full-time; the children go to a newly established day care center. Not very romantic, a far cry from Senator Barbara, but at least more than just Bill's Barbara. A realistic compromise. The main thing is that she is now financially independent.

Bill still provides for the children's support, of course. Until society accepts the responsibility for caring for its young, the individual parents must do so. Barbara isn't happy about raising her children in a father-less home, but she thinks that despite this, they are better off for having a mother who is happy with herself and enjoys them more.

"I realize that I'm lucky," says Barbara. "After all, my husband agreed to the divorce; in some states a divorce cannot be obtained unless both parties are in agreement. And he is willing to accept his responsibilities toward the children. I was also financially able to get the training I needed to become independent. Lots of women aren't that fortunate, and, of course, divorce is literally impossible for them. They're really stuck."

Barbara has made many new friends, among them several divorced women like herself. Together they have come to the conclusion that the institutions and social attitudes surrounding divorce must be changed. They are now engaged in drawing up what might be called "A Bill of Rights for Divorced Women." They propose:

1. That mechanisms be set up to give divorced women assistance in the form of housekeeping, baby-sitting and supplementary funds. The welfare laws provide *men* with these aids, why not women?

2. That halfway houses—physical centers of temporary refuge for the just-divorced or about-to-be-divorced woman and her children—be established in every major city. Divorce is a traumatic experience for a woman who has been dependent for so long. These centers would give her a chance to catch her breath and be sustained and supported by a community of other divorced women.

3. Financial subsidies for divorced women. Over half a million women get divorced every year. Many of them are thrown out into society without any training for productive work. If their career training could be subsidized, society would benefit from the useful work they could thereby learn to perform.

4. The establishment of divorce centers, staffed entirely by women, where divorced women could receive professional, legal and psychological help in meeting their new situation in life. If we have marriage counselors, why shouldn't we also have divorce counselors?

None of these proposals is outside the realm of possibility. If they come into being, one result would surely be an increase in the already high divorce rate. More important, the "Divorce Bill of Rights" might operate to keep more divorcees divorced. Husband-hunting would cease to be the prime occupation of formerly married women. Still more important, many more women might not get married at all.

Ideas like these, of course, threaten the foundations of the institution of marriage itself, a structure hitherto regarded as inviolable. No revolution, no social and economic upheaval, has yet dissolved that institution, and there is good reason for this. Society, as it is presently constituted, depends for its continued existence on the rigidly defined nuclear family structure. It provides a relatively inexpensive system of domestic maintenance and child-rearing. The nuclear family is the basic model for existing social order; no mere adjustments in the conditions of family life can change that. Adjustments have been made. Society "allows" women to work outside the home, provides women who can afford it with domestic help, encourages men to assist their wives in their housework and child-care responsibilities. But none of these modifications has altered woman's status as domestic laborer. The woman who works outside the home merely substitutes two jobs for one; she continues to assume responsibility for the house and children.

Meaningful change in the family system will occur when work roles are no longer predetermined by sex. The work of providing sustenance for the family and maintenance for the home should be shared equally between husband and wife. The increased interest in public or subsidized child-care centers; the mounting pressure for an end to job discrimination; the campaign for abortion law repeal are positive steps in this direction.

The opponents of these reforms frequently base their argument on the grounds that they all threaten the institution of marriage. They are quite correct. Any of these reforms, if adopted, would increase the independence of woman, and in so doing make marriage less attractive to her.

Barbara has been divorced for two years. Would she like to remarry?

"I don't think so," she says. "I do want to find a man with whom I can live and have a working relationship, because I'm still a romantic. I still believe in love. But I don't think marriage can give me that. Marriage does something to a woman, and it does something to love—turns it into a duty or an obligation, I guess. It's not for me. I'll have to find some other way."

Barbara has three children, all girls. Would she want them to marry when they grow up?

"I won't answer that question, because I have no right to. My daughters' choices in life must be their own. All I can tell you is that I am trying to raise them to regard themselves as full human beings, not as complements to men. I want them to take their desires and ambitions seriously and not to be diverted from them as I was. I want them to have identities of their own, outside of their identity as women."

FROM "THEORY OF SEXUAL POLITICS"
Kate Millett

Kate Millett's career illustrates both the barriers confronting women and their ability to surmount them. Born in 1934, an award-winning scholar at Oxford, she once found it extremely difficult to find a college teaching position. Today, however, as the author of *Sexual Politics* she is a celebrity, a leader in a revolutionary movement that eschews personalities. In Chapter Two, "Theory of Sexual Politics," which Miss Millett considers the most important part of her work, she explains that "sex is a status category with political implications" and that male domination is "perhaps the most pervasive ideology of our culture and provides its most fundamental concept of power." She then shows how a "man's world" uses every means available, including ideology, biology, myth, and psychology, to perpetuate the inferior status of women. This selection is an excerpt from Chapter Two. Miss Millett now lives in New York City, where she is a sculptor and a Women's Liberation advocate.

ANTHROPOLOGICAL: MYTH AND RELIGION

Evidence from anthropology, religious and literary myth all attests to the politically expedient character of patriarchal convictions about women. One anthropologist refers to a consistent patriarchal strain of assumption that "woman's biological differences set her apart . . . she is essentially inferior," and since "human institutions grow from deep and primal anxieties and are shaped by irrational psychological mechanisms . . . socially organized attitudes toward women arise from basic tensions expressed by the male." [1] Under patriarchy the female did not herself develop the symbols by which she is described. As both the primitive and the civilized worlds are male worlds, the ideas which shaped culture in regard to the female were also of male design. The image of women as we know it is an image created by men and fashioned to suit their needs. These needs spring from a fear of the "otherness" of woman. Yet this notion itself presupposes that patriarchy has already been established and the male has already set himself as the human norm, the subject and referent to which the female is "other" or alien. Whatever its origin, the function of the male's sexual antipathy is to provide a means of control over a subordinate group and a rationale which justifies the inferior station of those in a lower order, "explaining" the oppression of their lives.

[1] H. R. Hays, *The Dangerous Sex, the Myth of Feminine Evil* (New York: Putnam, 1964). Much of my summary in this section is indebted to Hays's useful assessment of cultural notions about the female.

The feeling that woman's sexual functions are impure is both world-wide and persistent. One sees evidence of it everywhere in literature, in myth, in primitive and civilized life. It is striking how the notion persists today. The event of menstruation, for example, is a largely clandestine affair, and the psycho-social effect of the stigma attached must have great effect on the female ego. There is a large anthropological literature on menstrual taboo; the practice of isolating offenders in huts at the edge of the village occurs throughout the primitive world. Contemporary slang denominates menstruation as "the curse." There is considerable evidence that such discomfort as women suffer during their period is often likely to be psychosomatic, rather than physiological, cultural rather than biological, in origin. That this may also be true to some extent of labor and delivery is attested to by the recent experiment with "painless childbirth." Patriarchal circumstances and beliefs seem to have the effect of poisoning the female's own sense of physical self until it often truly becomes the burden it is said to be.

Primitive peoples explain the phenomenon of the female's genitals in terms of a wound, sometimes reasoning that she was visited by a bird or snake and mutilated into her present condition. Once she was wounded, now she bleeds. Contemporary slang for the vagina is "gash." The Freudian description of the female genitals is in terms of a "castrated" condition. The uneasiness and disgust female genitals arouse in patriarchal societies is attested to through religious, cultural, and literary proscription. In preliterate groups fear is also a factor, as in the belief in a castrating *vagina dentata*. The penis, badge of the male's superior status in both preliterate and civilized patriarchies, is given the most crucial significance, the subject both of endless boasting and endless anxiety.

Nearly all patriarchies enforce taboos against women touching ritual objects (those of war or religion) or food. In ancient and preliterate societies women are generally not permitted to eat with men. Women eat apart today in a great number of cultures, chiefly those of the Near and Far East. Some of the inspiration of such custom appears to lie in fears of contamination, probably sexual in origin. In their function of domestic servants, females are forced to prepare food, yet at the same time may be liable to spread their contagion through it. A similar situation obtains with blacks in the United States. They are considered filthy and infectious, yet as domestics they are forced to prepare food for their queasy superiors. In both cases the dilemma is generally solved in a deplorably illogical fashion by segregating the act of eating itself, while cooking is carried on out of sight by the very group who would infect the table. With an admirable consistency, some Hindu males do not permit their wives to touch their food at all. In nearly every patriarchal group it is expected that the dominant male will eat first or eat better, and even where the sexes feed together, the male shall be served by the female.[2]

All patriarchies have hedged virginity and defloration in elaborate rites and interdictions. Among preliterates virginity presents an interesting problem in ambivalence. On the one hand, it is, as in every patriarchy, a mysterious good because a sign of property received intact. On the other hand, it represents an unknown evil associated with the mana of blood and terrifyingly "other." So auspicious is the event of defloration that in many tribes the owner-groom is willing to relinquish breaking the seal of his new possession to a stronger or older personality who can neutralize the attendant dangers.[3] Fears of defloration appear to originate in a fear of the alien sexuality of the female. Although any physical suffering endured in defloration must be on the part of the female (and most societies cause her—bodily and mentally—to suffer anguish), the social interest, institutionalized in patriarchal ritual and custom, is exclusively on the side of the male's property interest, prestige, or (among preliterates) hazard.

Patriarchal myth typically posits a golden age before the arrival of women, while its social practices permit males to be relieved of female company. Sexual segregation is so prevalent in patriarchy that one encounters evidence of it everywhere. Nearly every powerful circle in contemporary patriarchy is a men's group. But men form groups of their own on every level. Women's groups are typically auxiliary in character, imitative of male efforts and methods on a generally trivial or ephemeral plane. They rarely operate without recourse to male authority, church or religious groups appealing to the superior authority of a cleric, political groups to male legislators, etc.

In sexually segregated situations the distinctive quality of culturally enforced temperament becomes very vivid. This is particularly true of those exclusively masculine organizations which anthropology generally refers to as men's house institutions. The men's house is a fortress of patriarchal association and emotion. Men's houses in preliterate society strengthen masculine communal experience through dances, gossip, hospitality, recreation, and religious ceremony. They are also the arsenals of male weaponry.

David Riesman has pointed out that sports and some other activities provide males with a supportive solidarity which society does not trou-

---

[2] The luxury conditions of the "better" restaurant affords a quaint exception. There not only the cuisine but even the table service is conducted by males, at an expense commensurate with such an occasion.

[3] See Sigmund Freud, *Totem and Taboo,* and Ernest Crawley, *The Mystic Rose* (London, Methuen, 1902, 1927).

ble to provide for females.[4] While hunting, politics, religion, and commerce may play a role, sport and warfare are consistently the chief cement of men's house comradery. Scholars of men's house culture from Hutton Webster and Heinrich Schurtz to Lionel Tiger tend to be sexual patriots whose aim is to justify the apartheid the institution represents.[5] Schurtz believes an innate gregariousness and a drive toward fraternal pleasure among peers urges the male away from the inferior and constricting company of women. Notwithstanding his conviction that a mystical "bonding instinct" exists in males, Tiger exhorts the public, by organized effort, to preserve the men's house tradition from its decline. The institution's less genial function of power center within a state of sexual antagonism is an aspect of the phenomenon which often goes unnoticed.

The men's houses of Melanesia fulfill a variety of purposes and are both armory and the site of masculine ritual initiation ceremony. Their atmosphere is not very remote from that of military institutions in the modern world: they reek of physical exertion, violence, the aura of the kill, and the throb of homosexual sentiment. They are the scenes of scarification, headhunting celebrations, and boasting sessions. Here young men are to be "hardened" into manhood. In the men's houses boys have such low status they are often called the "wives" of their initiators, the term "wife" implying both inferiority and the status of sexual object. Untried youths become the erotic interest of their elders and betters, a relationship also encountered in the Samurai order, in oriental priesthood, and in the Greek gymnasium. Preliterate wisdom decrees that while inculcating the young with the masculine ethos, it is necessary first to intimidate them with the tutelary status of the female. An anthropologist's comment on Melanesian men's houses is applicable equally to Genet's underworld, or Mailer's U. S. Army: "It would seem that the sexual brutalizing of the young boy and the effort to turn him into a woman both enhances the older warrior's desire of power, gratifies his sense of hostility toward the maturing male competitor, and eventually, when he takes him into the male group, strengthens the male solidarity in its symbolic attempt to do without women." [6] The derogation of feminine status in lesser males is a consistent patriarchal trait. Like any hazing procedure, initiation once endured produces devotees who will ever after be ardent initiators, happily inflicting their own former sufferings on the newcomer.

[4] David Riesman, "Two Generations," in *The Woman in America,* edited by Robert Lifton (Boston, Beacon, 1967). See also James Coleman, *The Adolescent Society.*

[5] Heinrich Schurtz, *Altersklassen und Männerbünde* (Berlin, 1902) and Lionel Tiger, *op. cit.*

[6] Hays, *The Dangerous Sex,* p. 56.

The psychoanalytic term for the generalized adolescent tone of men's house culture is "phallic state." Citadels of virility, they reinforce the most saliently power-oriented characteristics of patriarchy. The Hungarian psychoanalytic anthropologist Géza Róheim stressed the patriarchal character of men's house organization in the preliterate tribes he studied, defining their communal and religious practices in terms of a "group of men united in the cult of an object that is a materialized penis and excluding the women from their society." [7] The tone and ethos of men's house culture is sadistic, power-oriented, and latently homosexual, frequently narcissistic in its energy and motives.[8] The men's house inference that the penis is a weapon, endlessly equated with other weapons, is also clear. The practice of castrating prisoners is itself a comment on the cultural confusion of anatomy and status with weaponry. Much of the glamorization of masculine comradery in warfare originates in what one might designate as "the men's house sensibility." Its sadistic and brutalizing aspects are disguised in military glory and a particularly cloying species of masculine sentimentality. A great deal of our culture partakes of this tradition, and one might locate its first statement in Western literature in the heroic intimacy of Patroclus and Achilles. Its development can be traced through the epic and the saga to the *chanson de geste*. The tradition still flourishes in war novel and movie, not to mention the comic book.

Considerable sexual activity does take place in the men's house, all of it, needless to say, homosexual. But the taboo against homosexual behavior (at least among equals) is almost universally of far stronger force than the impulse and tends to effect a rechanneling of the libido into violence. This association of sexuality and violence is a particularly militaristic habit of mind.[9] The negative and militaristic coloring of such men's house homosexuality as does exist, is of course by no means the whole character of homosexual sensibility. Indeed, the warrior caste of mind with its ultravirility, is more *incipiently* homosexual, in its exclusively male orientation, than it is *overtly* homosexual. (The Nazi experience is an extreme case in point here.) And the heterosexual role-playing indulged in, and still more persuasively, the contempt in which the younger, softer, or more "feminine" members are held, is proof that the actual ethos is misogynist, or perversely rather than positively hetero-

[7] Géza Róheim, "Psychoanalysis of Primitive Cultural Types," *International Journal of Psychoanalysis* Vol. XIII London, 1932.

[8] All these traits apply in some degree to the bohemian circle which Miller's novels project, the Army which never leaves Mailer's consciousness, and the homosexual subculture on which Genet's observations are based. Since these three subjects of our study are closely associated with the separatist men's house culture, it is useful to give it special attention.

[9] Genet demonstrates this in *The Screens;* Mailer reveals it everywhere.

sexual. The true inspiration of men's house association therefore comes from the patriarchal situation rather than from any circumstances inherent in the homo-amorous relationship.

If a positive attitude toward heterosexual love is not quite, in Seignebos' famous dictum, the invention of the twelfth century, it can still claim to be a novelty. Most patriarchies go to great length to exclude love as a basis of mate selection. Modern patriarchies tend to do so through class, ethnic, and religious factors. Western classical thought was prone to see in heterosexual love either a fatal stroke of ill luck bound to end in tragedy, or a contemptible and brutish consorting with inferiors. Medieval opinion was firm in its conviction that love was sinful if sexual, and sex sinful if loving.

Primitive society practices its misogyny in terms of taboo and mana which evolve into explanatory myth. In historical cultures, this is transformed into ethical, then literary, and in the modern period, scientific rationalizations for the sexual politic. Myth is, of course, a felicitous advance in the level of propaganda, since it so often bases its arguments on ethics or theories of origins. The two leading myths of Western culture are the classical tale of Pandora's box and the Biblical story of the Fall. In both cases earlier mana concepts of feminine evil have passed through a final literary phase to become highly influential ethical justifications of things as they are.

Pandora appears to be a discredited version of a Mediterranean fertility goddess, for in Hesiod's *Theogony* she wears a wreath of flowers and a sculptured diadem in which are carved all the creatures of land and sea.[10] Hesiod ascribes to her the introduction of sexuality which puts an end to the golden age when "the races of men had been living on earth free from all evils, free from laborious work, and free from all wearing sickness." [11] Pandora was the origin of "the damnable race of women—a plague which men must live with." [12] The introduction of what are seen to be the evils of the male human condition came through the introduction of the female and what is said to be her unique product, sexuality. In *Works and Days* Hesiod elaborates on Pandora and what she represents—a perilous temptation with "the mind of a bitch and a thievish nature," full of "the cruelty of desire and longings that

[10] Wherever one stands in the long anthropologists' quarrel over patriarchal versus matriarchal theories of social origins, one can trace a demotion of fertility goddesses and their replacement by patriarchal deities at a certain period throughout ancient culture.

[11] Hesiod, *Works and Days,* translated by Richmond Lattimore (University of Michigan, 1959), p. 29.

[12] Hesiod, *Theogony,* translated by Norman O. Brown (Indianapolis, Liberal Arts Press, 1953), p. 70.

wear out the body," "lies and cunning words and a deceitful soul," a snare sent by Zeus to be "the ruin of men." [13]

Patriarchy has God on its side. One of its most effective agents of control is the powerfully expeditious character of its doctrines as to the nature and origin of the female and the attribution to her alone of the dangers and evils it imputes to sexuality. The Greek example is interesting here: when it wishes to exalt sexuality it celebrates fertility through the phallus; when it wishes to denigrate sexuality, it cites Pandora. Patriarchal religion and ethics tend to lump the female and sex together as if the whole burden of the onus and stigma it attaches to sex were the fault of the female alone. Thereby sex, which is known to be unclean, sinful, and debilitating, pertains to the female, and the male identity is preserved as a human, rather than a sexual one.

The Pandora myth is one of two important Western archetypes which condemn the female through her sexuality and explain her position as her well-deserved punishment for the primal sin under whose unfortunate consequences the race yet labors. Ethics have entered the scene, replacing the simplicities of ritual, taboo, and mana. The more sophisticated vehicle of myth also provides official explanations of sexual history. In Hesiod's tale, Zeus, a rancorous and arbitrary father figure, in sending Epimetheus evil in the form of female genitalia, is actually chastising him for adult heterosexual knowledge and activity. In opening the vessel she brings (the vulva or hymen, Pandora's "box") the male satisfies his curiosity but sustains the discovery only by punishing himself at the hands of the father god with death and the assorted calamities of postlapsarian life. The patriarchal trait of male rivalry across age or status line, particularly those of powerful father and rival son, is present as well as the ubiquitous maligning of the female.

The myth of the Fall is a highly finished version of the same themes. As the central myth of the Judeo-Christian imagination and therefore of our immediate cultural heritage, it is well that we appraise and acknowledge the enormous power it still holds over us even in a rationalist era which has long ago given up literal belief in it while maintaining its emotional assent intact.[14] This mythic version of the female as the

[13] Hesiod, *Works and Days,* phrases from lines 53–100. Some of the phrases are from Lattimore's translation, some from A. W. Mair's translation (Oxford, 1908).

[14] It is impossible to assess how deeply embedded in our consciousness is the Eden legend and how utterly its patterns are planted in our habits of thought. One comes across its tone and design in the most unlikely places, such as Antonioni's film *Blow-Up,* to name but one of many striking examples. The action of the film takes place in an idyllic garden, loaded with primal overtones largely sexual, where, prompted by a tempter with a phallic gun, the female again betrays the male to death. The photographer who witnesses the scene reacts as if he were being introduced both to the haggard knowledge of the primal scene and original sin at the same time.

cause of human suffering, knowledge, and sin is still the foundation of sexual attitudes, for it represents the most crucial argument of the patriarchal tradition in the West.

The Israelites lived in a continual state of war with the fertility cults of their neighbors; these latter afforded sufficient attraction to be the source of constant defection, and the figure of Eve, like that of Pandora, has vestigial traces of a fertility goddess overthrown. There is some, probably unconscious, evidence of this in the Biblical account which announces, even before the narration of the fall has begun—"Adam called his wife's name Eve; because she was the mother of all living things." Due to the fact that the tale represents a compilation of different oral traditions, it provides two contradictory schemes for Eve's creation, one in which both sexes are created at the same time, and one in which Eve is fashioned later than Adam, an afterthought born from his rib, peremptory instance of the male's expropriation of the life force through a god who created the world without benefit of female assistance.

The tale of Adam and Eve is, among many other things, a narrative of how humanity invented sexual intercourse. Many such narratives exist in preliterate myth and folk tale. Most of them strike us now as delightfully funny stories of primal innocents who require a good deal of helpful instruction to figure it out. There are other major themes in the story: the loss of primeval simplicity, the arrival of death, and the first conscious experience of knowledge. All of them revolve about sex. Adam is forbidden to eat of the fruit of life or of the knowledge of good and evil, the warning states explicitly what should happen if he tastes of the latter: "in that day that thou eatest thereof thou shalt surely die." He eats but fails to die (at least in the story), from which one might infer that the serpent told the truth.

But at the moment when the pair eat of the forbidden tree they awake to their nakedness and feel shame. Sexuality is clearly involved, though the fable insists it is only tangential to a higher prohibition against disobeying orders in the matter of another and less controversial appetite—one for food. Róheim points out that the Hebrew verb for "eat" can also mean coitus. Everywhere in the Bible "knowing" is synonymous with sexuality, and clearly a product of contact with the phallus, here in the fable objectified as a snake. To blame the evils and sorrows of life—loss of Eden and the rest—on sexuality, would all too logically implicate the male, and such implication is hardly the purpose of the story, designed as it is expressly in order to blame all this world's discomfort on the female. Therefore it is the female who is tempted first and "beguiled" by the penis, transformed into something else, a snake. Thus Adam has "beaten the rap" of sexual guilt, which appears to be why the sexual motive is so repressed in the Biblical account. Yet the very transparency of the serpent's universal phallic value shows how uneasy the mythic mind can be about its shifts. Accordingly, in her inferiority and vulnerability the woman takes and eats, simple carnal thing that she is, affected by flattery even in a reptile. Only after this does the male fall, and with him, humanity—for the fable has made him the racial type, whereas Eve is a mere sexual type and, according to tradition, either expendable or replaceable. And as the myth records the original sexual adventure, Adam was seduced by woman, who was seduced by a penis. "The woman whom thou gavest to be with me, she gave me of the fruit and I did eat" is the first man's defense. Seduced by the phallic snake, Eve is convicted for Adam's participation in sex.

Adam's curse is to toil in the "sweat of his brow," namely the labor the male associates with civilization. Eden was a fantasy world without either effort or activity, which the entrance of the female, and with her sexuality, has destroyed. Eve's sentence is far more political in nature and a brilliant "explanation" of her inferior status. "In sorrow thou shalt bring forth children. And thy desire shall be to thy husband. And he shall rule over thee." Again, as in the Pandora myth, a proprietary father figure is punishing his subjects for adult heterosexuality. It is easy to agree with Róheim's comment on the negative attitude the myth adopts toward sexuality: "Sexual maturity is regarded as a misfortune, something that has robbed mankind of happiness . . . the explanation of how death came into the world."

What requires further emphasis is the responsibility of the female, a marginal creature, in bringing on this plague, and the justice of her suborned condition as dependent on her primary role in this original sin. The connection of woman, sex, and sin constitutes the fundamental pattern of western patriarchal thought thereafter.

MALE DOMINANCE? YES, ALAS. A SEXIST PLOT? NO.
Lionel Tiger

Lionel Tiger is the author of *Men in Groups* and an anthropologist at Rutgers. In this article he gives some corrective advice to those women who think that male and female roles are shaped more by culture than by biology and genetics. He directly or indirectly questions some basic premises and goals of the Women's Liberation movement, suggesting that personality differences between men and women are, in the case of aggressiveness—a primary source of male domination—a result of hormone differences and therefore unalterable; that women can't compete with men because they

From *The New York Times Magazine,* October 25, 1970. © 1970 by The New York Times Company. Reprinted by permission of International Famous Agency.

work ineffectively during the last week of their menstrual cycle; that such desirable schemes as day-care centers may be antithetical to inherited patterns of female behavior. To support his ideas, Tiger musters an impressive array of studies. He stresses the scientific quality of his argument and maintains that the feminists' view is "on generous scientific grounds . . . irresponsible" (though it should be stated that his estimations of what DNA research tells about inherited social behavior, are opinions, not facts). Given his views, it is easy to see why Kate Millett called Lionel Tiger a "sexual patriot."

The feminists' angry rebuke to us males could not be more correct and more justified. Women everywhere earn less money than men, possess less power over their communities than men, have more difficulty becoming eminent than men, and do so far less often; as a group they have lower status than men and less public prestige. Surely no one, myself included, would want to argue that such a situation is good or even tolerable: this must be the moral given or baseline from which all discussion of the feminist movement proceeds. However, if you want to change a system you have got to understand it.

The feminist critique is rooted in the assumption that there are no important differences between the sexes (except reproductive) which are not culturally determined and that, in fact, any differences which do exist result mainly from a universal conspiracy among males to keep females different—and inferior.

"Groups who rule by birthright are fast disappearing," says Kate Millett in her "Sexual Politics," "yet there remains one ancient and universal scheme for the domination of one birth group by another—the scheme that prevails in the area of sex." She claims that new research "suggests that the possibilities of innate temperamental differences seem more remote than ever. . . . In doing so it gives fairly concrete positive evidence of the overwhelmingly *cultural* character of gender, i.e., personality structure in terms of sexual category."

Not only do men keep women subordinate, goes the argument, they also make an elaborate pretense of placing them on a pretty pedestal— by means of literature and social science designed to make women feel they are most feminine, most productive and most natural when they raise men's children, cook men's food, share men's beds, and believe in the ideology that what's good for men and boys is best for women and girls.

As well as being of general intellectual interest, the feminists' attack on males is also one of the strongest indictments of science and the scientific method that it is possible to make. On generous scientific grounds, it seems clear to me that the evidence which feminists such as Kate Millett and Ti-Grace Atkinson use to support their case is, on balance, irresponsible in its selection and so narrowly and unfairly interpreted that it will finally do damage to the prospects of women's actual liberation.

Briefly, there is considerable evidence that differences between males and females do not result simply from male conspiracy, that they are directly related to our evolution as an animal, that they occur in such a wide variety of situations and cultures that the feminist explanation is inadequate in itself to help us understand them, and that there are biological bases for sexual differences which have nothing to do with oppressing females but rather with ensuring the safety of communities and the healthy growth of children. Furthermore, these differences reach back not only to the early states of our history as a civilization, but further back to our formative time as a species; accordingly, sexual differences in physique, hormone secretions, energy and endurance, and possibly even in ways of relating to other people, may be linked to our genetic heritage in direct and influential ways. To say that these differences have existed for a long time and have some biological basis is not —as some people too hastily conclude—to say that human beings are condemned to live in ancient arrangements with no hope of real change. But without understanding what they are and how they came about in the first place, the women and men who want to change our sexual patterns will fail.

First, we have to look at the unpleasant facts. In all communities, the central political decisions are overwhelmingly taken by males and the "public forum" is dominated by males. In a few progressive countries women may be actively involved in legislatures—for example, in Finland and Norway—but by and large the pattern is that even where females have had the vote for many years and where there is open encouragement of female political activity, the number of women participating in managing governments is tiny. The rule is, the higher up the hierarchy you look, the less likely it is you'll find a woman official. The same pattern applies in labor unions, businesses, recreational groups and religious hierarchies. All over the world armies and other fighting groups are all-male. In a few places where women are trained to fight, it remains unusual for them to join men in the front lines (except where defense of home territory is involved, as is sometimes the case for the Vietnamese, for example, and for Israelis living in some border kibbutzim). The task of forming a raiding and fighting party and leaving the home bases to attack elsewhere is universally and unexceptionally male. So is controlling other persons by force, as in police work and similar enterprises.

Other things being equal, women's work is of lower status than men's, and when women begin to move in on an occupation, it loses standing in comparison with others. Though in this country individual women have considerable power to dispose of family income and wealth, typically their investment decisions are guided by males; the products they buy and the manner in which they are stimulated to do so are managed by men. Even proponents of the kibbutz system in Israel —still the most radical, long-term effort at constructing the ideal society which we can observe—concede that insofar as relations between men and women are concerned, the result of over two generations of extremely shrewd and wholehearted effort is far from acceptable to sexual egalitarians. And in this country, those who have set up communes to avoid the effects of private property, patriarchy, restrictive sexual and familial life, and technocracy have discovered that simply because there is more heavy physical labor on the commune, the distinction between the men's work and women's work is far sharper than in the larger society from which they hope to escape.

The political misfortune in this is clear. However, the scientific question remains: why is this the case? I've already noted the feminist answer: patriarchy exists because it has existed for so long and so universally. Despite enormous variation in standard of living, religious belief, economies, ecologies, political history, ideology and kinship systems of different societies, the same pattern broadly prevails *because* males have always dominated females in an effective and widespread scheme. But coming from feminists, this is a curious explanation, because it implies that all men everywhere are sufficiently clever and persistent to subdue permanently all women everywhere. If this is so, the conclusion follows mercilessly that men *should* govern. And if women so universally accept this state of affairs, then perhaps they are actually incapable of political action. That is nonsense, and unflattering to women, and unduly optimistic about male political acumen.

In all this general discussion, one of the most useful laws of science has been overlooked, the so-called Law of Parsimony (or Occam's Razor). This dictates that you cannot explain a behavioral phenomenon by a higher, more complex process if a lower or simpler one will do. To take a simple case: The other day in the paperback section of Brentano's in Greenwich Village, a beautiful woman was looking at books. She wore no bra and her blouse was aggressively unbuttoned; all the supposedly cerebral men around couldn't take their horn-rimmed eyes off her. Now it is possible that the reason we stared was that we had been brainwashed by sexist books like Mailer's and Henry Miller's and our male chauvinist egos were aroused by the challenge of conquest. But the law of parsimony demands we consider that since sexual attraction is a basic signaling system which all animals have, this woman was signaling something which the men around her were dutifully responding to. Obviously, there were some higher processes involved, too, but the simple erotic one was probably primary in this case.

If male dominance extends over the whole species—and has existed for so long—we seem constrained by the law of parsimony to look first into the biological information and theory at our disposal for an explanation. This includes comparative information about the other primates who exhibit many of the behavior patterns which feminists claim are unique impositions on human females by human males. It also requires us to see what effect our evolution in the past has on our behavior in the present, which feminists—along with many of the social scientists they criticize—by and large are unwilling to do.

Their reasoning derives from the Pavlovian biology of the nineteen-twenties and thirties, which taught that habit and conditioning could account for almost all men's behavior—and inherited characteristics for very little. Like the Lysenkoists in Russia and the positivists in this country, the feminists believe that changing the environments of the human animal will soon change the animal itself. For this, there is no evidence. Moreover, the argument ignores the theory that remains one of the strongest in science today—Darwin's explanation of the evolution of the species through natural selection and inheritance.

Modern biology in part represents an extremely important synthesis of sociology and genetics: we are able to understand the complicated social behavior of animals and can also work out how this behavior can be transmitted in the genetic codes. By now, many people are familiar with the work of the animal ethologists such as Konrad Lorenz, George Schaller and Jane Goodall. Through their experiments and field studies, and those of their colleagues, we have come to appreciate that higher animals other than man also live in relatively elaborate social systems, with traditions, much learning, and considerable variation among different groups of the same species. And yet there remains a central pattern of behavior which is common to a species and appears to be passed down genetically from generation to generation. Three decades ago, how this was transmitted would have been difficult to say. But now we know that the intricate DNA genetic code makes it possible for the individual to inherit not only simple physical characteristics, such as size, shape and chemical makeup, but also a whole set of propensities for particular social behavior which goes with a given physiology. And we can deduce from systematic observations of behavior that these propensities can be inhibited or released in the encounter with other members of the species, and modified over generations by the process of natural selection. This is most important, because it is a decisive advance from the notion of "instinct," which was defined as a relatively automatic matter of feeling hunger, blinking, and kicking softly at the doctor who hits one's knee with a small hammer.

Now we see that the question of what can be inherited is much more complex than we once thought, that all animals are "programmed" not only to grow, come to sexual maturity, reproduce, become old and die, but also to interact with each other in rather predictable ways. Of course, there is considerable variation in how animals behave, just as there is in how they look, how quickly they run or swim, how much food they eat, and how large they grow. Just as with humans, there is considerable diversity but also a great amount of consistency and predictability.

We now want to know what the human biological inheritance is, or put another way, what is "in the wiring" of the average male and female, and how it got there. Almost certainly the most dismal difference between males and females is that men create large fighting groups, then with care, enthusiasm, and miserable effectiveness proceed to maim and kill each other. Feminists associate this grim pattern with *machismo*—the need for men to assert themselves in rough-and-tumble ways and to commit mayhem in the name of masculinity. Why men show *macho* and not women, the feminists do not wholly clarify, but the fact that women don't and men do is strikingly plain enough. Yet, among the possible reasons, there is a simple and clear biological factor the feminists overlook—the effect of the sex hormones on behavior.

In a report to a UNESCO conference on aggression I attended in Paris last May, David Hamburg of the department of psychiatry at Stanford described the role of testosterone in stimulating aggressive behavior. In experiments on primates, when both males and females are given extra testosterone, they show much more aggressive hyper-male activity. Humans have similar reactions under artificial manipulation of hormone levels. Among boys and girls before puberty, boys show more testosterone than girls. But at adolescence, the changes are startling: Testosterone in boys increases at least tenfold, and possibly as much as 30 times. On the other hand, girls' testosterone levels only double, from a lower base to begin with. These levels remain stable throughout the life cycle.

In one sense this seems unimportant, because the absolute amounts of these hormone substances are so tiny. And yet hormones are like poisons—a tiny amount can have a gross effect. Hence we see adolescent males—not only among humans but in some other primate species, too—flooded at puberty with a natural chemical which apparently stimulates marked aggressive behavior. When females are given extra amounts, their behavior—independent of socialization, advertising, the male conspiracy—becomes more male-like, more aggressive, more assertive. I choose the example of aggression to discuss "the wiring" and its effect on what we do because no one is likely to claim any longer

that the male capacity for violent corporate aggression is a sign of superiority or courage in the world we live in.

Other differences, too, are not unusual in the world of little boys and
girls. Parents and teachers are familiar with the marked difference in
the rate of maturity between girls and boys: the girls generally outpace
the boys for at least the first 14 years of life in school performance,
physical control, ability to withstand disease and accident, emotional
control, and capacity to engage in detailed work. The pattern persists
into sexual maturity; the earlier social competence of women is widely
recognized when women marry men some years older than they. Among
humans the contrast in rates of maturation are nowhere as marked as in
some of the primates—for example, those whose females may mature at
3½ years of age and males at 7. As John Tanner of London University
has shown in his book, "Human Growth," girls at adolescence are about
18 months ahead of boys, just as they have been physically more mature
than boys at all ages from birth. These differences are tangible, measur-
able and cross-cultural; they must reflect in some degree the genetic heritage which underlies such predictable regularities—though it must be
emphasized that we are speaking of propensities that overlap and not
absolute differences.

Now what could be the advantage to the human species of this extensive difference of male-female production of testosterone—given its implication for behavior? In a real if extremely simplified sense, evolution
is conditioning over time. In other words, just as dogs can be rewarded
for salivating at the sound of a bell, so members of a species do things
which become rewarded genetically by the greater ability of the performers of the effective actions to survive and to reproduce. So what
our information about sex hormones may mean is that there was an advantage to the evolving human species in selecting males with high testosterone levels and females with much lower levels. Our new information about human evolution from archeological research gives us a
reason for this difference: hunting.

From all the available evidence, hunting was the critical human adaptation as long ago as 2 million, or 14, or even 20 million years ago. We
have been farming for 13,000 years at most, and until about 5,000
years ago the majority of us were hunter-gatherers. We have been industrialized for barely 200 years. For 99 per cent of our history our
survival depended on what bio-anthropologist William Laughlin of the
University of Connecticut calls "the master pattern of the human spe-
ies."

During this vast time span, the hunting-based behavioral adaptations
which distinguish us from the other primates were selected in the same
way we evolved our huge higher brains, our striding walk, our upright

posture, and the apparatus for speech. And one of the most important of our evolutions underlies precisely the feminists' complaint: males hunted and females did not, and my suggestion is that, in addition to other indices such as size, running and throwing ability, and endurance, the differences between male and female hormone patterns reflect this reality.

It's worth reviewing this briefly. Among the other primates, an individual who is old enough gathers virtually all the food he or she will eat. Almost no primates eat meat, and there is no division of labor as far as getting food is concerned. Among humans, however, a division of work on the basis of sex is universal. A strong explanation for this is that our hunting past stimulated a behavioral specialization—males hunted, females gathered—which is clearly still very much part of us, though often in only symbolic and contorted forms. The ancient pattern seems to persist: men and women unite to reproduce young, but they separate to produce food and artifacts. Highly volatile adolescent males are subjected to rigorous and frequently painful initiations and training in the active manly arts; females—more equable, less accident-prone, less gripped by symbolic fantasies of heroic triumph—rarely undergo initiations as violent and abusive as those males suffer. That is, it appears that females are much less truculent, much less in need of control, much less committed to extensive self-assertion. The possibility must be faced that this general characteristic of the species reflects the physiological one—that female bodies are less driven by those internal secretions which mark the rambunctious and often dangerous males.

If millions of years of evolution have a lot to do with the temperament of the individual male, it may also help explain the deep emotional ties that bind men together in groups. In a book that I published last year, "Men in Groups," I suggested that there is a biological program that results in a "bonding" between males which is as important for politics as the program of male-female bonding is for reproduction. The results of this male bonding propensity could be seen easily and everywhere: in sports, rock groups (who ever said males weren't emotional?), the American Legion, the men's houses of Indians, the secret societies of both Yale seniors and Australian aborigines, and—most unhappily of all—the bizarre and fantasy-ridden male enterprises called armies.

So not only were there traditional and casual barriers to female participation in the powerful groups of human communities but more elusive and fundamental ones as well. It might take far more radical steps than we feared to approach the sexual equality we say we want.

I have said that males hunted and females gathered. This is not to imply that what females did was less valuable for survival. In his detailed studies of the Kalahari Bushmen, my colleague Richard Lee of Rutgers has shown that in this group, at least, the food women gather is 80 per cent of the diet. What the Kalahari males bring back from the hunt is useful, but not essential. How representative the Bushmen are of all hunters, and particularly of our ancestors, is another question, but Lee's general suggestion presumably applies in many hunting-gathering communities. Nonetheless, all societies make some distinction between men's work and women's work. As Cynthia Epstein of Queens College has pointed out in her excellent study, "Woman's Place" (the most sensitive and probing modern analysis of the sociology of female employment), these distinctions are not necessarily sensible or logical. Still and all, we are an animal as committed to sexual segregation for certain purposes—particularly those having to do with hunting, danger, war, and passionate corporate drama—as we are to sexual conjunction for others—in particular for conceiving and rearing children, and sharing food.

Once again, we get perspective of this matter from studying other primates. While among the other primates there is no sexual division of labor for food-getting, there is still considerable difference between what males and females do. In fact, from primatological work only now becoming available, an unexpected and fascinating body of information is emerging about encounters among primate females, their hierarchies, how they structure relationships over generations and how they learn their social roles. From the work of researchers at the Japanese Monkey Center, from Vernon Reynolds and his wife, Frankie, of Bristol University, from Jane Lancaster of Rutgers, Suzanne Ripley of the Smithsonian Institution and Phyllis Jay Dolhinow of the University of California, we are beginning to learn that there are indeed elaborate patterns of female bonding and that these are based to a large extent on kinship relationships rather than the political ones that frequently bind males. Furthermore, these kinship-like structures appear to be essential for comfortable and viable community life, and they provide security for the young in a web of affiliations which persist over their lifetimes. Hence, the core social bonds at the intimate level are mediated through the females, while at the public or political level, the central relationships remain very much a male monopoly. It is extremely unlikely for a female to assume political leadership of a group when a suitable adult male is available, even though the females may be far more experienced than a young leader-male, and though females seem perfectly capable of leading groups in interim periods when no suitable male is present.

One possible, if elusive, clue to the different social roles of male and female is suggested by research into the frequency of their smiles by Daniel G. Freedman of the Committee for the Study of Human Development at the University of Chicago. The underlying proposition is that smiling is an affiliative gesture of deference, a permissive, accommodating expression rather than a commanding or threatening one. Certainly among other primates, the smile is associated with fear, and humans too talk of the "nervous smile." Freedman and his associates found that among human infants two days old, females smiled spontaneously at a significantly higher rate than males. This was *eyes-closed smiling*—in the absence of a social relationship—and suggests the affinity for this particular motor pattern which girls have.

In another study—using the ingenious method of looking at photos of students in high school and college yearbooks since 1900—the same sexual difference was maintained. While everyone smiled less during periods of economic depression (they also had fewer babies), still the significant sexual difference persisted. And in his field studies of primates, Irven De Vore of Harvard University has found that females smile more often than males as a result of fear.

Intriguingly enough, some of the techniques of political organization which feminists are exploring suggest significant differences from conventional male procedures. For one thing, the principle of competitive, individual leadership is rejected in favor of an attempt at cooperative, group action. In their "consciousness-raising" sessions, the exchange and discussion of personal intimacies serves as a basis for eventual political activity; these groups gather in a circle, formalities are minimal and sisterhood is emphasized. In a sense, the feminist approach to politics is genuinely radical; if it works, it could well be an important contribution not only to the lives of women but to the political conduct of men and the body politic in general.

So far I have argued that the feminist critique takes for granted what important scientific evidence does not permit us to take for granted: that only explicit cultural control—in fact, conspiracy—lies behind the very great differences in certain male and female social behaviors. Feminists such as Kate Millett suggest that once upon a time there was a matriarchy that became corrupted by patriarchal force, which to this day oppresses women. However, the archeological facts available suggest that there is an unbroken line from the male-dominated primate systems I have described here through the hunting stage of our evolution—from which we have not changed genetically—to the most sophisticated and complicated, male-dominated technocratic societies.

Because they ignore biological factors (like many other reformers), the feminists run the risk of basing their legitimate demand for legal and economic equality on a vulnerable foundation. Their denial of significant physiological differences can also deter real occupational and educational success by women—a possibility that is suggested by a variety of studies of the menstrual cycle. The relationship of the cycle to social performance is by no means simple, nor is the evidence conclusive.

But studies such as those done over a period of some 15 years by Katherina Dalton of University College, University of London, must be considered: One of her estimates is that roughly 40 per cent of women suffer from a variety of distressing symptoms during the final week or so of the menstrual cycle (other researchers see a higher figure). Dalton's investigation of admission to mental hospitals revealed that 46 per cent of the female admissions occurred during the seven or eight days preceding and during menstruation; at this time, too, 53 per cent of attempted suicides by females occurred.

In another of her studies, 45 per cent of industrial employees who reported sick did so during this period; 49 per cent of crimes committed by women prisoners happened at this time and so did 45 per cent of the punishments meted out to schoolgirls. Dalton also discovered that schoolgirls who were prefects and monitors doled out significantly greater numbers of punishments to others during the menstrual period, and she raises the question of whether or not this is also true of women magistrates, teachers and other figures in authority.

She presents evidence that students writing examinations during the premenstruum earn roughly 14 to 15 per cent poorer grades than they do at other times of the month. If what happens in England also happens here (there could well be cultural and psychological differences between the reactions of the two female populations), then an American girl writing her Graduate Record Examinations over a two-day period or a week-long set of finals during the premenstruum begins with a disadvantage which almost certainly condemns her to no higher than a second-class grade. A whole career in the educational system can be unfairly jeopardized because of this phenomenon. In another sphere, a study by the British Road Research Laboratory suggests that about 60 per cent of all traffic accidents of females occur during about 25 per cent of the days of the month—apparently before and during menstruation. Since women are generally safer drivers than men, certainly in the younger age groups, this may not be a considerable hazard to the public. But for individual women driving cars or writing examinations, these findings may be relevant—and important.

So the paradox is that when they deny there are meaningful differences between males and females because of such a predictable phenomenon as menstruation, feminists may help make it more difficult for women to compete openly and equally for scholarships, jobs, entry to graduate schools, and the variety of other prerequisites of wealth and status. This emphatically does not mean women shouldn't have responsible or competitive jobs; it may mean that in a community committed to genuine equal opportunity examinations and schedules of work—for example, the flying time of women pilots—could be adjusted to the realities of female experience and not, as now, wholly to the male-oriented work week and pattern. (Interestingly, Valentina Tereshkova-Ni-kolayeva, the first woman astronaut, affirms that women can be as capable astronauts as men, but that allowance should be made for the effect of the cycle on physiology.)

The human species is faced with two overwhelming problems—war and overpopulation. The first results from the social bonding of males, and is not our concern here. The second results from the sexual bonding of males and females. Men and women make love and have children not simply because the patriarchal conspiracy offers women no other major form of satisfaction, but because an old pattern rooted in the genetic codes and reflected in our life cycles—particularly in the flurries of adolescence—draw men and women to each other and to the infants their conjunction yields.

There is no conspiracy in becoming adolescent and sprouting breasts and becoming interested in boys in a new way. Madison Avenue did not invent the fact that female bodies and the movement and sound of women are stimulating to men. Anyone who has pushed a baby carriage down the street will know how many passers-by peek at a young infant and how quickly the presence of a baby will help strangers talk. Throughout the primates, females with newborn infants enjoy high status and babies are enormously attractive to all members of the community. Can it be that human females, who have more of a stake in maternity than males, are responding to the crisis of population and devaluation of this role in the stringent, probing, feminist way? In other words, is the rhetoric about sexual politics really political, or is it, ironically, another expression of sexual difference? More poignantly still, may it perhaps reflect also the currently drastic excess of females over males of marriageable age—because of the disruptions of the Second World War and the baby boom which followed—and hence the probability that a huge number of mature women remain "sexually unemployed" insofar as they will probably be unable to arrange reproductive lives in the limited ways our sexual rigidities allow?

Child-rearing remains the most labor-intensive task left to members of mechanized societies, and it can't be speeded up. Day-care centers for children can obviously be a sensible feature of a civilized society. But it is another thing for Kate Millett to recommend that child care be entrusted to "trained persons of both sexes"—an idea which is not promising in view of the experiences of orphanages and foster homes. As John Bowlby has argued in his book on child-rearing and deprivation, "Attachment," children need inputs of behavior as much as they require food, and there is considerable evidence that those who do not have a mother or mother-figure on which to focus their affections and security in early childhood suffer irreparable difficulty later on.

Now, it is not clear that fathers cannot do as well. Millions of children are currently being raised by fathers without wives, and it is true that adult males obviously have, as Margaret Mead has suggested, a strong interest in infants. On the other hand, the long and intimate relationship a pregnant woman has with her gestating child must prime her to respond to the child differently from even the most doting father. Even if this has not been demonstrated conclusively, it remains a possibility, just as it is possible that breast-feeding mothers—still the majority at the present time—have, in comparison to fathers, some different if not more substantial commitment to their children because of the hormonal and other physiological processes involved. And if nothing else, the fact that the whole human species has overwhelmingly elected to have children raised at least in the first years by women suggests conformity to nature rather than to male conspiracy.

There is good psychological and primatological evidence that it is necessary for young children to separate themselves increasingly from their parents as they mature. But unless the daycare program of the women's liberationists takes carefully into account what mothers know too well—the routinely incessant and innocent demands of young children for both care and encounter—then too many women who have spent too many days with this understanding will reject the more appealing aspects of the movement. A rejection of the intimacies of family life such as they are, and an implication that females interested sexually in males as husbands and progenitors are somehow inferior and don't know their own minds, can also serve only to frighten off potential supporters.

The theorists who proclaim the withering away of the state of sexual differences may well be proved as wrong as those Marxists who assumed that the State would wither away once it had changed the social arrangements of the people. The problem the feminists face is not just to change a culture and an economy, but to change a primate who is very old genetically and who seems stubbornly committed to relatively little variation in basic sexual structures. This is not to say that some change cannot and will not be achieved, if for no other reason than that the population crush may affect this animal as it has some others—by drastically altering his behavior patterns (though we may as yet be far from the densities which will seriously inhibit breeding).

In an article on the relationship between women's rights and socialism (New Left Review, November–December, 1966), the English sociologist Juliet Mitchell called the feminist struggle "The Longest Revolution." If there is to be a revolution, it will be of infinitely greater duration than Mitchell anticipated. Our biological heritage is the product of millions of years of successful adaptation and it recurs in each generation with only tiny alterations. It is simply prudent that those concerned with changing sex roles understand the possible biological importance of what they want to do, and take careful measure of what these phenomena mean. If they do not, the primary victims of their mis-analysis, unfortunately, will be—as usual—women and their daughters.

WHAT IT WOULD BE LIKE IF WOMEN WIN
Gloria Steinem

Anyone who has read Gloria Steinem's essay knows that jokes and clichés do not do justice to the goals of the Women's Liberation movement. Miss Steinem, an author and editor of *New York Magazine,* well known as a political analyst and commentator on the contemporary scene, assures us that "women don't want to exchange places with men." Instead, they want something approaching an equitable relationship between men and women, free from sexist concepts of domination and subordination. If such a state could be brought to pass, women, men, children—everyone—would benefit. That the author considers her speculations "utopian" should not discourage current readers. One generation ago, such things as a guaranteed annual wage, civil rights for Negroes, and space travel seemed just as futuristic as free day-care centers, marriage and divorce reforms, and equal opportunities for women sound today.

Any change is fearful, especially one affecting both politics and sex roles, so let me begin these utopian speculations with a fact. To break the ice.

Women don't want to exchange places with men. Male chauvinists, science-fiction writers and comedians may favor that idea for its shock value, but psychologists say it is a fantasy based on ruling-class ego and guilt. Men assume that women want to imitate them, which is just what white people assumed about blacks. An assumption so strong that it may convince the second-class group of the need to imitate, but for both women and blacks that stage has passed. Guilt produces the question: What if they could treat us as we have treated them?

That is not our goal. But we do want to change the economic system to one more based on merit. In Women's Lib Utopia, there will be free access to good jobs—and decent pay for the bad ones women have been performing all along, including housework. Increased skilled labor might lead to a four-hour workday, and higher wages would encourage further mechanization of repetitive jobs now kept alive by cheap labor.

With women as half the country's elected representatives, and a

From *Time* magazine, August 31, 1970. Reprinted by permission of *Time.*

woman President once in a while, the country's *machismo* problems would be greatly reduced. The old-fashioned idea that manhood depends on violence and victory is, after all, an important part of our troubles in the streets, and in Viet Nam. I'm not saying that women leaders would eliminate violence. We are not more moral than men; we are only uncorrupted by power so far. When we do acquire power, we might turn out to have an equal impulse toward aggression. Even now, Margaret Mead believes that women fight less often but more fiercely than men, because women are not taught the rules of the war game and fight only when cornered. But for the next 50 years or so, women in politics will be very valuable by tempering the idea of manhood into something less aggressive and better suited to this crowded, post-atomic planet. Consumer protection and children's rights, for instance, might get more legislative attention.

Men will have to give up ruling-class privileges, but in return they will no longer be the only ones to support the family, get drafted, bear the strain of power and responsibility. Freud to the contrary, anatomy is not destiny, at least not for more than nine months at a time. In Israel, women are drafted, and some have gone to war. In England, more men type and run switchboards. In India and Israel, a woman rules. In Sweden, both parents take care of the children. In this country, come Utopia, men and women won't reverse roles; they will be free to choose according to individual talents and preferences.

If role reform sounds sexually unsettling, think how it will change the sexual hypocrisy we have now. No more sex arranged on the barter system, with women pretending interest, and men never sure whether they are loved for themselves or for the security few women can get any other way. (Married or not, for sexual reasons or social ones, most women still find it second nature to Uncle-Tom.) No more men who are encouraged to spend a lifetime living with inferiors; with housekeepers, or dependent creatures who are still children. No more domineering wives, emasculating women, and "Jewish mothers," all of whom are simply human beings with all their normal ambition and drive confined to the home. No more unequal partnerships that eventually doom love and sex.

In order to produce that kind of confidence and individuality, child rearing will train according to talent. Little girls will no longer be surrounded by air-tight, self-fulfilling prophecies of natural passivity, lack of ambition and objectivity, inability to exercise power, and dexterity (so long as special aptitude for jobs requiring patience and dexterity is confined to poorly paid jobs; brain surgery is for males).

Schools and universities will help to break down traditional sex roles, even when parents will not. Half the teachers will be men, a rarity now at preschool and elementary levels; girls will not necessarily serve cook-ies or boys hoist up the flag. Athletic teams will be picked only by strength and skill. Sexually segregated courses like auto mechanics and home economics will be taken by boys and girls together. New courses in sexual politics will explore female subjugation as the model for political oppression, and women's history will be an academic staple, along with black history, at least until the white-male-oriented textbooks are integrated and rewritten.

As for the American child's classic problem—too much mother, too little father—that would be cured by an equalization of parental responsibility. Free nurseries, school lunches, family cafeterias built into every housing complex, service companies that will do household cleaning chores in a regular, businesslike way, and more responsibility by the entire community for the children; all these will make it possible for both mother and father to work, and to have equal leisure time with the children at home. For parents of very young children, however, a special job category, created by Government and unions, would allow such parents a shorter work day.

The revolution would not take away the option of being a housewife. A woman who prefers to be her husband's housekeeper and/or hostess would receive a percentage of his pay determined by the domestic relations courts. If divorced, she might be eligible for a pension fund, and for a job-training allowance. Or a divorce could be treated the same way that the dissolution of a business partnership is now.

If these proposals seem farfetched, consider Sweden, where most of them are already in effect. Sweden is not yet a working Women's Lib model; most of the role-reform programs began less than a decade ago, and are just beginning to take hold. But that country is so far ahead of us in recognizing the problem that Swedish statements on sex and equality sound like bulletins from the moon.

Our marriage laws, for instance, are so reactionary that Women's Lib groups want couples to take a compulsory written exam on the law, as for a driver's license, before going through with the wedding. A man has alimony and wifely debts to worry about, but a woman may lose so many of her civil rights that in the U.S. now, in important legal ways, she becomes a child again. In some states, she cannot sign credit agreements, use her maiden name, incorporate a business, or establish a legal residence of her own. Being a wife, according to most social and legal definitions, is still a 19th century thing.

Assuming, however, that these blatantly sexist laws are abolished or reformed, that job discrimination is forbidden, that parents share financial responsibility for each other and the children, and that sexual relationships become partnerships of equal adults (some pretty big assumptions), then marriage will probably go right on. Men and women are, after all, physically complementary. When society stops encouraging men to be exploiters and women to be parasites, they may turn out to be more complementary in emotion as well. Women's Lib is not trying to destroy the American family. A look at the statistics on divorce—plus the way in which old people are farmed out with strangers and young people flee the home—shows the destruction that has already been done. Liberated women are just trying to point out the disaster, and build compassionate and practical alternatives from the ruins.

What will exist is a variety of alternative life-styles. Since the population explosion dictates that childbearing be kept to a minimum, parents-and-children will be only one of many "families"; couples, age groups, working groups, mixed communes, blood-related clans, class groups, creative groups. Single women will have the right to stay single without ridicule, without the attitudes now betrayed by "spinster" and "bachelor." Lesbians or homosexuals will no longer be denied legally binding marriages, complete with mutual-support agreements and inheritance rights. Paradoxically, the number of homosexuals may get smaller. With fewer overpossessive mothers and fewer fathers who hold up an impossibly cruel or perfectionist idea of manhood, boys will be less likely to be denied or reject their identity as males.

Changes that now seem small may get bigger:

Men's Lib. Men now suffer from more diseases due to stress, heart attacks, ulcers, a higher suicide rate, greater difficulty living alone, less adaptability to change and, in general, a shorter life span than women. There is some scientific evidence that what produces physical problems is not work itself, but the inability to choose which work, and how much. With women bearing half the financial responsibility, and with the idea of "masculine" jobs gone, men might well feel freer and live longer.

Religion. Protestant women are already becoming ordained ministers; radical nuns are carrying out liturgical functions that were once the exclusive property of priests; Jewish women are rewriting prayers—particularly those that Orthodox Jews recite every morning thanking God they are not female. In the future, the church will become an area of equal participation by women. This means, of course, that organized religion will have to give up one of its great historical weapons: sexual repression. In most structured faiths, from Hinduism through Roman Catholicism, the status of women went down as the position of priests ascended. Male clergy implied, if they did not teach, that women were unclean, unworthy and sources of ungodly temptation, in order to remove them as rivals for the emotional forces of men. Full participation of women in ecclesiastical life might involve certain changes in theology, such as, for instance, a radical redefinition of sin.

Literary Problems. Revised sex roles will outdate more children's books than civil rights ever did. Only a few children had the problem of a *Little Black Sambo,* but most have the male-female stereotypes of "Dick and Jane." A boomlet of children's books about mothers who work has already begun, and liberated parents and editors are beginning to pressure for change in the textbook industry. Fiction writing will change more gradually, but romantic novels with wilting heroines and swashbuckling heroes will be reduced to historical value. Or perhaps to the sado-masochist trade. (*Marjorie Morningstar,* a romantic novel that took the '50s by storm, has already begun to seem as unreal as its '20s predecessor, *The Sheik.*) As for the literary plots that turn on forced marriages or horrific abortions, they will seem as dated as Prohibition stories. Free legal abortions and free birth control will force writers to give up pregnancy as the *deus ex machina.*

Manners and Fashion. Dress will be more androgynous, with class symbols becoming more important than sexual ones. Pro- or anti-Establishment styles may already be more vital than who is wearing them. Hardhats are just as likely to rough up antiwar girls as antiwar men in the street, and police understand that women are just as likely to be pushers or bombers. Dances haven't required that one partner lead the other for years, anyway. Chivalry will transfer itself to those who need it, or deserve respect: old people, admired people, anyone with an armload of packages. Women with normal work identities will be less likely to attach their whole sense of self to youth and appearance; thus there will be fewer nervous breakdowns when the first wrinkles appear. Lighting cigarettes and other treasured niceties will become gestures of mutual affection. "I like to be helped on with my coat," says one Women's Lib worker, "but not if it costs me $2,000 a year in salary."

For those with nostalgia for a simpler past, here is a word of comfort. Anthropologist Geoffrey Gorer studied the few peaceful human tribes and discovered one common characteristic: sex roles were not polarized. Differences of dress and occupation were at a minimum. Society, in other words, was not using sexual blackmail as a way of getting women to do cheap labor, or men to be aggressive.

Thus Women's Lib may achieve a more peaceful society on the way toward its other goals. That is why the Swedish government considers reform to bring about greater equality in the sex roles one of its most important concerns. As Prime Minister Olof Palme explained in a widely ignored speech delivered in Washington this spring: "It is *human beings* we shall emancipate. In Sweden today, if a politician should declare that the woman ought to have a different role from man's, he would be regarded as something from the Stone Age." In other words, the most radical goal of the movement is egalitarianism.

If Women's Lib wins, perhaps we all do.

PART SIX

THE PROSPECT OF A FUTURE

"There is one bright spot and one only on my screen. I see wisps of hope in the young, in the blacks and browns, in the militants of all colors. They are the partisans of the new consciousness. But I do not want to idealize them. They are disorganized, rude, contemptuous. Sometimes they are even a tenth as violent as those beating on them. But they are thinking of the right things . . ."

W. H. FERRY

The last word on the 1970's will not be spoken until long after the decade has passed into history. So instead of concluding our survey of topical issues with definitive statements, we have chosen two essays which ask some unanswerable questions about the immediate future.

Beginning with the 1950's, each decade has witnessed an accelerated rate of technological and social change. In the first half of our century, aeronautical science increased man's airspeed tenfold. In the 1960's, science and technology took us to the moon. Now we speak of trips within our solar system by the mid-1980's. Social and political conditions have changed just as rapidly and dramatically. In the 1950's relatively few college students belonged to the Beat generation. Today, many college students, in every locale, know a new life style, whether they consciously advocate it or not. In

351

another area, the efforts to attain integrated schooling, which began in the 1950's, have taken surprising turns, with many blacks now demanding separate schools. The civil rights movement has broadened into a "third world" movement, which considers every walk of life as its domain. As the essays in the previous parts of the book suggest, we must learn to live with these and newer changes in the future.

Fittingly, then, the last two essays focus on the concept of change, its negative and positive consequences. While Eric Hoffer and Wilber H. Ferry approach the subject from different sides of the political spectrum, they agree that our times and institutions require a rebirth. Without this rebirth the new technology, new politics, and new morality will only accentuate the disruptive elements which make the future so bleak. Hoffer thinks that we will find the rebirth ritual inside our present institutions. Ferry is less optimistic, saying that radicalization is the only means of transformation. Like this book, neither essay has the final answer. But at least they raise important questions, small steps on a long journey, but ones in the right direction.

THE MADHOUSE OF CHANGE
Eric Hoffer

Eric Hoffer, a philosopher who worked for much of his life as a longshoreman, writes about the social and psychological consequences of change. He claims that "change . . . causes juvenilization" and that "the juvenile . . . is the archetypal man in transition." In order for a person or a society to cope successfully with change, there must be opportunities available for a rebirth or transformation. Mr. Hoffer's other works include *The True Believer, The Ordeal of Change,* and *Working and Thinking on the Waterfront.*

After the Second World War, I spent two years (1947–1948) writing a small book on the nature of mass movements, which Harper later published under the title *The True Believer.* These were two years of utmost concentration and absorption. Yet even as I was writing the book, there was something tugging at my mind, making me wonder whether my attempt to make sense of the Stalin-Hitler decades would have relevance to what was taking place in the post-War world, particularly to the strange goings on in Asia and Africa. On both continents, several countries won independence from foreign rule and began to modernize themselves in a hurry. The struggle for independence was relatively brief, but the attempt at modernization became a hectic affair, which turned every country into a madhouse. Now, modernization is not an occult process. It requires the building of roads, factories, dams, schools, and so on. Why should the accomplishment of such practical tasks require the staging of a madhouse?

I spent 18 years groping for an answer. Almost everything I have written during the past 18 years has dealt with some aspect of this problem. Every time I stumbled upon something that looked like an explanation, I wrote an essay. I acted on the assumption that in this sort of problem, all hunches and guesses were legitimate. It occurred to me, for instance, that modernization is basically a process of imitation— backward countries imitate advanced countries—and I wondered whether there might not be something bruising and antagonizing in the necessity to imitate a superior model. For the backward, imitation is an act of submission, and it is reasonable to expect that the sense of inferiority inherent in imitation should breed resentment. So I wrote an essay on "Imitation and Fanaticism," in which I suggested that the backward have to rid themselves of their feeling of inferiority, must demonstrate their prowess, before they will open their minds and hearts to all that the world can teach them. Most often in history, it was the conquerors who learned willingly from the conquered, rather than the other way around. There is, therefore, a kernel of practicalness in the attempt of a Nasser or a Sukarno to turn their people into warriors. It is a fact that nations with a warrior tradition, such as the Japanese or the inheritors of Genghis Khan in Outer Mongolia, find modernization less difficult than nations of subjected peasants, such as Russia and China. The essay also suggested that imitation is least impeded when we are made to feel that our act of imitation is actually an act of becoming the opposite of that which we imitate. Communism can be an effective agency for the transmission of Western achievements to backward countries, because it convinces the backward that by modernizing themselves they are actually becoming the opposite of the capitalist model they imitate. Finally, I pointed out that we are most at ease when we imitate a defeated or dead model, and that the impulse of the imitators is to defeat or even destroy the model they imitate.

I also noticed that the present modernization of backward countries is directed not by businessmen or traditional politicians but by intellectuals, and I blamed the madhouse on them. I wrote several essays in which I tried to prove that unlike prosaic men of action, the intellectual cannot operate at room temperature; that he pants for a world of magic and miracles, and turns everyday tasks into holy causes and Promethean undertakings. I suggested that should intellectuals come to power in an advanced country, it, too, would turn overnight into a madhouse.

The explanation that appealed to me most and to which I hung on longest was an unlikely one for an American. I became convinced that change itself is the cause of the madhouse; that change as such is explosive. It took me long to reach this conclusion. In this country, change is familiar and acceptable. We seem to change homes, jobs, habits, friends, even husbands and wives, without much difficulty. Actually, through most of history, change has been a rare phenomenon. Think of it: The technology perfected in prehistoric times served as a basis of everyday life down to the end of the 18th Century. Even in this country, people lived in 1800 A.D. the way men lived in 3000 B.C. George Washington would have felt at home in King Cheops' Egypt. The end of the 18th Century marks a sharp dividing line between an immemorial static world and a world of ceaseless change. It is obvious, therefore, that change is far from being as natural and matter of fact as we imagine it to be. Moreover, an observant person will notice that even in this country, change is never free of irritation and elements of fear. We adjust ourselves quickly to a new job or a new environment, but the moments of anxiety are there. And if we had to change our whole way of life as people have to do in the developing countries, we, too, would become upset and unbalanced.

The obvious fact is that we cannot prepare and fit ourselves for the wholly new. Skill and experience count for little and may even be a handicap. It takes time before we adjust ourselves to a wholly new situation and fit in. In other words, drastic change turns a whole population into misfits, and misfits live and breathe in an atmosphere of passion. We used to think that revolution is the cause of change. Actually, it is the other way around; revolution is a by-product of change. Change comes first, and it is the difficulties and irritations inherent in change that set the stage for revolution. To say that revolution is the cause of change is like saying that juvenile delinquency is the cause of the change from boyhood to manhood.

To understand what is going on in the developing countries, we must know what it is that misfits need above all. They need self-confidence, which means plenty of opportunities for successful action, for asserting themselves and proving their worth. Where there are such opportunities, change is likely to proceed without convulsions and explosions. We have seen it happen in this country. From the middle of the last century to the First World War, some 30,000,000 Europeans came to this country. They were, for the most part, peasants torn from the warm communal life of small towns and villages and dumped almost overnight on a strange, cold continent. If ever there was a drastic change, this was it. The immigrants went through an upsetting, irritating and painful experience. They were misfits in every sense of the word, ideal material for a revolution. Yet we had no upheaval. The immigrants adjusted themselves quickly to the new environment. Why? Because they had an almost virgin continent at their disposal and unbounded opportunities for individual advancement and self-assertion.

In most of the developing countries, there are only the meagerest opportunities for the individual to do something on his own. Most of these countries are unimaginably poor, with debilitated populations living on the edge of subsistence. Some countries, like Indonesia, are rich in natural resources, but their governments do not countenance individual enterprise and self-assertion. The intellectuals who are in charge derive their sense of usefulness from telling other people what to do, and see it as an infringement of their birthright when common people start to do things on their own. You cannot see a Sukarno or even a Suharto government telling the people of Indonesia to come and get it, the way America told the immigrants from Europe. Now, what do misfits do when they cannot win a sense of confidence and worth by individual effort? They reach out for substitutes. The substitute for self-confidence is faith, and the substitute for self-esteem is pride. Faith and pride in what? In a leader, a holy cause, a nation, a race. And it is easily seen that once you operate with faith and pride, you are going to have the bedlam atmosphere of a madhouse.

It is remarkable that all the years I was playing with these explanations I failed to see something that was staring me in the face. I failed to see that staging a madhouse in the course of rapid modernization was not peculiar to backward countries in Asia and Africa. It was only recently that it dawned upon me that Europe, too, has been living in an apocalyptic madhouse staged by Germany and Russia as they set out to modernize themselves at breakneck speed. The nationalist, racialist and revolutionary movements, and the great wars, which have convulsed the Occident during the past hundred years, were the by-product of a drastic change in the life of the European masses, when millions of peasants were transformed into urban, industrial workers. Seen against this apocalyptic background, my explanation of the explosiveness of change as due to the creation of a state of unfitness seemed pale and inadequate. I began to feel that change does more than create misfits, that it affects deeper layers of the psyche. Considering how rare change has been through most of history, it is legitimate to assume that change goes against human nature, that there is in man a built-in resistance to change. It is not only that we are afraid of the new. Deep within us there is the conviction that we cannot merely adjust to change, that we cannot remain our old selves and master the new; that only by getting out of our skins, by becoming new men, can we become part of the new. In other words, change creates an estrangement from the self and generates a need for a new identity and a sense of rebirth. And it depends on the way this need is satisfied whether change runs smoothly or is attended with convulsions and explosions.

Let us go back to the 30,000,000 immigrants who were dumped on our shores and see what really happened to them. I said that the reason they had adjusted themselves so quickly to the new environment was that they found abundant opportunities for individual advancement. Is this all there was to it? Actually, a whole lot more happened to them. The moment the immigrants landed on our shores, America grabbed hold of them, stripped them of their traditions and habits, gave them a new diet and a new mode of dress, taught them a new language and often gave them a new name. Here was a classical example of processing people into new men. Abundant opportunities for action by themselves could not have transformed the transplanted peasants so quickly and smoothly.

Immigration, then, is a potent agency of human transformation. It is, moreover, an agency the masses will resort to on their own accord whenever there is a drastic change in their way of life. It is significant that the rapid industrialization of Europe was attended not only by mass movements but also by mass migrations to the New World. Marx cursed the discovery of gold in California for cheating him of his foretold and prayed-for glorious revolution. He said it was the injection of gold from California that saved tottering Europe. Actually, it was the discharge of 30,000,000 immigrants to America that postponed Europe's apocalyptic denouement.

It should be obvious, of course, that immigration can effect a human transformation only when it is to a foreign country. Internal migration cannot do it. Even now, when you want to transform a Sicilian or Spanish peasant into an industrial worker, you can do it more effectively by transferring him to Germany or France than to Milan or Barcelona. The Sicilian peasant who goes to Milan is not automatically processed into a new man, and he is likely to satisfy his need for a sense of rebirth by joining the Communist Party or some other mass movement. Immigration to a foreign country is a do-it-yourself way for the masses to attain a sense of rebirth. When they achieve this sense by joining a mass movement, they avail themselves of a device staged for them by intellectuals. It is easy to forget that mass movements are the creation not of the masses but of the intellectuals. Now, what is likely to happen to a Sicilian peasant who becomes an industrial worker in Milan did happen to millions of European peasants who flocked to the cities of their native countries in the second half of the 19th Century: They attained a sense of rebirth and a new identity by joining the nationalist and revolutionary movements staged for them by poets, writers, historians and scholars, and their adjustment to a new life became a convulsive and explosive affair that eventually shook the Occident to its foundations.

Mass movements play a twofold role in the process of change. Firstly, they stage the drama of rebirth. By joining a mass movement, we become members of a chosen people—saints, warriors or pioneers showing the way to the rest of mankind. Secondly, by fusing people into a compact corporate body, a mass movement creates a homogeneous malleable mass that can be molded at will. We who have lived through the Stalin-Hitler decades know that one of the chief achievements of a mass movement is the creation of a population that will go through breath-taking somersaults at a word of command and can be made to love what it hates and hate what it loves.

There is one drastic change that no society can avoid; namely, the change from boyhood to manhood. It is a difficult and painful change, and we all know its explosive by-product of juvenile delinquency. How do ossified, changeless societies weather this change? I was particularly interested in primitive, tribal societies that have remained unchanged for millennia. When I first started to look into this matter, I had no idea what I would find. I happened to come upon a translation of Arnold van Gennep's *The Rites of Passage,* and as I turned the pages, I had the surprise of my life. There it was in black and white: The rites primitive societies stage to ease the boy's passage to manhood are the rites of death and rebirth. In the Congo, boys at the age of 15 are declared dead, taken into the forest and given palm wine until they pass out. The priest-magician watches over them. When they come to, he feeds them special food and teaches them a new language. During the rites of reintegration, the boys have to pretend that they do not know how to walk and that, like newborn children, they have to learn the gestures of everyday life. In several Australian tribes, the boy is taken violently from his mother, who weeps for him. He is taken into the desert, where he is subjected to physical and mental weakening to simulate death. He is then resurrected to live like a man.

In modern societies that have no rites of passage, the juvenile gropes his way to manhood on his own. He becomes an ideal recruit for mass movements. Indeed, the rapport between juvenile and mass movement is so striking—the two are so tailor-made for each other—that anyone of whatever age who joins a mass movement begins to display juvenile traits. This intimate linkage between juvenile and mass movement, and the fact that change readies people for mass movements, gave me a new view of the nature of change. Change, I realized, causes juvenilization; it turns a whole population into juveniles. It is as if the strain of change cracks the upper layers of the mind and lays bare the less mature layers.

Another way of putting it is that people who undergo drastic change re-
capitulate to some degree the passage from childhood to manhood, and
mass movements are in a sense the juvenile delinquency of societies
going through the ordeal of change.

The juvenile, then, is the archetypal man in transition. There is a
family likeness between juveniles and people who migrate from one
country to another, or are converted from one faith to another, or pass
from one way of life to another—as when peasants are turned into industrial workers, serfs into freemen, civilians into soldiers and people in
backward countries are subjected to rapid modernization. Even the old,
when they undergo the abrupt change of retirement, may turn, so to
speak, into senile juveniles. There is such a thing as senile delinquency.
Retired farmers and shopkeepers have made of Southern California a
breeding ground of juvenile cults, utopias and movements. The Birch
movement, with its unmistakable character of juvenile delinquency, was
initiated by a retired candymaker and is sustained by retired business
executives, generals and admirals. One need not strain the imagination
to visualize the juvenile madhouse we would have if rapid automation
should cause the retirement of millions of vigorous workers still hungry
for action.

It should be of interest to see what light these theories throw on one
of the most pressing changes that confront this country at present;
namely, the Negro's passage from inferiority to equality.

One sees immediately the almost insurmountable handicaps that beset
the Negro on every hand. Take the matter of *rebirth*. The fact that in
this country the Negro is a Negro first and only secondly an individual
puts the attainment of a sense of rebirth beyond his reach. No matter
what the Negro individual achieves or becomes, he remains a Negro
first. How can he ever feel that he is a new man reborn to a new life?
Think of the absurdities Elijah Muhammad and Father Divine had to
concoct in order to give the Negro some taste of rebirth. A decade of
fervent agitation, demonstrations, riots, court decisions and new laws
has not altered the fact that the white environment divests the Negro of
his individuality.

Or take *immigration*. Millions of Negroes have migrated from the
South to other parts of the country, but this mass migration has not
helped the Negro to change himself. It is an internal migration that, as
we have seen, cannot endow people with a new identity. The Negro
ghettos outside the South are a world of "nowhereness" and "nobodi-
ness" where the groping for identity assumes the aspect of a nightmar-
ish masquerade. It is of interest that Negroes who come to New York
from the West Indies, Panama or Africa do have the exodus experience,

and their performance is not utterly different from that of European immigrants.

Can *mass movements* do ought for the Negro? The answer is no. America is hard on mass movements. What starts out here as a mass movement ends up as a corporation or a racket. The Puritan and Mormon movements became training grounds for successful businessmen, and even the Communist movement is becoming a vehicle for the transformation of true believers into successful real-estate dealers. The Black Muslim movement is on the way to becoming a holding company of stores, farms and banks. The civil rights movement has been an instrument in the hands of the Negro middle class in its effort to integrate itself with the white middle class and force its way into the more privileged segments of American life. Used thus, the Negro revolution is not a movement but a racket. The Negro middle class has neither faith in nor concern for the Negro masses.

The fact is that the civil rights movement has not only failed to become a genuine mass movement but has also failed as a racket. Not only has it not achieved anything like a transformation of the average Negro but it has failed to give the Negro middle class the new life that seemed within its reach. The Negro middle class has fabulous opportunities for individual advancement, yet such opportunities cannot give the Negro a sense of fitness and an unequivocal sense of worth. Middle-class Negroes are finding out that what they need most is something that they as individuals cannot give themselves; something, moreover, that neither courts nor legislatures nor governments but only the Negro community as a whole can give them. Only when the Negro community as a whole performs something that will win it the admiration of the world will the Negro individual be able to be himself and savor the unbought grace of life. The Negro must have justified pride in the achievements of his people before he can have genuine self-respect. Another way of putting it is that at present the only way the Negro in America can attain a sense of rebirth is by giving birth to an effective Negro community. This cannot happen unless the Negro middle class reintegrates itself with the Negro masses and canalizes its energies, skills and money into the building of vigorous organs for mutual help, self-improvement and communal achievement. Demonstrations, riots, slogans, grandstanding and alibis cannot create one atom of pride.

The building of a Negro community will probably require a new type of leader—a leader who will know how to dovetail the Negro's difficulties into opportunities for growth. The renovation of the Negro slums has been crying out for the mass training of unemployed Negroes as carpenters, bricklayers, plasterers, plumbers, electricians, painters, etc., and their organization into a black union that later, when the slums have been rebuilt, could challenge the discriminating white unions to open up or be wiped out. There is no reason why the Negroes in America should not become world pioneers not only in the renovation of slums but in the overcoming of backwardness. It is to the 20,000,000 Negroes in America that the backward countries should turn for guidance.

I have said that everywhere in America at present, the Negro is a Negro first and only secondly a human being. This is not wholly true. There is one place, the U.S. Armed Forces, where the Negro is a human being first. By joining the Armed Forces, the Negro acquires a new identity and is reborn to a new life. His excellent performance in Vietnam is generating a pride that radiates across the Pacific and reaches into many Negro households. New Left activists who ring doorbells in Harlem and urge Negro housewives to make common cause with the Viet Cong are unceremoniously thrown out. It is not inconceivable that the new leaders who will eventually lead 20,000,000 Negroes to a promised land will be Negro veterans of the Vietnam war. The new type of leader will be without charisma, swagger or clownishness. When the task is done, the followers of such a leader will feel that they have done everything themselves and that they can do great things without great leaders.

THE UNANSWERABLE QUESTIONS

Wilbur H. Ferry

Will civilization survive? If it does, will man live in a world worth living in? Can we control the conditions of our daily lives? Can we resolve the race issue? Can Americans acquire the new consciousness required to give purpose and zest to their common life, and to redeem the nation's proclaimed ideals? These are some of the unanswerable questions which W. H. Ferry, formerly a Fellow of the Center for the Study of Democratic Institutions, asks. According to Ferry, our survival depends upon the answers. If there are to be any, he believes they will be found by the young: "In my mind the question is whether the small band of young people and blacks and idealists can, by demonstration, exhortation, confrontation, example, or raid, bring this nation to its senses before it undergoes the final great lesson of catastrophe, domestic or international. And this is the least answerable question of all."

The number of great issues to which no reasonable solution is possible appears to me to be growing almost daily. I am aware that mankind has

From *Center Magazine*, Vol. II, No. 4 (July 1969). Reprinted by permission of the Center for the Study of Democratic Institutions in Santa Barbara, California.

gone on for a long time with a considerable backlog of unanswered questions or, in any case, with questions that have been at best half-answered or have been resolved in the muffled tones of compromise. But it seems that today's backlog is different in important ways. Yesterday's questions tended to be local—for example, World War I only in a limited way had global dimensions. Today's questions, on the other hand, are nearly universal in their significance. Unless we have been misled, we shall have to call the next international conflict not World War III but Space War I.

There is the added sense that half-answers to today's questions cannot be satisfactory—or at least not satisfactory for very long. Mr. Micawber has been our proconsul for too many years. I think he must be retired instantly.

Reference to Mr. Micawber brings me to the first, the largest, and the most obvious of my questions: *Will civilization survive?* Man is now providing himself with the instruments of annihilation at a cost of almost two hundred billion dollars a year. Such is the fever pitch that the figure is probably now nearing the quarter-trillion-dollar mark. Most of this lunacy is taking place in the best-educated, best-informed, and most affluent nations in the world. No comparable figures for works of non-annihilation have been assembled, as far as I know. If one puts together expenditures for the United Nations and its satellites, plus the output for such items as aid to developing nations, and adds desultory efforts like disarmament commissions, world constitutions, and the like, a figure of around five to ten billion dollars can perhaps be reached for the works of survival, or about two to five per cent of the wealth expended on armaments. It must be agreed, I think, that there is little market for peace and an apparently insatiable one for the works of war. There arises the unhappy vision of mankind surviving only in nests of missiles and biological warfare installations, chattering across the barricades about peace "on our terms," in perpetual hock to fear. Will civilization survive? I deem the question unanswerable.

The second question is equally obvious: *If civilization survives, will man live in a world worth living in?* Since I am an American, let me localize this second question: I'll make it *Will democracy survive?* I have nothing complicated in mind here—by democracy I mean self-government.

The evidence is now plain that, in the minds of many Americans today, someone else in some other place is making all the decisions. There are many reasons for this increasing sense of political remoteness. All are of surface validity—for example, the sometimes incomprehensible interconnections of the industrial, internationalized state. But understanding these reasons does not change the citizen's feeling that politics is becoming form without substance. The notorious military-industrial complex has become an almost palpable presence in our lives. The citizen is talked *to* unceasingly—by the media, by politicians and self-seekers, but he has no way to talk back. The residents of Santa Barbara, where I live, looking across streaked beaches to a swiftly increasing grove of oil platforms in their channel, are discovering that the amenities of their city depend on such unintelligible factors as the world price of oil, the gaps and holes in the tax laws, and quiet agreements between magnates of industry and magnates of government thousands of miles away. Political scientists are in honest dispute as to the extent of democratic practice—not, mind you, democratic rhetoric—but all seem agreed that democratic practice is dwindling or is so changing in character as to call for a different name. Will democracy survive? Unanswerable again.

All unanswerable questions are not of this cosmic character. There are many homely examples. Consider, for example, whether we can, if we wish to do so, actually control the conditions of our daily lives. Posit a community of fifty thousand people, and suppose it to be in a setting pleasing to the inhabitants. Suppose further that the great majority of these inhabitants feel that their city is quite large enough and that they have no desire for an increase in population. Further suppose that, turning their backs on our alleged progress, they do not want any more industry, any more invading freeways. You may think these unlikely suppositions, but there is always a chance that some community will come to its senses and try to have something to say about its own development or non-development.

Let us suppose a few more things: that this community opts for home-owned businesses, for complete public control of the land within its boundaries, for privacy, and for freedom from the high decibels of crashing sound that have become commonplace in urban life, and also for a minimum of automobiles—say, one to a family. Supposing all such goals, could they be achieved? There is another unanswerable question. No one can confidently assert that such a community is impossible because it has never been tried. Nor can anyone say that it is possible if only the requisite determination can be achieved.

Now this is no frivolous set of suppositions. In my judgment there is an intense yearning among Americans for an environment that is manageable and small enough for citizens to lend their weight in the balance of decisions. The country is dotted with towns and small cities desperately seeking to resist a nearby megalopolis. The impulse is most clearly seen in the so-called outer suburbs. Are these communities at the mercy of the urban suction-pump or can they do something about it? Aside from these outer suburbs there are those more distant enclaves which still retain some sylvan charm. Trying to control one's own destiny took on a modern dimension when the suburbs finally cut themselves off from their parent cities and said, "We want a life different from yours." Of course most suburbanites never really meant this. What they really meant was that they wanted a quiet bedroom, better schools, and nothing but white faces in the neighborhood stores. The near-in suburbs have all but given up the struggle for real distinctiveness, but the effort goes on in the outer rings of megalopolis. And there are many communities, large and small, remote from the great centers, which are now watching their powers of self-government being eroded by distant forces that they cannot comprehend, much less regulate.

All this is only to say that many obstacles lie across the path of a community such as I have supposed. I pass over certain obstacles that will occur to everyone, such as the drive for super-efficient government, the difficulty of getting the citizenry to consider and debate significant issues, the indignation of neighboring communities about actions that injure them, and the subsequent reprisals of these neighbors. The less apparent obstacles are just as numerous. There is, for example, the homogenizing effect of television. Any effort to maintain a distinctive community in this country has the tube to contend with. Television decrees our national styles in attitude, dress, consumption, and who can say what else. Thus, to use a kitchen example, television is mainly responsible for the elimination of local cheese producers, so that we now have a choice only of rubbery samenesses on most of our supermarket cheese counters. Can a community, however determined it might be, prevail against such pressures?

The federal Constitution is, however, the chief obstruction, for it might well decree that our imaginary city could not ration births, halt the immigrant, deny the trespassing freeway-builder, or keep a second car out of the garage. Nonetheless, I do not consider this a conclusive objection, for the Constitution can always be changed. Indeed, it should be changed if it gets in the way of the human development of the nation. I would not care to argue that the Constitution ought to be amended or rewritten merely to meet the desires of my suppositious community. Perhaps a better way of stating the issue, then, is to ask whether the Constitution is facilitating undesirable development, so that under its permissive gaze we stand in danger of losing our souls as well as our water supplies, our clean air, and our arable land. Here, I believe, there is another unanswerable question: *Do we have the political wit or will to rewrite the Constitution to reflect what we have learned about ourselves and technical society in the past generation or two?*

To conclude the instance of the small city I have imagined, it would undertake to control its population. It would limit entry. It would work out a transportation policy based on the reasonable needs of the community. And so on and on. All such matters would require a communal dedication and enterprise in political action far beyond our current imagination. Combinations of persuasion and incentive and restraint, of which there is no modern example, would be called for.

Once again such a program will be dismissed as repugnant and regressive. Yet a good deal of the commotion today may be interpreted as efforts in that very direction. The traffic boss of New York City recently warned that private vehicles may soon have to be barred from the streets of that suffocating city. Los Angeles, a special example of demented mobility, is moving through smog in a similar direction, though no decisive action may be expected there until a few thousand citizens gasp to death. Garrett Hardin, of the University of California at Santa Barbara, proposes a tax in Los Angeles of a dollar a gallon on gasoline. The New York traffic boss and Professor Hardin and anyone like them trying to do what is necessary will, however, find themselves up against a constitutional challenge if they try to put their plans into effect.

As a final instance, consider some recent despairing words of Daniel Moynihan, President Nixon's adviser on the cities. Moynihan, ordinarily one of the most ebullient of men, said: "For reasons no one understands, government has been impotent in trying to solve urban problems. The inability of government to bring about urban change is a fundamental problem of government today. Our delivery systems are not in fact working."

I am trying to point out that the matters which have to be dealt with by a small city determined to keep its singular character are similar to those faced by every metropolis. But of course for most large cities it is already too late to think of finding human solutions. For these cities the big question is survival itself. Not long ago, *Newsweek* asked: "Can the suburban 'white noose' around the cities be broken by genuine integration? . . . Is there any real way to end the cycle of welfare dependency? Will better-paid, more mobile police cut the spiraling crime rate? Do decentralization and community control really promise better education? . . . Is big-city life still worth living?" The difference, it is clear, is one of degree. If the questions asked about the small city are unanswerable, all the more unanswerable are the questions being asked about the great cities.

We see in these issues some of what is agitating our young people. They have no care for a civilization held in thrall by questions that are at once awesome and unanswerable. Their plea for participation can be read as an appeal for intelligibility and manageability. A good deal of adult resentment of the young (which as often as not seems to verge on outright hatred) may arise from a subconscious realization that our children are stirring things up in favor of a *human* civilization, not a technical order, and in favor of restoring the kind of relations among people that adults themselves somehow let slip from their grasp. So there may be a heavy dose of envy mixed into the adult demand that the young be repressed and that they conform to a style of existence that their elders, in occasional fits of candor, acknowledge to be aimless and excruciatingly boring. It is a fair guess that adults do not want their children participating in any significant way in determining the conditions of their own lives if they themselves are not capable of doing so. In Kenneth Millar's phrase, the conservatism of despair holds them back.

Race is the next entry. I find some difficulty in phrasing the question correctly. The following will have to do: *Can we resolve the race issue, with freedom and justice for all?* This seems as unanswerable a query as any. On the one side we see millions of people getting to their feet, beginning to stand upright for the first time, experiencing a sense of selfhood and dignity that had been squashed throughout American history. Their talk is loud, angry, confused, and direct. Blacks are economically near-broke but spiritually and politically affluent—and I would like to come down hard on that word "politically." They are saying, we know what is best for ourselves, so please get that white hand off our shoulder.

On the other side there is a vast white majority that is frightened, with no genuine understanding of what the blacks are clamoring for in their campaigns for autonomy and for a culture based on black history. This white majority on the whole wishes its black colonial subjects well, and has even passed laws in evidence of its benign outlook. It hopes that the blacks succeed in improving their lot, but only if the improvement does not cost much and only if the blacks do not threaten white superiority or white peace of mind. The white majority is also heavily armed, officially and unofficially. These arms are intended for use any time the minority goes beyond the demilitarized zone that now by tacit consent separates blacktown and whitetown. Finally, the white majority says to the black minority: "We know better than you do what is best for you, and we'll see that you get it, even if you find it painful." The argument resembles the viewpoint of those who think we can best resolve the Vietnam dilemma by killing off all the Vietnamese.

I deny that there is an answer to the race question; I deny that we—that is, the conscientious members of the white majority—are really working at it and have achieved fair success already. I reject this whole line of argument, for on examination what we see is a series of compromises, or concessions, or half measures usually arrived at as a means of damping down explosive situations. Meanwhile the principal institutions of our racist society remain intact and unchanged, the towers of privilege are unshaken. Bargains and compromises, I am aware, are said to be the essence of American political life. But what, in this situation, has such an explanation to do with freedom and justice, let us say for the urban or rural blacks chained in their respective slums? I am reminded of one recent political bargain in Washington, under the terms of which starving black children are to be allowed—as an experiment—free food stamps for a while.

I conclude that race is a question without an answer in the United States, another problem to which there is no solution. There may well be a resolution of the matter, but it will in no sense be a genuine answer. I refer to the possibility of a civil war, which I regard as likely. But of course this resolution will not be a civil war but a pogrom, incited by those millions of whites to whom blacks today are almost as frightening a presence as Nat Turner and his band were to Southern plantation-owners. Such a resolution will necessarily have only a temporary effect in subduing blacks, will enormously increase the freight of white guilt, and will only compound the unanswerability of the question with which this article opened.

My last question is this: *Can Americans acquire the new consciousness required to give purpose and zest to their common life, and to redeem the nation's proclaimed ideals?* It may be thought that there is a preliminary query; namely, whether such a new consciousness is needed. Based on my view of the state of the nation, the answer has to be roaringly affirmative. A superficial casting-up of accounts establishes the United States as blessed beyond history's wildest intimations of success: a constitutional regime of two hundred years' stability, a plentiful domain moated by great oceans and friendly (or at least nonhostile) neighbors, propelled by an economic engine that year after year breaks records in all departments from G.N.P. to the amounts spent on noneconomic follies like arms and space, and constantly rising achievement in all the conventional indices from childhood mortality to literacy, to books and concert tickets sold, to salaries paid rock singers and football players. Such cataloguings of the American Way go on and on. They are all valid enough.

Yet this is not the central story of the United States today, only a small part of it. Such statistics are merely the backdrop of success against which the ironies stand forth plainly. Something has gone wrong. Erich Fromm says that Americans are "anxious, lonely, and bored." Wealth and accomplishment are not nearly enough. There is a hollowness at the center of the national life. Americans are cynical about politics and politicians and think that government is a matter of logrolling or of buying and selling favors. They are frightened by the prospects of abundance and leisure whether this leisure is for them or for their neighbors. Miracle-a-day science and technology fascinate them and at the same time bring forebodings as they sense their incapacity to deal with the moral issues generated in the laboratories. For example: What to do about the geneticists' alarming promise that we shall soon be able to determine the chief physical and mental characteristics of the population? What to do about our possession of enough poison to kill the people of the world ten times over, and enough deadly bugs and hydrogen bombs to eliminate any life that might manage to survive around the edges? What to do about the advent of a society in which relatively few people will have to work as the machine slaves take over?

We are distressed to discover that we have so misused nature as to put our grandchildren, if not our children, in danger of suffocation through lack of oxygen, or of being buried alive in their own garbage, or being carried off by lead poisoning. There is a halting recognition that as we pave our farmlands we may be doing away with croplands we shall one day need.

In the thoughtless and catastrophic attack on the environment, from the bottom of the sea to the outer envelope of the atmosphere, there may just be a new consciousness forming. Belatedly as always, the mass media are beginning to give a little alarmed attention to the rapid deterioration of our physical world. So at last we may be getting sensible and learning to fear the right things—not the Communists but our own suicidal practices. But I do not think that we will spend the billions needed to redeem our environment, nor, indeed, that we have the political machinery to carry on the great clean-up even if we were willing to tax ourselves for this purpose.

New orders of magnitude appear daily, and human beings become more dwarfed and insignificant. Size has always been a major criterion in the American consciousness—the bigger the better—but we are beginning to understand that size in the end is the death of individuality and distinctiveness. The illicit claims of bigness are apparent in the condition of our cities. They continue to grow, becoming less and less livable, each itself an increasing cluster of unanswerable questions. Citizens quiver in the drumhead tautness lying across metropolitan centers. The idea of community is itself the most conspicuous fatality of urban civilization. There can never have been a more sour joke than placing the label Fun City on New York. Our greatest metropolis is gritty with hatred and threatened with disintegration.

Like the earlier list, this catalogue of American ills could be extended indefinitely. Problems multiply at an unprecedented rate. I know that I shall be charged with having drawn an overblown picture. But it is the picture I see. There is little ease or serenity and little laughter among us. An uncommon malignity is beginning to mark our disputes. The legacy of America, as matters now stand, is not a life that is nasty, brutish, and short, but one that is apprehensive, surfeited, and long.

So I return to the question, Can Americans acquire a new consciousness? I believe this to be unanswerable. Americans must! cry the young. We will not, say the old. We cannot, intone the political pragmatists. It must be evident that I come down on the side of the young. The old consciousness is worn out. It has served it purpose and deserves respectful burial. But having cast my vote for the new consciousness, I have not answered the question whether we can achieve it, I have only declared my hope for its election. Nor is it within the scope of this article to discuss the *content* of the new consciousness. It is a separate matter—youth's dream of revolutionizing American morality, in John Updike's words. I do not mind, however, indicating the key to my understanding of this phrase. It takes in the word we hear more and more often from our young friends, the word "radicalization."

Radicalization is the process of looking afresh at the institutions and procedures of the society, beginning at their roots and working onward, taking nothing for granted or as being of continuing value except these indispensable things: community, self-rule, the integrity of the human person, and the necessity of living in harmony with the natural order. In this sense our protesting young people must be deemed not revolutionaries but counterrevolutionaries. They wish to undo or trip up the technical-industrial revolution and get back to prerevolutionary ideas like political participation and personal responsibility.

I take it that the new consciousness is aimed at doing something about all the conditions that cripple these essential aims. I wish its proponents well, for I cannot imagine how it will all end otherwise. It does not, I suppose, matter much whether a great civilization ends in a horrible bang or an ignoble whimper. The apocalyptic current in me has slowed down. Nor does my morose outlook incline me to suicide—men just don't seem to jump off the bridge often for big reasons, they usually do so for little ones.

Anyway, I have no taste for such long-range forecasts; the focus of this article is on the ambiance of life, the tone of hatred and suspicion and cynicism that we are coming to accept as part of what citizenship in post-industrial society means. Perhaps we shall never know when civilization, in the ordinary and honored sense, actually ends and refined barbarism takes over.

I realize that the mood of this essay has been unrelieved melancholy. This is partly because the topic is not a cheery one. It is mainly because no answers occur to me; and because I sense strongly that we have pushed our luck very near the breaking point. It is hard for me to accept that the human annals contain chapters as bleak and unpromising as the present one. There has surely never been so much morbid speculation amid plenty and apparent progress. Our hardest and most high-minded labors seem inevitably Sisyphean. Those who take comfort in the solidity of our institutions may do so; these institutions no longer feel solid to me. Those who derive confidence from our "tradition" are, I think, falsely led, for our tradition of justice, equality, fraternity, mutual respect is mostly a tissue of affectionate memory, not reality functioning in our lives except here and there along the margins. I do not know what to say to those asserting that God is working in history. That statement only recalls to me the frightening graffito reported from a San Francisco lavatory: "God has cancer." Our heroes are in outer space, on the basketball courts, or in the grave. Martin Luther King, Jr., is a hero, now that he is safely dead. President Eric Walker of the University of Pennsylvania has said that salvation is to be found in a rebirth of "practical know-how," and engineering on a gigantic scale. This strikes me as hair-of-the-dog advice, and about as effective.

There is one bright spot and one only on my screen. I see wisps of hope in the young, in the blacks and browns, in the militants of all colors. They are the partisans of the new consciousness. But I do not want to idealize them. They are disorganized, rude, contemptuous. Sometimes they are even a tenth as violent as those beating on them. But they are thinking of the right things, thinking of how to save our environment from human predators, thinking of how to retain their manhood as the structures of post-industrial society close in, thinking of how to convert accomplishment into human ends, thinking of how to achieve dignity. They are thinking of Malcolm X's wish that he might "save America from a grave, even fatal catastrophe." Their hope and mine rises as we consider that their efforts helped to drive a war-committed President from office, and as we see that genuine gains have been made in the independence of the black spirit.

Yet it must be conceded that these are minuscule breaches in the mighty wall of self-satisfaction and self-righteousness that is the chief defense of an overendowed society. In my mind the question is whether this small band of young people and blacks and idealists can, by demonstration, exhortation, confrontation, example, or raid, bring this nation to its senses before it undergoes the final great lesson of catastrophe, domestic or international.

And this is the least answerable question of all.